Gender and Politics Reimagined

CENTRING OCEANIC AND ASIAN LENSES

Gender and Politics Reimagined

CENTRING OCEANIC AND ASIAN LENSES

Edited by Tanya Jakimow,
Margaret Jolly, Sonia Palmieri
and Ramona Vijeyarasa

Australian
National
University

ANU PRESS

Plate 0.1: Elise Howard (right) with Mema Motusaga, Savaii, Samoa, 29 October 2022

Source: Photographed with Elise Howard's camera.

In memory of Elise Howard
A rare combination of selfless generosity and cheeky humour
Epicentre of brilliant collaborations
Much missed friend and colleague

Australian National University

ANU PRESS

Published by ANU Press
The Australian National University
Canberra ACT 2600, Australia
Email: anupress@anu.edu.au

Available to download for free at press.anu.edu.au

ISBN (print): 9781760467098
ISBN (online): 9781760467104

WorldCat (print): 1542889275
WorldCat (online): 1542890245

DOI: 10.22459/GPR.2025

Cover design and layout by ANU Press

This book is published under the aegis of the Social Sciences editorial board of ANU Press.

Contents

List of illustrations

Figures

Plates

Tables

Abbreviations

ANU	The Australian National University
ASEAN	Association of Southeast Asian Nations
CEDAW	*Convention on the Elimination of All Forms of Discrimination against Women*
DFAT	Department of Foreign Affairs and Trade (Australia)
GAD	gender and development
GIWL	Global Institute for Women's Leadership
IWDA	International Women's Development Agency
MP	Member of Parliament
NGO	nongovernmental organisation
PNG	Papua New Guinea
TSMs	temporary special measures
UK	United Kingdom
UN	United Nations
UPNG	University of Papua New Guinea
US	United States

Acknowledgements

This edited volume arose out of a three-day event 'Theorizing Gender and Political Leadership from Asia and the Pacific: Lessons for a more diverse political landscape in Australia' held at The Australian National University on 13–15 July 2022. It was a partnership between the School of Culture, History and Language (CHL) in the College of Asia and the Pacific, the ANU Gender Institute, The Australian National University's Global Institute for Women's Leadership and the ANU Centre for Asian-Australian Leadership. With appreciation to Fiona Jenkins, Natalie Barr and Jieh-Yung Lo for intellectual guidance and logistical and financial support.

Dr Elena Williams, a former PhD candidate at The Australian National University, was critical to the success of this event. She took a major role in organising the workshop-cum-conference from the beginning and was there each step of the way sharing the workload and emotional load. Without Ele, there would be no event, and no edited volume. The editors are grateful for this foundational work.

The event would have fallen apart were it not for Lea Collins from the CHL Professional team. Her time and experience to ensure the workshop ran smoothly, taking the stress away from the organising team, were greatly appreciated. Gouri Banerji and Stella Diao (CHL) provided marketing and administrative support, and Ricky Vuckovic and his team in the College of Asia and the Pacific ensured IT ran smoothly. Student volunteers also provided valuable assistance during the event.

The event was preceded by a workshop, 'Generating Change by Generations of Women in Oceania: A Pacific dialogue', organised by Margaret Jolly. Our thanks to the organising team for putting together such a fabulous event. Thank you to the participants who joined both the workshop and the broader event either in person or online, and especially to those who have contributed to either of the volumes.

Kathryn Allan provided wonderful assistance at various stages of this volume. She was a most committed volunteer at the workshop and has helped with administrative tasks and editing of draft chapters. Thank you also to Frank Bongiorno and the rest of ANU Press Social Sciences Editorial Board for your support of this project. We are grateful for the encouragement and feedback from two anonymous reviewers of the volume, and for the careful reading and feedback by Marian Sawer.

Tanya Jakimow was able to devote time to the event and consequent edited volume while on an Australian Research Council Future Fellowship (FT190100247). Parts of the introduction and afterword were written while a British Academy Visiting Scholar at the University of Birmingham (UoB) in the International Development Department (VF2\100361). I am grateful for the support of Professor David Hudson for facilitating that visit and to colleagues at UoB for many conversations about this volume and related areas of research. Working with Sonia, Ramona and Margaret has been one of the most rewarding experiences of my career and personally enriching. Thank you for your support and contributions to the event and for being the most wonderful, generous and inspiring co-editors and friends.

Margaret Jolly acknowledges the long-term support for her work on gender in the Pacific from the Australian Research Council, most recently for 'Engendering Climate Change, Reframing Futures in Oceania' (DP 180104224). I also warmly acknowledge the continuing support for my research in retirement as an Emerita Professor from Simon Haberle, Director of the School of Culture, History and Language, and the efficiency and grace of CHL administrative staff, including Joanna Cousins, Stella Diao and Jialing Sun. Several colleagues who offered helpful comments on my chapter are acknowledged here. I am especially grateful to Tanya Jakimow for inspiration and conscientious dedication to this project and to co-editors Ramona Vijeyarasa and Sonia Palmieri in what has truly been a 'Dream Team'.

Sonia Palmieri acknowledges the International Women's Development Agency and its project on Women's Leadership Pathways funded by the Government of the Netherlands from 2017 to 2020, which first introduced her to wonderful colleagues Camilla Batalibasi, Chandy Eng, Donna Makini, Melissa MacLean and Geraldine Valei. I have delighted in working with Vani Nailumu thanks to two Australian Government–funded programs: the Pacific Research Program, both Phase I (2017–21) and Phase II (2022–26), and 'Balance of Power'. Thanks also to colleagues in the Department of Pacific Affairs for unfailing support. Finally, a profound note of thanks to Tanya for inviting me to share her dream, to Margaret for being my role model of feminist Pacific inquiry and to Ramona for bringing cool, calm and compassionate consideration to every discussion.

Ramona Vijeyarasa thanks the Women's Leadership Institute Australia (Trawalla Foundation) for its generous support in providing a Research Fellowship (2022–25) that has enabled her to be a part of this project, and a Department of Foreign Affairs and Trade (DFAT) Aus4Skills grant in Vietnam in 2023 (with the Centre for Gender Studies and Women's Leadership) that has also shaped her perspectives as a contributor to this project. Thanks are also owed to my wonderful colleagues in the Faculty of Law at University of Technology Sydney. I first met Tanya at the Women in Asia Conference at the University of Western Australia in 2017. I will forever be grateful for that fortuitous opportunity to meet a kindred spirit and to the collaborations to which it has since given rise. My enormous thanks to Margaret, Sonia and Tanya for the rewarding journey and the unexpected friendship along the way.

Finally, to fellow members of the 'Dream Team': ours was a collaboration based on a shared vision, equal effort, mutual respect and collegiality. The work never felt like a burden; it was joyful and enriching. It has been a privilege to work with such inspiring and impressive women.

Contributors

Camilla Batalibasi is a solicitor from Solomon Islands. In her previous role as the Women in Leadership Officer with the Honiara-based nongovernmental organisation Women's Rights Action Movement, she was a lead researcher in the Women's Pathways to Leadership project supported by the International Women's Development Agency.

Longgina Novadona Bayo is a lecturer in the Department of Politics and Government, Gadjah Mada University, Indonesia. She is undertaking her PhD in Anthropology and Development Studies at the University of Melbourne, with the research project entitled 'Understanding Gender Dynamics and Women's Political Leadership in Eastern Indonesia'.

Bronwyn Anne Beech Jones is Assistant Lecturer in History at the University of Melbourne, where she also completed her PhD in 2024. Bronwyn's research centres on methods of narrating women's history and experiences, with a particular focus on Indonesia.

Rachael Diprose is an Associate Professor in the School of Social and Political Sciences at the University of Melbourne. Rachael has published widely on two interrelated streams of international development research, especially on Indonesia: sustainability, gender and social inclusion; and collective action, contestation and order.

Chandy Eng is the Executive Director of Gender and Development for Cambodia. In this role, she was a lead researcher in the Women's Pathways to Leadership project implemented by the International Women's Development Agency.

Serena Eleonora Ford is a PhD candidate at Monash University, where she is affiliated with the Global Peace and Security Centre and the Centre of Excellence for the Elimination of Violence against Women. She graduated from The Australian National University's School of Culture, History and Language with first-class honours in 2022.

Dr Elise Howard was a senior research officer and PhD candidate with the Department of Pacific Affairs at The Australian National University. Her doctoral research explores women's leadership and security in the context of climate change in the Pacific.

Tanya Jakimow is Professor of Anthropology in the School of Culture, History and Language, The Australian National University. She is an Australian Research Council Future Fellow, examining women's political labour and pathways to politics in Indonesia, India and Australia. She is the author of three books, most recently *Susceptibility in Development: Micropolitics of local development in India and Indonesia* (Oxford University Press, 2020).

Margaret Jolly AM, FASSA is an Emerita Professor at The Australian National University and a transdisciplinary scholar of gender and Pacific studies. She has published extensively on gender in Oceania, exploratory voyages and travel writing, missions and contemporary Christianity, maternity and sexuality, cinema and art and has a long-term interest in decolonial feminisms in Oceania.

Anna Kwai is an indigenous scholar from Solomon Islands. She is a PhD candidate in the Evolution of Cultural Diversity Initiative at The Australian National University. Anna's current research focus is on the historiography of traditional gender relations and their contemporary interpretation in Solomon Islands, using her cultural region of Kwara'ae on Malaita as a case study.

Ruby Y.S. Lai is an Assistant Professor in the Department of Sociology and Social Policy at Lingnan University, Hong Kong. Her research interests revolve around gender, family, reproductive politics, ethnicity, migration and space in Hong Kong and China.

Dr Salmah Eva-Lina Lawrence is a transformation strategist and social scientist. At the time of writing, Salmah was Director of Systemic Change and Partnerships at the International Women's Development Agency. She is a board member of WaterAid Australia, Honorary Associate Professor at The Australian National University, Fellow at Ormond College at the University of Melbourne and Adjunct Fellow at Macquarie University. She researches decolonial ethics and epistemology.

Melissa MacLean is an independent consultant, researcher and communicator specialising in international development, rights, gender and monitoring and evaluation. She formed part of the research support team in the Women's Pathways to Leadership project implemented by the International Women's Development Agency.

Donna Makini is a project officer with the Pacific Community and formerly the research and policy officer for the Women's Rights Action Movement in Solomon Islands. In this role, she was a lead researcher in the Women's Pathways to Leadership project implemented by the International Women's Development Agency.

Aparimita Mishra is an independent researcher based in New Delhi. She has a PhD in economics. She works in the areas of gender, grassroots governance, the environment and development.

Deepak K. Mishra is a Professor of Economics at the Centre for the Study of Regional Development, School of Social Sciences, Jawaharlal Nehru University, New Delhi. He has worked on agrarian change, labour migration and development. Recent books include *Global Poverty: Rethinking causality* (Brill, 2023), co-edited with Professor Raju Das.

Dr Mema Motusaga is the former Chief Executive Officer of the Ministry of Women, Community and Social Development, Samoa. Her doctoral thesis, 'Women in Decision Making in Samoa', includes a detailed discussion of the temporary special measures that resulted in the introduction of a gender quota in Samoa's parliament. Her research interests are good governance, gender equality, youth and children's development.

Vani Nailumu is Research and Communications Officer for the Pacific-led program Balance of Power. In this role, she has worked on several research projects that explore the social norms of women's leadership in the Pacific and, specifically, Fiji.

Sonia Palmieri is an Associate Professor and head of the Department of Pacific Affairs in the College of Asia and the Pacific at The Australian National University. Her research interests lie in the social and cultural conditions that legitimise women's leadership in political institutions, including parliaments. In parallel, Sonia explores with students and her disciplinary peers opportunities and strategies for more inclusive research methodologies, particularly feminist methodologies.

Ken M.P. Setiawan is Senior Lecturer in Indonesian Studies at the Asia Institute, University of Melbourne. Ken's research interests include globalisation and human rights, as well as historical violence and transitional justice. She has published widely on the politics of human rights in Indonesia.

Jaemin Shim is an Assistant Professor in the Department of Government and International Studies at Hong Kong Baptist University and a Research Associate at the German Institute for Global and Area Studies. His primary research interests lie in political representation, comparative welfare states, gender and legislative politics. He is the editor of *Mass–Elite Representation Gap in Old and New Democracies: Critical Junctures and Elite Agency* (University of Michigan Press, 2024).

Dr Elise Stephenson is a political scientist and international relations scholar focused on gender equality, feminist and queer theory, diplomacy, national security, government, entrepreneurship and diversity and inclusion. She is Deputy Director of the Global Institute for Women's Leadership at The Australian National University, a 2022 Fulbright Scholar and was recognised as one of Australia's Top 50 Outstanding LGBTI+ Leaders 2020.

Geraldine Valei is the Senior Field Officer with CARE International in Papua New Guinea. In her former role with the Bougainville Women's Federation, she was a lead researcher in the Women's Pathways to Leadership project implemented by the International Women's Development Agency.

Ramona Vijeyarasa is a Professor in the Faculty of Law at the University of Technology Sydney. Researching at the intersections of women's rights, law and technology, she is the author of *Rewriting the Rules* (University of California Press, 2026), *The Woman President* (Oxford University Press, 2022) and *Sex, Slavery and the Trafficked Woman* (Routledge, 2015) and editor of *International Women's Rights Law and Gender Equality: Making the law work for women* (Routledge, 2021).

1

Interrogating What Is Known About Gender and Politics: Vantage points from Oceania and Asia

Tanya Jakimow

The series of conversations that culminated in this edited volume began with the reading of a report in late 2020. *Women Political Leaders: The Impact of Gender on Democracy* (Cowper-Coles 2020) was produced in partnership by the Westminster Foundation for Democracy and the Global Institute for Women's Leadership (GIWL), King's College London. The report is a valuable resource. Based on an analysis of more than 500 pieces of research published over 25 years (1995–2020), it distils key lessons about women's political careers and the impact of their leadership on the quality of democracy and policymaking. A traffic-light system indicates findings for which the evidence base is solid (green), those for which further evidence is needed (amber) and remaining gaps in our understanding (red). The report hence provides a beneficial roadmap for research, including my own.

As a comprehensive review of the gender and politics literature, however, the report had notable absences. The number of studies from North America and Europe outnumbered those from all other regions put together. Only English-language evidence was synthesised. Tellingly, Cowper-Coles (2020) had to draw on area studies and development studies to fill the gaps in regional representation, revealing the underrepresentation of the 'majority world'[1] in political science journals. Apart from these disciplinary detours, most of the texts were from political science or sociology. Ethnographic writing on women in politics had been my primary resource as an anthropologist. The focus on everyday political practices and processes of sense-making and self-making within the political field provides incredibly rich insights into how politics and democracies work. These insights, and those of other disciplines such as history, law, geography, cultural studies and more, were largely missing. These limitations—which were acknowledged by the author—reflect the lopsided nature of scholarship and are not a deficiency of the report per se (see Medie and Kang 2018; Shim, Chapter 2, this volume).

Euro-American centrism and disciplinary parochialism are arguably stifling advancements in our understanding of gender and politics. We have at our disposal a toolbox of concepts, theories, methodologies and interpretative frames to examine the gendered nature of political institutions and the mechanisms that sustain male domination. Yet, despite this relative bounty, we remained caged by the dominance of particular geographical and disciplinary frames. Theories, concepts and analytical tools are overwhelmingly developed from studies in Euro-America and applied to other regions (for exceptions, see, among others, Bjarnegård 2013; Rai and Spary 2019; Piscopo and Kenny 2020; Baker and Palmieri 2021). Rarely is the majority world seen as a site of theory development that can illuminate the political institutions of the North Atlantic. Our imaginative resources are further constrained from citational practices that centre political science in studies of gender and politics. Insights from other disciplines may touch the margins, yet their capacity to advance the literature is dulled by their being corralled in disciplinary or area studies journals.

This volume seeks to offer a corrective of sorts by centring research from Oceania and Asia from a variety of disciplinary perspectives. We are not interested in simply presenting case studies that exhibit differences in countries outside the North Atlantic. Our ambitions are to make critical

---

1   Following Alam (2008) and Lawrence (forthcoming), I use 'majority world' to refer to the countries outside Europe and North America. As my focus is on scholarly dominance rather than economic relations, majority world does not map onto prior problematic categories of 'Third World' or 'developing countries'. I include all of Oceania and Asia (including West Asia or the Middle-East, Japan and South Korea), Latin America and Africa. A case can also be made for including countries in Eastern Europe that are marginalised in broader scholarship. Australia occupies a distinct position on the periphery that I explore below.

interventions in the literature, unearth fresh insights, develop innovative conceptual and theoretical tools and explore new research practices and sensibilities. In doing so, we aim to:

- Demonstrate the value in epistemologically decentring Euro-America by theorising from the majority world in research on gender and politics.
- Contribute to the re-envisioning of Asian Studies and Oceanic Studies by revealing the relevance of knowledge about these regions beyond them.
- Practise knowledge as social action (Collins 2019) through inclusive learning practices and critically interrogating knowledge hierarchies.

In this opening chapter, I examine each of these ambitions in turn, paying respect to the scholars who have made these ambitions urgent and outlining our contributions to broader agendas.

The primary methodology for this project was a workshop held over three days at The Australian National University (ANU) on 13–15 July 2022. It was a collaboration between four ANU entities: the School of Culture, History and Language within the College of Asia and the Pacific; the ANU Gender Institute; the sister institute of GIWL at The Australian National University; and the Centre for Asian-Australian Leadership. Three principles guided the event. First, we wished to revalue not only *research* from Asia and Oceania, but also *researchers*. Our invitation list targeted key scholars and activists located in institutions in these two regions. Second, we brought together two communities of practice: those studying gender and politics in Asia and/or Oceania, and those doing so in Australia. We aimed to show the possibilities for theorising from Asia and Oceania to address the deficiencies of political representation in multicultural settler states like Australia, while also providing a forum to discuss and strategise within these two communities. Our third principle was to break down the silos and hierarchies between 'scholarly' and 'practical' knowledge. We therefore invited people working in nongovernmental organisations (NGOs) and government departments and elected representatives to speak alongside academic researchers. Our aim was to co-produce rich knowledge with greater potential for social impact.

The different sets of participants at times added a certain *frisson* or productive discomfort. We aim to capitalise on the creative energy such tension unleashed at the workshop within this edited volume. This volume is a starting point, a call to action to provincialise, de-parochialise and decolonise knowledge production in gender and politics, but it merely scrapes the surface of its possibilities. In the conclusion to this volume, we draw out common lessons that are suggestive of new ways to advance gender and politics scholarship.

Centring Oceania and Asia

Ours is not the first edited volume to centre Asia and/or Oceania in the study of gender and politics. In 1992, a seminar held in Seoul resulted in the publication *Women in Politics in Asia and the Pacific* (UNESCAP 1993). More than 100 participants, including academics, Members of Parliament, ministers and representatives of women's organisations, attended, resulting in country papers and the adoption of the 'Seoul Statement on Empowering Women in Politics'. The Konrad Adenauer Foundation 'Political Dialogue Asia' office in Singapore carries on this important work to narrow the gender gap in politics through dialogue across sectors, with the resulting edited volumes valuable resources (Echle and Sarmah 2021; Joshi and Echle 2023). Regular academic events have resulted in several edited volumes that are classics in the study of gender and politics in Asia (Iwanaga 2008; Fleschenberg and Derichs 2012). Oceania has relatively fewer edited volumes, yet is often represented in chapters in books that take a global perspective (Howard et al. 2023; George 2020). Here, we outline how we are building on these volumes and what is distinct about our own.

First, what we do not do. This introductory chapter does not provide an overview of the state of women's political participation across Oceania and Asia, or globally. In part, this is because recent reviews exist (Prihatini 2021; Och 2023; Howard et al. 2023). But it is also due to the tendency of statistics to foreground phenomena that can be measured, while flattening what are complex pictures of women in politics within and across countries (see Batilabasi et al., Chapter 7; Vijeyarasa, Chapter 8, this volume). Data are more readily available in the minority world, with questions relevant to the United States prominent in comparative politics (Piscopo and Kenny 2020; Teele 2019). Statistics can also overlook the influence of women in political activities outside the formal political sphere that are less easily observed or enumerated, thereby perpetuating a deficiency narrative (Phua 2018; Waylen 1996). Nor is descriptive representation indicative of influence (Prihatini 2021), a sign that women's interests are being addressed (Vijeyarasa 2022) or fully explanatory of the conditions for obtaining political power. For these reasons, we have aimed for complexity and specificity in our stories of women's political participation, rather than broad statistical overviews.

The reader will also not find a historical narrative of gradual improvements in the status of women. Not only has this task been accomplished elsewhere, but also global accounts tend to privilege the story of women in the minority world (Celis et al. 2013; Och 2023). Often historicity is not extended to women in the majority world—most evident in the use of the term 'traditional' to refer to cultural barriers to women's political participation (Och 2023). Curiously underemphasised in both the global narrative and the defining of 'tradition' is the role of colonialism in transforming gender relations and hence enabling male dominance, even when the relatively recent nature of women's exclusion from the public sphere is acknowledged (Celis et al. 2013; see Hawkesworth 2012; Segato 2018). Colonialism's legacy extends beyond formerly colonised countries; the imperial project required and established gender relations at 'home' to contrast with the 'uncivilised' 'Other', with long-term effects for the position of women in these countries (Chakrabarty 2000; Hawkesworth 2012). We foreground the ongoing impact of colonialism on women's political participation through several chapters (Anna Kwai, Chapter 3; Salmah Eva-Lina Lawrence, Chapter 5; Margaret Jolly, Chapter 6; Novadona Bayo, Chapter 10), and in the afterword.

A valuable contribution of many edited volumes is a framework or analytical focal point that speaks to the commonalities of women across a region. Fleschenberg and Derichs (2012) centre the question of when women can be a springboard for democracy, seeking connections between gender exclusion, modalities of inclusion and how these shape democracies. Iwanaga's (2008) framework builds on the common categorisation of institutional, cultural and socioeconomic barriers by identifying 'facilitators' from the case studies to explain how women seek and gain political office in Asia. A challenge remains, however, that in attempting a regional overview of factors, certain features are inevitably highlighted. Such analysis often falls within a 'common denominator' frame of identifying what women have in common, which privileges the issues of the more powerful within a universal framework (Ciccia and Roggeband 2021). Conversely, privileging the experiences of women in the majority world bears the risk of presenting a unitary and essentialised 'woman', doing violence to the differences across and within places (Mohanty 2002; Waylen 1996), replacing one universalism with another without contending with transferability and partiality (Hawkesworth 2012).

Instead of a singular framework or orienting question, we therefore aim for dialogue across the different studies. It bears resemblance to a 'recognition of difference' approach, which eschews the search for commonalities in favour of recognising that differently positioned groups will have certain issues or ways of looking at issues (Ciccia and Roggeband 2021). Comparison remains central to the project, as differences and commonalities are the basis of analysis. As Chandra Mohanty (2002: 505) writes, 'specifying difference allows us to theorize universal concerns more fully'. Several comparative volumes achieve such a rich analysis. Commendable is the volume edited by Mariz Tadros (2014) that examines the informal repertoires of power for women across the majority world, identifying measures to increase women's political representation that are as valid in Australia as they are in Bangladesh. Other volumes that are more than the sum of their parts include the study of grammar and performance in politics edited by Rai and Reinelt (2014), of women and dynastic politics in Asia edited by Derichs and Thompson (2013) and the interrogation of substantive representation of women across Asia edited by Joshi and Echle (2023). We take inspiration from these volumes that extend our understanding of concepts or phenomena through comparative studies but revert to a bird's-eye view to identify the missing questions, theories and concepts that become visible when we privilege Oceania and Asia.

Texts from Oceania and Asia have, of course, already made important theoretical contributions to the gender and politics canon. The contributions in this volume build on excellent work in Thailand by Elin Bjarnegård (2013), the Pacific by Kerryn Baker (2019), Fiji by Nicole George (2012), Indonesia by Kurniawati Hastuti Dewi (2015) and India by Tarini Bedi (2016), among others. Nor is it true that disciplines outside political science and sociology have had no influence in shaping the field, with particular mention to anthropologist Emma Crewe (2021), historians J. Devika and Binitha Thampi (2012) and Shirin Rai (2017), whose disciplinary influences include performance studies. In bringing together texts with a particular regional or disciplinary focus, we seek insights across them, thereby contributing to the development of theory through the comparative project. In so doing, we aim to overcome several deficiencies in practices of knowledge production.

Disrupting canons; dismantling hierarchies

Demands to confront the hierarchies, absences and privileging within systems of knowledge production are rightly asserted in Australia and globally. Participants at the workshop shared their experiences of inequities and exploitation within academia and practice, directly confronting researchers whose voices are privileged. The resulting discomfort is necessary. To take even minor steps in the dismantling of knowledge hierarchies, it is not enough to provide space for researchers from the majority world. Minority-world researchers, especially 'white' researchers, must be wary of how they perpetuate these inequities. Naming and addressing racist and colonial systems of knowledge production are required for just and fair treatment of researchers. More importantly, failure to do so is one of the greatest impediments to advancing knowledge.

Raewyn Connell's (2007) book *Southern Theory* outlines the limitations of 'grand theory' produced from, and largely about, the 'metropole'. She argues that dominant theories in the social sciences are based on the experiences of Europe and North America, yet are presented as universal frames through which 'all societies are knowable' (Connell 2007: 44). Connell's observation that 'data gathering and application happen in the colony, while theorising happens in the metropole' (Connell 2007: ix) is relevant to the field of gender and politics. A review of article titles in leading journals shows how articles about the majority world inevitably include location—and hence their specificity and limited generalisation—while studies on Europe, and particularly the United States, are left unbound to particularities.[2] The experiences of the majority world are erased in the grounding of theory in the empirical, while knowledge of these places is framed through the theoretical problems and concepts of European society—the universal (Chakrabarty 2000; Morris-Suzuki 2020). Theory thus produced results 'not in minor omissions but in major incompleteness, and a profound problem about the truthfulness of arguments framed as universal generalisations' (Connell 2007: 226). To advance theory, we must not only include the ideas and experiences from the majority world, but also 'provincialise' knowledge produced in and about Euro-America (Chakrabarty 2000).

Doing so requires us to disrupt the canon of gender and politics— 'a privileged set of texts, whose interpretation and reinterpretation defines a field' (Connell 2007: 4). That such a canon exists in gender and politics is evident in the repetition of names in the bibliographies of leading journals, as well as the rejections authors face when they dare not give due reverence. 'Reading from the centre'—that is, referencing and positioning their own work in relation to other 'metropolitan theoretical

---

2   It is encouraging to see that the leading journal *Politics & Gender* now insists on the location in the title of all papers, including those from North America.

literature' (Connell 2007: 45)—leads to a limited framing of problems and conceptual tools. Teele (2019: 15) highlights the problem in comparative politics of the 'unreflexive importation of hypotheses from the American context' elsewhere without contextualisation. Lack of acknowledgement of the specificities of the United States' political system can lead to pursuing the wrong questions, being bogged down in details or overlooking other connections (Teele 2019; see also Liu 2018; Piscopo and Kenny 2020). Too often literature on gender and politics from Asia and Oceania also relies on the conceptual apparatus and analytical tools imported from Euro-America. Doing so can advance understanding, and authors in this book also draw on 'the concepts and techniques from the metropole' (Connell 2007: 223). Yet, theory is incomplete and limited in its empirical grounding and imaginative resources if it largely derives from the minority world.

In this volume, we aim to disrupt the canon or, in the least, expand it through theories and concepts developed in the majority world. As we outline below, and as elaborated in the chapters, this includes: historicisation that centres colonialism and decolonisation (see Hawkesworth 2012; Kauanui 2008; Teaiwa 2006); different ways of understanding and practising intersectionality, including recognising its long genealogies in feminist action (Ganesh 2016); processual understandings of democracy that excavate the importance of political subjectivities, cultural values and idioms (Michelutti 2007; Ciotti 2017); and reframing motherhood and domesticity in ways that revise conventional categorisations (Segato 2018; Waylen 1996). This ambition was realised in the selection of plenary speakers and presentations celebrating the work of overlooked feminist scholars from Oceania and Asia (see also Salmah Eva-Lina Lawrence, Chapter 5; and Margaret Jolly, Chapter 6, this volume). The theoretical resources in the work of these underappreciated women are rich, providing new frames to not only understand the experiences of women in Oceania, but also approach the study of gender and politics more generally. Further, as many of our authors are fluent in at least one Asian or Oceanic language, they have access to scholarship beyond English texts or translations. While authors could draw on the texts that most resonated with them, standard citational practices of 'reading from the centre' were discouraged.

In highlighting the value of overlooked scholars, the violence wrought by the absence of voices from the majority world becomes apparent. Mignolo (2011) shows how epistemological projects are also projects of control, not least of which is the project of 'modernity'. Knowledge is central, as it is 'the enactments of certain types and spheres of knowledge that frame the praxis of living' (Mignolo and Walsh 2018: 137). The theories of economics and politics came to produce economic and political institutions. Democratic institutions—a key part of modernity and an object of study in gender and politics—are part of modernising projects. Yet, the reverberations of colonisation and decolonisation in today's gender unequal politics are not a dominant theme in the literature. Focusing on many formerly colonial countries, these impacts are unavoidably foregrounded. Several chapters examine how processes of creolisation through the colonial encounter have led to political cultures and styles that privilege men, often obliterating more gender equal or feminine political cultures (Jolly, Chapter 6; Mostuga and Howard, Chapter 9; Novadona Bayo, Chapter 10, this volume). Political leadership has become more masculine, more hostile to women and embedded within racialised systems. Revealing these processes not only helps to understand the ongoing nature of coloniality, but also provides insights into how male dominance is produced anew over time (Segato 2018).

No discussion of hierarchies in systems of knowledge production would be complete without a discussion of 'whiteness'. The feminist values underpinning the identification of problems and priorities in gender politics too often end up being white feminist values (Mohanty 2002; Moreton-Robinson 2020). The initial framing of the workshop that centred leadership and representation was rightly taken to task for its narrow envisioning of what political participation is and the modalities through which change can happen. More so, racial hierarchies are all too present in our research practices. Some of the most powerful moments in the workshop came when participants such as Anna Kwai and Jennifer Kalpokas Doan called out the inequities: the tendency to juniorise researchers from Oceania and Asia; to under-recognise the value of PhD students from the region beyond being objects of 'capacity-building'; treating local collaborators as merely instruments for data collection rather than contributing expertise that would otherwise be missing. Nor are racialised hierarchies only evident in 'North–South' collaborations and relationships. Racialised and feminised bodies navigate invisibility/hypervisibility, marginalisation and discrimination within higher education systems where 'white' researchers are privileged (Barthwal-Datta 2023; Bhopal 2018). White academics have an obligation not only to renounce their privilege, but also to actively take part in dismantling white racial domination within knowledge institutions and practices (Leonardo 2004).

Scholars from Asia and Oceania have provided tools to challenge knowledge practices founded on racial domination and marginalisation. Māori scholar Linda Tuhiwai Smith's influential text *Decolonizing Methodologies: Research and Indigenous Peoples* laid bare 'the complex ways in which the pursuit of knowledge is deeply embedded in the multiple layers of imperial and colonial practices' (2005: 2). A decolonising methodology requires that Indigenous people lead the research process: the questions, the approach, the uses. This disruption of the 'regular rules' for research is not only an ethical and political necessity; it is also crucial for producing richer and more truthful knowledge.[3] Anna Kwai (Chapter 3) shows how research on minority gender and development approaches applied in Solomon Islands by external researchers were driven by Orientalist discourses that fitted within a global development discourse of the Pacific as 'backward'. Misrepresentations were based on false evidence and an exclusion of Solomon Islands women from knowledge-making practices. Indeed, including the lived experiences of women is another way in which we should disrupt the canon of gender and politics. Workshop participants spoke of the need to make visible the generations of women who have been seeking change and elevate them in our theorising. Their lived experiences of movement and solidarity-building may not have achieved the hoped-for transformations, but they are uncovering inequalities and forging new places from which women can seek change (see Ruby Lai, Chapter 12; Rachael Diprose et al., Chapter 13; Serena Ford, Chapter 14).

These necessary changes to our research practices come up against the neoliberal and neocolonial university. With universities as institutions of knowledge authority, academics are rewarded for being *the* experts, made legible through the number of first or sole-authored publications. Collaboration is encouraged—particularly when it brings in grant money— but the redistribution of resources and devolving of power/authorship are not. Nonetheless, and with no easy answers, contributors have explored ways to conduct research more ethically, with a focus on the quality of knowledge, not individual accolades. Chapter 7 by Camilla Batalibasi, Chandy Eng, Melissa MacLean, Donna Makini, Vani Nailumu, Sonia Palmieri and Geraldine Valei most explicitly addresses this issue, outlining a collaborative, non-hierarchical model of sense-making around their common experience of interviewing women political leaders in Asia and Oceania. In questioning research practices and seeking new forms of collaboration, we argue that fresh insights, new conceptualisations and theoretical contributions are possible.

---

3   See Connell (2007) on questions of truthfulness in social sciences.

Thinking anew about area studies

Our ambition to rethink how we do scholarship extends to studies of Asia and Oceania. The value of Asian and Pacific studies is particularly pertinent to three of the co-editors and an additional four authors, all of whom have their institutional home in the College of Asia and the Pacific (CAP) at The Australian National University. The college is critical to The Australian National University's special status as producing knowledge and expertise about the regions in which we are situated. Institutional survival depends, in part, on demonstrating the value of this enterprise—narrowly in terms of Australia's national interests and broadly in terms of global scholarship. The workshop aimed to take advantage of the critical mass of scholars working on gender and politics in Asia and the Pacific located in CAP, but also to bring fresh ideas about where the value of this scholarship lies. We aimed to do so by disrupting the boundary between area studies and knowledge produced for, and about, Australia (and, by extension, other countries).

But first, an explanation on our approach to defining the regions. We are mindful of the relegation of the Pacific as an add-on to the Asia-Pacific: a hyphenate descriptor popular among policymakers. Often the countries of the Pacific are almost entirely absent in maps of the Pacific Rim, which show a vast, empty ocean at its centre (Jolly 2007). We therefore use, where appropriate, 'Oceania', which more accurately reflects the relations and connections across the 'sea of islands with their inhabitants' (Hau'ofa 1994: 153). Further, we treat neither Asia nor the Pacific as natural entities, but recognise their constructed, fluid and contested boundaries (Morris-Suzuki 2020). The Australian geopolitical imaginary has strong framings of the two regions: Asia as the future promise of capitalism; the Pacific as an object for development intervention (Jolly 2007). The developmentalism discourse that simplifies and generalises the Pacific (Teaiwa 2006) is particularly present in knowledge institutions in Australia, where government funding rewards the production of solutions for the 'development' problems of near neighbours. We hence want to be very clear that neither the Pacific nor Asia is the focus of this volume because they have an unusually acute problem of women's marginalisation in politics. Rather, we see male dominance of politics as a global phenomenon, with experiences from Asia and Oceania valuable in expanding our knowledge of this shared problem.

To achieve this potential, studies of Oceania and Asia must overcome some of the problems of area studies. Area studies has been critiqued for being part of the modernist project of the colonial era and thereafter providing intelligence for Cold War governments (Goss and Wesley-Smith 2010). From our perspective, however, the most pressing problem is that the theories that inform the interpretation of 'the diverse complexities of the particular region' remain driven by the 'West' (Morris-Suzuki 2020: 15). As Tessa Morris-Suzuki (2020: 15) argues, this reliance on Western frameworks dulls understanding and frustrates the necessary task of 'rethinking of the vision of "Western civilisation" as interpreter of the world, and as crucible of the modern'. Yet, in more recent iterations, area studies can be an antidote to Euro-American dominance in grand theory. Scholars such as Gayatri Spivak and Arif Dirlik have drawn on 'non-Western discourses, epistemologies, societies and cultural formations to critique Euro-Amerocentrism and to develop more comprehensive theories of global phenomena' (Jackson 2019: 57). If a major criticism of grand theory in the social sciences is its erasure of the experiences of most of humankind, then rich empirical studies grounded in deep cultural and linguistic familiarity with Asia and Oceania can correct its inadequacies.

The interdisciplinarity of area studies further overcomes the limitations of knowledge produced within the narrow confines of one discipline. Peter Jackson (2019) argues that disciplinary studies are based on Euro-American intellectual and political hegemony. He pinpoints political science as one discipline that is so narrow in its geographical focus that it could be considered a disguised Western area studies. With the failure of discipline-based studies to explain 'globalizing processes beyond the West' (Jackson 2019: 58), area studies' cross-disciplinarity is a strength. Teresia Teaiwa (2010: 116) similarly sees the value of Pacific studies to 'the humanities and social sciences [as] a space for conscientious interdisciplinary engagement'. She notes that the field of Pacific studies enables cross-pollination across the stacks of single-discipline monographs and theses on the Pacific, with different disciplinary viewpoints brought together for a more holistic account. For our purposes, the need for cross-disciplinarity arises not to know a region, state or peoples, but to address a complex and shared problem of male political dominance.

So, while Asian studies and Pacific studies are valued for their production of rich knowledge of regions crucial to Australia's interests, we argue that their greater contribution is in advancing empirical, conceptual and theoretical resources to understand common research problems. While not all authors in this volume would identify as a scholar in Asian and/or Pacific studies, all contribute to developing a wider empirical basis for grounding theory. Unlike the cursory treatment of countries to find generalisable patterns in comparative social science, these studies are grounded in deep familiarity and specificity. Against the argument that depth results in endless particularity with limited relevance beyond the locality, it is this attention to detail that enables the unearthing of hidden processes and avoids the missteps of misinterpretation (Ingold 2018; van der Veer 2016). Our cross-disciplinary approach allows us a wider range of methodological, theoretical and conceptual tools to understand the problem of male dominance in politics, and to reveal the processes that lend it remarkable durability across geographical contexts.

Our engagement with Asia and Oceania is therefore not as a region or regions per se, but for the potential of studies grounded in places outside Euro-America to advance understandings *beyond* these regions. Bringing these regions together is not with an ambition to produce a grand narrative with disproportionate weight on commonalities in histories and experiences. Our approach to comparison is more anthropological than sociological, aiming for the 'elucidation of complex phenomena through comparison without "generalism" or modelling of "social systems"' (van der Veer 2016: 148). In this way our ambitions align with what Morris-Suzuki describes as an 'anti-area studies' that does not use 'modern Western academic theories to elucidate the peculiarities of places in Asia or elsewhere' (2020: 22), but instead 'uses knowledge of a variety of places and a variety of disciplinary approaches to elucidate problems that cross boundaries' (p. 23). In so doing, we also question the validity of theories from the minority world and interrogate the knowledge practices that produce them. This involves interrogating the borders of artificial constructs such as Asia and Oceania. Ramona Vijeyarasa (Chapter 8) takes on the task of seeing what and how we can learn across the regions, urging us to challenge our sense of boundaries and borders rather than compartmentalise and categorise in ways that lose sight of experiences and the lessons to be learnt.

As demonstrating the relevance of studies of Oceania and Asia beyond the regions was central to our aims, a key measure of success of the workshop was the dialogue between researchers working in these regions and those in Australia. Conventionally, research from and about Oceania and Asia is seen as relevant to Australia only in as much as it satisfies the national interest to know its neighbours. When Australia seeks to know itself, it turns to the United Kingdom, the United States and Canada. There are good reasons to do so. Australia is a settler state, a multicultural nation and has a Westminster-style democracy. Yet, to ignore the rich insights from Asia and Oceania is to limit the creativity with which we tackle fundamental problems. Particularly pressing is the problem of the underrepresentation of people of non-European ancestry in our political institutions, especially Asian Australians (Song 2023; Pietsch 2018). By bringing together two communities of practice—those working in Asia and/or Oceania and those working in Australia—we aimed to show the possibilities for theorising from these regions to address the deficiencies of political representation in countries like Australia.

These possibilities come in two shapes. The first operates at the meso-level of theory development, with the claim that theories developed from Asia and Oceania provide tools for understanding beyond these regions, as outlined above. The second answer responds to Australia's status as a multicultural nation. While the influence of the United Kingdom on Australia's political system is widely accepted, less so are the influences of diasporas on emergent political styles and cultures. Zappala (1998) notes the different political cultures of minority 'ethnic groups' compared with those of Anglo-Australian ethnicity (see also Sheppard et al. 2020). He argues for greater understanding of the way ethnic communities have changed the political culture in Australia, including in more mainstream ways. Nonetheless, such research remains rare, perhaps due to the focus in political science on formal political institutions—which remain British influenced—compared with the more informal institutions and political cultures. Without ignoring the dangers of reifying and essentialising fragmented and diverse 'ethnic groups' (Ang 2014), and of the way naming a diaspora 'stamps it with ethnic, national or racial characteristics that survive despite all differences' (Dirlik 2005: 166), understanding the styles of political engagement across Asia and Oceania can help us understand Australia's political cultures (in the plural), their dynamics and complexities.

These are the kinds of possibilities that we sought to explore in the workshop. Whether we succeeded in this aim is a different matter. The workshop split largely into two groups and, while some participants attended the entire three days, the majority kept to their own communities of practice. A special issue that presents the research from the papers on Asian Australian leadership and cultural citizenship has been published by *Peril* magazine, edited by three leading scholars of this field: Mridula Chakrabarty, Olivia Khoo and Jacqueline Lo. While these volumes are notable outcomes from the workshop, more must be done to bring this parallel scholarship into greater conversation.

Knowledge as social action

A final ambition of the workshop was to break down the false distinction between theory and practice. Inspired by Patricia Hill Collins (2019), we conceived the workshop as a form of social action in two senses. First, we theorise not for theory's sake, but to see academic practice as an integral part of social change. As Stuart Hall (2016) encouraged and practised, theory provides a map to navigate the world so that we may intervene in ways that effect positive change. As the world is messy and dynamic, so too must our theories capture complexity and be forever contingent. Collins (2019) also advocates theory oriented to criticising social inequalities and changing the world from what it is. In this respect, theory—and perhaps especially the 'grand theory' that promises overarching and durable explanations of the world—can help maintain, as much as challenge, the status quo. We must therefore be not only attentive to how our own knowledge projects act on the world, but also critical of the knowledge projects that perpetuate injustices (Collins 2019).

The second sense is that social action is itself a form of knowledge production (Collins 2019). Subordinated groups have rich knowledge of systems of oppression and vast experience in navigating and labouring to transform the status quo. Their vested interest in understanding and resisting oppression makes their theories and experiences crucial resources. Patricia Hill Collins proposes intersectionality as a methodology that goes beyond academia. She writes: 'Rather than rejecting experience and social action as dimensions of its critical theorizing, I suggest that intersectionality would do better to redefine social action as a way of knowing that, because it valorizes experience, potentially strengthens intersectional theorizing' (Collins 2019: 13). In recognition of the value of social action for theorising, we invited to our workshop people working in nongovernmental organisations, feminist organisations, government departments and elected representatives. Our aim was to co-produce rich knowledge with greater potential for social impact.

Social activists were some of the most committed participants, with their questions and responses to research papers particularly productive. My favourite moment was when a 'culturally and racially marginalised'[4] female political actor challenged the critical analysis of ethnic politics in

---

4   Following the Diversity Council of Australia, I prefer the term 'culturally and racially marginalised' to refer to people who are racialised in the Australian context, which often has a cultural element, especially religion.

Australia. Her inflamed response provided not only a correction, but also experiential knowledge of the power relations that prevent women from racialised backgrounds from progressing in politics. We also convened two panels comprising people in roles focused on practical changes on the ground. Their insights help us see how we can achieve knowledge as social action through partnerships. It became clear that development agencies are as attuned as academics to rethinking knowledge practices. Panellists spoke of the need to learn from lived experience, be that the lived experience of their own relative privilege or that of the women with whom one is working. While they acknowledged the challenge of different motivations and constraints between practitioner–academic partnerships, open dialogue can ameliorate the threat. While much needs to be done in thinking creatively and reflecting critically about how we collaborate in knowledge projects, the workshop and chapters that explore these questions (Lawrence, Chapter 5; Batalibasi et al., Chapter 7) give us much food for thought.

But, like the other ambitions in this volume, breaking down the boundary between theory and practice has been only partially realised. Ideally, we would ask practitioners to review chapters and pinpoint actionable insights. Dialogue might identify models of partnerships in which the synergies across academia and practice could be realised. But time to review, comment and engage is in short supply in both sectors. We are reminded of the way neoliberal economies, with their audit culture and cost-cutting, have squeezed out time for the more impactful and arguably most satisfying parts of our work (Fleming 2021). Durable systems of value also present barriers. Among some disciplinary communities, the work of academic activists is looked down on and their careers stall. Nonetheless several chapters bring together practice and theory either through the composition of authors or by movement between sectors. Salmah Eva-Lina Lawrence (Chapter 5) shows how she has brought deep decolonial thinking into the knowledge practices of the International Women's Development Agency. Balitabasi et al. (Chapter 7) reflect on their experiences working across sectors in a research project. While knowledge as social action remains by necessity an incomplete project, we hope to have taken steps in showing its importance and potential in gender and politics scholarship.

This volume

Considering the aim and politics of this edited volume—centring knowledge and researchers from Oceania and Asia—it is of some regret that the four editors are Australian researchers based in Australian universities: Margaret, Sonia and Tanya at The Australian National University and Ramona at the University of Technology Sydney. The editorial team emerged from those most active in making the workshop a success, and who had the time and editorial skills required. Such a project can be a risk, and hence prior successful working partnerships were valued. Nonetheless, having an editorial home in Australia has consequences that we explore below. We achieved more regional representation among authors, with 15 of the 24 authors based in Asia or Oceania, with three of these currently holding positions (Salmah Eva-Lina Lawrence) or pursuing PhD study (Anna Kwai and Longgina Novadona Bayo) in Australia. All knowledge is situated knowledge (Haraway 1988), and we encouraged authors to reflect on their positionality in their respective chapters. Here, we consider how the volume was shaped by it being edited from Australia.

Workshop participants from Oceania noted that they are overly determined by their positionality. They are assumed to be speaking from somewhere, whereas researchers from the minority world are free to speak from a disinterested position, to be experts of, and beyond, a region. Universities in Australia are filled with such 'expert' researchers, with their expertise sought by policymakers and high-ranking public servants. This is especially true of The Australian National University, with its historical role in advancing the nation's interests and its location in Canberra—the seat of federal government. The different levels of authority afforded the voices of Australia-based researchers, particularly those not from the regions, was a reality that hung heavy over the workshop. We hope to have captured some of that tension in this volume, rather than smoothing over these inequitable realities.

That productive tension should prompt reflection among Australia-based researchers as to the value and costs of their doing research in Oceania and Asia. The workshop was held mid-2022 after two years of closed international borders and consequent reconfiguring of our research partnerships with international collaborators. The devolving of power and leadership to local partners was a logistical necessity, but also reflected the localisation agenda in development practice and efforts to decolonise the academy. What, then, is the role of country experts outside the country? What legitimacy do they have to direct efforts for change through the knowledge they produce? Will they expend the same efforts and bear the equivalent personal costs as those living the struggle? As Vijeyarasa (2022: 87) writes, in many countries, academics and researchers cannot avoid activism, as 'there is always something going on which calls for intervention and protest'. Is the compulsion the same for academics working internationally? Questions remain about how they render themselves accountable to their countries of focus.

Australia occupies a curious place in global systems of knowledge production. It has the resources and ability to play the rankings game that allows its scholars a prominent voice in global scholarship. At the same time, being on the periphery of the Global North, separate from but still connected to the debates and theories that are dominant in Euro-America, lends the antipodes a unique perspective (Schech 2012). We are arguably less parochial in our scholarship and more outward-facing in our learning from other contexts. Forceful critiques by First Nations scholars have demanded introspection and provided the tools to reflect on, and be accountable in, our research relationships, even as epistemic violence remains an ongoing problem (Moreton-Robinson 2020; Watego 2021). At the same time, in claiming an antipodean perspective as privileged Australian scholars, we are mindful of distracting from 'contributions to social theory from those who are more truly "Southern" in "our part of the world", for example, Indigenous Australians ... and Indigenous Pacific peoples', as Margaret Jolly (2008) writes. Our positioning shapes the aims of this volume to decentre Euro-America and disrupt knowledge hierarchies, but we must be clear on our position of privilege within them, with its attendant limitations.

Remaining questions

Knowledge projects are always contingent and incomplete. As with the GIWL report that catalysed this project, ours also has limitations. Yet, the questions asked of the report remain valid. Would the starting questions and distillation of 'common lessons' look different from the 'majority world'? Would we have the same core findings with the same degree of certainty? Would we prioritise different areas for future research? The answer in each case is yes. The key task now is to derive these common lessons, the strength of evidence and priority research areas. Yet, this volume is not an overview of all the literature that has come out of Oceania and Asia on gender and politics. It is a collective effort to add empirically rich and grounded studies that contribute an evidence base, from which we can develop new theoretical and conceptual lenses. We discuss the crosscutting themes in the afterword. Here, I provide my tentative responses to these questions based on what I have learnt from this exercise.

The centrality of the postcolonial experience[5]

As noted above, centring Asia and Oceania necessarily entails centring historical experiences of colonialism, decolonialisation and the forging of new political institutions. Many of the lessons gleaned through this volume come through comparing these experiences and their impact on gender and politics.

The footprint of past colonial and continuing neocolonial relations is visible in the very framing and naming of the countries of Asia and Oceania. There was a wide diversity of political forms across this region before the incursions of Euro-American and, in some cases, Asian imperialism. In many parts of Oceania, precolonial polities were small, stateless entities. This was true of what is now Papua New Guinea (PNG), Vanuatu, Solomon Islands and other parts of the Western Pacific, where there was and is extraordinary cultural and linguistic diversity. Both achieved and ascribed patterns of leadership tended to elevate men as big-men or chiefs, especially in relations of war and peace with other polities. Women exerted power through sacred kinship connections to place and through their potency in producing food and bringing forth new life. In eastern Oceania, in Samoa, Tonga and Hawai'i, for example, archipelagos were more culturally and linguistically homogeneous, more integrated hierarchical polities prevailed and here rank was more important than gender in exerting power and influence. Women could be high-ranking, titled chiefs (see Jolly, Chapter 6; Motusaga and Howard, Chapter 9, this volume).

Although the precolonial political patterns of Asia were far more diverse, with a range of princely states and Asian empires that pre-dated European imperialism, the borders of countries still largely bear the imprint of later colonial impositions and postcolonial processes—most visibly perhaps in the violent processes of the Partition of India and Pakistan in 1947 and

---

5   Margaret Jolly wrote much of this subsection. I am grateful for her generosity in allowing me to use it in the introduction without co-authorship—indicative of her collegiality from which I have learnt and benefited.

later the emergence of Bangladesh from what was East Pakistan. The crucial point here is that despite the diversity of cultures and histories, many of these political entities in Asia and Oceania, most of them parties to the international system of states through the United Nations, emerged from the turbulent cauldron of violent colonial histories and movements of anticolonial resistance and decolonisation. These histories influenced not just their shape and borders but also what constituted 'politics' and the masculinism that saturated state-based politics.

Against this background, this volume is in part a search for analytical lenses through which to read *across* studies of gender and politics in postcolonial states in Oceania and Asia. Why did masculinist states emerge and how is masculine dominance reinscribed over time? Answering this question foregrounds processes that are arguably underexamined within the gender and politics literature, with relevance not only for postcolonial countries, but also for settler states and former colonial powers. Within this volume these processes include knowledge practices (Kwai, Chapter 3), the introduction of novel gender ideologies (Jolly, Chapter 6), the framing of politics through borrowed cultural idioms (Bayo, Chapter 10) and the construction of the places of politics from masculinist repertoires (Howard and Motusaga, Chapter 9). Attentiveness to how history and sociocultural settings shape democracy as an unfolding cultural practice has revealed the mechanisms that privilege male political leadership in the majority world, but rarely have these theoretical tools been used to shed light on gender and politics in the minority world.

A distillation of common lessons from comparing Asia and Oceania suggests three research priorities. The first is to show the importance of history. How do the experiences of being a colonial power (and the loss of that power), the establishment of settler colonies and frontier wars resonate in today's political institutions in the minority world? How have racial and gendered systems of power emerged that sustain white-male dominance? The second priority is to deploy the concepts and theories that elucidate these processes in the majority world to the minority world. How do discourses and ideologies produce the 'political' in ways that exclude, make invisible or diminish women's political action? How do the cultural idioms through which we make sense of the political sustain male dominance? The final priority is arguably the most important: radically reimagining what democracy (or even politics) is and can be. Precolonial political systems remind us that there is nothing inevitable or sacred about electoral democracy, while the diversity of vernacular democracies invites a search for new cultural practices. What would a vernacular democracy look like as scripted by women? As our volume reiterates, these exercises in imagination must be led by Indigenous researchers in a decolonial praxis (Lawrence, Chapter 5) and involving women with diverse lived experiences. It is also worth reiterating that reimagining political systems is as necessary in Euro-America as it is in Asia, Oceania and the rest of the majority world.

Unsettling certainties

This volume also raises questions about the certainty of 'common lessons' arising from a Euro-American–dominated literature. I identify three 'certainties' (though admittedly I use the term lightly) that our volume challenges. The first is the certainty over what counts as a subject in gender and politics, and who is a political actor. Kwai (Chapter 3) notes the harm caused by a 'spotlight' that shines a light on remarkable women but casts a shadow over others and the work that they do. Intersecting axes of youth, gender, sexuality, ethnicity and disability push many 'out of the spotlight' to the peripheries of political action (Stephenson, Chapter 4). These peripheries can nonetheless be a space where women can exercise more informal, and at times less confrontational, forms of power, be that in village women's groups and networks (Diprose et al., Chapter 13) or through democratic practices in domestic spaces (Bayo, Chapter 10). Other chapters highlight women's political action that is largely overlooked in gender and political scholarship, including in church groups, regional organisations, NGOs and women's activist groups (Jolly, Chapter 6; Ford, Chapter 14). While this political action deserves greater attention and celebration, the costs of its peripheralisation should not be overlooked, including reinforcing exclusionary structures (Stephenson, Chapter 4). These chapters also, however, show the limitations of a frame of exclusion for understanding male political dominance. These women are not excluded from political systems as much as adversely incorporated—that is, included, but in ways in which their political action is minimised, made invisible, appropriated or rendered marginal (see Jakimow 2024). Unsettling who counts as a political actor also means unsettling the dominant framing of 'exclusion' in gender and politics literature.

Several chapters also suggest the need to unsettle the common axes of intersectionality. Race, gender and, to a lesser extent, class have dominated understandings of how intersecting power relations influence political systems (Brown 2014; Crowder-Meyer 2020; Murray 2023). Stephenson (Chapter 4) is the most explicit in calling for greater attention to ethnicity, sexuality, age and disability in majority-world contexts, adding to the relatively smaller bodies of work exploring these axes of dis/advantage in minority-world contexts (Chou et al. 2021; Evans and Reher 2022; Meekosha 2006; Waltz and Schippers 2021). Other chapters point to the need to include other power relations within gender and politics scholarship. Jolly (Chapter 6) highlights differences in high-ranking and low-ranking women—a form of hierarchical differentiation requiring careful translation from Oceanic to other contexts, *and vice versa*. Mishra and Mishra (Chapter 11) note the significance of ethnicity as an enabler and disabler of women's political participation. The relative absence of discussions of clan, caste and religion in intersectional readings of politics, despite their significance across much of Oceania and Asia, is a missed opportunity. In this context, Lai (Chapter 12) offers a valuable contribution by proposing a strategy of 'intersectional specialisation', living up to Patricia Hill Collins's (2019: 2) ambition of '*intersectionality* as a tool for social change'.

The final certainty that I wish to unsettle is 'what works' to increase female representation. Female role-models, properly implemented quotas and political funding are the ingredients for women's political careers in the Cowper-Coles (2020) report. Yet, the evidence is perhaps shakier than the 'green light' rating implies. Liu (2018) found that rather than the role-model effect seen in Western democracies, female political leaders in South-East and East Asia can create a backlash that depresses women's political participation. While I have not encountered evidence that suggests political funding has a negative impact anywhere, it may not be a viable strategy in clientelist political cultures (Harahap et al. 2022). Contributions by Vijeyarasa (Chapter 8) and Mishra and Mishra (Chapter 11) point to the limitations of quotas, even when implemented properly. It is important to capture the potential negative consequences of quotas—such as a demand for women's time and the perpetuation of narratives that minimise women's contributions—alongside the positive impacts. Perhaps the uncertainty that is being unsettled is the ability to identify universal lessons of 'what works' at all. We need new ways to learn from the lessons of others, requiring cultural fluency (Lawrence, Chapter 5) and a nuanced appreciation of the lived experiences of women political actors (Batalibasi et al., Chapter 7).

It is not sufficient to acknowledge that we know more about Euro-America than the rest of the world; we must inquire into how this imbalance impacts the field of gender and politics (see Shim, Chapter 2). One impact is the missed opportunity for theoretical development. Another is overconfidence in certain findings derived from limited contexts and their extension in practice to others. In this final section, I have shared what I have learnt from reading the rich knowledge contained in this volume and how it responds to my discomfort with the existing gender and politics literature. My hope is that readers will also derive lessons from many, if not all, of the chapters; that they prompt new questions, draw attention to overlooked phenomena, suggest productive analytical lenses and refresh knowledge-making practices, regardless of the contexts in which they work.

Overview of chapters

This book is divided into four parts. Chapters in Part I each identify ways that the existing gender and politics literature is limited. Jaemin Shim provides evidence of publishing inequalities through a review of journal articles and book chapters on gendered media coverage in politics. He finds that most authors are based in Western Europe and English-speaking settler colonies. Studies from these areas are also overrepresented and have a disproportionate visibility in the literature. Anna Kwai offers a sharp critique of knowledge-making practices about Solomon Islands. She shows how Western-centric and uncorroborated portrayals of Solomon Islander women inaccurately make them victims of their own culture. She interrogates how such inaccuracies persist and their political effects. Elise Stephenson's chapter focuses on the political pathways of gender-diverse young people in South-East Asia and Australia—a group that has garnered only sporadic attention in the literature. She shows how constructive gaps have emerged that provide space for diverse political participation, albeit in ways that do not fit conventional framings of politics. Through examining the limits of scholarship, these chapters also identify alternative ways of knowing and doing politics.

The chapters in Part II define, interrogate and practise decolonisation in gender and politics scholarship. Salmah Eva-Lina Lawrence aims to recover the political potential of 'decolonisation' in development programs supporting women's leadership. Through engagement with Pasifika women scholars, she introduces two concepts to make theoretical interventions in decoloniality relevant for practice: Indigenisation and cultural fluency. Margaret Jolly's chapter continues the task of celebrating Pasifika women thinkers and activists who have regretfully remained external to the gender and politics 'canon'. She shows how their work not only expands our understanding of gender relations in politics, but also offers alternative ways of thinking about the political project of decolonisation from a Pasifika standpoint. The chapter by Camilla Batalibasi, Chandy Eng, Donna Makini, Vani Nailumu and Geraldine Valei, with Sonia Palmieri and Melissa MacLean, puts words into action on the methodological challenges and opportunities of researching women's political leadership in Cambodia, Bougainville, Fiji and Solomon Islands. Experiences as 'local' researchers reveal subtleties in how power works in and through gendered bodies, while, as a collective, they reflect on their collaboration through a decolonial lens.

Part III, 'Reframing the Narrative, Reclaiming Space', expands our imaginative horizons through fresh ways of looking at gender and politics. Ramona Vijeyarasa goes beyond the usual question of how women reach the top levels of power, to examine what happens when they do. In answering this question for women presidents in Asia, she both deconstructs the idea of 'Asia' as a distinct region and points to the possibilities of producing global theory from distinctly 'Asian' commonalities. Mema Motusaga and Elise Howard examine the discursive power of narratives to construct political spaces as gendered spaces that exclude women in Samoa. They propose 're-storying' as a respectful process to reclaim and restore women's political power, but in ways that challenge Eurocentric notions of politics. Longgina Novadona Bayo challenges assumptions that domestic spaces are apolitical, seeing them as sites for women to learn and practise political leadership in West Timor, Indonesia. She shows how domestic cooking sites are places where relationships are forged and affective investments made that support political ambitions. Deepak Mishra and Aparimita Mishra further interrogate the spatiality of gender and politics—in this case, by revealing the distinct possibilities for women's political leadership in the frontier region of Arunachal Pradesh, India. They demonstrate how ethno-politics and patronage fundamentally shape these possibilities and present news ways of understanding the effects on women's political participation.

Part IV turns to the movements and solidarities that are challenging male domination of politics. Ruby Y.S. Lai's chapter introduces the concept of a 'self-limiting movement' to understand how feminist movements in Hong Kong have modified their advocacy to ensure their continuity in a shifting political culture. She points to the need to recognise women's movements in their plurality and to theorise the ways they change in response to fast-moving conditions. Rachael Diprose, Bronwyn Anne Beech Jones and Ken M.P. Setiawan examine rural women's practices of 'networked collective action' through the building of muti-actor coalitions of women's groups in Indonesia. These networks of solidarity, mutual support and resource-sharing are a means for women from non-elite backgrounds to engage in decision-making spaces. Serena Eleonora Ford's chapter shows how feminist activists can resist the depletion through social reproduction of Vietnamese trainees in Japan's Technical Intern Training Program. Through acts of replenishment, activists across borders sustain women's wellbeing within gendered systems of exploitation. These chapters centre the actions of feminist activists and women organisers, and thereby the knowledge with which they interpret and act on male political domination.

By way of conclusion, the afterword returns to the questions sparked by the Cowper-Coles report. Ramona Vijeyarasa, Sonia Palmieri, Margaret Jolly and Tanya Jakimow identify key insights and research priorities that emerge when we centre Asia and Oceania and take a cross-disciplinary approach to politics and gender.

References

Alam, Shahidul. 2008. 'Majority World: Challenging the West's Rhetoric of Democracy.' *Amerasia Journal* 34, no. 1: 88—98. doi.org/10.17953/amer.34.1. l3176027k4q614v5.

Ang, Ien. 2014. 'Beyond Chinese Groupism: Chinese Australians between Assimilation, Multiculturalism and Diaspora.' *Ethnic and Racial Studies* 37, no. 7: 1184–96. doi.org/10.1080/01419870.2014.859287.

Baker, Kerryn. 2019. *Pacific Women in Politics: Gender Quota Campaigns in the Pacific Islands*. Honolulu: University of Hawai'i Press. doi.org/10.2307/j.ctv7r42qp.

Baker, Kerryn, and Sonia Palmieri. 2021. 'Can Women Dynasty Politicians Disrupt Social Norms of Political Leadership? A Proposed Typology of Normative Change.' *International Political Science Review* 44, no. 1: 122–36. doi.org/10.1177/01925121211048298.

Barthwal-Datta, Monika. 2023. 'On In/Visibility.' *Journal of Critical Southern Studies* 4, no. 3: 1–14. doi.org/10.3943/jcss.45.

Bedi, Tarini. 2016. *The Dashing Ladies of Shiv Sena: Political Matronage in Urbanizing India*. Albany: SUNY Press. doi.org/10.1515/9781438460321.

Bhopal, Kalwant. 2018. *White Privilege: The Myth of a Post-Racial Society*. Bristol: University of Bristol Press. doi.org/10.56687/9781447335986.

Bjarnegård, Elin. 2013. *Gender, Informal Institutions and Political Recruitment: Explaining Male Dominance in Parliamentary Representation*. London: Palgrave Macmillan. doi.org/10.1057/9781137296740.

Brown, Nadia E. 2014. 'Political Participation of Women of Color: An Intersectional Analysis.' *Journal of Women, Politics and Policy* 35, no. 4: 315–48. doi.org/10.1080/1554477X.2014.955406.

Celis, Karen, Johanna Kantola, Georgina Waylen, and S. Laurel Weldon. 2013. 'Introduction.' In *The Oxford Handbook of Gender and Politics*, edited by Georgina Waylen, Karen Celis, Johanna Kantola, and S. Laurel Weldon, 1–19. Oxford: Oxford University Press. doi.org/10.1093/oxfordhb/9780199751457.013.0034.

Chakrabarty, Dipesh. 2000. *Provincializing Europe: Postcolonial Thought and Historical Difference*. Princeton: Princeton University Press.

Chou, Mark, Lesley Pruitt, and Luke Dean. 2021. 'Too Young to Run? Young Political Candidates and the 2020 Victorian Local Government Elections.' *Australian Journal of Political Science* 56, no. 4: 428–44. doi.org/10.1080/1036 1146.2021.1998345.

Ciccia, Rossella, and Conny Roggeband. 2021. 'Unpacking Intersectional Solidarity: Dimensions of Power in Coalitions.' *European Journal of Politics and Gender* 4, no. 2: 181–98. doi.org/10.1332/251510821X16145402377609.

Ciotti, Manuela. 2017. *Unsettling the Archetypes: Femininities and Masculinities in Indian Politics*. New Delhi: Women Unlimited.

Collins, Patricia Hill. 2019. *Intersectionality as Critical Theory*. Durham: Duke University Press.

Connell, Raewyn. 2007. *Southern Theory: The Global Dynamics of Knowledge in Social Science*. Sydney: Allen & Unwin. doi.org/10.4324/9781003117346.

Cowper-Coles, Minna. 2020. *Women Political Leaders: The Impact of Gender on Democracy*. Report for the Global Institute for Women's Leadership and the Westminster Foundation for Democracy. London: King's College London. www.wfd.org/what-we-do/resources/women-political-leaders-impact-gender-democracy.

Crewe, Emma. 2021. *The Anthropology of Parliaments: Entanglements in Democratic Politics*. London: Routledge. doi.org/10.4324/9781003084488.

Crowder-Meyer, Melody. 2020. 'Baker, Bus Driver, Babysitter, *Candidate*? Revealing the Gendered Development of Political Ambition Among Ordinary Americans.' *Political Behavior* 42: 359–84. doi.org/10.1007/s11109-018-9498-9.

Derichs, Claudia, and Mark Thompson, eds. 2013. *Dynasties and Female Political Leaders in Asia: Gender, Power and Pedigree*. Berlin: LIT Verlag.

Devika, J., and Binitha V. Thampi. 2012. *New Lamps for Old?* New Delhi: Zubaan.

Dewi, Kurniawati Hastuti. 2015. *Indonesian Women and Local Politics: Islam, Gender and Networks in Post-Suharto Indonesia*. Singapore: NUS Press and Kyoto University Press. doi.org/10.2307/j.ctv1nth4c.

Dirlik, Arif. 2005. 'Asia Pacific Studies in an Age of Global Modernity.' *Inter-Asia Cultural Studies* 6, no. 2: 158–72. doi.org/10.1080/14649370500065870.

Echle, Christian, and Megha Sarmah, eds. 2021. *Women, Policy and Political Leadership: Regional Perspectives*. Singapore: Konrad-Adenauer-Stiftung. www.kas.de/en/web/politikdialog-asien/single-title/-/content/women-policy-and-political-leadership-1.

Evans, Elizabeth, and Stefanie Reher. 2022. 'Disability and Political Representation: Analysing the Obstacles to Elected Office in the UK.' *International Political Science Review* 43, no. 5: 697–712. doi.org/10.1177/0192512120947458.

Fleming, Peter. 2021. *Dark Academia: How Universities Die*. London: Pluto Press. doi.org/10.2307/j.ctv1n9dkhv.

Fleschenberg, Andrea, and Claudia Derichs, eds. 2012. *Women and Politics in Asia: A Springboard for Democracy*. Singapore: ISEAS Publishing.

Ganesh, Kamala. 2016. 'No Full Circle: Revisiting My Journey in Feminist Anthropology.' *Contributions to Indian Sociology* 50, no. 3: 293–319. doi.org/10.1177/0069966716657456.

George, Nicole. 2012. *Situating Women: Gender, Politics and Circumstance in Fiji*. Canberra: ANU E Press. doi.org/10.22459/SW.11.2012.

George, Nicole. 2020. 'Women in Politics: Pacific Islands and New Zealand.' In *Women, Policy and Political Leadership: Regional Perspectives*, edited by Christian Echle and Megha Sarmah, 141–58. Singapore: Konrad-Adenauer-Stiftung.

Goss, Jon, and Terence Wesley-Smith. 2010. 'Introduction: Remaking Area Studies.' In *Remaking Area Studies: Teaching and Learning Across Asia and the Pacific*, edited by T. Wesley-Smith and J. Goss, ix–xxvii. Honolulu: University of Hawai'i Press. doi.org/10.21313/hawaii/9780824833213.001.0001.

Hall, Stuart. 2016. *Cultural Studies 1983: A Theoretical History*. Durham: Duke University Press. doi.org/10.2307/j.ctv11cw8wg.

Harahap, Aida Fitra, Tanya Jakimow, Asima Yanty Siahaan, and Yumasdaleni. 2022. 'Is Money an Insurmountable Barrier to Women's Political Representation in Transactional Democracies? Evidence from North Sumatera, Indonesia.' *Politics, Groups and Identities* 11, no. 4: 733–49. doi.org/10.1080/21565503.2022. 2041442.

Haraway, Donna. 1988. 'Situated Knowledges: The Science Question in Feminism and the Privilege of Partial Perspective.' *Feminist Studies* 14, no. 3: 575–99. doi.org/10.2307/3178066.

Hauʻofa, Epeli. 1994. 'Our Sea of Islands.' *The Contemporary Pacific* 6, no. 1: 148–61. hdl.handle.net/10125/12960.

Hawkesworth, Mary. 2012. *Political Worlds of Women: Activism, Advocacy and Governance in the Twenty-First Century*. London: Routledge.

Howard, Elise, Kerryn Baker, and Sonia Palmieri. 2023. 'Oceania.' In *Women and Politics: Global Lives in Focus*, edited by M. Och, 223–50. Santa Barbara: ABC-CLIO. doi.org/10.5040/9798216183723.ch-008.

Ingold, Tim. 2018. *Anthropology: Why it Matters*. Cambridge: Polity Press.

Iwanaga, Kazuki. 2008. *Women's Political Participation and Representation in Asia*. Copenhagen: NIAS.

Jackson, Peter. 2019. 'South East Asian Area Studies beyond Anglo-America: Geopolitical Transitions, the Neoliberal Academy and Spatialized Regimes of Knowledge.' *South East Asia Research* 27, no. 1: 49–73. doi.org/10.1080/0967 828X.2019.1587930.

Jakimow, Tanya. 2024. 'The Affective Economy of Democracy: Women's Adverse Incorporation in Party Politics in Dehradun, North India.' *HAU: Journal of Ethnographic Theory* 14, no. 2: 436–49. doi.org/10.1086/730690.

Jolly, Margaret. 2007. 'Imagining Oceania: Indigenous and Foreign Representations of a Sea of Islands.' *The Contemporary Pacific* 19, no. 2: 508–45. doi.org/ 10.1353/cp.2007.0054.

Jolly, Margaret. 2008. 'The South in *Southern Theory*: Antipodean Reflections on the Pacific.' *Australian Humanities Review* 44 (March): 75–99. doi.org/ 10.22459/AHR.44.2008.05.

Joshi, Devin, and Christian Echle. 2023. *Substantive Representation of Women in Asian Parliaments*. London: Routledge. doi.org/10.4324/9781003275961.

Kauanui, J. Kēhaulani. 2008. *Hawaiian Blood: Colonialism and the Politics of Sovereignty and Indigeneity*. Durham: Duke University Press. doi.org/10.1215/ 9780822391494.

Lawrence, Salmah Eva-Lina. Forthcoming. *Decolonising International Development: The View from the Majority World.* London: Bloomsbury.

Leonardo, Zeus. 2004. 'The Color of Supremacy: Beyond the Discourse of "White Privilege".' *Educational Philosophy and Theory* 36, no. 2: 137–52. doi.org/10.1111/j.1469-5812.2004.00057.x.

Liu, Shan-Jan Sarah. 2018. 'Are Female Political Leaders Role Models? Lessons from Asia.' *Political Research Quarterly* 71, no. 2: 255–69. doi.org/10.1177/1065912917745162.

Medie, Peace A., and Alice J. Kang. 2018. 'Power, Knowledge and the Politics of Gender in the Global South.' *European Journal of Politics and Gender* 1, nos 1–2: 37–54. doi.org/10.1332/251510818X15272520831157.

Meekosha, Helen. 2006. 'What the Hell Are You? An Intercategorical Analysis of Race, Ethnicity, Gender and Disability in the Australian Body Politic.' *Scandinavian Journal of Disability Research* 8, nos 2–3: 161–76. doi.org/10.1080/15017410600831309.

Michelutti, Lucia. 2007. 'The Vernacularization of Democracy: Political Participation and Popular Politics in North India.' *Journal of the Royal Anthropological Institute* 13, no. 3: 639–56. doi.org/10.1111/j.1467-9655.2007.00448.x.

Mignolo, Walter. 2011. *Darker Side of Western Modernity: Global Futures, Decolonial Options.* Durham: Duke University Press. doi.org/10.1215/9780822394501.

Mignolo, Walter, and Catherina Walsh. 2018. *On Decoloniality: Concepts, Analytics, Praxis.* Durham: Duke University Press. doi.org/10.1215/9780822371779.

Mohanty, Chandra Talpade. 2002. '"Under Western Eyes" Revisited: Feminist Solidarity through Anticapitalist Struggles.' *Signs: Journal of Women in Culture and Society* 28, no. 2: 500–35. doi.org/10.1086/342914.

Moreton-Robinson, Aileen. 2020 [2000]. *Talking Up to the White Woman: Indigenous Women and Feminism.* Brisbane: UQP.

Morris-Suzuki, Tessa. 2020. *On the Frontiers of History: Rethinking East Asian Borders.* Canberra: ANU Press. doi.org/10.22459/OFH.2020.

Murray, Rainbow. 2023. 'It's a Rich Man's World: How Class and Glass Ceilings Intersect for UK Parliamentary Candidates.' *International Political Science Review* 44, no. 1: 13–26. doi.org/10.1177/01925121211040025.

Och, Malliga, ed. 2023. *Women and Politics: Global Lives in Focus.* Santa Barbara: ABC-CLIO. doi.org/10.5040/9798216183723.

Phua, Mei Yen. 2018. 'Gendered Political Participation and Grassroots Activism in Hyderabad, India.' *Asian Anthropology* 17, no. 2: 151–63. doi.org/10.1080/1683478X.2018.1458402.

Pietsch, Juliet. 2018. *Race, Ethnicity, and the Participation Gap: Understanding Australia's Political Complexion.* Toronto: Toronto University Press. doi.org/10.3138/9781487519544.

Piscopo, Jennifer M., and Meryl Kenny. 2020. 'Rethinking the Ambition Gap: Gender and Candidate Emergence in Comparative Perspective.' *European Journal of Politics and Gender* 3, no. 1: 3–10. doi.org/10.1332/251510819X15755447629661.

Prihatini, Ella. 2021. 'Women in Politics.' In *Women, Policy and Political Leadership: Regional Perspectives*, edited by Christian Echle and Megha Sarmah, 33–47. Singapore: Konrad-Adenauer-Stiftung. www.kas.de/en/web/politikdialog-asien/single-title/-/content/women-policy-and-political-leadership-1.

Rai, Shirin. 2017. 'Performance and Politics: An Approach to Symbolic Representation.' *Politics, Groups and Identities* 5, no. 3: 506–11. doi.org/10.1080/21565503.2017.1321996.

Rai, Shirin, and Janelle Reinelt, eds. 2014. *The Grammar of Politics and Performance.* London: Routledge. doi.org/10.4324/9781315879871.

Rai, Shirin, and Caroline Spary. 2019. *Performing Representation: Women Members in the Indian Parliament.* Oxford: Oxford University Press. doi.org/10.1093/oso/9780199489053.001.0001.

Schech, Susanne. 2012. 'Development Perspectives from the Antipodes: An Introduction.' *Third World Quarterly* 33, no. 6: 969–80. doi.org/10.1080/01436597.2012.681498.

Segato, Rita. 2018. 'A Manifesto in Four Themes.' *Critical Times* 1, no. 1: 198–211. doi.org/10.1215/26410478-1.1.198.

Sheppard, Jill, Marija Taflaga, and Liang Jiang. 2020. 'Explaining High Rates of Political Participation Among Chinese Migrants to Australia.' *International Political Science Review* 41, no. 3: 385–401. doi.org/10.1177/0192512119834623.

Song, Jay. 2023. 'Political Representation of Asian Australians in Liberal Nationalist Multiculturalism.' *Australian Journal of Political Science* 58, no. 2: 157–74. doi.org/10.1080/10361146.2023.2166810.

Tadros, Mariz, ed. 2014. *Women in Politics: Gender, Power and Development.* London: Zed Books. doi.org/10.5040/9781350224070.

Teaiwa, Teresia K. 2006. 'On Analogies: Rethinking the Pacific in a Global Context.' *The Contemporary Pacific* 18, no. 1: 71–87. doi.org/10.1353/cp.2005.0105.

Teaiwa, Teresia K. 2010. 'For or *Before* an Asia Pacific Studies Agenda? Specifying Pacific Studies.' In *Remaking Area Studies: Teaching and Learning Across Asia and the Pacific*, edited by T. Wesley-Smith and J. Goss, 110–24. Honolulu: University of Hawai'i Press. doi.org/10.21313/hawaii/9780824833213.003.0006.

Teele, Dawn Langan. 2019. 'Resisting the Americanization of Comparative Politics.' *APSA-CP Newsletter* 29, no. 1: 15–21.

Tuhiwai Smith, Linda. 2005. *Decolonizing Methodologies: Research and Indigenous Peoples*. London: Zed Books.

United Nations Economic and Social Commission for Asia and the Pacific (UNESCAP). 1993. *Women in Politics in Asia and the Pacific: Proceedings of the Seminar on the Participation of Women in Politics as an Aspect of Human Resources Development, Seoul, 12–20 November 1992*. New York: UNESCAP. hdl.handle.net/20.500.12870/5072.

van der Veer, Peter. 2016. *The Value of Comparison*. Durham: Duke University Press.

Vijeyarasa, Ramona. 2022. *The Woman President: Leadership, Law and Legacy for Women Based on Experiences in South and Southeast Asia*. Oxford: Oxford University Press. doi.org/10.1093/oso/9780192848918.001.0001.

Waltz, Mitzi, and Alice Schippers. 2021. 'Politically Disabled: Barriers and Facilitating Factors Affecting People with Disabilities in Political Life within the European Union.' *Disability and Society* 36, no. 4: 517–40. doi.org/10.1080/09687599.2020.1751075.

Watego, Chelsea. 2021. *Another Day in the Colony*. Brisbane: UQP.

Waylen, Georgina. 1996. 'Analysing Women in the Politics of the Third World.' In *Women and Politics in the Third World*, edited by Haleh Afshar, 7–24. London: Routledge.

Zappala, Gianni. 1998. 'Clientelism, Political Culture and Ethnic Politics in Australia.' *Australian Journal of Political Science* 33, no. 3: 381–97. doi.org/10.1080/10361149850534.

Part I: Exposing Limits, Exploring Alternatives

Introduction

Sonia Palmieri

When asked, I have readily described myself as a classically trained feminist political scientist. After all, I began to study gender and politics in the early 1990s in what was then called a 'department of government'. I learned about the entrenched nature of political party discipline, the efficacy of electoral gender quotas and the centrality of a critical mass to women's descriptive and substantive representation. These remain foundational concepts in the gender and politics literature, allowing continued intellectual focus on the experiences and challenges faced by women in political institutions.

But these are not universal experiences or challenges. Indeed, years of travelling to parliaments around the world have crystallised in my mind the danger of universalising minority-world or Euro-American experience. Political parties operate in vastly different ways in each context; gender quotas work when local rules—written and unwritten—are heeded in their design and implementation; and the specific institutional norms in which politicians, of any gender, work weigh heavily on their ability to perform substantive representation.

As the chapters in this section make clear, a majority-world approach and a multidisciplinary lens expand our appreciation of diverse critical actors in advancing gender equality in the political sphere and the contexts in which they live and work. Each in their own way—Jaemin Shim, Anna Kwai and Elise Stephenson—exposes the limits of dominant research approaches to our collective body of knowledge about gender and politics. These chapters methodically outline the injustice of theoretical and empirical exclusion in this majority-world–focused literature and present cogent examples of what a more inclusive approach would look like.

In perhaps the most empirical of all our chapters, Jaemin Shim presents compelling evidence of the inequality of authorship and citation practice in the gender, politics and media literature. Having purposively curated a robust database of articles and book chapters from the discipline's two most used scientific search engines, Shim finds the literature substantially overrepresents authors from the 'minority' world, compared with what he calls their 'demographic weight'. Studies covering minority-world countries—in particular, the United States, the United Kingdom, Canada and Australia—tend to be cited more and published in journals with higher impact scores. More disconcertingly, however, theorisation of gender, politics and media continues to rely on the experience of women (and men) in the minority world, with more than 90 per cent of the theory used in this literature drawn from studies in these countries and less than 3 per cent derived from authors based in the majority world.

With strong intrinsic motivation to question the gender and development discourses often imposed in her country of Solomon Islands (and beyond), Anna Kwai poetically describes the damaging consequences of colonial misinterpretations of culture. Drawing on the inspirational work of Edward Said, Sally Engle Merry and Anne Dickson-Waiko, Kwai identifies the complex relationship between colonialism and patriarchal cultures that global gender and development practitioners have underappreciated in their quest for gender equality. Kwai's is an eloquently written cautionary tale of the 'gender equality saviour' who fails to grasp the intricate web of gender relations and dynamics in Pacific settings.

With their respective interdisciplinary lenses, both these chapters invite us to reconsider foundational concepts and theories used in mainstream gender and politics narratives. Can we continue to speak of a 'gender gap' in the reporting of news media if the examples used to develop this concept rely on the experience of women in a handful of English-speaking countries? Can we advocate for gender equality in the communities of Pacific nations when the term continues to be contested?

Similarly, can we continue to understand political participation when significant populations feel they have been marginalised from mainstream institutions? In the final chapter of the section, Elise Stephenson delves deeply into questions of intersectionality to consider alternative ways in which diverse young people engage in politics and understand their pathways to politics. Revisiting the concept of 'proxies'—or alternative understandings of politics as formal representation—Stephenson suggests that marginalised actors construct their participation in creative industries, entrepreneurship and non-profit activism as meaningful forms of political participation. Stephenson explores these alternative pathways to politics for actors who identify across several axes of diversity: youth, gender, sexuality, ethnicity, disability. This is a strong call for diversity of pathways that legitimise a wider range of actions that can have significant impact on our polity. If our democracies are to truly listen to all, the very mechanisms by which diverse voices are heard must themselves be diverse and accessible for all.

These chapters show us the value in exposing the limits of our traditional framings and narratives on gender and politics. With lived experience of diversity, Shim, Kwai and Stephenson compel us to see the world through their lenses to find innovative, alternative answers.

2

Geographic Publication Inequality and Bias: A critical review of the gender, politics and media literature

Jaemin Shim

Beginning with Kahn and Goldenberg's seminal work 'Women Candidates in the News' (1991), the field of gender, politics and media has become an increasingly significant area of interdisciplinary study, the primary analysed content of which straddles the borders between political science, communication and gender studies. For instance, the literature frequently examines the gendered media coverage of male and female politicians in terms of quantity, tone and masculine or feminine stereotypes.

The media gender bias is crucial for politicians because voters primarily learn about politicians and political issues and develop criteria for evaluating them through the media (Brady and Johnston 1987; Lyengar and Kinder 1987). Relatedly, extant research demonstrates that the media's gender bias can have real-world political consequences ranging from voter likeability (Bligh et al. 2012) to perceived viability, actual electoral performance (Kahn 1992; Kasadha and Kantono 2021) and even to future political ambition (Haraldsson and Wängnerud 2019). Reflecting the significance of analysing media from a gender lens, there have been related peer-reviewed academic journals—for example, *Feminist Media Studies* and *Women's Studies in Communication*—in which pertinent research from around the globe is regularly published. Moreover, the importance of examining media sexism has reached beyond the academic setting. For instance, the resource portal Who Makes the News (WMTN) hosts the Global Media Monitoring Project and provides data on media coverage from its monitoring of multiple gender-related media indicators every five years since 1995.

Against this background, the primary purpose of this chapter is to examine the state of the gender, politics and media field based on published empirical works. Specifically, it investigates studies touching on the field's primary concern: gendered media coverage of politicians. Three decades since the field's inception, a large database of research has been generated. Reflecting the substantial knowledge accumulation in the field, several meta-analyses have been conducted lately to synthesise findings on the gendered mediation theme—for example, Sazali and Basit (2020), van der Pas and Aaldering (2020) and Winfrey and Schnoebelen (2019). However, a study that takes a step back and reflects on the publication patterns of the field itself has not yet been undertaken. This chapter fills that gap. I draw on the work of Jane H. Bayes (2012), who pointed out that the production of knowledge in the gender and politics discipline is not free from a Western-centric global hierarchy. Indeed, while recent studies show that gender research has become increasingly 'mainstream' in terms of the overall quantity of publications (Tsay and Li 2017) and its representation in top political science journals (Barnett et al. 2022), it remains to be examined whether the discipline's increased saliency and influence have been driven equally by research from the world's different regions.

In this chapter, I assess the extent to which the gender, politics and media field is built on research that equally represents the state of play across the world's diverse regions, including Asia and the Pacific. To do this, I define the regional representation of this literature in two ways: first, in relation to authorship, by exploring the relative representativeness of this research; and second, by examining the content of the research and its impact, defined in terms of its visibility and theoretical contribution. In relation to authorship, I find that two-thirds of the scholarship produced in this field comes from authors based in the United States, the United Kingdom, Canada and Australia, and that studies by scholars based in the minority world are, on average, cited nearly five times more than those based in the majority world (following the definition of this volume, Western countries correspond to the 'minority region', while the remaining countries fall into the 'majority region'). In relation to content, I find that more than 90 per cent of the theory used in this literature is drawn from references written by authors from the minority world; less than 3 per cent is derived from authors based in the majority world. Finally, I uncover that while the field has enjoyed increased visibility over the past three decades, research produced by authors in minority-world countries is legitimised more than that produced in majority-world countries.

My perspective in this chapter stems from my position as an East Asian early career scholar who has had to navigate the international academic job market in which individuals' peer review publication record is the key currency. After completing my PhD dissertation on welfare politics in South Korea, Japan and Taiwan, I shifted my focus to the topic of political representation for my postdoctoral project. In this field, I began to research gender and politics in East Asia, including legislative behaviour, career paths and media portrayals of female politicians. As I explored this research topic, I had to meet specific expectations for journals and requests from journal editors and reviewers in the review process, which motivated me to write this chapter.

First was the request to write more about the countries I analyse for the journal readership. I questioned why we should take for granted the readers' ignorance about the countries I cover. As the journals in which I tried to publish increasingly reduce the word limit of each article, sacrificing the findings and methods for basic country context seemed to me unjustifiable. The second issue relates to the Western case–dominant theory build-up. Many journals expect a theoretical contribution and implicit in this is building on the findings published in other well-indexed high-impact journals or salient books published at university presses. I noticed these are predominantly based in Western countries. Yet, the findings derived from Western countries were often treated as generalisable at the global level and the norm was to build on them. With the help of bibliometric analysis, I hope the findings shared in this chapter make these implicit publication biases in the field more explicit.

The following section describes the sampling strategy employed to identify relevant studies in the field. Subsequently, I present empirical evidence demonstrating regional inequality in the publications using a range of descriptive indicators. I then present several possible explanations for this inequality and conclude with my thoughts on their implications and suggestions to improve the current inequalities in the field.

Literature identification: Applied method and sampling

To examine publication inequality in the gender, politics and media field, this chapter employs a bibliometric analysis. The method can be defined as a statistical analysis of publication data (Pritchard 1969) that enables researchers to systematically examine many publications in a research field over time. It complements the classical literature overviews or meta-analyses, the focus of which tends to be substantive findings on a specific topic. Bibliometric studies in social science and humanities are still rare, yet their share is growing—for instance, in political science (for example, Metz and Jäckle 2017; Kristensen 2012; Jensen and Kristensen 2013; Russett and Arnold 2010).

To identify studies in the gender, politics and media field, I used search function tools from the two largest global scientific citation databases: Web of Science and Scopus. These databases were chosen in view of their established status and vast coverage of scientific studies spanning multiple disciplines over the past decades. The following search criteria were used: 1) research published in social science or humanities fields; 2) research published as journal articles, books or book chapters; and 3) studies simultaneously including keywords related to 'gender' and 'politicians' and 'media outlets' and 'coverage' in the title.[1] This returned 1,993 studies from Web of Science and 1,702 from Scopus. I then removed duplicates between the two search databases and narrowed it further to only studies that fulfilled the following four criteria: 1) the study explicitly analyses gender bias in the media with politicians (either one or both genders) as the subject; 2) the author of gender bias in the media is a journalist; 3) the analysis was conducted based on traditional media, such as newspapers, TV and radio;[2] and 4) the research is published in English.[3] This screening process was based on reading the study title and abstract and, if still inconclusive,

---

1   More specifically, the search conducted on 17 January 2022 used the following keywords: (gender OR sex OR male OR female OR men OR women) AND (media OR news OR TV OR television OR press) AND (politician OR candidate OR president OR legislator OR MP OR lawmaker OR official OR leader) AND (report OR coverage OR portray* OR frame OR stereotype OR representation).
2   Narrowing the sample to analyses of traditional media excludes new (social) media outlets such as Facebook, X (Twitter) and Instagram. The exclusion has to do with the fact that, for social media outlets, journalists do not have to be the authors of the content and journalistic norms and news values are not leading.
3   Studies selected from both search engines were published in 23 different languages. However, English publication makes up 93 per cent and the remaining 7 per cent written in other languages is excluded in this study due to the linguistic limitations of the author.

the main text content. As a result, 222 studies were identified as relevant.[4] The bibliometric analysis in this chapter is therefore based on these 222 studies, which comprise 212 articles and 10 book chapters.[5]

Geographical representation of authors

Underrepresentation of the majority world

Based on the full samples, I examined the academic saliency of the field over time. After dividing the total publication period into four eight-year intervals—1991–98, 1999–2006, 2007–14 and 2015–22—the result points to the increasing number of related publications. These samples suggest that the field has become increasingly salient over time. If the total publication period is divided into four equal time frames, the number of publications has increased significantly: 10 articles and book chapters were published between 1991 and 1998; 29 between 1999 and 2006; 66 between 2007 and 2014; and 117 between 2015 and 2022. The increasing academic salience echoes that of the broader gender and politics discipline noted earlier; and the publication growth rate surpasses that of the political science discipline (Shim and Farag 2025).

Despite this positive trend, the equality of geographic representation across the field is a separate question. To consider this, I examine the state of authorship inequality by looking at both the country of origin and the citation prevalence of this scholarship. As noted earlier, the primary goal of this chapter is to investigate the global publication hierarchies in the gender, politics and media field. Following the framing of this edited volume (see Jakimow's Chapter 1), the reference point for comparison is between the majority world and the minority world. In this chapter, I consider the minority world inclusive of 'advanced Western democracies' and define it as the 19 countries of Europe[6] and four English-speaking democracies outside Western Europe: Aotearoa New Zealand, Canada, the United States and Australia. Analyses hereafter will be based on this distinction.

---

4   For the screening, I tested an intercoder reliability between two coders and came to high degrees of agreement, with Krippendorff's alpha coefficient reaching 0.94 (p < 0.01).
5   For books with multiple chapters with separate analyses on the media's gender bias towards politicians, only the first chapter is selected as the study sample.
6   Austria, Belgium, Denmark, Finland, France, Germany, Greece, Iceland, Ireland, Italy, Luxembourg, Malta, Netherlands, Norway, Portugal, Spain, Sweden, Switzerland and the United Kingdom.

An examination of the single/first authors[7] among the 222 studies in the sample suggests that the field is not dominated by a small circle of individuals. In fact, 173 different single/first authors produced these 222 studies. Despite this numerical diversity, authors' countries of origin are not particularly diverse, indicating that the field suffers from regional overconcentration. Here, the geographical location of the single/first author is assigned based on the author's institutional affiliation at the time of writing. While the 222 studies are written by single/first authors from 42 different countries, Table 2.1 indicates that 65 per cent of the field's scholarship comes from authors in just four of those countries: the United States, the United Kingdom, Canada and Australia. The level of regional overconcentration of authorship resembles findings from other bibliometric analyses in social science (for example, Carammia 2022; Goyal 2017; Schulte 2019).

Table 2.1: Top 10 countries by author's institutional affiliation

Rank	Country name	Proportion (%)
1	United States	38.3
2	United Kingdom	13.1
3	Canada	9.9
4	Australia	4.1
5	Israel	3.2
6	Germany	2.7
7	Mexico	2.7
8	Belgium	1.8
9	Aotearoa New Zealand	1.8
10	The Netherlands	1.8

Notes: 'Proportion' is calculated by dividing 'the number of studies having a particular country as the single/first author's geographic location' by 'the number of all studies'.

Source: Author's calculation based on the samples selected for bibliometric analysis.

Under-referencing of the majority world

Regional inequality persists when we consider citation practices in the field. To do this, I examined Google Scholar citations for each of the publications in my sample and identified the citation numbers. The results show that studies by scholars based in the minority world are, on average, cited nearly

---

7   First authorship is determined by which author's name appears first in the list of all contributing authors.

five times more than those based in the majority world, with scores of 58.91 compared with 12.42, respectively. Even after considering the passage of time since publication (dividing the total citation numbers by the number of years since publication), the citation disparity gap persists: minority-world scholars tend to attract, on average, 5.62 citations a year compared with 2.24 citations a year for majority-world scholars.

Centrality of content

There has been an ongoing theoretical dependence on the scholarship derived from the minority world. In this section, I investigate this theoretical dependence by considering both the country focus of research in the field and the literature from which theories are developed and extended.

Table 2.2: Top 10 countries by study focus

Rank	Country name	Proportion (%)
1	United States	28.2
2	United Kingdom	7.6
3	Canada	6.9
4	Australia	5.1
5	Belgium	2.5
6	Germany	2.5
7	Aotearoa New Zealand	2.5
8	Spain	2.5
9	France	2.2
10	Israel	2.2

Note: 'Proportion' is calculated by dividing 'the number of studies having a particular country as the single/first author's geographic location' by 'the number of all studies'.

Source: Author's calculations based on the samples selected for bibliometric analysis.

Scholars based in the minority world can, of course, study countries beyond their country of origin/location. This being the case, I was interested in the geographical spread of scholarship in the gender, politics and media field. For each study in my sample, I identified the country of focus. I found that 59 countries were studied in this sample, covering each of the world's regions. However, as Table 2.2 shows, there is disproportionate representation in the most studied countries. While more than 80 per cent of the studies cover 23 developed Western democracies, together, the United States and the United Kingdom account for more than 35 per cent of the focus of scholarship.

To put this in perspective, the gendered media depiction of US politician Hillary Clinton has been at the centre of 32 studies from 1996 and 2020 (almost 15 per cent), which is equivalent to the total number of studies covering 28 countries at the bottom of the frequency table appearing in this study.

Publication centrality: Country of focus and region citations

Examining how many countries are covered per study, the results show that just over 90 per cent of studies in my sample focus on only one country; 4 per cent compare two countries; and 3 per cent cover three countries. Comparing the location of single/first authors (presented in Table 2.1) with the countries on which their research is focused, these are not independent of each other. That is, 88 per cent of the studies in the sample focus on the country where the authors' affiliated institutions are located. Moreover, an inward-looking bias was more prominent among authors from the minority world, with 97 per cent of these scholars examining their local contexts, compared with 68 per cent of those located in the majority world. Similarly, I note that there is a citation bias by region: studies that cover the minority world are more likely to be cited (with Google Scholar scores of 60.49) than those that focus on the majority world (16.27). This translates to a score of 5.80 citations a year for minority-world–based scholarship, compared with 2.38 citations a year for those in the majority world.

Publication centrality: Theoretical dependence

I also examined the extent to which each study's theoretical section relies on references whose analyses are based on minority-world countries. To tease out the theoretical basis for each study, I considered sections labelled clearly with a heading (or subheading) that reviewed relevant theories rather than discussions of method, data or study implications.[8] Most frequently, these sections of the studies in my sample are literature reviews from which authors derive theoretical expectations for their analysis. A total of 177 studies (80 per cent of the sample) clearly included a distinctive theory section. On average, these studies cited 33 theory-informing references.[9]

---

8   Where there was more than one section, I counted references from all relevant sections.
9   Often, the same references are cited more than once. Removing duplicate references, the theoretical part, on average, had 22 references.

I further examined these sections by coding whether each reference cited is based on research from either the majority world or the minority world. I did this for both the authorship origin and the country of focus.[10]

Table 2.3 confirms the gender, politics and media field's theoretical dependence on the minority world. More than 90 per cent of the theory used in this literature is drawn from references written by authors from the minority world; less than 3 per cent is derived from authors based in the majority world. A similar—if not slightly worse—trend is evident when we consider the country of focus of the references used to build theory in this literature.

Table 2.3: Geographic inequality in theoretical dependence of gender, politics and media studies (per cent)

		Minority	Minority and majority	Majority
Author origin	Minority	93.7	3.9	2.5
	Majority	65.8	6.8	27.3
Country of focus	Minority	94.6	3.8	1.5
	Majority	67.5	6.1	26.4

I considered two additional indicators of centrality: the inclusion of the country name in the study title, and whether the substantive text of the research pieces includes an explanation of the country studied. Figure 2.1 (top) clearly illustrates the geographic inequality. Studies that are focused on the minority world were less likely to include the name of the countries studied in the title (43 per cent compared with almost 94 per cent for majority-world studies). The exceptionally high proportion of majority-world country names included in the title could be taken as a sign of marginalisation, because it gives the impression that the focus of study is idiosyncratic, not generalisable and not mainstream. It is noteworthy that only 28 per cent of the studies analysing the United States include the country name in the title.

---

10 I categorised references that did not have a clear connection to a specific country (or countries)—for example, purely theoretical works or experiment-based works—as 'others' and removed them from the analysis.

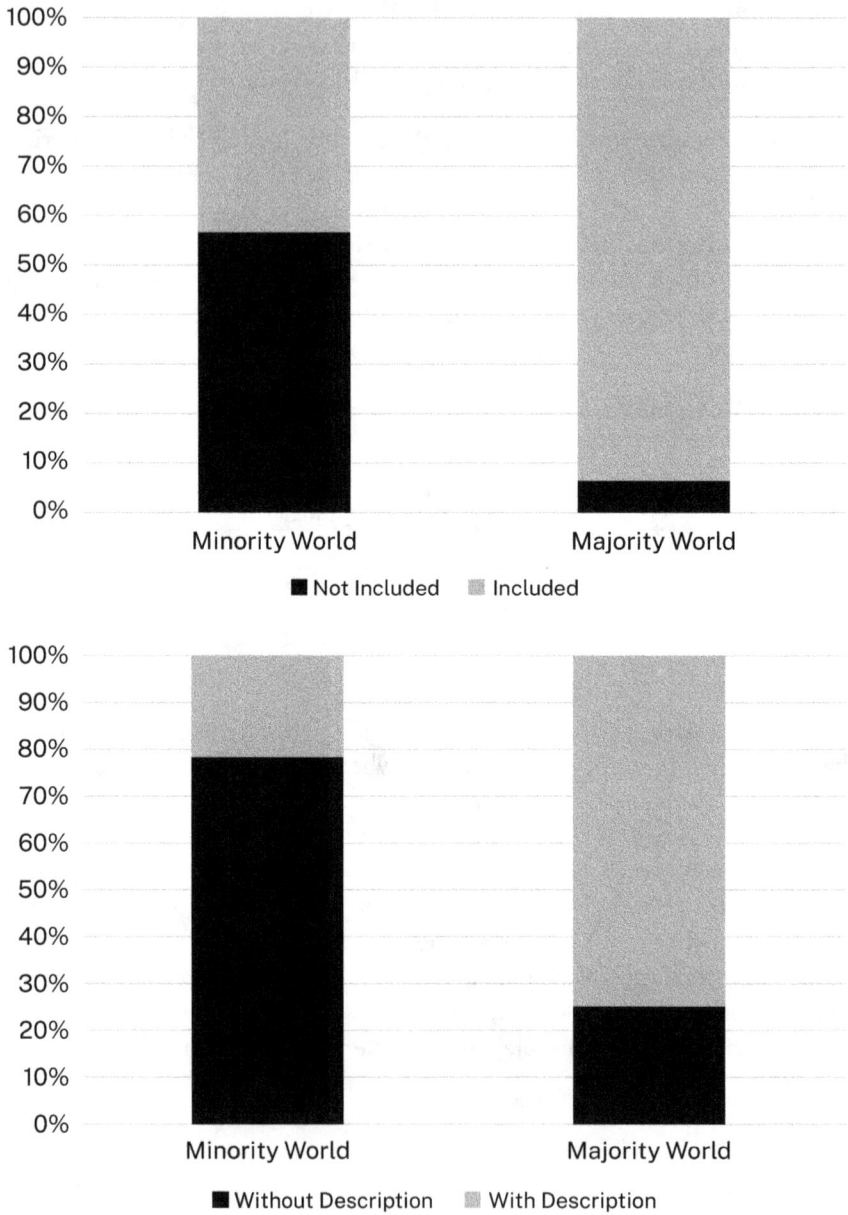

Figure 2.1: Country name inclusion in the title (top) and country description in the text (bottom)

The marginalised status of majority-world research is also demonstrated in the explanations provide for the focus countries in the main text of the study. I examined whether a published study had a separate section (with a separate heading or subheading) offering introductory information about the country of interest, such as the media landscape, women and politics, politics in general and/or the status of gender (in)equality (see Figure 2.1 (bottom)). Again, regional differences are apparent. Studies from the minority world are less likely to provide a separate country description (21 per cent), compared with 75 per cent of majority-world countries. Implicit in the inclusion of these introductory explanations is an expected or taken-for-granted ignorance among readers about the analysed majority-world countries and, conversely, an expected or taken-for-granted familiarity with the background of countries like the United States and the United Kingdom. As with including a country name in the study title, this implies the non-mainstream or non-standard nature of the majority world. Moreover, a separate country description within the main text could be problematic in view of the limited word count. For studies analysing countries in the majority world, an average of 630 words was devoted to introducing the country. Based on my calculations,[11] these additional words make up about 7 per cent of the total word count, which is not a negligible proportion.[12]

Visibility and legitimacy of authorship and content

Publication visibility: Journal indicators

Having examined the state of inequality in authorship and content centrality, I now examine the visibility of studies in this field.

To begin with visibility, journals publishing media gender bias articles have become more visible over time. Table 2.4 compares the average scientific journal ranking (SJR) of each of the studies in my sample between the

---

11 The total number of words was counted using the online word count tool Word Counter (onlinecountwords.com/). For the country-level description, I copied and pasted all the words under the pertinent heading/subheading. In the case of total word count per study, I uploaded the downloaded file for the counting; for book chapters, I scanned each chapter as a PDF, used OCR function to make it text-recognisable, then uploaded to Word Counter for the word calculation.

12 If we assume that the reference part takes up, say, 15 per cent of the total word count and exclude it from the total world count, 7 per cent increases to 8 per cent.

time of publication and 2020.[13] The SJR measures the scientific influence of scholarly journals by taking into account both the number of citations received by a journal and the importance or prestige of the journals from which the citations come.[14] The higher the score, the more influence a journal is considered to have—for example, an increase of 0.3 between the time of publication and 2020 specified in Table 2.4 means that the journals publishing media gender bias articles have, on average, become more prominent over time. The scores presented in Table 2.4 are also differentiated by the origin of the author and the region covered in the article.[15]

Table 2.4: Academic salience of the gender, politics and media literature

			At the time of publication	2020	Difference
SJR score	Total		0.81	1.11	+0.30
	Author origin	Minority	0.89	1.23	+0.34
		Majority	0.48	0.56	+0.08
	Region covered	Minority	0.85	1.18	+0.33
		Majority	0.72	0.88	+0.16

Although the field as a whole has become increasingly visible, regional inequality is apparent. Journal articles written by scholars based in the minority world begin with higher SJR scores than those of majority-world–based scholars at the time of publication. Comparing the SJR score from 2020, regional inequality had worsened. That is, the magnitude of change in visibility is greater in research produced by authors in minority countries, compared with majority countries (+0.34, compared with +0.08; t-test p-value < 0.001). Similarly, the magnitude of change is much greater in research that looks at the minority world compared with that which considers the majority world (+0.33, compared with +0.16; t-test p-value <0.01).[16]

---

13   The year 2020 was selected as the comparative year because SJR scores were available for 196 of the 212 journal publications (just over 92 per cent) included in the sample. More than half of the journals did not yet have SJR scores for 2021 or 2022 at the time of writing. Specific scores for each journal are available at Scimago Journal and Country Rank: www.scimagojr.com.

14   A journal's SJR indicator is a numeric value representing the average number of weighted citations received during a selected year per document published in that journal during the previous three years, as indexed by Scopus.

15   Five studies examined *both* Western and non-Western countries in one journal article and were left out of the sample.

16   The average year of publication between the minority and the majority worlds differed by 3.8 years for author origin and 2.8 years for covered region. Factoring the average number of years since publication did not alter key differences presented in Table 2.4.

Explaining geographic publication inequality

Can the observed geographical concentration in the minority world be explained by geographic weight? To begin, I consider descriptive representation. Widely used in the gender politics literature and often referred to as 'standing for' representation, the term is often used to examine to what extent representatives mirror the sociodemographic characteristics of constituents such as race, ethnicity and gender (Pitkin 1967). In a similar vein, here I compare the presence of the 23 minority-world countries vis-a-vis 179 UN-registered countries for which I could secure the necessary data. Based on the most straightforward measure, the population size in 2020, minority-world countries make up 11 per cent yet represent 81 per cent of the countries covered in the gender, politics and media field. Given that minority-world countries are overrepresented by 70 per cent, population size clearly does not explain the current state of regional overconcentration in publications.

An alternative explanation for the disproportionate representation of minority-world literature might be 'need'. For instance, research suggests that the elderly population incurs medical expenses greater than their proportional representation in society (OECD 2016). However, this is acceptable because they are more likely to fall ill due to their age and, as a result, are in greater need of medical attention. Likewise, regional publication inequality may be explained based on the state of gender inequality in the minority world compared with the majority world. To verify the need-based explanation, I examined the gender inequality index (GII) (UNDP 2019) and gender equality in the news media index (GEM 6) (Färdigh et al. 2020). The former measures global gender inequality based on reproductive health, empowerment and labour market inequality (the lower the score, the more equal are genders). The latter measures global gender equality in the news based on women's presence in the news and as reporters, women's presence as a covered topic about the economy and politics and women's role as spokespeople or experts (the closer the score is to zero, the closer is the country to gender equality). Table 2.5 shows the average scores and ranking for each index; and both clearly demonstrate that the minority world is not faring worse on either indicator.

Table 2.5: Gender inequality comparison between the West and the rest

	GII		GEM 6	
	Score	Ranking	Score	Ranking
Minority world	0.07	16	–48.31	48
Majority world	0.38	92	–52.21	67

If this does not explain publication inequality, are there other reasons? A first potential explanation relates to language. That is, the countries with English as the dominant language (or with high levels of English fluency) have a natural advantage in producing more globally accessible studies. In this sense, it is no coincidence that the top-four countries in which the authors are based are the United States, the United Kingdom, Canada and Australia (see Table 2.1); similarly, Belgium, the Netherlands and Germany are included in the top-10 countries (see Table 2.1) and, at the same time, their English level is categorised as 'very high proficiency', according to the English Proficiency Index (Education First 2022). Considering that the two major citation databases, the Web of Science and Scopus, primarily index studies published in English, the scholars who do not or cannot write their studies in English will be disadvantaged in terms of international visibility. And, for non-native English speakers, as shown by research in linguistics, writing a peer-reviewable scholarly article in English is a considerable challenge (Flowerdew 1999; Vasconcelos et al. 2007). To begin with, it takes more time to write in English and, to make matters worse, if the communicative convention of the author's native language is reflected in English, this can be treated as academic incompetence by Western scholars (Canagarajah 1996). It is often financially burdensome for authors to write in another language and have their work professionally translated into English, particularly for scholars in developing countries or those without sufficient research funds.

Second, resource-related factors can also influence regional publication inequality. For instance, the authorship origin–based top-10 countries (Table 2.1) spend on average 2.5 per cent of their gross domestic spending on research and development (OECD 2020). In the case of the gender, politics and media field, it might be easier to gather and process media-related data in the minority world. For instance, having a powerful media search engine can facilitate collection of newspaper coverage of politicians. Moreover, in the minority world, there might be more classes related to gender and media or more gender and politics themes offered at the university level from which one can build the foundation for pertinent analyses. Institutional support facilitating international journal publications can be another advantage. Offering publication seminars by editors of renowned journals is a fitting example, and perhaps such opportunities are more readily available in the minority world, where most of the journal editors are based.

Conclusion

The primary purpose of this chapter has been to investigate the global publication hierarchy in studies examining the media coverage of politicians from a gendered perspective. For this goal, I applied bibliometric techniques to 222 related studies from the past three decades and compared the publication inequality between the developed Western democracies (that is, minority-world countries) and others (that is, majority-world countries). First, the chapter examined the publication patterns based on geographical representation and the result demonstrates a clear bias. The data on both authorship origin and covered countries show that the field lacks balanced regional representation. Minority-world countries, particularly English-speaking ones, have dominated the field. Second, and going further, the chapter makes clear the state of marginalisation by conducting an interregional comparison of publication centrality and visibility. Results show that studies covering majority-world countries tend to be marginalised judging by their heavy reliance on minority-world–based theories and the burden of demonstrating their non-standard/mainstream status vis-a-vis minority-world countries. Moreover, studies authored by minority-world–based authors or that cover minority-world countries tend to be cited more and published in journals with higher visibility. To make matters worse, the regional inequality in publication visibility has widened over time.

I regard openness and diversity as intrinsic qualities of the gender and politics field. As can be clear from the frequent application of the 'descriptive representation' concept in its research (for example, Wängnerud 2009; Shim 2022; Tan 2016; Childs 2008), gender and politics is a discipline particularly sensitive to the underrepresentation of minorities. It is also the discipline that first paid attention to the fact that multiple layers of minority identity—for example, gender, race, age, disability, ethnicity, class or religion—intersect simultaneously and reinforce disadvantage (for example, Crenshaw 1994; Anthias and Yuval-Davis 1992). It is therefore imperative for the discipline to be aware of the extant regional parochialism and address it to avoid reinforcing the existing West-centric global publication hierarchy.

A field whose knowledge accumulation is based on a broader geographical scope would open itself to new theoretical insights, as well as solutions to present problems. A case in point is the emergence of numerous innovative works in gender and politics drawn from non-Western cases—for example, Bjarnegård (2013), Rai and Spary (2019), Barnes (2016) and Jones (2016). Moreover, global-level analyses are needed because we cannot simply extrapolate to the majority world what is observed in the minority world. For instance, one might argue that the media sexism in visibility should be less concerning since some of the latest findings drawn from Anglo-European democracies point out that such gendered visibility bias is either weakening or has disappeared (for example, Brooks 2013; Hayes and Lawless 2016). However, latest worldwide analyses including both Western and non-Western regions demonstrate that gendered media bias still exists globally and is often more evident in the non-Western regions (for example, Joshi et al. 2020; Ross et al. 2020). This must change.

Beyond knowledge accumulation purposes, geographical diversity in publications should be upheld to equalise professional career opportunities in global academia. Nowadays, publishing in highly regarded international outlets is central to academic careers and the measurement of performance in numerous countries around the globe (for example, Plümper and Radaelli 2004; Flowerdew 1999). For instance, at the institutional level, publications and citations in internationally peer-reviewed journals are crucial for determining the distribution of public funds to universities and research institutes. Moreover, publication performance directly affects the global university or department rankings to which prospective students pay attention.[17] At the individual level, increasingly, publication in top-tier journals or presses is connected to faculty members' salary level, promotion chances and teaching load (for example, Strathman 2000). If researching or being based in the majority world disadvantages one from publishing in globally recognised journals and gathering citations, it is natural for career-conscious scholars to avoid the majority region. This, in turn, can perpetuate geographic inequality in academic career opportunities between scholars focused on or based in the minority world and those focused on or based in the majority world.

---

17 For instance, publication performance/influence are explicitly included as part of their evaluation components by the two most reputable global university ranking survey agencies: Times Higher Education ranking (evaluation includes citations and publication numbers) and QS University Ranking (evaluation includes citations).

How, then, can the field become more inclusive of majority-world authors and experiences? First, we must minimise the language/resource gap between the majority and minority worlds. Considering that English has de facto become the *lingua franca* of research and publication (Swales 1990), there should be more support provided by publishers for English editing and translation. Submitting papers or book chapters in well-written English is important to give good impressions to editors, who are the gatekeepers of the peer-review process. Not doing so often results in desk rejection. Recognising the importance of English writing, many publishers offer professional editing or translation services. However, the service fee is often beyond the affordable range of many scholars in the majority world, most of whom are in developing countries.[18] In light of this, like differentiated pricing schemes adopted in conference registration fees—for example, by the International Political Science Association—I propose that the level of editing support should be offered based on the author's professional status and country affiliation. In addition, publication-related seminars offered at major academic conferences and leading academic institutions can be made public using video conferencing tools. Due to the Covid-19 pandemic, many conferences in the past few years have adopted a hybrid mode of conference participation and video-recorded key panels. Some include publication-related roundtables by editors of key journals or scholarly publishing houses, shared with the public.[19] Opportunities like this can offer valuable insights into the publication process, particularly for those who cannot easily travel to major conferences for financial or visa-related reasons.

Second, we must do more to identify and remove existing publication bias against the majority world. On this, as gatekeepers to publishing, editors and reviewers can play a crucial role. For instance, for empirical studies, editors could impose consistency when it comes to specifying the country or countries in the paper's title. In this regard, the latest author instructions at *Politics & Gender* journal are exemplary in setting the requirement that '[a]uthors of empirical papers should specify the country/countries under investigation in the title and/or abstract'. In a similar vein, for empirical studies claiming or assuming broad applicability, the theoretical build-up and testing sections ought to reflect findings from multiple world regions. To establish this practice, both editors and reviewers must start treating

18 For instance, at the time of writing, the price quoted for editing an 8,000-word piece ranged from US$400 (SAGE Publications) to US$2,000 (Taylor & Francis).

19 A model example is conference highlights offered by the European Consortium of Political Research (ECPR) through its ECPRDigital YouTube channel.

geographical diversity in references as an important criterion of the study's quality. Moreover, editors can conduct a thorough survey of potential geographic publication inequality with the submission data they have in hand. The evidence included in this chapter is based on published studies, so it leaves out those that have not reached the publication stage. With the full submission data, one can document important pieces of information by geographic region or country, such as the total number of submissions; review progress status—for example, desk rejection, rejection after the first-round peer review, acceptance; and the reasons behind the rejection—for example, ignores literature, too narrow, no theory, undeveloped argument. Going further, editors can conduct a more sophisticated analysis of whether the author's country/region or analysed country/region affects their publication chances. For instance, Garand and Harman (2021) examined the relationship between the author's country/region and desk rejection likelihood, and we need more analyses like this.

Third, we must actively promote and incentivise majority-world–based research projects and publications. For instance, there should be increased research funding for cross-regional projects collecting and sharing data at the global level. In gender and media scholarship, the Global Media Monitoring Project is an exemplary case in this regard. To incentivise this, major research funding bodies can explicitly prioritise cross-regional projects, including scholars from diverse world regions. Beyond data collection, more publication opportunities ought to be offered for cross-country collaboration. Model examples are edited volumes like *The International Encyclopedia of Gender, Media and Communication* (Ross et al. 2020), which involves numerous authors from all major world regions. Another way to increase the presence of majority-world–based publications is increasing the number of journals that explicitly include geographic diversification in publication as one of their core missions. Benchmark examples can be found in the social policy discipline, which has journals such as *Global Social Policy, International Journal of Sociology and Social Policy* and the *Journal of International and Comparative Social Policy*.

References

Anthias, Floya, and Nira Yuval-Davis. 1992. *Racialized Boundaries: Race, Nation, Gender, Colour and Class and the Anti-Racist Struggle*. London: Routledge.

Barnes, Tiffany. 2016. *Gendering Legislative Behavior*. Cambridge: Cambridge University Press. doi.org/10.1017/CBO9781316534281.

Barnett, Carolyn, Michael FitzGerald, Kate Krumbholz, and Manika Lamba. 2022. 'Gender Research in Political Science Journals: A Dataset.' *PS: Political Science & Politics* 55, no. 3: 511–18. doi.org/10.1017/S1049096522000385.

Bayes, Jane H. 2012. 'Introduction: Situating the Field of Gender and Politics.' In *Gender and Politics: The State of the Discipline*, edited by Jane H. Bayes, 11–32. Opladen: Barbara Budrich Publishers. doi.org/10.2307/j.ctvddzq1d.5.

Bjarnegård, Elin. 2013. *Gender, Informal Institutions and Political Recruitment: Explaining Male Dominance in Parliamentary Representation.* London: Palgrave Macmillan. doi.org/10.1057/9781137296740.

Bligh, Michelle C., Michèle M. Schlehofer, Bettina J. Casad, and Amber M. Gaffney. 2012. 'Competent Enough, But Would You *Vote* for Her? Gender Stereotypes and Media Influences on Perceptions of Women Politicians.' *Journal of Applied Social Psychology* 42, no. 3: 560–97. doi.org/10.1111/j.1559-1816.2011.00781.x.

Brady, Henry E., and Richard Johnston. 1987. 'What's the Primary Message: Horse Race or Issue Journalism?' *Media and Momentum*: 127–86.

Brooks, Deborah J. 2013. *He Runs, She Runs: Why Gender Stereotypes Do Not Harm Women Candidates.* Princeton: Princeton University Press. doi.org/10.1515/9781400846191.

Canagarajah, A. Suresh. 1996. '"Nondiscursive" Requirements in Academic Publishing, Material Resources of Periphery Scholars, and the Politics of Knowledge Production.' *Written Communication* 13, no. 4: 435–72. doi.org/10.1177/0741088396013004001.

Carammia, Marcello. 2022. 'A Bibliometric Analysis of the Internationalisation of Political Science in Europe.' *European Political Science* 21: 564–95.

Childs, Sarah. 2008. *Women and British Party Politics: Descriptive, Substantive and Symbolic Representation.* London: Routledge. doi.org/10.4324/9780203019443.

Crenshaw, Kimberlé Williams. 1994. 'Mapping the Margins: Intersectionality, Identity Politics, and Violence Against Women of Color.' In *Public Nature of Private Violence*, edited by Martha Albertson Fineman and Roxanne Mykitiuk. New York: Routledge.

Education First. 2022. *English Proficiency Index: A Ranking of 111 Countries and Regions by English Skills.* Lucerne: Education First. www.ef.com/assetscdn/WIBI wq6RdJvcD9bc8RMd/cefcom-epi-site/reports/2022/ef-epi-2022-english.pdf.

Färdigh, Mathias A., Monika Djerf-Pierre, Maria Edström, with Carolyn M. Byerly, Sarah Macharia, Claudia Padovani, and Karen Ross. 2020. *The GEM Dataset, Version 1*. Gothenburg: Comparing Gender and Media Equality (GEM) Project, Department of Journalism, Media and Communication, University of Gothenburg.

Flowerdew, John. 1999. 'Writing for Scholarly Publication in English: The Case of Hong Kong.' *Journal of Second Language Writing* 8, no. 2: 123–45. doi.org/10.1016/S1060-3743(99)80125-8.

Garand, J.C., and M. Harman. 2021. 'Journal Desk-Rejection Practices in Political Science: Bringing Data to Bear on What Journals Do.' *PS: Political Science & Politics* 54, no. 4: 676–81. doi.org/10.1017/S1049096521000573.

Goyal, Nihit. 2017. 'A "Review" of Policy Sciences: Bibliometric Analysis of Authors, References, and Topics during 1970–2017.' *Policy Sciences* 50, no. 4: 527–37. doi.org/10.1007/s11077-017-9300-6.

Haraldsson, Amanda, and Lena Wängnerud. 2019. 'The Effect of Media Sexism on Women's Political Ambition: Evidence from a Worldwide Study.' *Feminist Media Studies* 19, no. 4: 525–41. doi.org/10.1080/14680777.2018.1468797.

Hayes, Danny, and Jennifer L. Lawless. 2016. *Women on the Run: Gender, Media, and Political Campaigns in a Polarized Era*. Cambridge: Cambridge University Press. doi.org/10.1017/CBO9781316336007.

Jensen, Mads Dagnis, and Peter Marcus Kristensen. 2013. 'The Elephant in the Room: Mapping the Latent Communication Pattern in European Union Studies.' *Journal of European Public Policy* 20, no. 1: 1–20. doi.org/10.1080/13501763.2012.699656.

Jones, Nicola. 2016. *Gender and the Political Opportunities of Democratization in South Korea*. Berlin: Springer.

Joshi, Devin K., Meseret F. Hailu, and Lauren J. Reising. 2020. 'Violators, Virtuous, or Victims? How Global Newspapers Represent the Female Member of Parliament.' *Feminist Media Studies* 20, no. 5: 692–712. doi.org/10.1080/14680777.2019.1642225.

Kahn, Kim Fridkin. 1992. 'Does Being Male Help? An Investigation of the Effects of Candidate Gender and Campaign Coverage on Evaluations of U.S. Senate Candidates.' *The Journal of Politics* 54, no. 2: 497–517. doi.org/10.2307/2132036.

Kahn, Kim Fridkin, and Edie N. Goldenberg. 1991. 'Women Candidates in the News: An Examination of Gender Differences in US Senate Campaign Coverage.' *Public Opinion Quarterly* 55, no. 2: 180–99. doi.org/10.1086/269251.

Kasadha, Juma, and Rehema Kantono. 2021. 'Media Representation and Its Impact on Female Candidates' Electability in Parliamentary Elections: A Content Analysis of Three Ugandan Newspapers.' *Journal of Public Affairs* 22, no. 4: E2616. doi.org/10.1002/pa.2616.

Kristensen, Peter M. 2012. 'Dividing Discipline: Structures of Communication in International Relations.' *International Studies Review* 14, no. 1: 32–50. doi.org/10.1111/j.1468-2486.2012.01101.x.

Iyengar, Shanto, and Donald R. Kinder. 1987. 'News That Matters.' In *Public Policy: The Essential Readings*, edited by Stella Theodoulou and Matthew Cahn, 295–305. Upper Saddle River: Pearson.

Metz, Thomas, and Sebastian Jäckle. 2017. 'Patterns of Publishing in Political Science Journals: An Overview of Our Profession Using Bibliographic Data and a Co-Authorship Network.' *PS: Political Science & Politics* 50, no. 1: 157–65. doi.org/10.1017/S1049096516002341.

Organisation for Economic Co-operation and Development (OECD). 2016. *Health Expenditure by Disease, Age and Gender*. Policy Brief, 14 April. Paris: OECD Publications. www.oecd.org/en/publications/health-expenditure-by-disease-age-and-gender_7b219798-en.html.

OECD. 2020. 'Gross Domestic Spending on R&D.' *Indicators*. [Online]. Paris: OECD. www.oecd.org/en/data/indicators/gross-domestic-spending-on-r-d.html.

Pitkin, Hanna F. 1967. *The Concept of Representation*. Berkeley: University of California Press.

Plümper, Thomas, and Claudio Radaelli. 2004. 'Publish or Perish? Publications and Citations of Italian Political Scientists in International Political Science Journals, 1990–2002.' *Journal of European Public Policy* 11, no. 6: 1112–27. doi.org/10.1080/1350176042000298138.

Pritchard, Alan. 1969. 'Statistical Bibliography or Bibliometrics?' *Journal of Documentation* 25, no. 4: 348–49.

Rai, Shirin M., and Carole Spary, eds. 2019. *Performing Representation: Women Members in the Indian Parliament*. Oxford: Oxford University Press. doi.org/10.1093/oso/9780199489053.001.0001.

Ross, Karen, Ingrid Bachmann, Valentina Cardo, Sujata Moorti, and Cosimo Marco Scarcelli, eds. 2020. *The International Encyclopedia of Gender, Media, and Communication*. 3 vols. Hoboken: Wiley-Blackwell. doi.org/10.1002/9781119429128.

Ross, Karen, Marloes Jansen, and Tobias Bürger. 2020. 'The Media World Versus the Real World of Women and Political Representation: Questioning Differences and Struggling for Answers.' In *Comparing Gender and Media Equality Across the Globe: A Cross-National Study of the Qualities, Causes, and Consequences of Gender Equality in and through the News Media*, edited by Monika Djerf-Pierre and Maria Edström, 233–57. Gothenburg: Nordicom.

Russett, Bruce, and Taylor Arnold. 2010. 'Who Talks, and Who's Listening? Networks of International Security Studies.' *Security Dialogue* 41, no. 6: 589–98. doi.org/10.1177/0967010610388205.

Sazali, Hasan, and Lutfi Basit. 2020. 'Meta Analysis of Women Politician Portrait in Mass Media Frames.' *Jurnal Komunikasi: Malaysian Journal of Communication* 36, no. 2: 320–34. doi.org/10.17576/JKMJC-2020-3602-19.

Schulte, Felix. 2019. 'Publication and Collaboration: Patterns in Autonomy Research—A Bibliometric Analysis.' *Journal of Autonomy and Security Studies* 3, no. 2: 38–65.

Shim, Jaemin. 2022. 'Substantive Representation of Women and Policy–Vote Trade-Offs: Does Supporting Women's Issue Bills Decrease a Legislator's Chance of Reelection?' *The Journal of Legislative Studies* 28, no. 4: 533–53. doi.org/10.1080/13572334.2021.1902645.

Shim, Jaemin, and Mahmoud Farag. 2025. 'Blind Spots in the Study of Democratic Representation: Masses and Elites in Old and New Democracies.' *International Political Science Review* 46, no. 2: 91–107. doi.org/10.1177/01925121231219045.

Strathman, James G. 2000. 'Consistent Estimation of Faculty Rank Effects in Academic Salary Models.' *Research In Higher Education* 41: 237–50. doi.org/10.1023/A:1007047322146.

Swales, J. 1990. *Genre Analysis: English in Academic and Research Settings*. Cambridge: Cambridge University Press.

Tan, N. 2016. 'Gender Reforms, Electoral Quotas, and Women's Political Representation in Taiwan, South Korea, and Singapore.' *Pacific Affairs* 89, no. 2: 309–23. doi.org/10.5509/2016892309.

Tsay, Ming-Yueh, and Chia-Ning Li. 2017. 'Bibliometric Analysis of the Journal Literature on Women's Studies.' *Scientometrics* 113: 705–34. doi.org/10.1007/s11192-017-2493-9.

United Nations Development Programme (UNDP). 2019. *Gender Inequality Index (GII)*. New York: United Nations Development Programme.

van der Pas, Daphne Joanna, and Loes Aaldering. 2020. 'Gender Differences in Political Media Coverage: A Meta-Analysis.' *Journal of Communication* 70, no. 1: 114–43. doi.org/10.1093/joc/jqz046.

Vasconcelos, S.M.R, M.M. Sorenson, and J. Leta. 2007. 'Scientist-Friendly Policies for Non-Native English-Speaking Authors: Timely and Welcome.' *Brazilian Journal of Medical and Biological Research* 40, no. 6: 743–47. doi.org/10.1590/S0100-879X2007000600001.

Wängnerud, Lena. 2009. 'Women in Parliaments: Descriptive and Substantive Representation.' *Annual Review of Political Science* 12: 51–69. doi.org/10.1146/annurev.polisci.11.053106.123839.

Winfrey, Kelly L., and James M. Schnoebelen. 2019. 'Running as a Woman (or Man): A Review of Research on Political Communicators and Gender Stereotypes.' *Review of Communication Research* 7: 109–38. www.ssoar.info/ssoar/bitstream/document/61203/1/ssoar-rcr-2019-winfrey_et_al-Running_as_a_woman_or.pdf.

3

Kalsa blong hu nao woman no garem raet? Rethinking the culture and gender narrative in Solomon Islands

Anna Kwai

In 2015, I had a short-term engagement with the Australian Department of Foreign Affairs and Trade (DFAT) in Honiara. One of my first tasks in my new role was to develop a gender action plan. The most fascinating thing about this was the realisation that many versions of a 'bucket list' of activities for this program had been produced but never implemented. With the drive to produce a list of activities that could work, I launched into a series of consultations with local women within DFAT and across the Solomon Islands Government. These consultations evolved into informal chats over morning tea, lunch and beyond. These conversations left an impression on me as they revealed the opinions and concerns of local women that were raised but often brushed aside by their superiors or experts in the gender and development (GAD) field. These conversations also revealed a particularly concerning trend; I found great hesitancy among Solomon Islanders about when and where to draw the line in the discussion of culture and its compatibility with key tenets of the GAD framework. Trained as a historian and with a rural upbringing that was entrenched in both Christian and cultural processes, I am troubled by the confusion brought by GAD. I always see women in my culture of Kwara'ae as central and crucial to the stability of the community but why are they reduced so significantly in GAD literature to be victims of the same culture that holds them in such high esteem? This quandary became the motivation for this chapter.

In this chapter, I use the metaphor of the spotlight to argue for the prominence of culture for women and their prominence within culture as individual members of Indigenous societies.[1] The word 'spotlight' has been widely used in GAD literature to celebrate, promote, publicise, bring attention to and/or acknowledge women's achievements in various sectors of society.[2] Metaphorically, the spotlight can be projected onto someone or something to highlight a positive or a negative, or can highlight something positive yet yield a negative result. The same goes for shining the spotlight on something negative for a positive result. While to spotlight someone or something is a useful tool in GAD, the practice of picking an individual to showcase creates a group of women who are deemed remarkable—and not by the society as a whole. The curated nature of this approach to women's profiles may lead to a lack of broader relatability and the stigmatisation of featured individuals, while simultaneously oversimplifying the complex challenges women face on a daily basis. This is symbolic of the interpretative metaphor of the spotlight. It can only shine exclusively at a certain spot in each time and fails to capture women's activities and accomplishments in areas beyond its reach. This singular focus can be to the detriment of the bigger, more comprehensive picture. The exclusive light shone by the spotlight and, importantly, those shining the spotlight ignore and thereby misinterpret the larger context. To lessen this risk, I suggest that the spotlight should either be moved around constantly or GAD practitioners must be more attentive to the areas surrounding the spotlight that are not captured.

This chapter use the interpretative spotlight metaphor to engage in a historical analysis of the relationality of gender and culture in Solomon Islands. The chapter begins by discussing the problems with GAD as a discourse and where it fails to see Indigenous cultures as an asset in its practice. It then uses the metaphor of the spotlight to consider three ways in

---

1   Anna Naupa used the term 'spotlight' during her presentation at the Gender Institute signature event 'Generating Change by Generations of Women in Oceania: A Pacific Dialogue' in July 2022. She emphasised the importance of highlighting the leadership engagements of rural women in Vanuatu. Although 'spotlight' has been used as a synonym for recognising women's leadership and accomplishments in the GAD literature, it was through Naupa's presentation that I began to imagine the limitations and possibilities of the term as an interpretative metaphor.

2   An example of how women are brought under the spotlight is to recognise and celebrate their achievements in society. 'Spotlight' is also used in philosophy through the spotlight theory of time (Deasy 2015; Skow 2009), which is beyond the scope of the discussion in this chapter.

which its light, or focus, has been to the detriment of women in Solomon Islands: in GAD analysis, historical photography and the contemporary understanding of bride price. Finally, I consider the implications of the spotlight analysis and offer some suggestions that development practitioners might find useful when working in projects that focus on gender in Solomon Islands and beyond.

The GAD discourse in Solomon Islands

As a discourse, GAD has its shortfalls. Edward Said's publication of *Orientalism* (1978) marked a period of rethinking discourse and the ways in which knowledge was produced and maintained by Western institutions. Said saw a problem with the portrayal, characterisation and perception of cultures and peoples of the Middle East. He argues that the perception and portrayal of the East through Western scholarship and media are a 'political intellectualism' of 'self-affirmation' (Said 1978). In this context, the relevance of the narrative to peoples of the West has nothing to do with the realities of the existence of those in the East.[3] Yet, the inaccurate knowledge of 'the Orient' persists because it was reinforced over time through various mediums including colonial governments. Drawing on Michel Foucault,[4] Said saw that power and knowledge propel the West's conceptualisation of the East.

To the extent that Western scholars were aware of contemporary Orientals or Oriental movements of thought and culture, these were perceived as silent shadows to be animated by the Orientalist and brought into reality by them or as a kind of cultural and international proletariat useful for the Orientalist's grander interpretative activity (Said 1978: 208).

---

3   While I understand that binaries such as East–West (Said 1978) and urban–rural (Guha 1982; Spivak 1988) are simplistic in broader contextual applications, they can be useful to see where marginal voices can or cannot be found or where Indigenous voices can fit in. It is also important to note that categories such urban–rural may not be applicable in island nations with small populations, where such divisions do not exist at all or where they manifest differently. In a country such as Nauru, a rural–urban divide may not be present.

4   One of the key insights of Michel Foucault's theory of power and knowledge is that power functions not only in a linear way; rather, it operates in a multidimensional manner. Foucault (1988) also argues that power can dictate the terms of knowledge. While his scholarship is quite complex to grapple with, it allows us to reason with the relationality of power and knowledge and the effects of this relationship, as in the case of Said (1978). To an extent, the victimisation of women in their cultures, as alluded to in the GAD discourse, gives men a greater sense of power to dictate the forms of knowledge produced within GAD.

Said's criticism of Orientalism also resonates with the observations of prominent subaltern scholars such as Ranajit Guha (1982), Gayatri Spivak (1988) and Dipesh Chakrabarty (2000). Similarly, in the Pacific, the transition from postcolonialism to decolonisation has created a space for colonised voices such as Epeli Hau'ofa (1994), Konai Thaman (2003) and Tracey Banivanua-Mar (2006), among many others. While the decolonising approach of Pacific scholarship is gaining traction, the GAD literature seems mired in the decades-old culture-blame narrative that is often at odds with Indigenous epistemologies, traditions and culture more broadly. Culture and traditions that form the complex and changing fabric of Pacific societies became oversimplified in a one-size-fits-all category (Guttenbeil-Likiliki 2020, 2022). Yet, the assumption that gender–culture relations in Fiji must be the same as in Papua New Guinea or Solomon Islands has become the epitome of gender analysis, action plans, reports and policy documents (see, for instance, DFAT 2021).[5]

In a 2003 article, Sally Engle Merry observes that the language and idea of culture as a monolithic essence stem from global knowledge production, driven in many cases by non-Indigenous peoples. The process of producing reports against international standards such as the UN *Convention on the Elimination of All Forms of Discrimination against Women* 'is a very legalistic domain of activity' (Merry 2003: 60) that sees the cultures of developing nations as being of an unchangeable primitive nature that is detrimental to women and 'a barrier to progress'. Merry (2003: 60) notes that the critique of culture in this context 'builds on imperial understandings of culture as belonging to the domain of the primitive or backward, in contrast to the civilisation of the coloniser. Residues of this understanding of culture emerge in contemporary human rights law.' Such residues seem to permeate knowledge production at both the international and the local levels of development practice. Culture and traditions within this context and especially of developing nations become classified as 'obstacles to human rights', as Margaret Jolly (1996) observes in the case of Vanuatu.

---

5   This is not to criticise DFAT or the stakeholders who are pioneering the crucial Pacific Women Lead program. But it is important to point out that if promoting gender equality at the bilateral level is challenging, how accessible would transformational change be at the regional level? The 'Pacific values and principles' echoed through the document are impossible to imagine from the margins of remote rural communities. As such, the promotion of Pacific values assumes there is consistency in the values and principles of various Indigenous communities in the Pacific.

The concept of 'gender equality/inequality' is also relatively new in the case of Solomon Islands society. Gender-related developments only began in 1975 with the establishment of the Young Women's Christian Association, followed by the Solomon Islands Council of Women in 1983 (Solomon Islands in Focus 2015–25). These institutions became active advocates for the elimination of violence against women and the collective voice for the equal participation of women in political decision-making. In 1994 the country signed the *Pacific Platform for Action on Gender Equality and Women's Human Rights* and the following year ratified the *Beijing Declaration and Platform for Action* (Mulder 2019).[6] As part of the Solomon Islands Government's commitment to the *Beijing Platform for Action*, the Department of Women, Youth and Sports and the Child Care and Social Welfare Unit within the Ministry of Education and Human Resources Development were formed in 1997.[7]

By the dawn of the new millennium, the global movement for gender equality had accelerated in response to national commitments to the Millennium Development Goals and, subsequently, the Sustainable Development Goals, in 2015. Yet at this time, Solomon Islands faced civil unrest and the collapse of law and order. The Regional Assistance Mission to Solomon Islands (RAMSI) contingent arrived in the country in 2003 to begin the peace-building process. Local advocacies regained momentum under RAMSI's presence and the movement for women's rights and equality regained traction. The narrative during this period maintained the dominant understanding of men as active participants in the conflict and women as active peacemakers (Pollard 2000). Women who were participants in the conflict who were known to many locals were rarely mentioned or referenced (if at all) because their participation fitted neither the context of violence as a masculine activity nor the feminine role of a peacemaker.

By 2007, the Solomon Islands Government finally formed the much-needed Ministry of Women, Youths, Children and Family Affairs, which became the government arm responsible for drafting legislation and implementing, monitoring and evaluating the national gender plan, among other ministerial responsibilities. The presence of RAMSI during this period also saw an increased production of GAD grey literature (mostly technical

---

6   See also the discussion of the effects of the second-wave feminism in the process of decolonisation in Papua New Guinea by Anne Dickson-Waiko (2013).

7   Solomon Islands became independent when the second wave of feminism gained momentum in the 1970s. By the time the ideologies of this wave gained traction in Solomon Islands in the early 2000s, categories such as 'gender' and 'gender perspectives' were well established in academia.

reports) resulting from an increase in stakeholders participating in GAD programs in Solomon Islands. In 2010, the Solomon Islands Government endorsed the *Gender Equality and Women's Development Policy* and the Family Protection Bill passed parliament in 2014, becoming the *Family Protection Act*, making Solomon Islands one of the leading Pacific countries in the push for gender equality.

With the recent transition from GAD to gender equality, disability and social inclusion in the aid and development space, the emphasis firmly centres on human rights (see Hermkens 2013; Jolly 2000). A development bulletin by Corrin Care (2000) on customary law and women's rights in Solomon Islands emphasises the incompatibility of customary law and human rights ingrained in the country's Constitution. As Corrin Care notes: 'Customary law is based on male domination … [while] human rights … are founded on principles of equality' (2000: 20). Corrin Care makes a careful discussion of cases that show where state law and customary law disagree in practice. Although both categories of law are recognised by the Constitution, their conflicting functions, as Corrin Care concludes, are the result of the 'assumption by the British drafters that international human rights norms are universal'. Corrin Care argues that the approach to recognise both strands of law 'fails to take into account the fact that traditional Solomon Islands societies are founded on community values and duties, rather than on individual rights' (2000: 22). It is hard to imagine that the colonial drafters of Solomon Islands' Constitution could assume that human rights norms were universal. By 1978, Solomon Islands societies had endured more than eight decades of colonial rule over their affairs and had well embraced and were reliant on the colonial rule of law. There was no customary law like the one recognised by the Constitution in Solomon Islands traditional societies before colonialism. The male-dominated customary law critiqued by Corrin Care was created and enforced by the colonial state. Traditional societies were also made up of individuals who collectively determined which values and duties to abide by as a community. It is odd to suggest that 'community values and duties' as a static entity determine where human rights lie in local context. Traditionally, physical spaces were never permanent and people moved constantly either to a new location within an existing village or hamlet or to a completely new location. Such patterns of movement are important to understand to grasp the fluidity of communities and individual (not just men's) influence within such fluid spaces.

While human rights arguments are important contributions to the discussion of the inequalities and forms of discrimination women face in contemporary society, they minimise and exclude the complex entanglements of cultural change that slowly overwhelmed island societies over decades of encounters with Western cultures, peoples, institutions and processes. Those encounters were often violent and forced on islanders under circumstances of deliberate inequality that was overwhelmingly racial in nature (see Banivanua-Mar 2006). In Solomon Islands, for instance, by the time political autonomy was transferred to islanders in 1978, they had experienced more than eight decades of colonialism. That time (and the years before) entailed decades of normalising a white male–dominated system of colonial governance and religion. It is important to point out that Solomon Islands women did not struggle for voting rights nor were they legally barred from opportunities, employment or education at the time of independence. However, this does not mean that women have equal access to opportunities within the masculinist structure of a colonial state, or even in the postcolonial state, which continues to uphold the legacy of its predecessor. In other words, the inherent examples of a male-dominated structure of colonialism— embedded in governance institutions and amplified by the processes of missionisation and modernity—became a widely accepted norm in societies throughout Solomon Islands by the late 1970s. Certainly, the 'structural bias' towards men inherited from such a long history cannot be overstated.

In her chapter in the 2007 edited volume *Britishness Abroad*, Anne Dickson-Waiko analyses the 'colonial enclaves and domestic spaces' of British New Guinea. She argues that the demarcation of spaces for the colonised and the coloniser was not the only example of spatial limitation. Indigenous peoples of British New Guinea were further divided into categories based on the status of their engagement in the colonial enclave.[8] While white women in the 'colonial enclave' experienced 'racial dominance', they were also subjected to the 'misogynist notions transplanted from the metropole', which placed them in a less equal position to men in the colony (Dickson-Waiko 2007: 210). But their experiences were different from those of Indigenous women. Their space within these segregated enclaves (colonial, domestic as well as mission), as Dickson-Waiko shows in the case of British New Guinea, were 'legally enforced' by the coloniser (see also Hall 1992).

---

8   Dickson-Waiko (2007: 209) notes that the categories of 'signed-on boys' and 'village natives' were used to divide and identify Indigenous New Guineans based on their employment status: 'Signed-on boys were those under indenture, while village natives were those who remained in their villages.'

In terms of the mission enclave, Dickson-Waiko (2007: 206) found that it extended the colonial enclave beyond the urban environment to create a 'new layer of patriarchy'.[9] She argues:

> It was the European missionaries and their wives who cultivated the cult of domesticity and the civilising mission among the colonised through Christianity and mission education. A model of clean Christian living formed an essential part of the nuclear family unit as represented by the missionaries. (Dickson-Waiko 2007: 210)

In the Solomon Islands public service, Pauline Soaki (2017) observes that structural bias is one of the reasons it is difficult for women to be elected to parliament and hold leadership positions, even today. Yet, as both Debra McDougall (2014) and Dickson-Waiko (2007) note, masculine bias was a colonial strategy to restrict the 'movement and settlement' of colonised peoples in colonisers' spaces. Even keeping women in villages was a colonial strategy that, as McDougall argues,

> ensured that men would return there when their labour was no longer required, that wages would not have to be high enough to support whole families, and that labour would be available for the rural cash cropping that was the heart of the economy. (2014: 199)

McDougall notes that women were faced with overwhelming domestic responsibilities in the men's absence from villages. This observation resonates with Margaret Jolly's (1991: 39) observation in Vanuatu that Western perceptions of domesticity became models for colonised peoples and especially girls, who were groomed in schools run by missionaries in the proper behaviour and manners that would make them into an ideal Christian wife and hence produce a civilised family. However, Hyaeweol Choi and Margaret Jolly (2014: 4) argue that the ambition to create an ideal Christian wife of Indigenous girls is a paradox as missionary women were allowed to work in the 'public sphere, even at a global level'.

---

9   See also Heywood (2007), who shows how the concept of patriarchy varies in its application. Different strands of feminism use the concept to refer to forms of gendered power relations. Liberal feminists, for instance, use patriarchy to draw attention to the underrepresentation of women in various sectors of society. Some socialist feminists, on the other hand, see patriarchy and capitalism as interlinked. Hence, gender subordination and class inequality are intertwined systems of oppression. Radical feminists see patriarchy as a systematic, institutionalised and pervasive form of male power that is rooted in the family. In other words, the pattern of female subordination and male domination within domestic spaces reflects the broader power imbalances in the society at large.

In Canada, Kiera Ladner (2009) found that the internalisation of colonialism by Indigenous peoples was in many cases involuntary. The 1867 *Indian Act* in Canada, for instance, was a colonial effort to civilise and integrate Indigenous peoples into the newly created white society. The provisions of the Act were predominantly patriarchal yet translated into policies and practices that 'eliminate[d] the "Indigenous" and replace[d] it with the "civilised"' (Ladner 2009: 65). Ladner argues that the patriarchal provisions of the Act, such as status and rights (both political and property), became pathways through which colonialism was internalised by Indigenous peoples. Such internalisation, as Ladner (2009: 65) argues, resulted in the 'inharmonious plurality of cultural identities and understandings of gender' by Indigenous peoples. As Macintyre and Spark (2017: 13) note in the case of the Pacific, consequently:

> The changes in gender relations since colonisation, and in ways of life more generally, ensure that what counts as 'traditional' is often quite different from past construction of customary practices and values.

While knowledge production in general is a key component of awareness of social issues, its context-specific positionality means it does not always fit other cultural contexts. Development practitioners must be cautious in their application of frameworks and concepts that are not culturally monolithic.

Monolithic culture and patriarchy in GAD analyses

The shortcomings of GAD as a discourse become clearer as we move our spotlight to different areas. First, GAD analyses in reports systematically fail to see the value of local cultures to women. Culture and women appear in GAD analysis as contradictory categories (Merry 2003). Phrases such as 'Solomon Islands' cultures are predominantly patriarchal' (Homan et al. 2019), 'patriarchal society' (DFAT 2021), '[p]atriarchal systems of social organisation reinforce the dominance of men and boys over women and girls' (World Vision 2024), 'patriarchal attitudes and gender stereotypes are pervasive in Solomon Islands' (Equal Rights Trust 2016) and 'culture is a barrier' (Hedditch and Manuel 2010) are just a few examples of the references characterising women's societal position in culture in GAD reports and analyses.

An Asian Development Bank (ADB) country gender assessment report carries a similar message on culture and traditional norms to explain the context of gender inequality:

> Customary norms may be invoked throughout Solomon Islands in relation to issues such as men's and women's control over family decisions, land rights, marriage and bride-price, division of labor, and the custody of children. Custom is often used to justify the notion that women are inferior to men, and that men's oppressive behavior and violence is acceptable. This places Solomon Islands women in a dilemma, as few wish to criticise their traditional culture in defense of their rights, although a few courageous writers have done so. (ADB 2015: 5)

If we broaden the spotlight to understandings of culture, however, a new dimension of knowledge emerges. The reference to 'courageous writers' who wish to criticise their traditional culture in the quote above refers to a series of poems written and published by Solomon Islands poet Jully Makini (later Jully Sipolo) under the title of one of the poems in the series, *Civilized Girl* (Sipolo 1981).[10] Among the 20 poems published in this series, 'A Man's World' is the only one with a direct reference to culture and gender norms. But this poem is more than just a criticism of culture; it is a description of the struggle of maintaining traditions in a society that is becoming more and more pressurised because of modernity and in which men are seeing themselves as more powerful or at least are regarded as such by women. Sipolo speaks of the struggle to maintain traditions within a household that comprises both male and female members of the family living under the same roof, which entails negotiating different power dynamics daily.

In the case of Kwara'ae, there used to be greater gender separation between older children and adults. Men used to live in a separate hut (*heara*, also spelt *heralfera*) from women and younger children in the village. This practice loosely continues in many villages of Kwara'ae where unmarried men live in a separate hut in the village until they are married. I have witnessed during my lifetime the normalisation of young men in rural eastern Kwara'ae living under the same roof as their parents and siblings—more like in urban areas. While gendered habitation may be seen as segregation, for Kwara'ae people, it was a practice that upheld morality and ensured societal sanctity. Unlike cultures such as the Huli in Papua New Guinea, where polygyny was practised and co-habitation involved much negotiation between spouses

---

10   For an analysis of the series of poems, see Marsh (2015).

(Wardlow 2006), it is uncommon in Kwara'ae for men to openly practise *tau'wunga ang* or polygamy. Rather, Kwara'ae married couples in the past lived in separate domestic spaces. This was seen as an efficient way to uphold morality and mitigate the risk of the spread of diseases, sickness and death within the village. For instance, women in Kwara'ae were responsible for younger children from birth up to an age when boys were old enough to move to the *heara/hera* to be under the daily guidance of their father and male relatives. However, these were very fluid spaces. Even places such as *bis* ('menstruation huts') were not inaccessible to men and there are many local stories of men who courted or eloped with women from the safety of the *bis*. These domestic spaces became infiltrated and fractured with the introduction of foreign diseases and eventually demoralised by the processes of colonisation and missionisation in their creation of an ideal Western-centric domestic space.

A broader spotlight also highlights the fact that non-local gender 'experts'—often consultants of institutions who have little understanding and knowledge of local cultures and cultural processes—wrote most of these reports. It is important to note that most of the international institutions that are based in countries such as Solomon Islands are very risk-averse and work diligently to ensure the maintenance of a favourable public image. In other instances, they present an unfavourable image on the situation to create a humanitarian need or to justify the institution's position as an advocate for the needy. The narrative used in this case is often to maintain or further that public image. Where qualitative evidence is used as the basis for such assertions, it draws excessively from ethnographies by Western anthropologists and scholars who did research at some point in the country. When they are drawn from local scholars, as in the previous paragraphs, they become a conflation of poor cultural understanding (for example, in the application of Pollard 2000) with a disregard for the broader context of discussion (for instance, in the application of Sipolo 1981). When local women produce consultation reports, these are often heavily edited by overseeing experts or aligned closely to fit the mainstream GAD narrative. In the case where quantitative research substantiates the claims made, it is either based on an urban sample or with questionnaires formulated by technical expertise[11] that has not considered or concisely incorporated local cultural knowledge.

---

11 Although it is changing, in many international NGOs working in the Pacific, most technical expert or advisor roles are filled by international experts—expatriates rather than locals.

By directing our spotlight onto individuals who work in GAD institutions, we can also see the manifestation of the 'saviour complex'. Lila Abu-Lughod (2013) captured this perception succinctly in her monograph *Do Muslim Women Need Saving?*, in which she sees that 'gendered Orientalism' has clouded conceptualisations and the global, predominantly Western imagination of Muslim women and culture to a degree that distracts from the real need to listen to women's voices. Such conceptualisations become a blanket that covers the need to be more attentive to other cultures, women's voices and their position within their own societies. Cecile Jackson (2006) argues that feminist epistemologies can be a crucial contributor as they can move the spotlight to women's testimonies of lived experiences. But Jackson cautions that the interpretation of personal testimonies risks women's voices being treated as either a 'conflation of individual voices with collective representation' or a 'recognition of false consciousness' (Jackson 2006: 539; see also Torjer 2017). Such false consciousness can mischaracterise muteness as either an indication of feminine subordination or a form of agency. So often when Indigenous women's voices are captured, they are reduced to the simplistic and 'readily put down to the mystification of gender inequality' (Jackson 2006: 539), as in the case of Jully Sipolo's poetry.

It does not require much research to see the overall picture of the absence (or sporadic presence) of women, their voices and how they have been characterised in the broader historiography of Solomon Islands. In the precolonial and colonial past, the literature on people, society, culture and environment was driven predominantly by European/white male explorers, from those as early as Álvaro de Mendaña de Neira (Amherst and Thomson 1901) to naturalists like Charles Woodford (Lawrence 2014), missionaries, scholars (anthropologists, linguists and so on) and photographers (like Northcote Deck and John Beattie). Their work is essential yet offers us very little on gender relations in history to reconstruct feminine agency that is absent from written records of our past.[12] When feminine agency is discussed, it is in the context of pollution, taboos, sorcery, suicide or the effects of these practices on women (Garrett 1992). In 1985, Roger Keesing revealed what is seen as a change in his perception of Kwaio women's social status in their societies. Keesing observes that the Kwaio culture exemplifies a 'sexually polarised Melanesian society', in which women were ethnographically perceived as inferior to men in social and religious rituals.

---

12 Assessing the historiography of women's presence in the broader literature of Solomon Islands is a key component of my current research and one that is beyond the scope of this chapter.

However, as Keesing observes from his long engagement with the Kwaio people, the opposite was true. Kwaio women held esteemed positions in their communities and were central to social life and religious rituals (1985: 28). Keesing states that in a deeper understanding of the Kwaio society, he observes that 'domestic male–female relations were characteristically close rather than antagonistic' and, because of this closeness, women's 'bodies and reproductivity are sources of power that have to be properly compartmentalised (as does contact with the ancestors) but are not inherently polluting' (1985: 28). However, not all scholars of contemporary Solomon Islands studies engaged at a level of interactions as deep as Keesing's in the communities in which they worked to be able to project the spotlight in areas that Keesing projected his. Those who relied predominantly on local surveys to collect data and fill questionnaire sheets had a much narrower perception of aspects of local culture.[13]

Oral history and my personal experiences also counter the view that women assume a submissive role in all spheres of life in my culture.[14] Yet, the manifestation of gender inequalities fashioned by the processes of colonisation and missionisation that could explain the historical discrepancies in gender roles that are assumed by the GAD discourse to be qualities of Indigenous cultures are rarely criticised. Why, then, should institutions and individuals who produce knowledge continue to snuff out Indigenous cultures when they know little about them to begin with? In a recent interview with elders of my society, I was schooled in the crucial space women occupy in our culture and the agency of their voice and actions. There is a concern among the elders that contemporary cultural change is influencing the way many men regard women in society. As an Indigenous woman of Kwara'ae, phrases such as *bib ahn hanoa* ('main fabric' or 'foundation of the society'), *aeh iontwa'a* ('an important woman') and *aeh aub* ('a sacred woman') matter for me personally. When those terms are used to describe my place in society, it reasserts my agency as a woman and

---

13 Scholars and individual researchers from universities are also part of this process but, in many cases, they exercise more profound and longer engagement with host communities, often as part of research for a higher degree (such as the work of Keesing himself; Monson 2022; McDougall 2016; Dureau 2010). While the development literature often benefits from the more substantial academic literature produced by extended fieldwork and presence in rural communities, it also often cherry-picks the most useful references for its purposes or fails to grasp concepts concisely due to positionality barriers.

14 Malaita culture and society have always been seen as among the more patriarchal cultural groups in Solomon Islands. However, phrases that speak to the status of women in my region of Kwara'ae resonate a deeper sense of women's status and importance that are not captured in the literature on women and gender relations in Solomon Islands (see Keesing 1985; Akin 2003).

valued member of my society. However, the absence of such language in the Kwara'ae literature means these words mean nothing to the non-Kwara'ae people who write about Kwara'ae women. It is evident, then, that what is crucial is an intimate knowledge and experience of culture that many non-Kwara'ae scholars lack. The solution here is to redirect the spotlight onto Indigenous cultures, practices of Indigenous knowledge production and the recognition of forms of Indigenous women's agency in local communities.

Historical photographs: Men as warriors, not fathers

The historical literature on Indigenous peoples is ridden with the white saviours' desire to rescue Third World/Indigenous women from the madness of our own cultures and the backwardness of our state of being. Irrespective of how gender was perceived by our ancestors and in our own ways of knowing, the hierarchy of gender roles was projected onto us by our white saviours from first contact. Men were regarded with high esteem as warriors, not as fathers, and women were seen as no different to domestic slaves. Women are never portrayed as warriors. Yet, when we redirect our spotlight onto early colonial photography, we see gender relationships that were more fluid and dynamic than our contemporary ones. These discrepancies are likely not conceptualised in gender analysis because of poor cultural awareness. On childrearing, for instance, an NGO shadow report for the period 2002–12 claims that men 'often refuse to participate in unpaid work in the home, including child-rearing, as it is customarily perceived by many men and women as the role of a woman' (Christian Care Centre et al. 2012: 16–17). While this statement holds some truth to the extent that domestic responsibilities vary between families, it is also shows a fixation on a cultural deficit that is arguably a product of the gender imbalance due to the absence of men since the onset of depopulation from introduced diseases, the labour trade, colonial labour migrations throughout Solomon Islands and the patriarchal nature of Christian biblical teachings. At a time when photographic technology required people to sit still, young children were not ideal subjects for the lens, so were often excluded, although there are some images of men holding their babies (see Plates 3.1a and 3.2).

Plate 3.1a: The original caption for this image by John Watt Beattie read, 'Cannibal men at [Fote], Malaita, Solomon Islands, 1906'
Source: PIC Album 463 #PIC/7580/, National Library of Australia, nla.gov.au/nla.obj-141127709/view.

Photography and Indigenous cultural experiences disturb the notion of a disrespectful and sexist culture. Yet, these are often ignored, poorly explained or brushed aside as irrelevant to the context of perceived feminine marginality. For instance, Plate 3.3, a photo taken by Australian photographer John Watt Beattie in 1906, originally captioned 'Local people gathered near the women's landing place of Ferasiboa, Malaita, Solomon Islands, 1906',[15] clearly contradicts a UN Women article that states:

> The list of things women shouldn't do according to Solomon Islands' culture is long: no wearing shorts, no lingering eye contact with men, no sitting near your brothers and no speaking up, among them. The rules are nuanced and vary by province and tribe. But overall, cultural predispositions across the country leave women without the same level of respect and representation as men. (UN Women Asia and the Pacific 2019)

---

15 The 'Beattie' photographs of Solomon Islands are available online from the National Library of Australia's collection *Scenery and Peoples of the Islands in the South and Western Pacific*: nla.gov.au/nla.obj-141125607. In many coastal villages in the past, women and men were said to have separate canoe-landing areas. This was also where women's canoes were stored.

Plate 3.1b: Beattie's photo as edited and reproduced in *A Solomon Islands Chronicle*, with the man holding the baby and the boy cropped out

Source: Alasa'a et al. (2001).

Through the spotlight, Plate 3.3 portrays a vibrant society with less restrictive gender disparities than is often characterised in contemporary gender analysis and reporting. This image disputes assumptions that women did not have the same respect as men. The images that follow also feature fathers holding their children rather than the selective image of all men as warriors.

Plate 3.2: Northcote Deck, 'Lau men and a toddler (Malaita)' (c. 1908?), lantern slide

Source: The Trustees of the British Museum. Shared under CC BY-NC-SA 4.0 International license. www.britishmuseum.org/collection/image/563277001.

Plate 3.1a, also taken by Beattie in the same visit in 1906, is yet another pictorial example of an important detail that is often ignored in such reproductions. Originally captioned as 'Cannibal men at [Fote], Malaita, Solomon Islands', the photo is often reproduced in the context of male agency, ignoring the man on the right who is holding a baby and sometimes the older child on the left because they disturb a narrative of masculine agency, tribalism or the integration of superior European materials, especially weapons, into local cultures (see Plate 3.1b).[16]

16　The photo in Plate 3.1b is reproduced in Alasa'a et al. (2001).

Plate 3.3: The original caption for this image by John Watt Beattie read, 'Local people gathered near the women's landing place of Ferasiboa, Malaita, Solomon Islands, 1906'

Source: PIC Album 463 #PIC/7580/794, National Library of Australia, catalogue.nla. gov.au/catalog/6387675.

Tampering with images is not a new thing in photography; it is, to some extent, part of the art of photography itself. Photographs are sometimes altered to make a point, as in the case of the photograph in Plate 3.1b, or as in the case of American photographer Edward Curtis (Lawlor 2005). Curtis, who aimed to depict Native American life before colonisation, is known for manipulating his images by editing and airbrushing out objects of European origin to re-enact his perception of an authentic Indigenous culture and give a sense of Native Americans as a vanishing race confronting modernity. Altering images, whether by cropping or airbrushing, serves a particular narrative that critically removes details that are essential to our present understanding of specific periods in Indigenous cultures.

Reflections on traditional practice: The case of bride price

Although it has been two decades since Solomon Islands signed the 1994 *Pacific Platform for Action*, the concept of gender and the associated discourse are still new. This does not mean that individual Solomon Islanders are content with issues of gender inequality or human rights violations or ignorant of the growing advocacy for gender equality, but the discourse on gender offers a new lens through which to evaluate domestic and societal relationships. Sociocultural practices that weave together tradition, reciprocity, individuality and kinship have been filtered through this new lens. An elaborate example is the stereotype of bride price that is used to rationalise the threat of culture to women's aspirations for progress in the country. A development report produced by the International Finance Corporation (Hedditch and Manuel 2010) emphasises the damage done to women's entrepreneurial aspirations by the 'bride price system'. A textbox with a quote from a foreign-born male businessowner in the country is used as evidence of this damage:

> It's a male dominated culture here [in Solomon Islands]—it comes from the bride price system. Men think they own women. If a woman starts a business and her husband doesn't like it, he says stop and she does. Society here says if a woman wants to achieve something she can't because she's just a woman. (Hedditch and Manuel 2010: 7)

In Kwara'ae the tradition of *daurai'ia* (poorly translated as 'bride price') is at the forefront of criticisms of gender inequalities on islands such as Malaita, yet many individuals who are outspoken against these traditions are often active participants in such practices.[17] The danger of such filtering is that women are now seen as monetised, branded commodities, who can be owned. When such branding is normalised, it gives male perpetrators power and the excuse to be abusive and violent towards their female partners

---

17 Personally, I have paid compensation (*ha'abua'a*) demanded by other families of my family, contributed financially towards *daurai'ia*s and have immediate family members, both men and women, who have demanded *ha'abua'a* from other people in response to social issues. This is because such social traditions are an essential part of the fabric of society—a twine of interdependence that links alliances, reciprocates relationships and brings people together even today. While the influence of the cash economy, modernity and new concepts such as gender equality challenge the relevance of such traditions in the contemporary setting, it does not mean that people have lost sight of their importance.

(Honda et al. 2022).[18] While this could be a result of modernisation and a rapidly changing society (and culture), it is also the direct outcome of a discourse that demonises our cultural processes. In Are'are, Pollard (2000) explained that bride price is a matrimonial gift-exchange ceremony that brings families, clans and communities together and is not perceived as transactional. In Kwara'ae, the term 'bride price' or its contemporary equivalent, '*huail kin ang*', became a catchphrase to simplify what Underhill-Sem (2010) referred to as a 'complex constellation of power'. Within this constellation, all the participants have some power to leverage or contribute. As Underhill-Sem (2010: 7) warns,

> [S]implistic accounts of bride price, bride wealth and marriage exchanges expose contemporary prejudices against 'Melanesian countries', and often diverts attention from more systematic practices that belittle many women in the Pacific in the contemporary era.

Traditional practices that persist in Solomon Islands today warrant a clear understanding as these are essential to the fabric of many societies in the Pacific. It is important to point out that traditions such as *daurai'ia* were for decades among the key foundations for peaceful coexistence and holding perpetrators accountable in precolonial societies, and even in societies today where the presence of state policing falls short (Braithwaite et al. 2010; Braithwaite 2002).[19] As John Cox (2017) observes in the Western Solomons, accepting the notion of the incompatibility of equality and *kastom* ignores the diverse ways and initiatives of Melanesian women in their engagement with modernity to make their relationships with men more equal and less prone to violence. The challenge for researchers and policymakers is to ensure that these traditional practices and their functions in the contemporary context are more deeply understood.

What intrigues me as a Solomon Islands woman, reading about the vilification of the 'bride price' tradition in the GAD literature, is the preoccupation with the deficit of the tradition in the contemporary economy. Again, by moving the spotlight away from the deficit to local experiences and knowledge of the practice, a different picture emerges. In Kwara'ae for instance, the phrase *huail kin ang* implies the presence of a transaction, which indicates that

---

18 While the report by Honda et al. (2022) is not about cultural branding, it highlights that pride price is a cultural practice that reinforces violence against women.

19 It is important to understand that in most rural areas in Solomon Islands, there is no law enforcement presence. Instead of critiquing traditional social practices such as bride price and compensation, maybe we should ask how effective these practices are in holding perpetrators of violence accountable while maintaining peace and stability in rural societies where the state fails miserably.

the term itself could have been a reversed translation of the Western term 'bride price'. The term for what is now a bride-price ceremony is *daurai'ia* in Kwara'ae and in Langalanga it is called *kwatena*, which is best translated as 'giving' (Guo 2020). The tradition of *daurai'ia* in Kwara'ae and many cultures of Malaita is only one component in the process and celebration of a marriage. Language, as part of culture, changes over time. These changes are important to understand, especially in traditions that continue in the present, because it shows the deeper impact of the inclusion of money rather than Indigenous valuables as well as the effects of the influx of imported commodities and the capitalistic language of property (Monson 2022). But, most importantly, our spotlight must capture these changes in the present to accommodate cultural inclusivity in gender practices.

Implications of the spotlight analysis

By introducing the spotlight metaphor, I have shown that GAD practices have produced a narrow focus on Indigenous cultures, with a sometimes negative effect. Broadening the spotlight is useful as it can reveal different images or perspectives in the ongoing practices of producing knowledge. Often what is referred to as 'culture' by many in contemporary Solomon Islands is the intersection of mission and colonial cultures and their incorporation into Indigenous cultures by islanders themselves (Robbins 2004).[20] While culture changes with time and complex hybridisation[21] can occur, the relative newness of the gender equality movement in places such as Solomon Islands means that culture as a concept must be explicitly understood before it is applied to gender analysis.

A video made by the International Women's Development Agency is important to discuss here as it echoes the views and experiences of Solomon Islands women who engaged in gender advocacy and who are discussing the opportunities and challenges that culture poses to their work promoting

---

20 Robbins also observes that individualism has been emphasised in the evangelical and Pentecostal Christian sects. Christianity emphasises a nuclear domestic structure with the man as the head of the family. Such a structure may empower women to disregard societal norms, but it does not necessarily mean that it improves their lives. It simply introduces new dynamics of inequality that may not bear the same cultural meanings that define women's position in society.

21 Homi Bhabha's theory of hybridity recognises that multiculturalism enables new cultural forms to materialise. Bhabha argues that while colonialism (and its processes) can be seen as 'in the past', its legacy lingers in the present. Therefore, our understanding of cross-cultural relations and intersections must be on par.

gender equality (IWDA 2012). However, it also shows the challenges of differentiating culture in a hybridised context. All the women who speak in this video emphasise the important social structure and presence of chiefs as mediators in their advocacy work. There is a strong emphasis on respect for women and elders by men in rural communities. Flora Lasi, who works for a local NGO, emphasises in her interview that, in her experience, men have great respect for women and encourage women to participate in community activities including gender workshops. But it is often women's perceptions of their place in the home that catalyses their hesitation to engage. A similar observation was made by Judith Siota, who observes that men in Solomon Islands have immense respect for women, but it is at the domestic level that inequalities are prevalent. When asked about the challenges culture poses to gender issues, the responses varied. The challenges identified include stereotypes of men that prevent them doing domestic chores, the lack of capacity by advocates to translate messages about gender inequality for local communities, the exclusion of men from gender advocacy work as well as an observed poor understanding of the traditional practice of bride price among Solomon Islanders themselves. These responses are crucial as they point to a much deeper gap in the historiography of the gender discourse in Solomon Islands that forms the essence of the problematic use of the term 'culture'.

Fundamentally redirecting the spotlight onto local women can allow them the space to objectively articulate their approval and disapproval of their own culture. But it must be done without judgement or criticism from outside gender and human rights experts. Institutions that practice GAD can usefully begin with the local women they employ in this process by allowing the space, time and opportunity to engage them in candid discussions about culture, the role of the church and modernity and its influence on their wellbeing as individuals. Such a focus has the potential to shine a spotlight on an area that has less to do with cultural processes than with the contemporary challenges of modernity, or intersections between the two. Ultimately, this will lead to more positive analyses and understandings of culture in gender discussions.

To conclude, I have shown in this chapter some examples of the discrepancies in the development discourse about culture and gender in Solomon Islands. I argue that women are key players in society and important participants in knowledge production and cultural continuity, and do not conceptualise themselves as marginal in their own cultures. Rather than criticisms of gender disparities and culture, what must be recognised is the historical discomfort of women's marginal representations in the narratives so excessively produced by non–Solomon Islanders since first contact. For it is through the non–Solomon Islands lens of characterisation that women's status and position in local societies have been viewed over the course of history. While culture may have its defects, understanding its complexity in its entirety is an essential first step for outside researchers, gender experts, advisers, consultants, advocates and activists to form a baseline understanding of its gender-related functions.

References

Abu-Lughod, Lila. 2013. *Do Muslim Women Need Saving?* Cambridge: Harvard University Press. doi.org/10.4159/9780674726338.

Akin, David. 2003. 'Concealment, Confession, and Innovation in Kwaio Women's Taboos.' *American Ethnologist* 30, no. 3: 381–400. doi.org/10.1525/ae.2003. 30.3.381.

Alasa'a, Samuel, Ben Burt, and Michael Kwa'ioloa. 2001. *A Solomon Islands Chronicle*. London: British Museum Press.

Amherst, William Amhurst Tyssen-Amherst, Baron, and Basil Thomson. 1901. *The Discovery of the Solomon Islands by Alvaro de Mendana in 1568*. Translated from the original Spanish manuscripts, edited with introduction and notes by Lord Amherst of Hackney and Basil Thomson. London: Hakluyt Society.

Asian Development Bank (ADB). 2015. *Solomon Islands: Country Gender Assessment*. Manila: Asian Development Bank. www.adb.org/sites/default/files/institutional-document/176812/sol-country-gender-assessment.pdf.

Banivanua-Mar, Tracey. 2006. *Violence and Colonial Dialogue: The Australian-Pacific Indentured Labor Trade*. Honolulu: University of Hawai'i Press.

Beattie, John W. 1906. *The Scenery and Peoples of the Islands in the South and Western Pacific*. PIC Album 461-463. Canberra: National Library of Australia.

Bhabha, Homi K. 1994. *The Location of Culture*. London: Routledge.

Braithwaite, John. 2002. 'Setting Standards for Restorative Justice.' *The British Journal of Criminology* 42, no. 3: 563–77. doi.org/10.1093/bjc/42.3.563.

Braithwaite, John, Sinclair Dinnen, Matthew Allen, Valerie Braithwaite, and Hilary Charlesworth. 2010. *Pillars and Shadows: Statebuilding as Peacebuilding in Solomon Islands*. Canberra: ANU E Press. doi.org/10.22459/PS.11.2010.

Chakrabarty, Dipesh. 2000. *Provincializing Europe: Postcolonial Thought and Historical Difference*. Princeton: Princeton University Press.

Choi, Hyaeweol, and Margaret Jolly, eds. 2014. *Divine Domesticities: Christian Paradoxes in Asia and the Pacific*. Canberra: ANU Press. doi.org/10.22459/DD.10.2014.

Christian Care Centre, Family Support Centre Organisation, Gizo, People with Disabilities Solomon Islands, Sistas Savve Group, White River, Solomon Islands National Council of Women, Solomon Islands Planned Parenthood Association, YWCA Solomon Islands, Vois Blo Mere, Women's Rights Action Movement, Western Provincial Council of Women, Gizo, and World Vision Solomon Islands. 2012. *NGO Shadow Report on the Status of Women in Solomon Islands: Initial, Second and Third Report (2002–2012)*. Geneva: Office of the United Nations High Commissioner for Human Rights. www2.ohchr.org/English/bodies/cedaw/docs/ngos/SolomonIslandsJointNGOCEDAWShadowReport.pdf.

Corrin Care, Jennifer. 2000. 'Customary Law and Women's Rights in Solomon Islands.' *Development Bulletin*, no. 51: 20–22. www.toksavepacificgender.net/wp-content/uploads/2021/03/Corrin-Care_J_2000.pdf?utm_source=website&utm_medium=website&utm_campaign=PDF_Download.

Cox, John. 2017. 'Kindy and Grassroots Gender Transformations in Solomon Islands.' In *Transformations of Gender in Melanesia*, edited by Martha Macintyre and Ceridwen Spark, 69–93. Canberra: ANU Press. doi.org/10.22459/TGM.02.2017.03.

Deasy, Daniel. 2015. 'The Moving Spotlight Theory.' *Philosophical Studies: An International Journal for Philosophy in the Analytical Tradition* 172, no. 8: 2073–89. www.jstor.org/stable/24703966.

Department of Foreign Affairs and Trade (DFAT). 2021. *Pacific Women Lead: Investment Design*. Policy Document, July. Canberra: Australian Government. www.dfat.gov.au/sites/default/files/pacific-women-lead-design-framework.pdf.

Dickson-Waiko, Anne. 2007. 'Colonial Enclaves and Domestic Spaces in British New Guinea.' In *Britishness Abroad: Transnational Movements and Imperial Cultures*, edited by Kate Darian-Smith, Stuart Macintyre, and Patricia Grimshaw, 205–30. Melbourne: Melbourne University Press.

Dickson-Waiko, Anne. 2013. 'Women, Nation and Decolonisation in Papua New Guinea.' *The Journal of Pacific History* 48, no. 2: 177–93. doi.org/10.1080/00223344.2013.802844.

Dureau, Christine. 2010. 'Mixed Blessings: Christianity and History in Women's Lives on Simbo, Western Solomon Islands.' PhD diss., Macquarie University, Sydney. doi.org/10.25949/19431431.v1.

Equal Rights Trust. 2016. *Stand Up and Fight: Addressing Discrimination and Inequality in Solomon Islands*. Report. London: Equal Rights Trust. www.equalrightstrust.org/resources/stand-and-fight-addressing-discrimination-and-inequality-solomon-islands.

Foucault, Michel. 1988. *Power/Knowledge: Selected Interviews and Other Writings, 1972–1977*. Edited by Collin Gordon. Translated by Collin Gordon, Leo Marshall, John Mepham, and Kate Soper. New York: Pantheon Books.

Garrett, John. 1992. *Footsteps in the Sea: Christianity in Oceania to World War II*. Suva: Institute of Pacific Studies, University of the South Pacific.

Guha, Ranajit. 1982. *On Some Aspects of the Historiography of Colonial India: Subaltern Studies. Volume 1*. Delhi: Oxford University Press.

Guo, Pei-Yi. 2020. 'Marriage-Related Exchanges and the Agency of Women among the Langalanga, Solomon Islands.' *Oceania* 90, no. 3: 273–91. doi.org/10.1002/ocea.5281.

Guttenbeil-Likiliki, 'Ofa-Ki-Levuka Louise. 2020. *Creating Equitable South–North Partnerships: Nurturing the Vā and Voyaging the Audacious Ocean Together*. Melbourne: IWDA. www.sistalibrary.com.vu/wp-content/uploads/2021/03/Creating-Equitable-South-North-Partnerships_Full-Report.pdf.

Guttenbeil-Likiliki, 'Ofakilevuka. 2022. 'Enough is Enough: Audaciously Decolonising the Development and Humanitarian Nexus.' *Devpolicy Blog*, 15 December. Canberra: Development Policy Centre, The Australian National University. devpolicy.org/decolonising-the-development-and-humanitarian-nexus-20221215/.

Hall, Catherine. 1992. *White, Male and Middle Class: Explorations in Feminisms and History*. London: Wiley & Sons.

Hedditch, Sonali, and Clare Manuel. 2010. *Solomon Islands: Gender and Investment Climate Reform Assessment*. Washington, DC: International Finance Corporation. openknowledge.worldbank.org/server/api/core/bitstreams/c1a30286-2728-54f6-b28a-f548c29fdea1/content.

Hermkens, Anna-Karina. 2013. '"Raits Blong Mere"? Framing Human Rights and Gender in Solomon Islands.' *Intersections: Gender and Sexuality in Asia and the Pacific* 33. doi.org/10.25911/QNC9-HK75.

Heywood, Andrew. 2007. *Political Ideologies: An Introduction*. 4th edn. London: Palgrave Macmillan.

Homan, Sarah, Tomoko Honda, Loksee Leung, Emma Fulu, and Jane Fisher. 2019. *Transforming Harmful Gender Norms in Solomon Islands: A Study of the Oxfam Safe Families Program*. October. Melbourne: The Equality Institute, Monash University and Oxfam Australia.

Honda, T., S. Homan, L. Leung, A. Bennett, E. Fulu, and J. Fisher. 2022. 'Community Mobilisation in the Framework of Supportive Social Environment to Prevent Family Violence in Solomon Islands.' *World Development* 152: 105799. doi.org/10.1016/j.worlddev.2021.105799.

International Women's Development Agency (IWDA). 2012. *Gender & Culture in the Solomon Islands*. [Documentary]. Melbourne: IWDA. www.youtube.com/watch?v=8QqIjBnwi3U.

Jackson, Cecile. 2006. 'Feminism Spoken Here: Epistemologies for Interdisciplinary Development Research.' *Development and Change* 37, no. 3: 525–47. doi.org/10.1111/j.0012-155X.2006.00489.x.

Jolly, Margaret. 1991. '"To Save the Girls for Brighter and Better Lives": Presbyterian Missions and Women in the South of Vanuatu, 1848–1870.' *The Journal of Pacific History* 26, no. 1: 27–48. doi.org/10.1080/00223349108572645.

Jolly, Margaret. 1996. 'Women's Rights, Human Rights and Domestic Violence in Vanuatu.' *Feminist Review* 52, no. 1: 169–90. doi.org/10.1057/fr.1996.14.

Jolly, Margaret. 2000. '"Woman ikat raet long human raet o no?" Women's Rights, Human Rights and Domestic Violence in Vanuatu.' In *Human Rights and Gender Politics*, edited by Anne-Marie Hilsdon, Martha Macintyre, Vera Mackie, and Maila Stevens, 124–46. London: Routledge.

Keesing, Roger M. 1985. 'Kwaio Women Speak: The Micropolitics of Autobiography in a Solomon Island Society.' *American Anthropologist* 81, no. 1: 27–39. doi.org/10.1525/aa.1985.87.1.02a00040.

Ladner, Kiera L. 2009. 'Gendering Decolonisation, Decolonising Gender.' *Australian Indigenous Law Review* 13, no. 1: 62–77.

Lawlor, Laurie. 2005. *Shadow Catcher: The Life and Work of Edward S. Curtis*. Lincoln: Bison Books, University of Nebraska.

Lawrence, David. 2014. *The Naturalist and His 'Beautiful Islands': Charles Morris Woodford in the Western Pacific*. Canberra: ANU Press. doi.org/10.22459/NBI.10.2014.

Macintyre, Martha, and Ceridwen Spark, eds. 2017. *Transformations of Gender in Melanesia*. Canberra: ANU Press. doi.org/10.22459/TGM.02.2017.

Marsh, Selina Tusitala. 2015. 'Un/Civilized Girls, Unruly Poems: Jully Makini (Solomon Islands).' In *Huihui: Navigating Art and Literature in the Pacific*, edited by Jeffrey Carroll, Brandy McDougall, and Georganne Nordstrom, 46–62. Honolulu: University of Hawai'i Press.

McDougall, Debra. 2014. '"Tired for Nothing"? Women, Chiefs, and the Domestication of Customary Authority in Solomon Islands.' In *Divine Domesticities: Christian Paradoxes in Asia and the Pacific*, edited by Hyaeweol Choi and Margaret Jolly, 199–224. Canberra: ANU Press. doi.org/10.22459/ DD.10.2014.07.

McDougall, Debra. 2016. *Engaging with Strangers: Love and Violence in the Rural Solomon Islands*. London: Berghahn Books. doi.org/10.2307/j.ctvgs09mh.

Merry, Sally Engle. 2003. 'Human Rights Law and the Demonization of Culture (And Anthropology Along the Way).' *Political and Legal Anthropology Review* 26, no. 1: 55–76. doi.org/10.1525/pol.2003.26.1.55.

Monson, Rebecca. 2022. *Gender, Property and Politics in the Pacific: Who Speaks for Land?* Cambridge: Cambridge University Press. doi.org/10.1017/97811 08953672.

Mulder, Stella. 2019. *Wave: Women and Political Leadership in Solomon Islands— Literature Review*. Research Report. Melbourne: International Women's Development Agency.

Pollard, Alice A. 2000. *Givers of Wisdom, Labourers without Gain: Essays on Women in Solomon Islands*. Suva: Institute of Pacific Studies.

Robbins, Joel. 2004. *Becoming Sinners: Christianity and Moral Torment in a Papua New Guinea Society*. Berkeley: University of California Press.

Said, Edward. 1978. *Orientalism*. New York: Pantheon Books.

Sipolo, Jully. 1981. *Civilized Girl*. Suva: South Pacific Creative Arts Society.

Skow, Daniel. 2009. 'Relativity and the Moving Spotlight.' *The Journal of Philosophy* 106, no. 12: 666–78. www.jstor.org/stable/20620219.

Soaki, Pauline. 2017. 'Casting Her Vote: Women's Political Participation in Solomon Islands.' In *Transformations of Gender in Melanesia*, edited by Martha Macintyre and Ceridwen Spark, 95–114. Canberra: ANU Press. doi.org/ 10.22459/TGM.02.2017.04.

Solomon Islands in Focus. 2015–25. 'SINCW.' *Solomon Islands in Focus*. [Online]. www.solomonislandsinfocus.com/sincw.htm.

Spivak, Gayatri C. 1988. 'Can the Subaltern Speak?' In *Marxism and the Interpretation of Culture*, edited by Cary Nelson and Lawrence Grossberg, 271–313. Urbana: University of Illinois Press.

Thaman, Konai Helu. 2003. 'Decolonizing Pacific Studies: Indigenous Perspectives, Knowledge, and Wisdom in Higher Education.' *The Contemporary Pacific* 15, no. 1: 1–17. doi.org/10.1353/cp.2003.0032.

Torjer, Olsen A. 2017. 'Gender and/in Indigenous Methodologies.' *Ethnicities* 17, no. 4: 509–25. doi.org/10.1177/1468796816673089.

Underhill-Sem, Yvonne. 2010. *Gender, Culture and the Pacific*. Asia-Pacific Human Development Report Background Papers Series 2010/05. New York: United Nations Development Programme.

UN Women Asia and the Pacific. 2019. 'Meet the Women Pushing for Equal Representation in Solomon Islands Provinces.' *News*, 8 March. Bangkok: UN Women Asia and the Pacific. asiapacific.unwomen.org/en/news-and-events/stories/2019/05/meet-the-women-pushing-for-equal-representation-in-solomon-islands-provinces.

Wardlow, Holly. 2006. *Wayward Women: Sexuality and Agency in a New Guinea Society*. Berkeley: University of California Press. doi.org/10.1525/9780520938977.

World Vision. 2024. 'Tackling Gender-Based Violence in the Solomon Islands: Channels of Hope Driving a Shift in Cultural Attitudes to Violence.' [Online]. Melbourne: World Vision Australia. www.worldvision.com.au/global-issues/work-we-do/poverty/tackling-gender-based-violence.

4

Political Proxies: Gender-diverse young people's alternative paths to politics in South-East Asia and Australia

Elise Stephenson

It is not new to claim that previous conceptions of gender and political life have been limited by a singular focus on women or men, and in a binary and heteronormative fashion. Yet, queering the study of gender and politics—particularly in the cases of South-East Asia and Australia—remains largely underdone. To 'queer' research on gender and politics enables the production of new knowledge and exposes the limits of relatively insular disciplinary conversations and conceptualisations.

This chapter therefore invites a deconstruction of political power by studying the alternative paths to politics across several axes of diversity: youth, gender, sexuality, ethnicity and disability. It shows that while too often excluded from formal institutions that are accorded the title of 'politics', young diverse and marginalised groups are hardly politically inactive. Through alternative forms of political participation via 'proxies', diverse young people both reflect the constraints of current archetypical political systems and prise open constructive gaps. They can—and do— make themselves heard through non-traditional political means, with mixed results in gaining traditional political effects. Where traditional political impact is witnessed, it is to significant effect. Where traditional political impact is not evidenced or possible, ongoing challenges are highlighted in translating power to the margins. Yet, that does not leave the margins powerless, as individual and communal forms of power are wielded, even without traditional political representation.

This research finds diverse young people need not be engaged in traditional politics to be deeply political. Proxies for traditional political participation exist, such as through non-profit organisations, creative arts or entrepreneurship. This allows young people to wield substantial individual and communal levels of power and, at times, also impact broader traditional and structural politics and society. Yet, proxies have limits. Restricting historically marginalised groups 'only' to these spheres replicates existing power structures that exclude them from traditional politics. Further, a devaluation of these institutions is evident, resulting in further social capital and economic inequalities. Ultimately, the ability to be engaged in any political action—traditional or through novel or informal means—is a privilege.

The implications of this research are threefold. First, young people are not (just) disengaged, passive victims of a hierarchical political structure, but are political actors in their own right. Second, to support more diverse voices in politics, those recruited for politics and supported into the political pipeline could and should come through much more diverse means. Seeking out or supporting those already active in political 'proxies' may be one such avenue of recruitment. Third, traditional politics still matters, but it is not all that matters. Studies of gender and politics must do better to incorporate alternative paths to and practices of politics.

Ultimately, the concept of a 'path to politics' fails to incorporate the true nature of how young diverse people see their political representation and political action—as multidimensional and not constrained only to established paths and political norms. Further, there are several possibilities that come from queering the gender and politics literature: challenging the heteronormative domination of feminist and non-feminist understandings of politics, and 'seeing' those who have been minoritised and marginalised even within gender studies.

An insider's account: A pracademic, critical feminist friend approach

Being a scholar-entrepreneur or 'pracademic' first inspired this semi-insider account of diverse young people's paths to political influence across Australia and South-East Asia. Walker describes two facets necessary for a pracademic:

1. A solid grounding in experience in the field to appreciate nuances and subtle signals that the environment emits and 2. Rigorous academic research and reflective analysis training to be able to make sense of situations encountered and to be able to probe deeply into causal issues and to understand implications for practice. (Walker 2010: 2)

From 2017 to 2020, I travelled more than 75,000 kilometres by road around Australia while completing my PhD and running a social enterprise I co-founded, which worked with non-profits, activists and social entrepreneurs across rural and regional Australia, as well as across South-East Asia. My PhD was in women's leadership in international affairs, while the work I was leading with my enterprise encompassed running youth-led, youth-focused public diplomacy programs for Australia's premier public diplomacy initiative, 'Australia now'. The point where my research and entrepreneurial work intersects inspired this chapter, which shares research on the alternative paths to politics, power and social impact for young gender-diverse individuals across Australia and South-East Asia.

While my approach to this research began in 2017, the bulk of the data informing this chapter were generated over three years from 2019 to 2022 while running a flagship public diplomacy program throughout Australia and South-East Asia, the Young Entrepreneurs and Leaders Speaker Series (funded by the Australian Department of Foreign Affairs and Trade) (Plates 4.1 and 4.2). After running 76 workshops, events and media engagements with roughly 3,600 young people throughout South-East Asia (in person in Vietnam, Cambodia, Laos, Brunei and Malaysia, and online with the rest of the member countries of the Association of Southeast Asian Nations, or ASEAN) and Australia (online) about topics as diverse as gender equality, LGBTIQ+ rights, climate change, sustainability and fashion, social enterprise, human rights and more, critical key themes of young people's activism and participation in the development of their nations that warranted analysis and sharing came to the fore. In particular, the stories of how gender and sexuality-diverse young people, ethnic minorities and people with disabilities who seldom held 'traditional' roles of authority were crafting policy, representing their communities in national and international forums and advocating for politics pushed me to better understand the themes I had observed.

Plate 4.1: Elise Stephenson speaking at the Young Entrepreneurs and Leaders Speaker Series engagement at UN headquarters, Hanoi, Vietnam, 2019

Source: Elise Stephenson.

Plate 4.2: Workshopping approaches to gender equality for Gender Month, Vietnam, 2019

Source: Elise Stephenson.

Subsequent to completing my final series of workshops in Malaysia in March 2022, I sought qualitative interviews with 16 young gender-diverse people to explore how they conceptualised politics and power, whether they had run for politics (or politics-adjacent forms of activism), the challenges experienced by gender, sexuality, ethnically and other diverse individuals, and what they would like to see change to allow more diverse and representative forms of political representation in the region. This 'pracademic' approach allowed me to anchor my scholarship and work in a practical setting, with academic credibility, tools, techniques and ways of thinking that typically set pracademic researchers apart from those without substantial experience of practice. Doing so allows this research to 'build a bridge between theory and practice', to understand the lived realities of young people across time, geography, political settings and individual identities (Walker 2010: 3).

To go deeper into the trends observed from the 76 workshops and events, 16 in-depth interviews were sought across a range of participants from throughout the region, seeking a broad regional picture of diversity in paths to politics, rather than case-by-case study. Participants who met the following criteria were sought over a six-week period in 2022: between 18 and 35 years of age; had run for politics, were interested in running for politics or were otherwise engaged in politics; and based in South-East Asia or Australia. Of the 16 interviewed, eight (50 per cent) identified as male, five (31 per cent) as female and three (19 per cent) as nonbinary or transgender. The average age of participants was 26, with the youngest 19 and the oldest 35 years of age. Ten (62.5 per cent) identified as 'straight', with six (37.5 per cent) identifying as LGBTIQ+. Four interviewees came from the Philippines, three from Indonesia, two each from Australia and Vietnam and one each from Brunei, Malaysia, Cambodia, Thailand and Myanmar. Among them, six (37.5 per cent) identified as Indigenous or from an ethnic minority. Two (12.5 per cent) identified as having a disability. Two (12.5 per cent) had run for politics and 11 (68 per cent) desired to run for politics. Participants in this chapter have been de-identified and a pseudonym has been used to share their perspectives. The ethical components of this research were granted human ethics approval through The Australian National University (Protocol 2022/359).

While a scholar-academic or pracademic approach formed the genesis of this research, I also undertook this project using a 'critical feminist friend' approach, allowing me to understand the gendered, racialised, heteronormative, ableist political and social institutions within which I was 'entangled'. Critical feminist friend (Stephenson 2024; Chappell and Mackay 2021) approaches enable researchers to build collaborative, long-term relationships with the institutions studied, while maintaining autonomy, researcher integrity, an ability to 'see clearly' and analyse critically and align researcher and institutional goals. This approach enabled me not only to conduct observational analysis during the many workshops and events run across multiple years, but also to see opportunities to dig deeper through qualitative interviews to validate findings after completion of the speaker series.

The enmeshing of these research approaches was critical for understanding the delicate contours of minoritised young people's experiences of politics and the political advocacy approach. Large-scale observation across the workshops and events provided me with a glimpse into the 'everyday' processes and practices that I would not have gleaned through interviews alone. It also provided me with an opportunity to witness the movements, creativity and entrepreneurship young people pioneered and experience it in real time. The interviews, on the other hand, allowed me to contextualise what I had observed and gain participants' understandings of their actions, enterprises, creative processes and perspectives. While recognising that such a unique methodological approach may not be well suited to all kinds of research, it did have inherent benefits for reaching young people whose work and experiences simply may have been missed without it. Not all can access political action or research on politics in the same ways, as it may be doubly distanced from their everyday lived realities.

Understanding the context: Diversity in politics in South-East Asia and Australia

In relation to South-East Asia, Australia operates as a middle-power country, variably seen as a critical player in the region with 'special proximity' (Epstein 2017: 15) to South-East Asia, on the one hand, and on the other, absent and unhelpful, with Singapore's former prime minister Lee Kuan Yew famously warning that Australia risked becoming the 'poor white trash of Asia' (Dobell 2015). While Australia and countries across South-East Asia may not be seen as a natural grouping of nations, all share geopolitical interests, proximity, strategic engagement and South-East Asian prioritisation in Australian foreign policy. Australia is a strategic partner to ASEAN (comprising the 10 nations studied: Singapore, Malaysia, Myanmar, Thailand, Vietnam, Laos, Cambodia, the Philippines, Indonesia and Brunei) and ASEAN is one of Australia's top-three trading partners (PM&C n.d.). The nations share many similar demographic features such as the underrepresentation in politics of women, LGBTIQ+, Indigenous and ethnic minority groups and people with disability, and significant youth populations or a youth 'bulge' impacting political outcomes. Yet, there are great differences not only between Australia and South-East Asia, but also within.

Political systems across Australia and South-East Asia vary greatly, from democracies to hybrid regimes to authoritarian states. Australia is a representative democracy, with features such as compulsory voting and enshrined values around freedoms, equality and representation in government. The Philippines and Indonesia are presidential or semi-presidential republics, which Croissant and Lorenz (2018) classify as defective democracies, where elements of their democratic systems are 'insufficiently institutionalised' or partial (Croissant and Merkel 2019: 439). Cambodia and Malaysia are constitutional monarchies, while Singapore and, until recently, Myanmar have parliamentary republic systems. These last four countries can be grouped as having electoral authoritarian systems (CountryReports 1997–2025). Thein-Lemelson (2021: 3) has argued that since the 2021 coup, Myanmar manifests longstanding 'politicide': patterns of 'systematic violence perpetrated against political groups and social movements that challenge military control and dominance'.

At the other end of the democratic spectrum, Brunei, Laos, Vietnam and Thailand have closed autocratic systems (Croissant and Lorenz 2018). Vietnam has a single-party system governed by the Communist Party of Vietnam, like Laos, which is governed by the Lao People's Revolutionary Party. Brunei's context is particularly unique when considering diversity in politics, as it is an absolute monarchy where freedom of speech is highly restricted. Political participation is near impossible for those outside the royal family or regime and politics is closely tied to religion, with Islamic Sharia law implemented throughout the country (Freedom House 2020).

Great variation in political systems is evident among South-East Asian countries and this impacts the level and diversity of political participation that can be achieved. Across the countries studied in the region, according to Freedom House, Australia scores the highest on global freedom (measured by political rights and civil liberties), at 95 out of 100 in 2021, while Myanmar scores the lowest in the region with only 9 out of 100 (Freedom House n.d.).

Young people and politics

When it comes to the involvement of young people in politics across Australia and South-East Asia, states are witnessing an increased incidence of youth political activism, yet politics remains exclusionary and exclusive to youth voices. Societies in South-East Asia are traditionally paternalistic, hierarchical and male dominated, making it challenging for young people to permeate existing political structures (UNDP 2014). Velasco (2005) finds that significant institutional and societal obstacles prevent meaningful youth participation in politics. Young people are often dismissed as inexperienced or naive, and countries such as Cambodia and Indonesia lack articulated youth policies to shape and encourage political involvement (Velasco 2005). In Myanmar, Ebead and Hirakawa (2022) observe the significant impact of autocratic military rule on the marginalisation of women, youth and ethnic minorities in formal political processes. Youth (people aged 15 to 35) make up 33 per cent of Myanmar's population and have historically spearheaded the fight against repression. Mass protests after the February 2021 military coup were partially driven by young people advocating for democratic accountability and transitional justice (Ebead and Hirakawa 2022). However, Ebead and Hirawaka (2022) identify several barriers to political participation, including sociocultural norms and perceptions, limited political awareness, financial hurdles and a lack of legal and institutional measures to encourage youth inclusion.

Socioeconomic challenges are particularly prominent in preventing young people from participating in politics in South-East Asia. A 2018 study by the Economic and Social Commission for Asia and the Pacific (ESCAP) found that marginalisation in education or employment influences inclusion in other areas of society, including civic engagement and political participation. Given that average enrolment rates for secondary and tertiary education are 77 per cent and 30 per cent, respectively, in the Asia-Pacific (ESCAP 2018), this remains a barrier to effective political participation by young people. Moreover, youth are found to be highly disenfranchised by formal politics. A study by the United Nations Development Programme (UNDP 2014) finds that there is a low level of trust in institutions among young people. In Australia, trust in political institutions is falling, with Fu et al. (2021) arguing that there is a 'democracy gap' for Australian youth, who distrust traditional politics (but are still focused on civic-mindedness). This dissatisfaction with current political regimes is seeing young people increasingly turn to non-electoral participation in politics through social media, protests and demonstrations, as well as through other proxies for political action, as will be explored in this chapter, to make their voices heard (ESCAP 2018). Information and communication technology is expanding opportunities for youth political engagement (UNDP 2014), with this providing a possible avenue for political change driven by young people. However, social, economic and institutional barriers continue to pose a challenge for young people seeking to participate in politics in Australia and South-East Asia.

Despite the barriers, youth participation in politics has increased in recent years. In the 2019 Indonesian election, nearly half of eligible voters were aged between 17 and 35 (Siahaan 2019). This strongly influenced political parties' campaign strategies. The creation of the Indonesian Solidarity Party (Partai Solidaritas Indonesia, PSI) in the 2019 election was specifically aimed at garnering votes from young people, with PSI advocating tolerance, human rights, democratic values, freedom of speech and greater social inclusion (Siahaan 2019). PSI failed to win a seat in the House of Representatives, however, this example still demonstrates the growing influence of youth voters on the political landscape in South-East Asia. Similarly, the Future Forward Party (FFP) established in 2018 in Thailand opposes military oppression and seeks to uphold human rights and transparency. The FFP secured 31 constituency seats in the Thai Parliament and the third-largest number of votes in the 2019 elections (Siahaan 2019)—again illustrating the impact of young people on politics. Syed Saddiq became Malaysia's youngest cabinet minister in 2018 at age 25 and founded the Malaysian United Democratic Alliance (MUDA) in 2020. Saddiq envisions MUDA as 'a team of great young potentials ready to change Malaysia's political landscape', who will build on substantial work started by Undi18, a youth-led movement that managed to successfully lower the voting age from 21 to 18 in 2019 (Anand 2022). In Australia's 2022 federal election, young people were similarly a decisive force, voting for climate action and gender equality. The election saw the rise in 'Teal' independent candidates appealing to both a more diverse and a younger audience, and the re-election of one of Australia's youngest parliamentarians, 28-year-old Senator Jordon Steele-John, a representative of the Australian Greens party and a disability rights advocate. Despite challenges, opportunities for young people to engage in politics are evident across the region, although much greater efforts are required to overcome socioeconomic, institutional and cultural barriers.

Gender and politics

While the attempt by young people to gain representation in politics in South-East Asia and Australia remains incomplete, the same is true for gender diversity, with women remaining underrepresented in formal politics in the region and trans and nonbinary individuals almost entirely unrepresented and invisible. Iwanaga (2008) argues that politics is often associated with violence, bribery and corruption, which contradicts the view that women are innocent and peaceful. Further, by enforcing gender stereotypes and expectations, patriarchal systems mean women are largely perceived as incapable of entering politics (Devasahayam 2019). Iwanaga (2008) also explores more specific individual factors, with social background, education, experience and connections impacting the ability of women to participate in politics. Where women come from low socioeconomic backgrounds or have lower educational attainment, breaking into public office is particularly difficult, highlighting the duplicative, intersecting nature of identity on the challenges experienced (Richter 1990). Where women have been successful in obtaining political leadership positions, Richter (1990) finds that this has largely been the result of familial ties to prominent male politicians. Political dynasties can facilitate women's political leadership by legitimising their involvement on moral grounds in patriarchal systems but do not create pathways for other women from low socioeconomic backgrounds, reinforcing social divisions (Choi 2019). Further, in her book *The Woman President*, Vijeyarasa (2022: 254) notes that for those women who achieved the highest offices of power in Asia, 'gender for the woman president is a second skin that cannot be shed', with their presence in politics remaining exceptional and improbable. The most significant barriers to women's participation in politics in Australia and South-East Asia are therefore entrenched patriarchal attitudes and norms, financial challenges and socioeconomic divisions that are reinforced by political dynasties.

LGBTIQ+ people and politics

The political representation of LGBTIQ+ people—particularly within South-East Asian and Australian contexts—has not been widely examined in the academic literature. Although some South-East Asian nations are becoming more progressive, religious and political systems and public attitudes are still significant barriers to recognition and respect for LGBTIQ+ people and their rights (Root 2022), and political participation is unattainable for the LGBTIQ+ community in much of the region.

ASEAN has pledged to become more 'people-oriented' and adopted its own Bill of Rights in 2012. However, rights regarding sexual orientation, gender identity and gender expression (SOGIE) were controversially excluded from this (Langlois 2018). Legislation in some South-East Asian nations prevents LGBTIQ+ people from openly expressing their identity. For example, homosexual acts are punishable by the death penalty in Brunei and can incur a prison sentence in Malaysia and Myanmar. Conversion practices still occur in countries including Indonesia, Malaysia and the Philippines (Root 2022). Homosexual conduct is criminalised in Singapore, although this law is rarely upheld and the country celebrates the Pink Dot Festival annually in support of the LGBTIQ+ community, demonstrating inconsistency between legal frameworks and practices (Wilkinson et al. 2017).

Even in countries where legislation is changing to decriminalise homosexual acts and ban conversion therapy, as in Singapore and Vietnam, respectively, in 2022 (Root 2022), religious practices present another barrier for the LGBTIQ+ community. Langlois (2022) explores the juxtaposition between historical religious traditions that included transgender people and the influence of religion on modern society. Transgender ritual specialists held key symbolic roles in their communities in countries including Indonesia, Malaysia and the island of Borneo (which is now shared by both countries and Brunei). However, contemporary society is broadly traditional and conservative in these countries, and Indonesia has seen a regression in terms of tolerance of sexuality and gender diversity since 2016 (Langlois 2022). Similarly, Sanders (2020) examines the role of religion in state governance in countries such as Brunei and Malaysia, where Islam is the official state religion. Given that Islamic laws are highly conservative and do not support homosexuality (Wilkinson et al. 2017), there is little opportunity for political change in these countries at present and religion still presents a barrier to the recognition and political participation of LGBTIQ+ individuals.

Moreover, public attitudes towards the LGBTIQ+ community present a challenge to political participation. Even in countries where near-full legal equality has been achieved, LGBTIQ+ people remain significantly more likely than heterosexual or cisgender people to experience prejudice or discrimination (Manalastas et al. 2017). Manalastas et al. (2017) conducted a study of attitudes towards lesbians and gay men in Indonesia, Malaysia, the Philippines, Singapore, Thailand and Vietnam. The research found that 66 per cent of respondents in Indonesia and 59 per cent in Malaysia reject lesbians or gay men as neighbours. The country with the greatest tolerance for same-sex neighbours was the Philippines, at 28 per cent. Homosexuality was found to be least acceptable among Indonesians, followed by Vietnamese and Malaysians (Manalastas et al. 2017). The ASEAN SOGIE Caucus (2021) also finds that social and cultural prejudices in the region uniquely disempower and oppress sexual and gender diversity. While LGBTIQ+ political candidates are beginning to appear in countries such as the Philippines, Vietnam and Thailand (Langlois 2018), attitudes among civil society must shift before real change can occur in the political arena regarding the inclusion of LGBTIQ+ people in politics. Additionally, in Australia, where queer politicians exist, Stephenson et al. (forthcoming) find that LGBTIQ+ politicians face significant trolling and online abuse. Significant legal, religious and societal barriers in South-East Asia and Australia currently hinder progress towards recognition of LGBTIQ+ people in some countries, let alone the full political participation of this community.

Ethnic diversity and politics

Ethnic minorities in Australia and South-East Asian countries face significant barriers to political participation. The concept of ethnic minorities is not defined in international legal documents (Yen and Thang 2022), so definitions vary in academic literature. Yen and Thang (2022: 288) explore several definitions but concur with the statement that an ethnic minority 'is any group of persons which constitutes less than half of the population in the entire territory of a State whose members share characteristics of culture, religion or language, or a combination of any of these'. This definition encompasses defining features of ethnic minorities highlighted by other scholars.

Pholsena (2016) identifies the divide between majority and minority groups as a dominant feature of society and a barrier to political participation, with ethnic minorities sometimes still perceived as backward or untrustworthy and therefore unfit to hold political office. Gaining recognition as citizens is still a prominent issue for ethnic minorities in mountainous communities in Thailand, with 40 per cent of the highland population lacking Thai citizenship in 2005 (Pholsena 2016). This prevents participation of any sort in society, including in politics. Rural-based ethnic communities in Cambodia, Thailand, Laos and Vietnam are found to generally underperform in economic and social development. Higher levels of poverty, lower access to education and health facilities and lower participation in state education are all identified as barriers to achieving equality in these countries, including in the political sphere (Pholsena 2016). Furthermore, ethnic minorities in South-East Asia often reside in mountainous areas. These communities are often underdeveloped, with children sometimes unable to access education or struggling to use official languages in school. This creates a barrier to political participation for ethnic minorities (Children of the Mekong n.d.).

Tan and Preece (2022) provide a more positive analysis of ethnic minorities in Singapore. Quotas require 18.3 per cent of national legislature members to be from ethnic minority groups, guaranteeing representation of minorities such as Malays and Indians. This quota has been surpassed, with 29 per cent of current legislators coming from minority ethnic groups (Tan and Preece 2022). However, their study also highlights that Malays have historically been disadvantaged in Singapore and trail behind in education, employment and income outcomes. Socioeconomic and structural inequalities persist between the dominant Chinese and minority Malay groups, making this a challenge to achieving substantive political representation (Tan and Preece 2022). Barriers to political participation among ethnic groups in South-East Asia therefore include socioeconomic inequalities, lower access to education, electoral vote-splitting and weak party institutionalisation.

Political representation of diverse young people in Australia and South-East Asia

Overall, there are several gaps in the academic literature on political pathways, participation and experiences among young people, women, LGBTIQ+ people and ethnic minorities in South-East Asia. Region-wide studies often fail to fully comprehend the impact of political regimes on political choices, while considerable variation within the region makes it difficult to draw generalisations. The intersectionality of identity remains understudied, with most research focused on a single axis of identity or inequality, lacking nuance and in-depth exploration. While this literature review has attempted to understand overlapping aspects of identity, it is noted that the paucity of research on people with disability and politics has constrained analysis. Overall, the political landscape in Australia and South-East Asia can be characterised as ethnically homogeneous, heterosexist and male. The overwhelming focus on politics as formal representation inhibits scholarly and practical conceptions of informal politics (or proxies—activism in non-profits, through social entrepreneurship or the creative industries, for instance) as politics. Except for scholarship on young people, which considers informal methods of participation such as protests and social media activity, literature on informal political participation remains missing. Given there are potentially fewer barriers for diverse groups to participate informally in politics, this remains an important area for study.

How do gender-diverse young people define politics and see their path to politics?

While much of the literature defines political participation as participation in formal politics, young people in this research held a much more expansive definition of politics and political participation. Their conceptualisations varied from seeing politics as a neutral 'process of shaping social structures and power' to one of 'debate and negotiation'. In Cambodia, one participant, Chea, even described politics positively: '[W]e all subscribe to democracy, we adhere in our institutions, to our constitution around liberal democracy. Everyone has an opportunity to actively engage in politics and also be a political representative.'

Yet, the bulk of participant responses highlighted negative associations with politics, using words such as 'violent', 'competition', 'paternalistic', 'corruption', 'nepotism', 'seniority', 'nonsense' and 'dirty'. It is seen as difficult, exclusionary and dangerous, with Linh noting that 'to participate in politics is a risk of its own'. Abdul notes that in Indonesia, politics is seen as being close to crime: 'Indonesia has done very good in eradicating corruption, but still it happens in many places, which makes many young people not interested in politics.' For others, there was a perception that you would only go into politics for yourself (ego) or money, and the barriers were seen as myriad: lack of finance and resources; perceived lack of experience; lack of political ties or connections; royalty; nepotism; sexism; ageism; ableism; and societal and individualised homophobia, biphobia and transphobia.

Despite the largely negative connotations surrounding perceptions of politics and barriers to participation, young people were politically active and many identified that they were on the path to politics—seeking future election or representation in 'traditional' politics. Many viewed their own political engagement as responding to some of the negative aspects of traditional politics: they were trying to make it safer and less paternalistic, bring about good governance and be impactful in their communities. But being on the 'path to politics' was also an incomplete definition of how they saw what they did; although not elected officials, many felt they were already 'in' politics. The definition of their own political action was not viewed purely through a traditional lens of party membership and political elections.

In the Philippines, Pearl characterises young people's engagement in politics as multidimensional:

> Maybe you comment on the climate crisis, or maybe you create art that focuses on the lived experience of queer women. Maybe your activism is through art, maybe it's through doing your own climate tech startup … [Y]ou're not wrong for entering a particular space or doing a particular thing, build[ing] your own path.

While many of these actions could be seen as political engagement, infrequently have they been equated with direct and specific political representation or action. The political engagement spoken about was seen not merely as being part of their pathway to politics, but as already political. This was a clear and consistent message reinforced throughout this research. Politics is contextual and often rooted in intentions rather than methods.

This had clear benefits for participants, as well as constraints. Linh, who identifies as nonbinary and is from Vietnam, highlights the nuances:

> [P]olitics, for someone with my profile right now, does not feel right … I would think of grassroots organisations, calling that a form of democracy, political actions, that would be something I'd be involved in. But if we talk about the usual politician's career and election, that would not be the case.

While two participants in this study had run for election before, the types of political engagement usually engaged in included:

- starting an initiative or project
- founding a social enterprise, enterprise or non-profit
- artistic output: cartoons, comics, drawings, paintings, digital art
- protests (for example, Strike for Climate)
- petitions
- sharing information on social media
- fundraising

- content creation (blogs, vlogs, TikTok)
- voting
- joining a political party or student political party
- running for politics
- research
- developing resources for particular causes (for example, anti-racism kit)
- small-scale diffused, local volunteering
- overseas study or work
- being an influencer or celebrity.

Their experiences reinforced the idea that if more diverse actors are sought for traditional representation in politics, more diverse pathways to politics must also be recognised. It was clear that it is not only those who run for student politics, join a political party or study political science who are on the 'path to politics'. While the barriers to political participation were significant—and warrant due exploration beyond the limitations of this chapter—the analysis of constructive gaps that follows highlights initial attempts to re-characterise pathways to politics.

Constructive gaps: Gendered authority from the margins

Entrepreneurship, creative industries, volunteering and other pursuits are not always viewed as part of a path to politics or as explicitly political representation or action. However, this research found that these same actions were seen as a legitimate political tool and, in some cases, a proxy for 'traditional', formal political participation. This section breaks down some of the core trends in mechanisms used by young people to be politically active across Australia and South-East Asia, including building credibility, reframing, leveraging regional and international partnerships, informal participation in politics, using the novel, embodying power and combining impact and income. This allowed young people to circumvent hierarchy, gain traction, model inclusion, maintain distance and boundaries and sustain action, as explored in Figure 4.1.

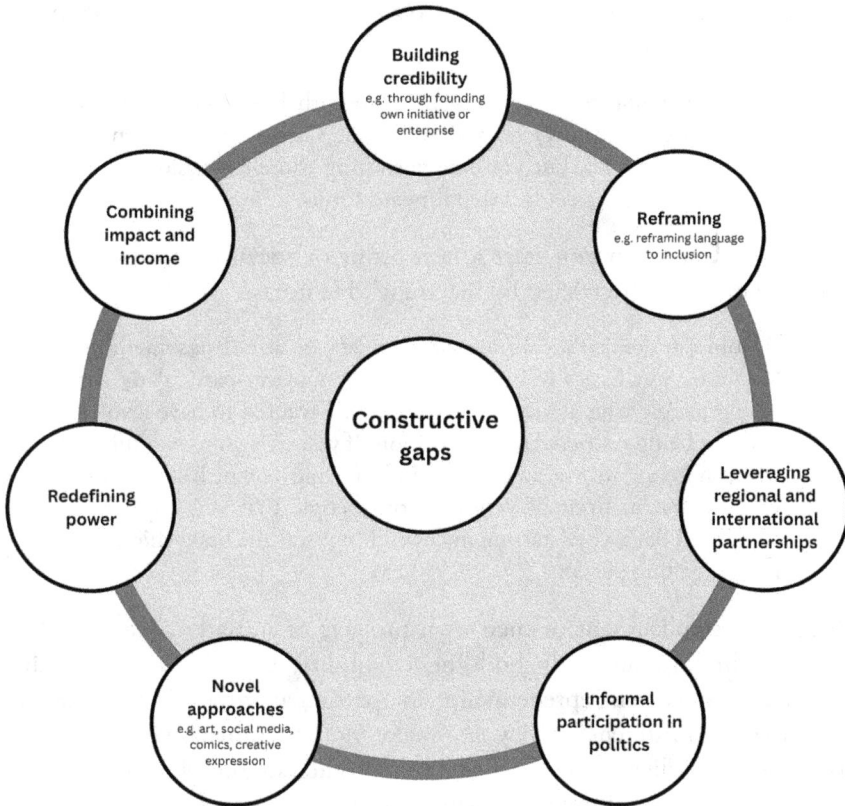

Figure 4.1: Constructive gaps used by gender and ethnically diverse young people to wield political power

Building credibility

As many of the challenges experienced by participants when engaging with politics are reinforced throughout the literature—ageism, sexism, homophobia—building credibility was a strong theme that emerged as a constructive gap used by young people to wield influence. Starting a social enterprise or initiative enabled participants to build credibility. Sal notes:

> You're able to show the numbers and the stories at the same time. By establishing yourself as a leading practitioner/thought leader, you're able to have conversations with communities, help them in a certain way, and that gives us an added boost to slowly introduce or influence policies here in the country.

Founding an initiative or enterprise also gave participants an opening to talk with senior leaders. As Sal explains:

> We're not going to be able to come up with laws and legislation because we're not lawyers, and we're not actually a congressman or congresswoman, but you know, starting those discussions with [senior leaders] is already a step forward for us.

Tim notes that when you start a non-profit or social enterprise yourself, individuals are not 'restricted by hierarchy'. He notes:

> If I join a student political group or interned with an MP or something like that, you basically have a hierarchy in place, particularly for young people who are less experienced ... I wanted to have a voice without being restricted by my position. If you start your own thing, you can be a leader at any age, and if your movement has support, you can get in front of very powerful people that you ordinarily couldn't. That's why [starting my own thing] was the best vehicle for me as a young person.

Using the establishment of their own projects or initiatives was therefore a critical link to not only building credibility, but also circumventing hierarchy. Social entrepreneurship in particular gives individuals an opportunity to influence policy *plus* make money, connect with audiences, consumers or clients in a different way, and so on, which could be enormously beneficial to young people from diverse backgrounds who may otherwise face extensive barriers.

Reframing

In the creative industries, many note that the open-ended nature of creative expression means that more controversial or progressive political stances can go unnoticed or be reframed to protect the artist/activist, while still having duplicative meanings used to spread information, garner support or influence policy and politics. The use of motifs such as rainbows was employed to signal LGBTIQ+ inclusion or a specific message. Additionally, reframing was used in some countries hostile to LGBTIQ+ people to specifically support LGBTIQ+ communities by reframing a focus on service delivery to mandate the 'inclusion of all people'—setting the precedent for inclusion without needing to call out specific target audiences who might otherwise be at risk. Reframing was also applied at a national level. Where participants had a hard time engaging politically in their own country, they advocated for a more regional approach and getting involved in initiatives and campaigns that were regionally based, taking a multi-country approach to political influence. Often this was around a specific issue or cause, such as LGBTIQ+ rights or climate change, and many regional youth networks are backed by international donors and regional bodies (the United Nations or ASEAN) or governments (the United States, United Kingdom, Australia).

Leveraging regional and international partnerships

The use of partnerships to participate in politics was a strategy employed to undertake 'politics at a distance'. In Cambodia and Laos, youth organisations are often unregistered (which comes with its own constraints) or, for local government–backed organisations, proximity to existing government institutions can result in a degree of organisational restraint and following the status quo. However, by partnering with international governments and donors, youth organisations (even government-backed ones) are sometimes able to take a more progressive and contentious position on topics than if no partnership options are available. In Cambodia, Chea noted that NGOs could get their message to a third party (international embassy or donor), which then reflected their desired policy ideas back to the Cambodian Government. In Laos, by partnering with the Australian Government under the Australia Now program, the Lao Youth Union ran events on progressive topics such as mental health and LGBTIQ+ and domestic violence, which otherwise might not have been possible.

Through using these approaches, young people were able to get around some of the barriers instituted by governments, with Chea noting that otherwise 'the government would not give us credit to talk with them because we're young, we don't have a proper [legal] organisational structure'. Similar methodologies were employed in linking young people with international journalists who could write about their causes in international forums, influencing foreign governments and donors, who could then apply pressure to internal political systems.

Informal participation in politics

Some young people used informal participation in politics to engage in contentious ideas in a safe and exploratory space. In Cambodia, Chea engaged with other young people over football, coffee and chess to learn the 'culture of debate and negotiation' and engage a wider group of young people who could become informed about politics. It was seen as a more effective approach than having a teacher talk for a whole day and lecturing or dictating what young people should do. It was also a pragmatic choice: many non-profit or activist organisations in Cambodia operate under intense police and political scrutiny.

Using the novel

For Zara, a nonbinary comic artist from Malaysia, their art was not always political, but it became political because Zara would try to use their voice to

> make light of sexual harassment issues and, at that point, there was no-one else that did ... comics like I did, which got a lot of attention from people, and I got women personally messaging me saying her experience and saying thank you for making light of this issue.

Initiatives as diverse as the Teach Us Consent movement in Australia, Strike for Climate Action, the youth resistance in Myanmar, the boycott over Brunei's repressive stance on LGBTIQ+ rights and more garnered additional strength by drawing on novel approaches—the use of social media, art, poses and hand signs—that were helpful for both media attention and gaining financial and other support for their political influence.

Embodying power

One of the defining features of young diverse people's engagement in politics across Australia and South-East Asia was the concept of power. The constraining factors of gender, ethnicity, age, sexuality and disability all impacted on participants' feelings of power and powerlessness. However, many participants spoke of knowing their own power, confronting it and redefining it. Arif noted that some of his work caught the attention of the president's office and he was offered an internship in government. He asked what the program would entail and was told administration and logistics for events and programs. Arif said it would involve

> helping out with the drinks, helping out with the food, carrying tables, and I was very upset. I said, 'No, there is no way that my organisation will engage in this sort of way that disrespects the participation of youth.' ... [Then] she genuinely did ask how would young people like to engage, and I said, if you want to bring us into your work, let us have a substantial role in communications, shaping public policy.

His example demonstrates the benefits of pushing back against what is offered and shaping a more collaborative, equal engagement style.

Combining impact and income

Social entrepreneurship in particular gives individuals an opportunity to influence policy *plus* make money and connect with audiences, consumers or clients in a different way that could be enormously beneficial to young people from diverse backgrounds who may otherwise face extensive barriers. Ahmad notes that being a founder of a social enterprise 'really put me in a lot of different spaces, from Indonesian Parliament, or talking to young people'. He also notes how important it is to use social enterprises as a space to help marginalised people, influence policy and get by. He notes that many of those with whom he now works in government or leadership have 'never been as poor as I am, or they haven't been as poor as others whom [I help]'. Social enterprise was seen as an even more viable option to influence policy, given the prevalence of volunteering among young people and the recurrent complaint that only those privileged enough could participate in politics; financial resourcing and remuneration were critical, but frequently inaccessible.

Enabling factors

Young diverse people's ability to participate in politics and use these constructive gaps to influence policy did share many common enabling factors. These included having: enough financial privilege to dedicate time and/or resources to volunteering or starting something; politically engaged parents or other community figures (education, religion); role models and mentors; educational experiences that enabled women and historically marginalised groups to step out and speak up; and experiences of marginalisation, conservativism, personal or social challenge that motivated or inspired individuals to act. Ahmad additionally notes that education is critical—both achieving a high enough level and the 'right kind'. He notes that where you go to university (and whether you go to university or finish education at all) acts as a filter that screens many out of the pipeline to politics. Reinforced by the nature of this study, which was undertaken in English, English-language skills were seen to give individuals more prestige and more useable capital to aid their political participation.

Additionally, political participation by young diverse and historically marginalised groups is evidently a privilege. It means individuals have enough time and resources to step out of their day-to-day professional and personal lives. Non-profits, creative industries and social enterprises are historically notoriously devalued, which has implications for the degree to which these avenues are viable constructive gaps to pursue in the first place.

Implications

As Baker and Barbara (2020: 135) note: 'Understanding how citizens participate in politics is important because it shapes political culture and the tenor of democracy.' Indeed, they note in their research on the Pacific that the standard research framing of politics 'is looking increasingly tired and is poorly serving the Pacific region by framing core research questions too narrowly' (Baker and Barbara 2020: 136). The narrowness of our studies and understandings of politics is reinforced in this study, which highlights three critical learnings. First, young people are not (just) disengaged, passive victims of a hierarchical political structure, but are political actors in their own right. Second, to support more diverse voices in politics, those recruited for politics and supported into the political pipeline could and should come through much more diverse means. Seeking out or supporting those already active in political 'proxies' may be one such avenue of recruitment. Third, traditional politics still matters, but it is not all that matters. Studies of gender and politics must do better to incorporate alternative paths to and practices of politics.

While proxies have been a powerful lens through which to view youth political action in this study, proxies do have limits, and warrant further investigation. Restricting historically marginalised groups 'only' to these spheres risks replicating existing power structures that exclude them from traditionally defined formal politics. This research therefore sits in an uncomfortable space: highlighting the strength of young people's alternatives to traditional political participation risks pigeon-holing their political activism to *just* these spheres, rather than fundamentally encouraging the transformation of politics. This highlights the need to continue to be critical of representative political ideals: the process of representing the people is incomplete without actual representation, which cannot be replaced or substituted purely with alternative forms of participation. It remains to be seen whether current 'politics as usual' can allow young people to ultimately exist, let alone thrive, and it is therefore questionable whether reform is truly possible. This is reinforced by Lee and Craney (2019: 19), who note that in the Pacific:

> Youth are often not taken seriously as political subjects within their own societies; their activism is not viewed as a right and it is sometimes dismissed, sidelined or, even worse, assumed to be anarchic or even criminal behaviour that needs to be controlled.

In this context, to what degree is political institutional change possible?

Relatedly, participants still raised considerable challenges to using their political power: trolling and threats, balancing mental health concerns with staying well, navigating financial barriers and overcoming ageism, sexism and homophobia, to name a few. These barriers will be further explored in additional publications, yet highlight the narrow (traditionally recognised) pathway to politics and the deeply ageist, ableist, gendered, heteronormative and ethnically homogeneous political context in which they operate.

Reflections on disability and queering the gender and politics literature

The participants living with disability or who identified as queer in this study were tired of not being seen, even in forums and literature aligned to their empowerment—such as feminist spaces. The Australian Feminist Foreign Policy Coalition's issue paper on *Furthering LGBTIQ+ Inclusion and Rights through Feminist Foreign Policy* argues this in the case of human rights defenders: '[S]ome human rights defenders are sexist, some feminists are transphobic and homophobic, and some LGBTIQ+ advocates [are] racist' (Stephenson et al. 2022: 1). The intersectional nature of both privilege and oppression reinforces the importance of 'building' attention to queerness and disability into gender and politics research. The work of gender and politics researchers is incomplete without queer and disability perspectives, with Henrickson et al. (2020: 9) noting that centring 'the knowledges of racialized and otherwise minoritized and marginalized gender and sexually diverse people can affirm their lives, histories, and subjugated standpoints'. Further, the credentials of critical feminist research (which seeks to be empowering) are ultimately severely impacted by the continued marginalisation of queer and disabled people and perspectives in politics.

To be queer is to question existing power structures, subvert norms, make the invisible visible and critique heteronormative, hegemonic masculinised and normative spaces and institutions (see Butler et al. 1994; McCann and Monaghan 2019). Queer theory traces its academic roots to gay and lesbian studies, however, it now makes key theoretical contributions across related interdisciplinary fields, from politics to entrepreneurship, focusing on relational power, identity, subversion and disruption (Jagose 1996). While there is a growing field of research of queering politics, much of the research on gender and politics focuses on women and is 'binary' in approach. The prevalence of research on 'both' men and women (as if there were only two genders) or only ciswomen (to the exclusion of trans and nonbinary genders) works to continue to silence and render invisible gender diversity in politics. It also presents an incomplete analysis of the gendered dynamics of politics. This is further problematised by the rise of 'gender-critical feminist' perspectives in politics, which exacerbate an already embedded exclusion faced by many queer people. Simply put, what was once conceptualised as trans-exclusionary radical feminism/feminist (TERF) is now more often referred to as 'gender-critical feminism/feminist' to represent a 'linguistic pivot from "anti-trans" to "pro-woman"' (Thurlow 2022: 962). Agendas such as these that are ultimately reliant on 'transphobic tropes, moral panics and essentialist understandings of men and women' further distance queer people from political spaces that could be integral to their empowerment (Thurlow 2022: 1).

Queer politicians, and those on the 'path', are already more likely to attract high levels of public scrutiny due to there being 'something sufficiently novel, interesting, [and] important' about them to 'attract close attention and interference from observers and exchange partners' (Sutton and Galunic 1996: 205). The consequence of this 'risky visibility' in public spheres is the exacerbation of the 'moral regulation of non-traditional lifestyles and identities' already imposed on gender and sexual minorities in a heterosexist society (Stephenson et al. forthcoming; Wagner 2021: 502). Queer activism and political movements can be viewed as 'threats' to political hegemony, whether overtly or subconsciously, by the media, politicians, community and constituents alike (Taylor and Pye 2019). This drives an environment that is increasingly hostile to any attempts to subvert traditional gender and social roles and identities in political paths, too. For many queer individuals, therefore, the hostility and harassment perceived as part of entering public office are often considered not worth the stress (Wagner 2021).

This is reinforced and complicated by disability. Politics is a game of endurance and resilience that some in the system have additional privilege and support to be able to navigate. The impact of living with disability had a dual impact on my research participants, affecting their experiences and participation and impacting on their choice to opt out of the system that so constrained them. If our studies on gender and politics remain focused only on those who 'made it', there are critical implications for all those who did not, could not or opted not to 'make it' due to the systemic pressures (and individual circumstances) stacked against them. This reinforces my own research's focus on not only a much broader definition of politics (including the 'path'), but also depth: going beyond what we 'know' of challenges to those seldom discussed. As Thomas (2013: 58) notes, twentieth-century 'feminism singularly failed to address the question of disability, and can actually be accused of contributing to disablist discourses and practices either by omitting to consider disability at all, or through its practice of uncritically reproducing disablist ideas'.

Ultimately, my own reflections on incorporating queer and disability perspectives within gender and politics research reinforce the importance of critiquing work that merely seeks to add women to existing political systems—without reflecting on the system itself. Queering understandings of politics and 'seeing' those who have been minoritised and marginalised even within gender studies are important. Disability studies further aligns the emancipatory promise of feminist research on gender and politics to see and understand those most minoritised and be reflective of biases we build in when studying only those who have 'made it' to politics.

Conclusion

This chapter has sought to situate young people—particularly of diverse genders, sexualities, ethnicities and abilities—as experts and change agents. Queering politics through this research has sought to disrupt narratives about whose voice is credible and heard on political knowledge and expertise, as well as explore ethical forms of social action and political inclusion from those creating it. Ultimately, diverse young people need not be engaged in traditional politics to be deeply political. Proxies for traditional political participation exist—through non-profits, creative arts and entrepreneurship, at a minimum. This allows young people to wield substantial individual and communal levels of power and, at times, also impact broader traditional and structural politics and society. Arif notes:

> For me, entrepreneurship is always a fantastic and important pursuit that every young person should foster ... Why don't we view entrepreneurship in the same lens of the civil society space? What does entrepreneurship represent? It represents disruption, it represents innovation, it represents change, it represents a drive to shift the momentum for the better, and I think that's really what's missing in the civil society space.

Yet, proxies have limits. Restricting historically marginalised groups 'only' to these spheres replicates existing power structures that exclude them from traditional politics. Further, a devaluation of these institutions is evident, resulting in further inequalities in social and economic capital. Ultimately, the ability to be engaged in any political action—traditional or through novel or informal means—remains a privilege. Incorporating the perspectives and paths of young people of diverse genders, sexualities, cultures and experiences of disability not only helps rectify silences in feminist political research but also contributes critical insights to a body of work that may otherwise fall short of its true emancipatory potential.

References

Anand, Adhiraaj. 2022. 'Youth Politics in East and Southeast Asia.' *The Interpreter*, 1 April. Sydney: Lowy Institute. www.lowyinstitute.org/the-interpreter/youth-politics-east-southeast-asia.

ASEAN SOGIE Caucus. 2021. 'Sexual Orientation, Gender Identity and Expression, and Sex Characteristics (SOGIESC) and the UN Human Rights Mechanisms in Southeast Asia (2017–2020).' Fact Sheet. Quezon City: ASEAN SOGIE Caucus. www.aseansogiecaucus.org/images/resources/publications/2021 0706%20ASC%202021%20Fact%20Sheet%20UN%20Mechanisms%20 SOGIESC%20SEA%202017-2020.pdf.

Baker, Kerryn, and Julien Barbara. 2020. 'Revisiting the Concept of Political Participation in the Pacific.' *Pacific Affairs* 93, no. 1: 135–56. doi.org/10.5509/ 2020931135.

Butler, Judith, Lynne Segal, and Peter Osborne. 1994. 'Gender as Performance: An Interview with Judith Butler.' *Radical Philosophy* 67: 32–39. www.radical philosophy.com/interview/judith-butler.

Chappell, Louise, and Fiona Mackay. 2021. 'Feminist Critical Friends: Dilemmas of Feminist Engagement with Governance and Gender Reform Agendas.' *European Journal of Politics and Gender* 4, no. 3: 321–40. doi.org/10.1332/ 251510820X15922354996155.

Children of the Mekong. n.d. 'Ethnic Groups in Southeast Asia.' [Online]. London: Children of the Mekong. www.childrenofthemekong.org/priorities/ethnic-minorities/#:~:text=Children%20of%20the%20Mekong%20have,break%20 the%20cycle%20of%20poverty.

Choi, Nankyung. 2019. 'Women's Political Pathways in Southeast Asia.' *International Feminist Journal of Politics* 21, no. 2: 224–48. doi.org/10.1080/14616742.2018. 1523683.

CountryReports. 1997–2025. 'Countries in Asia.' [Online]. Pleasant Grove: CountryReports. www.countryreports.org/countries/asia.htm.

Croissant, Aurel, and Philip Lorenz. 2018. 'Government and Political Regimes in Southeast Asia: An Introduction.' In *Comparative Politics of Southeast Asia: An Introduction to Governments and Political Regimes*, edited by Aurel Croissant and Philip Lorenz, 1–14. Cham: Springer. doi.org/10.1007/978-3-319-68182-5_1.

Croissant, Aurel, and Wolfgang Merkel. 2019. 'Defective Democracy.' In *The Handbook of Political, Social, and Economic Transformation*, edited by Wolfgang Merkel, Raj Kollmorgen, and Hans-Jürgen Wagener, 437–46. Oxford: Oxford University Press. doi.org/10.1093/oso/9780198829911.003.0041.

Department of the Prime Minister and Cabinet (PM&C). n.d. *ASEAN–Australia Overview*. Canberra: Australian Government. aseanaustralia.pmc.gov.au/ resources/asean-australia-overview.

Devasahayam, Theresa W. 2019. 'Politics in Southeast Asia: Where are the Women?' In *Women and Politics in Southeast Asia: Navigating a Man's World*, edited by Theresa W. Devasahayam, 1–16. Liverpool: Liverpool University Press. doi.org/ 10.2307/j.ctv3029j6z.7.

Dobell, Graeme. 2015. 'Lee Kuan Yew and Oz: White Trash or White Tribe of Asia (2).' *The Strategist*, 9 April. Canberra: Australian Strategic Policy Institute. www. aspistrategist.org.au/lee-kuan-yew-and-oz-2/.

Ebead, Nathalie, and Atsuko Hirakawa. 2022. *Inclusion and Gender Equality in Post-Coup Myanmar: Strategies for Constitutional and Democratic Reform*. Stockholm: International Institute for Democracy and Electoral Assistance. doi.org/10.31752/ idea.2022.35.

Economic and Social Commission for Asia and the Pacific (ESCAP). 2018. *Realizing Youth Inclusion for a More Sustainable Asia and the Pacific*. Draft report. Bangkok: United Nations.

Epstein, David. 2017. 'No Longer at the Centre: Australia's Real Relationship with Asia.' In *Disruptive Asia: Asia's Rise and Australia's Future. Volume 1*, 13–17. Sydney: Asia Society. disruptiveasia.asiasociety.org/no-longer-at-the-centre-australias-real-relationship-with-asia.

Freedom House. n.d. *Global Freedom Status*. [Online]. Washington, DC: Freedom House. www.freedomhouse.org/explore-the-map.

Freedom House. 2020. 'Brunei.' *Freedom in the World 2020*. [Online]. Washington, DC: Freedom House. www.freedomhouse.org/country/brunei/freedom-world/2020.

Fu, Jun, Johanna Wynn, and Brendan Churchill. 2021. 'Australia's Gen Y Democracy Gap.' *Pursuit*, 20 September. Melbourne: University of Melbourne. www.pursuit.unimelb.edu.au/articles/australia-s-gen-y-democracy-gap.

Henrickson, Mark, Sulaimon Giwa, Trish Hafford-Letchfield, Christine Cocker, Nick Mule, Jacob Schaub, and Alexandre Baril. 2020. 'Research Ethics with Gender and Sexually Diverse Persons.' *International Journal of Environmental Research and Public Health* 17, no. 18: 6615. doi.org/10.3390/ijerph17186615.

Iwanaga, Kazuki. 2008. 'Women and Politics in Asia: A Comparative Perspective.' In *Women's Political Participation and Representation in Asia: Obstacles and Challenges*, edited by Kazuki Iwanaga, 1–23. Copenhagen: NIAS Press.

Jagose, Annamarie. 1996. *Queer Theory: An Introduction*. New York: NYU Press.

Langlois, Anthony J. 2018. 'No Regional Pattern: LGBTIQ Rights and Politics in Asia.' In *Routledge Handbook of Human Rights in Asia*, edited by Fernand de Varennes and Christie M Gardiner, 322–32. London: Routledge. doi.org/10.4324/9781315720180-22.

Langlois, Anthony J. 2022. *Sexuality and Gender Diversity Rights in Southeast Asia*. Cambridge: Cambridge University Press. doi.org/10.1017/9781108933216.

Lee, Helen, and Aidan Craney. 2019. 'Pacific Youth, Local and Global.' In *Pacific Youth: Local and Global Futures*, edited by Helen Lee, 1–31. Canberra: ANU Press. doi.org/10.22459/PY.2019.01.

Manalastas, E.J., T.T. Ojanen, B.A. Torre, R. Ratanashevorn, B.C.C. Hong, V. Kumaresan, and V. Veeramuthu. 2017. 'Homonegativity in Southeast Asia: Attitudes Toward Lesbians and Gay Men in Indonesia, Malaysia, the Philippines, Singapore, Thailand, and Vietnam.' *Asia-Pacific Social Sciences Review* 17, no. 1: 25–33. doi.org/10.59588/2350-8329.1120.

McCann, Hannah, and Whitney Monaghan. 2019. *Queer Theory Now: From Foundations to Futures*. London: Bloomsbury.

Pholsena, Vatthana. 2016. *SEATIDE Integration in Southeast Asia: Trajectories of Inclusion, Dynamics of Exclusion Ethnic Minorities, the State, and Beyond: Focus on Mainland Southeast Asia*. Research Report. Singapore: Ecole française d'Extrême-Orient, National University of Singapore. shs.hal.science/halshs-01963789v1/document.

Richter, Linda K. 1990. 'Exploring Theories of Female Leadership in South and Southeast Asia.' *Pacific Affairs* 63, no. 4: 524–40. doi.org/10.2307/2759914.

Root, Rebecca L. 2022. 'LGBTI Rights: Many Challenges in Southeast Asia Remain, Despite Victories in Singapore and Vietnam.' 14 September. London: International Bar Association. www.ibanet.org/LGBTI-rights-Many-challenges-in-Southeast-Asia.

Sanders, Douglas. 2020. 'Sex and Gender Diversity in Southeast Asia.' *Journal of Southeast Asian Human Rights* 4, no. 2: 357–405. doi.org/10.19184/jseahr.v4i2.17281.

Siahaan, Gabriele Natalia. 2019. 'Youth Engagement in Southeast Asian Elections.' *Australian Outlook*, 9 July. Sydney: Australian Institute of International Affairs. www.internationalaffairs.org.au/australianoutlook/comparing-youth-political-engagement-three-major-southeast-asian-elections/.

Stephenson, Elise. 2024. *The Face of the Nation: Gendered Institutions in International Affairs.* Oxford: Oxford University Press. doi.org/10.1093/oso/9780197632727.001.0001.

Stephenson, Elise. 2019a. *Elise Stephenson speaking at the Young Entrepreneurs and Leaders Speaker Series engagement at UN headquarters in Hanoi, Vietnam, 2019.*

Stephenson, Elise. 2019b. *Workshopping approaches to gender equality for Gender Month, Vietnam, 2019.*

Stephenson, Elise, Jack Hayes, and Matcha Phorn-In. 2022. *Furthering LGBTIQ+ Inclusion and Rights through Feminist Foreign Policy.* AFFPC Issue Paper Series, Issue 5, August. Melbourne: Australian Feminist Foreign Policy Coalition. iwda.org.au/assets/files/AFFPC-Issue-Paper-FFP-and-LGBTQI-Inclusion-and-Rights_Stephenson-et-al.pdf.

Stephenson, Elise, Blair Williams, Gosia Mikolajczak, and Jack Hayes. Forthcoming. '"Risky Visibility": The Layered Harassment of Queer Politicians Online.' *International Feminist Journal of Politics.*

Sutton, Robert I., and D. Charles Galunic. 1996. 'Consequences of Public Scrutiny for Leaders and Their Organisations.' *Research in Organisational Behaviour* 18: 201–50.

Tan, Netina, and Cassandra Preece. 2022. 'Ethnic Quotas, Political Representation and Equity in Asia Pacific.' *Representation* 58, no. 3: 347–71. doi.org/10.1080/00344893.2021.1989712.

Taylor, Mary Anne, and Danee Pye. 2019. 'Hillary Through TIME: The (Un) Making of the First Woman President.' *American Behavioral Scientist* 63, no. 7: 807–25. doi.org/10.1177/0002764217711801.

Thein-Lemelson, Seinenu M. 2021. '"Politicide" and the Myanmar Coup.' *Anthropology Today* 37, no. 2: 3–5. doi.org/10.1111/1467-8322.12639.

Thomas, Carol. 2013. 'Feminism and Disability: The Theoretical and Political Significance of the Personal and the Experiential.' In *Disability, Politics & the Struggle for Change*, edited by Len Barton. London: Routledge.

Thurlow, Claire. 2022. 'From TERF to Gender Critical: A Telling Genealogy?' *Sexualities* 27, no. 4: 962–78. doi.org/10.1177/13634607221107827.

United Nations Development Programme (UNDP). 2014. *Youth and Democratic Citizenship in East and South-East Asia*. Bangkok: United Nations Development Programme. www.undp.org/asia-pacific/publications/youth-and-democratic-citizenship-east-and-south-east-asia.

Velasco, Djorina. 2005. 'Introduction: Youth and Politics in Southeast Asia.' In *Go! Young Progressives in Southeast Asia*. 2nd edn. Manila: Friedrich Ebert Stiftung.

Vijeyarasa, Ramona. 2022. *The Woman President: Leadership, Law and Legacy for Women Based on Experiences from South and Southeast Asia*. Oxford: Oxford University Press. doi.org/10.1093/oso/9780192848918.001.0001.

Wagner, Angelia. 2021. 'Avoiding the Spotlight: Public Scrutiny, Moral Regulation, and LGBTQ Candidate Deterrence.' *Politics, Groups, and Identities* 9, no. 3: 502–18. doi.org/10.1080/21565503.2019.1605298.

Walker, Derek H.T. 2010. 'Being a Pracademic: Combining Reflective Practice with Scholarship.' Keynote Address to Australian Institute of Practice Management (AIPM) Conference, 10–13 October, Darwin. www.researchgate.net/publication/267995102_Being_a_Pracademic_-_Combining_Reflective_Practice_with_Scholarship.

Wilkinson, Cai, Paula Gerber, Baden Offord, and Anthony J. Langlois. 2017. 'LGBT Rights in Southeast Asia: One Step Forward, Two Steps Back?' *IAFOR Journal of Asian Studies* 3, no. 1: 5–17. doi.org/10.22492/ijas.3.1.01.

Yen, Nguyen Thi Hong, and Nguyen Toan Thang. 2022. 'The Right to Political Participation of Ethnic Minority Women in Vietnam: Barriers and Challenges.' *Asia-Pacific Journal on Human Rights and the Law* 23, no. 3: 281–314. doi.org/10.1163/15718158-23030001.

Part II: Decolonising Knowledge and Practice: A question

Introduction

Tanya Jakimow

The term 'decolonising' was debated among the editorial team before we settled on the title of this section. Ubiquitous in higher education and development institutions, 'decolonising' often amounts to what Salmah Eva-Lina Lawrence in Chapter 5 describes as 'thin decolonisation', compared with the transformative practices required of 'thick decolonisation'. Performative acts, such as labelling a section in an edited volume, can, and should, become a lightning rod for critique: provocative not because they challenge power, but because they do not.

We have stuck with 'decolonising', but as a question, not a claim. That what constitutes decolonising—and related terms decolonisation and decoloniality—should be kept open is demonstrated in Margaret Jolly's Chapter 6 (and indeed her larger oeuvre). She shows that 'authoritative' definitions—even in the plural—still largely overlook the intellectual thought and action beyond the Americas, Africa and Asia. In Jolly's and Lawrence's chapters, the contributions of scholar-activists from Oceania are centred, offering correctives and insights not only for knowledge or action for gender equity in politics, but also for the open and ongoing process of defining (in order to practice) decoloniality in and beyond the region.

'Decolonisation' adds further value to a project like ours through its demand for historicity. Margaret Jolly's chapter shows how gender inequality is deeply rooted in colonialism and the introduction of novel binaries that profoundly changed gender relations in Oceania. Oceanic feminist and decolonial lenses reveal that achieving national independence further strengthened male dominance in politics and reinforced women's subordination. While the gender and politics literature has (belatedly) acknowledged colonialism as introducing novel forms of gender inequities that persist today, Jolly reminds us that the history of 'decolonisation' itself also needs critical feminist attention for its contemporary legacies.

Salmah Eva-Lina Lawrence locates colonial and decolonial legacies in international development. She, too, shows how feminist/activist thought from Oceania is crucial to interrogating contemporary harms, including the damage caused by the neglect of this knowledge in dominant epistemic frames. She gifts the reader conceptual tools such as cultural fluency, methodological tools such as relational 'both/and' thinking and new lines of sight, including state power and gendered violence. By showing the fecundity of scholarship from Anne Nealibo Dickson-Waiko, J. Kēhaulani Kauanui, Teresia Teaiwa and Orovu Sepoe—scholar-activists largely absent from the gender and politics canon—Lawrence and Jolly demonstrate the urgent need to centre such thinking in our reimagining of the field.

At the same time, I share Lawrence's discomfort with our section title. Even as we reject the label of decolonising project in the Introduction, our ambition to centre Asia and Oceania in thinking about gender and politics faces the knotty reality that all the co-editors are based in institutions in settler Australia. How does someone like me—a white feminist working in a well-resourced institution—contribute to decoloniality? Contrary to representations, I come across very few feminists who are white and privileged who are not grappling with what our positions in global racial hierarchies mean for practice. How do we cede space, speak with but not over, while taking responsibility and sharing the burden of meaningful action?

The point is not to answer the question, but to grapple with it. This 'grappling' with decolonising practices is exemplified in Chapter 7 by Camilla Batalibasi, Chandy Eng, Donna Makini, Vani Nailumu and Geraldine Valei with Sonia Palmieri and Melissa MacLean. It starts by privileging the voices of 'local' researchers through methodologies such as autoethnography and collaborative writing practices. They use institutional power to facilitate access and enable transformative research, but also demonstrate the necessity of what Lawrence describes as 'cultural fluency'. By putting aside predefined questions, the researchers excavated stories not commonly told about women's political leadership. Distinctly different to standard narratives in the gender and politics literature, they invite new questions, new frames and new levels of understanding.

The three chapters in this section underline the importance of keeping 'decolonising' as an open question and, with every humility, an ambition. In so doing, we aim to disrupt the canon of gender and politics, celebrate and learn from activists and/or scholars from overlooked regions, gain new conceptual, theoretical and methodological tools and, importantly, produce grounded, nuanced knowledge of the lives and experiences of a much wider pool of women in (or excluded from) politics.

5

Whose Knowledge Matters: Subjugation and the hegemony of whiteness in international development

Salmah Eva-Lina Lawrence

This is a chapter about knowledge of gender and development theory and praxis. More specifically, it is about whose knowledge is privileged, whose knowledge is not privileged and why that matters. This, of course, is part of challenging ongoing systems of colonisation, known as coloniality.

Papua New Guinean women have had to endure a colonialism that devalued them based on gender and race, and which at the same time empowered their men beyond what was permissible before colonisation (Dickson-Waiko 2008, 2010, 2013). Now in the era of developmentalism, as the United Nations prods countries towards greater gender equality, one could rejoice in the greater focus of international development on gender equality. But what does this mean for Papua New Guinean women? What changes are possible if the coloniality of gender and the coloniality of knowledge that underpinned colonialism persist through developmentalism?

To begin to answer these questions, we must start with an understanding of decolonisation and decoloniality. I then look across the works of two Papua New Guinean scholar-activists, Dr Anne Dickson-Waiko and Dr Orovu Sepoe, excavating key ideas on the coloniality of gender and the coloniality of knowledge. The invisibility or (wilful) ignorance of feminist or women-centred thought from Papua New Guinean women is a symptom and a cause of the dominant epistemic frame in gender theory in international development that contributes to multiple harms. I end by outlining key principles to mitigate those harms and work towards epistemic justice.

Majority world

Before I explicate some thoughts on decolonisation, I will introduce key vocabulary that I employ as part of my activism and in my scholarly work. Like photojournalist Shahidul Alam (2008), who has advocated for the use of 'majority world since the 1990s', since 2014, I have used 'Majority World' in place of 'developing' and 'minority world' in place of 'developed'. The difference in capitalisation is a deliberate gesture to emphasise magnitude.

The Majority World is both a global demographic and a sociological majority.[1] The global population in July 2021 was estimated by the United Nations to be 7.9 billion, the majority of whom live in countries classified as in need of some form of development. Among this vast population are shared ethics, ontology and epistemology based very broadly on relationality and holism in contrast to the individualism and reductivism of the minority world—an understanding shared by decolonial theorists from Aníbal Quijano in 1992 (pp. 18–19) to Boaventura de Sousa Santos in 2013 (pp. 188–206).

I acknowledge that many of the following concepts are contested, nonetheless, I deliberately use the terms 'whiteness', 'West', 'Global North', 'Eurocentric' and 'minority world' interchangeably to demonstrate the hierarchies of modernity/coloniality. Furthermore, although there simply is no way to describe in opposing binaries the diversity and complexity of humanity and human social organisation, I employ the opposing binary of Majority World/minority world since this is based on the fact of a demographic and sociological global majority, unlike other binaries such as developed/developing, which are arbitrary indicators useful to maintain the dominance and control embedded in the modernity/coloniality matrix that I unpack further below.

---

1 The contours of international development discourse and practice suggest an embedded and unchanging hierarchy in which the 'developed' coloniser of the West/Global North occupies the apex and all others are infantilised as needing development, reiterated through the legacy ordinal numbering of worlds as first, third, etcetera. This othering narrative also psychologically reinforces the idea that 'developing' communities are lacking, rendering invisible cultural, social and environmental wealth. I expand on these ideas in Lawrence (forthcoming).

The use of Majority World brings into relief the inequities and injustices of a global demographic majority continuing to be subjugated in various ways by a global demographic minority. This understanding gives shape to the various demands for decolonisation that are sweeping the planet.

Decolonisation

I understand that this chapter is to appear in a section in this book that speaks to decolonisation. Decolonisation is fast becoming a buzzword. Tuck and Yang (2012) remind us that it is not a metaphor. Decolonisation speaks to the transformation of all kinds of power relationships: social, geopolitical, economic, and so on. It can never be a performative act and it will always be an uncomfortable space as those holding power seek to protect and maintain their privilege even as the subaltern pushes back. I call these performative acts 'thin decolonisation' and I use 'thick decolonisation' to refer to transformative practices (Lawrence forthcoming).

I admit to my own discomfort in possibly being complicit in thin decolonisation by contributing to a book that is framed through decolonisation when this text is produced by an institution that is located on unceded land. To speak of decolonisation in the face of this fact, to merely acknowledge that the land is unceded, is to use decolonisation as a metaphor since an aspect of decolonisation is to return what was stolen by the coloniser. Land. Sovereignty. Self-determination. The right to practise on one's own land one's own ways of being, knowing and ethics. Metaphorical uses of decolonisation do not address these issues or offer meaningful redress for the significant violence and harms of colonisation and coloniality—a term coined by Aníbal Quijano (1992, 1999) to refer to ongoing practices of domination through various technologies of power, some of which I address below.

Although decolonisation has a spectrum of meanings depending on location, self-determination is central to it. Self-determination has conventionally been thought of as political independence, but this juridical sovereignty is of little value if people do not also have epistemic, economic, social and cultural self-determination. Epistemic self-determination follows from epistemic decolonisation—another phrase coined by Quijano (1992: 19). In his groundbreaking critique of modernity as being inseparable from practices and processes of coloniality, Quijano argued that power is enacted through epistemic processes.[2] Within modernity, that means that all other ways of knowing, conceptualisation and representation have been subjugated and subordinated to a Eurocentric epistemological perspective (Quijano 2000; Mignolo 2002). This coloniality of knowledge fuels contemporary demands for decolonisation in the international development sector. At the heart of these demands is the desire for epistemic self-determination: the freedom for individuals and collectives to know, conceptualise and re/present themselves and their worlds free of subjugation.

Within international development, Indigenisation is one strategy through which self-determination—and therefore decolonisation—can be progressed. For instance, Papua New Guinea is populated by people Indigenous to the island of New Guinea, who have been there for millennia. Much of the landmass of Papua New Guinea is still under customary governance. Sovereignty and the return of stolen land, therefore, are not the issues in decolonisation. Rather, it continues to be how to Indigenise development in a manner that enables epistemic, economic, social and cultural self-determination. I define Indigenisation not as a process of translation but as a nonlinear social process undertaken by people Indigenous to that context, which involves identifying, adapting and adopting what is useful from the new and introduced, and building on what already exists. The process can be both organic and systematic. Inextricably linked to Indigenisation is cultural fluency.

I define cultural fluency as the highest level of contextual knowledge. Just as linguistically a native speaker is the expert in their language, the cultural native possesses the highest level of cultural knowledge. A foreigner living in a Majority-World country for a few years does not qualify as culturally fluent, just as an immigrant in a white settler society needs years of lived experience and language education to become at least culturally competent in the host culture. Because so much cultural knowledge is not transmitted orally, even foreigners who study cultures that are not their own can never attain the highest levels of cultural fluency by virtue of not having been present through the formative years of childhood and adolescence.

Returning to decolonisation, despite independence arising from political decolonisation, true self-determination remains an issue because the global order and its governance structures have emerged from colonisation. These structures, whether the World Trade Organization, the World Bank or the

---

2　Feminists have also argued this point. See, for example, Fricker (2007).

UN Security Council, privilege a particular world view—one that is for the most part steeped in whiteness. The structures themselves are rigid and unchanging; witness, for example, the permanent members of the UN Security Council or the leadership of the International Monetary Fund (IMF), which, though rotating, is drawn from the United States or the European Union.

This global power order to a large extent (but not entirely) no longer explicitly colonises. Instead, it pursues integration into the structures of a global governance system. Sundhya Pahuja (2011) writes of how in the heady early days of achieving independence from the colonisers, many newly formed states dared to imagine a more equitable world but found themselves instead confronted by the reality of colonial powers refusing to relinquish control of global trade and financial flows.[3] Integration of the formerly colonised into these inequitable systems has often meant subjugation within a particular hierarchy underpinned by whiteness.

Whiteness is used by critical race theorists to mean practices and processes that produce and sustain white people's dominance, privilege and supposed superiority (Mills 1997; Sullivan 2006). Central to whiteness, and thus, central to upholding the superiority of whiteness, is the idea that the only valid and valued knowledge is that produced by white people or the processes and practices of whiteness.

---

3   Regarding the World Trade Organization (WTO), the growth of economic nationalism in the interwar years of the 1920s is cited as a contributor to World War II by way of reducing global trade, which instigated the Great Depression, which in turn generated fascism and eventual war. The link, seemingly direct, between economic nationalism and war so influenced US planning for the postwar era that global institutions were created to promote the counter position, that of economic liberalism— supposedly a path to peace. The global regime of trade is today governed by the WTO. In its first institutional incarnation as the General Agreement on Tariffs and Trade (GATT), signed in 1947, the free-trade regime sought to reduce trade barriers. As the WTO, its mandate has broadened to include regulation of trade in services and intellectual property, as well as a dispute-resolution mechanism. This mandate has not been without controversy. While free trade has indeed increased interdependence and has not triggered war, the free-trade regime has generated criticisms of and concerns about distributive justice and the democratic legitimacy of the system (Esty 2002) as it does not allow for many Majority-World countries to be treated fairly in the global arena. Joseph Stiglitz (2003: 6) has been vocal about the West's hypocrisy in pushing for the elimination of trade barriers, while simultaneously erecting them. Others argue that '[t]he prevailing pattern of protection in the world today is biased against the poor in that barriers are highest on goods produced by poor people' (Hoekman 2002: 41). Regarding the IMF, voting is weighted in favour of the minority-world donors with the effect that the many people in the Majority World who are 'stakeholders in global political problems that affect them … remain excluded from the political institutions and strategies needed to address these problems' (Held 2006: 166). A further concern about inclusiveness and diversity of views relates to the identities and interests of IMF staff, who, coming mostly from the same demographic and educational background, are hardly able to represent the diversity of stakeholders in today's world.

To summarise, the existing global governance system was designed by colonial powers and is thus underpinned by whiteness. It is a global order built on coloniality through various technologies of power such as the coloniality of race, the coloniality of gender and the coloniality of knowledge (Mignolo 2009; Quijano 2007a, 2007b; Grosfoguel 2002; Lugones 2008). I expand on these technologies of power in the next section. Suffice to say here that the coloniality of knowledge is central to enabling the privilege and maintaining the superiority of whiteness and white people. Thus, for example, we have a global economic system that continues to favour wealth extraction from the Majority World for the primary benefit of the white minority world, in which the latter's consumption of planetary resources far exceeds that of the billions of bodies in the Majority World. In this context of ongoing coloniality in a supposedly postcolonial world, Linda Tuhiwai Smith (2012) has written that we, the peoples of the Majority World, know we are still being colonised.

What, then, is decolonisation when, as mentioned earlier, our different histories and geopolitics position us to fight for different outcomes? Perhaps it is easier to define first what it is not or cannot be. *Decolonisation can never be defined by the coloniser since to do so is to continue to colonise.* Second, at its broadest reach, beyond a mere critique of power, decolonisation as framed by the theorists of decoloniality is a *process* of continuously understanding how people with different world views can share this planet equitably and peacefully.[4]

If decolonisation represents a spectrum of practices, processes and outcomes, decoloniality occupies the very thick core of decolonisation spiralling outwards. Decoloniality seeks to transform power relations by addressing root causes. Decoloniality is relational thinking that recognises the complexity of human social life—what Mignolo (2011) calls the pluriverse—nestled within and influenced by an even more complex natural world. For me, decolonial practice is a process of building understanding, a cycle of learning and unlearning. It is not a means of subjugating different world views and different ethical, political, legal and epistemic systems into a single paradigm that replaces one hierarchy with another, albeit with different dominant parties. For Pasifika peoples, it is a continued process

---

4   Enrique Dussel's work on liberatory ethics intersects with the theoretical school of modernity/coloniality to propose a decolonial ethics towards liberation from oppression and subjugation. See Alcoff (2012); Allen and Mendieta (2021).

of Indigenisation. Just as Pasifika peoples have successfully Indigenised Christianity, so, too, can we successfully Indigenise other introduced ways of being and knowing—should we choose to.

Let me return to where I started in this section.

Land.

Land is my starting point because colonisation involved usurping land and was often accompanied by a loss of authority that many Majority-World women had previously enjoyed.[5] Later in this chapter I draw on the works of Papua New Guinean scholars Anne Dickson-Waiko and Orovu Sepoe to analyse that loss of authority and its implications.

Land is my starting point because theorising as a person from the Majority World—more specifically, as a Pasifika person—is to acknowledge that land and belonging to the land are central to Indigenous Oceanic societies, whether matricentric or otherwise. In the Suau language of the Milne Bay Province of Papua New Guinea, *eanua* is the land and associated relationships to which I belong. Since Milne Bay is a maritime province, the relationship to the ocean is also embedded within one's *eanua*, such that *eanua* is one's country, encompassing relationships of both land and ocean.[6] Whether or not the relationship to ocean is embedded in other Pasifika languages, it is the case that many of our different languages have cognates that attest to the importance of the relationship to land, to country:[7] in the Motu language of the Central Province of Papua New Guinea, the word is *hanua*; in Fiji and Vanuatu, it is *vanua*; in te reo Māori, it is *whenua*; in Samoa, it is *fanua*; in Tongan, *fonua*; and in Hawai'i, it is *honua*.

Eanua and the Majority World are part of my epistemic frame.

I mention matricentricity as part of emplacing myself; I am a woman from a society that organises and functions through matrilineal descent, which is about bodies of land as much as it is about bodies of people. It is not just about emplacing myself to make visible to others the influences on my

---

5   For example: the Great Mahele, the division of communal lands in Hawai'i in 1846–55 (Stauffer 2003); Indigenous Australians in *Our Land is Our Life* (Yunupingu 1997).

6   See Epeli Hau'ofa (2008) on how the ocean unites rather than divides Pasifika peoples.

7   This relationship to Country is also significant to First Nations Australians, who are considered by many Pasifika peoples to be part of the Pasifika community.

being and thinking; it is also acknowledging that, as a Papua New Guinean from a matricentric society that includes matrilocal residence,[8] I am deeply rooted in the land of my ancestors.

I mention this because as feminists have long known—at least since Donna Haraway's (1988) seminal paper—all knowledge generated by individuals is partial (Harding 1993; Longino 1993; On 1993; Alcoff and Potter 1993b; Dalmiya and Alcoff 1993) and influenced by individual histories, geographies, bodies and geopolitics. The knowledge that I share in this chapter is informed by my experience of being shaped by and belonging to a community in which girls, boys, men and women are equally valued as necessary members of a balanced society.[9] I grew up knowing of, if not directly, my female kin who had scaled the Owen Stanley Range in the 1700s, purchased land in the 1800s to establish matrilines, travelled the world (Australia, India, England, Ireland) in the mid-1900s, been the first to be accepted into Australian universities in the 1960s, the first female journalist, and so on. Gender was not a barrier for these Milne Bay women.[10]

Yet, in the 2022 PNG elections in which women won only two of the 118 seats, their gender continued to be a monumental barrier. Why? Why is it that Milne Bay women are unsuccessful in national politics when in their matricentric communities these women are explicitly valued? My curiosity is not just as a woman from Papua New Guinea. I also work in international development, currently as director of systemic change and partnerships for a feminist international NGO located in the minority world.[11] My curiosity is thus both personal and professional.

To answer this question, I start by exploring the coloniality of gender and the coloniality of knowledge—two technologies of power articulated through the theoretical lens of the modernity/coloniality matrix. To situate this theoretical framing, I then read across the works of Papua New Guinean scholars Anne Dickson-Waiko and Orovu Sepoe.

---

8   After marriage, couples live primarily on land belonging to the wife and her matriline.

9   See also Demian (2000, 2006).

10   My mother, Dineheilo Dickson Lawrence, was the first Papuan woman to be accepted into an Australian university; my great aunt Alice Wedega was in the Legislative Council of the Territory of Papua and New Guinea. On her travels, she was once in Northern Ireland, where, to my astonishment, she lectured the Irish on peace; my cousin Pauline Bona was the first female journalist in Papua New Guinea.

11   The IWDA works to support partner organisations across the Pacific and Asia and is committed to decolonising its practice.

Technologies of power: The coloniality of gender and the coloniality of knowledge

The theories of modernity, coloniality and decoloniality explain that there is an underside to modernity. The successes of European modernity gained through the scientific and technological progress that began with the European Age of Enlightenment have been made possible only through the violence that was enacted on others through expropriation, enslavement and colonisation (Quijano 1992, 1999; Mignolo 1995, 1998). It is a violence that remains hidden yet continues to be enacted through various technologies of power, including: the coloniality of race (Quijano 1995), which speaks to intentional actions to entrench white men at the top of a race hierarchy followed by white women, with black women occupying the lowest rung; the coloniality of gender (Lugones 2007, 2008) or the oppositional binary gender norms of whiteness; and the coloniality of knowledge (Quijano 1992, 1999; Mignolo 1995, 1998, 1999, 2009),[12] which, underpinned by the coloniality of race and the coloniality of gender, privileges knowledge produced through a lens of whiteness—primarily knowledge produced by white men and secondarily knowledge produced by white women.

Let me illustrate the coloniality of knowledge and gender with an anecdote.

Some time ago I came across an online news item about an Australian volunteer in the PNG Highlands. Alas, I did not keep a copy. However, according to the article, the volunteer was teaching the women from the Highlands agricultural skills. Now the Highlands of Papua New Guinea is an area in which agriculture has been practised continuously for the past 10,000 years. Indeed, the Kuk Early Agricultural Site (or the Kuk Swamp in the Wahgi Valley) has been designated a World Heritage Site by the United Nations Educational, Scientific and Cultural Organization (UNESCO) for its extant evidence of cultivation. According to archaeologists: 'Multidisciplinary investigations at Kuk Swamp in the Highlands of Papua New Guinea show that agriculture arose independently in New Guinea by at least 6950 to 6440 calibrated years before the present' (Denham et al.

---

12 Although Aníbal Quijano (1999) coined the phrases 'coloniality of power', 'coloniality of knowledge' and 'epistemic decolonisation', Walter Mignolo is better known in the Anglophone world for theorising modernity/coloniality and decoloniality. Mignolo (1998: 22), however, acknowledges that 'the contribution of Aníbal Quijano ... is a fundamental theoretical turn in outlining the conditions under which the coloniality of power ... was and is a strategy of "modernity"'.

2003).[13] The evidence also reveals systems of drainage to enhance cultivation and to address the challenges of feeding growing populations (Bellwood 2017: 36).

Given this evidence of millennia of agricultural practices in the Highlands, what, I wondered, could this white (according to the accompanying photograph) Australian woman teach Papua New Guinean Highlanders about agriculture? As it transpired, according to the article, she demonstrated how to cultivate tomatoes and lettuce—foods that are not part of the daily diet and would presumably have been grown to sell. Nonetheless, the knowledge that was shared hardly rates alongside the technological and technical complexities that the ancestors of the Highlanders negotiated and mastered and the knowledge that was then passed down the generations to the present day—complexities that included both cultivation and domestication.[14]

This anecdote is a manifestation of an ongoing practice of injustice that excludes and/or devalues knowledges held and produced by particular groups of people and which contributes to and maintains the colonial hierarchies of knowledge that are embedded in the modernity/coloniality matrix. It is a twofold problem of gendered epistemic injustice highlighted by feminists (Alcoff and Potter 1993a) and the epistemic racism made visible by decolonial scholars and activists (Grosfoguel 2002, 2007). The embedded assumption is that the knowledge held by a white woman must be superior to that held by black women.

Furthermore, this coloniality of knowledge, acutely inflected by both race and gender, is deeply embedded in the international development sector in which I work.[15] The coloniality of gender and the coloniality of knowledge are two technologies of power that are used to continue to subjugate Majority-World peoples.

---

13 See also Haberle et al. (2012).
14 'Cultivation and domestication are not one and the same thing' (Bellwood 2017).
15 See Lawrence (2023).

PNG feminist theory: Anne Dickson-Waiko and Orovu Sepoe

The peoples of Papua New Guinea have undergone tremendous social change over the past century and a half. The first missionary landed on Papuan shores in the 1870s and Papua was shortly after annexed by the British before becoming an Australian protectorate in 1901 on Australia's Federation. New Guinea, which had been annexed by the Germans in 1884, also became a protectorate of Australia, in 1906. Independence came in 1975 but the promise of self-determination has been fleeting.

Without excusing the corruption, nepotism and bad governance, the challenge of development and providing services to Papua New Guineans has been exacerbated by a quadrupling of the population in the period since independence, numbering 9.3 million in 2022 (UNFPA 2024). On the positive side, the 800-odd different linguistic groups and associated cultures by and large live together peacefully with high levels of intermarriage between peoples of coastal and island provinces.

However, Papua New Guinean women have had to endure a colonialism that devalued them based on gender and race, and which at the same time empowered their men beyond what was permissible before colonisation (Dickson-Waiko 2008, 2010, 2013). Now in the era of developmentalism, as the United Nations prods countries towards greater gender equality, one could rejoice in the greater focus of international development on gender equality. But what does this mean for Papua New Guinean women? What changes are possible if the coloniality of gender and the coloniality of knowledge that underpinned colonialism persist through developmentalism?

The women on whose work I draw here do not necessarily identify as feminists but their work in scholarship and activism is firmly rooted in challenging gendered power structures to enable the greater participation of their countrywomen in the political and economic spheres of modernity.

Dr Anne Dickson-Waiko

The late Dr Anne Dickson-Waiko left a treasure of papers concerned with the position of women in Papua New Guinea. Like many Papua New Guinean women, Dickson-Waiko did not call herself a feminist. Nonetheless, the critique she offers of patriarchy and of the gendered relationship between the PNG state and its citizens could be claimed as feminist—more specifically, a decolonial feminist critique. I define a decolonial feminist not merely by geopolitical and cultural location, but also as one whose ethical framework explicitly recognises that all cultures have both positive and negative gender norms (Lawrence, forthcoming). A decolonial feminist understands that the global order of modernity operates through various technologies of power, including the coloniality of gender, the coloniality of race and a corresponding racialised and gendered epistemic hierarchy. A decolonial feminist also understands and practices the principles of decoloniality—principles that are embedded in the writings of decolonial scholars and the praxis of activists (Lawrence, forthcoming).

One of the decolonial principles in Dickson-Waiko's work is the application of BOTH/AND logic. This is the logic of accepting that two opposing situations can and do coexist in the same space–time continuum in lieu of a logic that insists on one OR the other of a polarising oppositionality. The way it plays out in her work is through the recognition of the existence of *both* positive *and* negative gender norms across Papua New Guinea. This stance contrasts with non-decolonial feminists, who, out of ignorance or to justify requests for funding or for some other reason, focus exclusively on the harmful norms that serve to position them as saviours of victims. This stance is as harmful as the negative norms to which they object. It is harmful because focusing only on the negative creates the potential for the wholesale demonisation of cultures.[16] Furthermore, the singular focus on the negative generates resistance among both men and women to this one-sided portrayal of what it means to be Papua New Guinean.[17] This makes the work of enacting systemic change towards gender equality more difficult than a balanced approach that recognises that all cultures possess harmful gender norms just as all cultures also possess norms that are life-enhancing.

Dickson-Waiko's positionality as a Papua New Guinean scholar enabled her access to multiple sources of data and information: recorded data, oral histories and, as importantly, experiential knowledge. This experiential knowledge stemming from cultural fluency puts Dickson-Waiko and other Indigenous scholars in a much stronger position in understanding context than researchers, policymakers and program designers and implementers who do not have that fluency. Triangulating these sources enabled Dickson-Waiko to identify what I see as the recurrent theme across her writing: that

---

16 Sisonke Msimang (2022) writes about this in relation to Indigenous Australians.
17 See also Papua New Guinean Mercy Masta's (2021) research into Papua New Guinean masculinities.

the colonial and postcolonial structures of government and governance have been harmful to the rights of the women of Papua New Guinea (Dickson-Waiko 2001, 2003, 2007, 2008, 2009, 2013). Indeed, both structures have consistently stripped women of the freedoms—including economic independence—that they enjoyed before the arrival of whiteness.

Papua New Guinean women always had productive and reproductive roles that were valued in their communities. The separation of the domestic and public spheres by missionisation and colonisation—continuing today under developmentalism—is one of the critical factors through which Papua New Guinean women have become devalued under modernity. From the onset of colonisation to the creation of an independent state, men were the ones who were favoured to participate in the public spaces (Dickson-Waiko 2001, 2003). Dickson-Waiko argues that due to the history of colonialism in Papua New Guinea, which from the outset engaged men in roles away from their villages, men have entered the state as citizens and as both individual and relational beings. Women, however, because of their absence from colonial interactions and transactions, are relational beings only, not individuals with rights in the way men have been constructed. This mirrors the way the minority world, through whiteness, has historically constructed gender relations. The relational identity is not valued: the outputs and outcomes of relational labour, though necessary for social wellbeing and cohesion, are still not counted as part of gross domestic product (GDP).

As with other Pasifika women working towards the development of their countries, and as is common among decolonial feminists, Dickson-Waiko's work did not stop at critique. She identified promising pathways of change, the most significant of which was leveraging existing church women's groups to strengthen a fledgling women's rights movement (Dickson-Waiko 2003). Notwithstanding the church's initial historical role in the construction of a predominantly individualised personhood, Dickson-Waiko posited that the church had also become a path for women to participate in the public sphere of community politics. She writes:

> What is perhaps not widely known is that the catalyst for women's activism right across the Pacific region has been provided by church women's organizations. A combination of religion and feminism—an unlikely marriage in the eyes of many modern 'Western' feminists—remains buried under the label 'Church Women's Fellowships' and is kept inconspicuous by the image the women project. (Dickson-Waiko 2003: 99)

Moreover, development workers and scholars marginalise church women because their agendas do not mirror feminists' expectations (Dickson-Waiko 2003: 115). For Dickson-Waiko, women are the missing rib in PNG politics and government, and church women's groups are the missing rib in feminist understandings of Pacific women.

Dr Orovu Sepoe

Dr Orovu Sepoe, also a PNG scholar of gender, like Dickson-Waiko, suggests that strengthening the women's movement in Papua New Guinea is necessary for increasing women's political participation. Sepoe makes a similar argument for community women's groups—groups that might include church women's groups but might also coalesce around matters other than religion. She argues that community women's groups are a means through which women exercise decision-making and political power:

> Conventional studies of the political tend to maintain a dichotomy between institutional and community politics ... The dichotomy also extends to development practice so much so that women's organizations are predominantly perceived as 'just women's groupings'. The dichotomy serves to marginalise issues concerning women, and the agendas and activities of women organising. (Sepoe 2000: vii)

Sepoe's experiential knowledge coupled with her research led her to a similar understanding to Dickson-Waiko of gender roles in precolonial Papua New Guinea, how these have changed and the impact on women. Her insights include that '[s]ettled, subsistence agriculture has been, and remains the mainstay of household economic activity' (Sepoe 2000: 2). Women continue to play a significant role in this as they did in the past. Triangulating experiential knowledge with anthropological literature, she surmises that in precolonial times:

> Women's and men's roles were separate and different but these roles were of mutual value, contributing to the total wellbeing of their respective community. The checks and balances of these pre-colonial societies ensured that both men's and women's designated roles served the interests of the community as a whole. The separate roles of women and men did not necessarily correspond with a devaluing of their place and status in society, since they had their specific spheres of influence. (Sepoe 2000: 3)

The balance of these separate and different roles of mutual value was upended by both Christianisation and colonisation, but in different ways. Both introduced the idea of opposition: the oppositional gender roles of whiteness and the opposition of public and domestic necessary to uphold the oppositional gender roles. But there are significant differences in the approaches used by missionaries and colonisers.

Christianity has been Indigenised to the extent that it is part of the identity of most Pasifika peoples today. This adoption was made possible largely by what Sepoe (2000: 6) refers to as the missionary practice of 'evangelism through localisation'. As I, too, have written about the Kwato people of the mission of the same name, the extent of the uptake of Christianity relied on two things: first, that Christian values of communality echoed extant values of relationality; and second, it was locals who drew on their kinship and trade networks to exponentially multiply congregations of believers (Lawrence 2018). The process of 'localisation' resulted in Indigenisation. As stated earlier, I define Indigenisation not as a process of translation; rather, it is a process of building on what already exists. In this context, it is building on values and ways of being that already existed. Importantly, during this period, men and boys were not lured away from their villages in the same way that colonial administrations and economies centred men in growing towns and on plantations. In the mission at Kwato Island, local men and women worked together to grow the mission and, in this matricentric region, Indigenous women in the mission were also teachers, plantation managers and preachers.

Outside the mission, however, and across the two territories of Papua and New Guinea, men dominated the colonial administration even in the last decades of colonial rule. Sepoe writes:

> In 1963 ... there were 6000 officers in the public service, of whom only 16 were women. In the private sector, women comprised only 3% out of a total 57,200 employees. On the eve of self-government, in 1971, of a total paid workforce of 132,632, only 12% were women. (2000: 9)

With such a bias in favour of men's representation and participation, '[t]he emerging formal and informal structures and processes privileged men more than women' (Sepoe 2000: 11). Furthermore, she argues it is not just economic structures and processes that are gendered, so, too, is male bias embedded in political structures and processes (Sepoe 2000: 22), and whiteness, modernity and coloniality devalue women's work in relation to men's because 'development assistance and interventions often exclude the work that women perform' (p. 24). Sepoe is also concerned that a focus on women's representation is at the expense of women's participation in decision-making.

What can we determine about the coloniality of knowledge vis-a-vis the scholarship of Dickson-Waiko and Sepoe and the anecdote about agriculture that preceded this section? We know from feminist scholars that within whiteness gender has been a factor in the validity of knowledge claims (Alcoff and Potter 1993a). And we know from decolonial scholars (Mignolo 2002) that the coloniality of race is the racial hierarchy that inflects the coloniality of knowledge such that knowledge produced by white men and white women is knowledge that is valued. But, according to the logic of whiteness, knowledge produced by black women is an oxymoronic phrase since black women and their contributions are so devalued in these hierarchies of race and gender. It is, therefore, unsurprising, in the context of this racialised knowledge hierarchy, that a white woman should pronounce that she is teaching agriculture to black women who, along with their ancestors, have been practising for some 6,000 years the very thing said to be taught! And it explains why Dickson-Waiko's and Sepoe's feminist analyses are not prominent in the theory, discourse and praxis of international development actors working on gender in Papua New Guinea. They do not belong to the dominant epistemic frame.

The dominant epistemic frame and its role in subjugation in international development

That the discourse and praxis of aid and international development are an expression of neocolonialism is accepted by scholars and activists of the Majority World (Escobar 1992, 1995), including the Pacific (Hau'ofa 1994, 2008; Duituturga 2017; Lagi 2017; Va'ai 2017). Indeed, 'aid' is a contentious word. The theories of modernity, coloniality and decoloniality make very visible the ongoing harms of coloniality even after the end of colonisation and in the era of political independence. Resources extracted from the Majority World have historically and in contemporary times served to enrich the minority world. In addition, minority-world consumption patterns and the underlying economic systems are a significant contributing factor to the changing climate (Pörtner et al. 2022). Majority-World peoples thus continue to be harmed in multiple ways. In this context, 'aid' should be seen as part of a package of reparations for historical and ongoing systemic harms caused by the minority world and endured by the Majority World. But the conceptualisation and meaning given to 'aid' within the international development praxis and popular conceptions are blind to the harms of modernity because the dominant epistemic frame does not acknowledge these harms.

The impact of the dominant epistemic frame, coupled with the colonialities of race and gender, is one of exclusion. Making an argument about the education received by those working in human rights and social justice—which can equally be applied to international development practitioners—Godoy (2022: 5) writes that 'education is often rooted in Eurocentric assumptions about modernity, the state, and the autonomous individual in ways that, far from challenging hegemonic approaches, may in fact reproduce them'. Indeed, it reproduces hegemony and subjugation because the dominant epistemic frame excludes the history and context experienced by most peoples on this planet. This continues to be the case even in feminism. Just as Sepoe and Dickson-Waiko have demonstrated, and as Connell (2018: 23) recognises, '[t]he social experience of the colonized world is historically different, and the practical work of feminism, in the settings where the majority of the world's people live, requires theory that responds to this history'. To this I would add that feminist values existed in many Majority-World cultures long before colonisation, as have diverse gender roles that do not correspond to minority-world framing.[18]

Dickson-Waiko's and Sepoe's work also reflect the ways that Connell (2018) has identified in which Majority-World gender scholarship differs in its focus. The four concerns of Majority-World gender and feminist scholarship centre on: state and power, identity as collective, methodology and land. Individual personhood and the construction of womanhood are not a primary concern, which is not to say that cultures are collective only. Many Majority-World cultures, such as matricentric Milne Bay in Papua New Guinea, support BOTH the collective AND the individual. The many commonalities across Majority-World cultures suggest also that Majority-World theory must be considered together. Indeed, according to Connell (2018: 31):

18 Oyèrónké Oyěwùmí (1997) writes of female husbands in precolonial Nigeria—a reflection of gender roles very different to those in the minority world.

> It is not enough to have work from India, South Africa, the Maghreb, Brazil, Mexico, and Australasia separately. It is by seeing this work together that we become conscious of a body of knowledge with a scope and sophistication comparable to the output of the metropole.

We of the Majority World have far more in common with each other than we do with the minority world.[19]

Reading across Dickson-Waiko and Sepoe is a reminder about whose knowledge is centred in gender and development interventions in Papua New Guinea. Since the theories of gender that underpin these development interventions are generated in the minority world, it is safe to say that minority-world knowledge is centred on development interventions in Papua New Guinea. Indeed, despite all the talk across the sector of the importance of context, the coloniality of knowledge persists because of the centring of minority-world theories.

What might happen if we centred Papua New Guinean feminist thinkers? Let us take a couple of Dickson-Waiko's and Sepoe's insights, arranged through some of the concerns that Connell identified as features of Majority-World gender and feminist scholarship and generate some exploratory questions from those.

State and power: Coming to terms with legacies of gendered colonial violence

To understand the many forms of contemporary violence against Papua New Guinean women it is necessary to make visible colonial violence and the gendered nature of state formation. Without this recognition, any approach to address gender equality will not be addressing one of its root causes. The acknowledgement of this root cause opens questions such as: if Papua New Guinea is a liberal state in name only, what does this mean for interventions based on gender mainstreaming and the assumption that increasing the number of women will lead to greater equality as in a liberal state? This equalising of gender certainly has not played out in national politics. Likewise, the problematic assumption of liberal feminism that teaching women 'leadership' skills (as if they did not already possess these) will be sufficient to influence an extremely gendered national political process and structure. If the political process and structure are gendered,

---

19   Argued in my book (Lawrence forthcoming) and my thesis (Lawrence 2018).

what women need, according to Dickson-Waiko and Sepoe, is a movement to shift that structure and the norms underpinning it. Furthermore, the strengthening of individuals' capacities must attend to how to negotiate the processes and structures of national politics in Papua New Guinea because these privilege men. It is for this reason that not even women from matrilineal societies in Papua New Guinea can penetrate contemporary national politics and no amount of leadership training of individual women is going to shift this.

Applying relational methodologies/acknowledging relational identities

Indigenous methodologies of the Majority World are relational, as are decolonial methodologies. The lens of knowledge creation is constructed around the existence of BOTH this AND in lieu of EITHER this OR that. In Papua New Guinea, as in other parts of the Majority World, identity is constructed as BOTH collective AND individual.

How might the BOTH/AND lens work to support gender equality in Papua New Guinea? Let us look at this in the context of eliminating gender-based violence. Dickson-Waiko wrote of Papua New Guinean women's concern about not alienating men. Indeed, the development narrative about PNG masculinities is a harmful one as it focuses on the negative norms of gender-based violence (Masta 2021). It is a discourse that generates resistance to the language and practice of gender equality and, unsurprisingly, this one-dimensional perspective of PNG masculinity alienates many Papua New Guinean men.

Recognition of BOTH the collective AND the individual nature of PNG societies with the deliberate use of a BOTH/AND methodology would open questions such as: How might interventions support bringing men on a shared journey instead of alienating them through representation based on a single masculinity steeped in violence? What might be the impact on the desired systemic change of BOTH identifying and celebrating positive norms AND working against negative norms? In lieu of an oppositional stance, what would allyship look like and what might it yield? Furthermore, why assume that interventions by international actors applying theories generated in the minority world will lead to transformational change? If Papua New Guineans are going to enact transformational change it will be because there is a cause around which people (that is, women and men) can unite and mobilise, such as through the movement-building suggested by Dickson-Waiko and Sepoe. To understand what will inspire people to unite and how to mobilise them requires a great deal of cultural fluency. Indeed, the early Papuan missionaries in Milne Bay very successfully created large movements that translated into thousands of converts to Christianity (Lawrence 2018; Wetherell 1986, 2012).

The need for cultural fluency

Both Dickson-Waiko and Sepoe are Papua New Guinean feminist experts in the field of gender and gender relations. In their texts, they acknowledge the complexity of gender in this ethnically, linguistically and culturally diverse nation. If they as Papua New Guineans find the terrain challenging, on what basis can a foreigner claim gender expertise in Papua New Guinea? Moreover, their insights point to many pathways through which women's equality and rights can be pursued and enhanced. It is far from clear that gender programming by international actors draws on this expertise. In fact, when I shared this chapter with white women who work as gender 'experts' in Papua New Guinea they acknowledged that they had never heard of Dickson-Waiko though some had met Sepoe. They also acknowledged that the theories, insights and questions I raised above had never occurred to them. One could read into this that cultural fluency is necessary to enact social transformation and that an absence of cultural fluency is harmful because it serves to maintain the status quo. That status quo unfolds as the subjugation of both PNG feminist knowledge and Papua New Guinean women because development interventions create piecemeal change but are ineffective at enabling transformation.

What, then, is the relationship of cultural fluency with epistemic injustice? Since epistemic injustice is the privileging of knowledge generated only through one lens and the coloniality of knowledge plays out as the imposition of that knowledge on peoples from different geographies with different histories, politics and ethics, epistemic justice and decoloniality are both necessary to the practice of do no harm or do the least harm. And part of the practice of decoloniality is to centre cultural fluency through both experiential and academic knowledge.

Epistemic justice is more than the development buzzword of 'contextualisation' since this contextualisation in development practice has meant the superficiality of attempting to retrofit minority-world theories to PNG contexts. Indigenisation is true contextualisation. And Indigenisation, as the uptake of Christianity in Papua New Guinea demonstrates, is most successfully done by those with cultural fluency through processes and language that are culturally appropriate. Indeed, epistemic justice demands the recognition of local knowledge and centres situated knowledge over universal knowledge claims.

As an aside, and to those who might want to regurgitate old arguments about cultural relativism, decolonisation from the decolonial perspective requires recognition and acknowledgement of the harms caused by universals that are generated from a single cultural context. When we all recognise this, we will be able to negotiate whether we agree on any social knowledge that is truly universal. To get to that point first requires the practise of epistemic justice. With regard to gender theory, Connell (2018: 22) recognises that

> [t]he problem is not a deficit of ideas from the global periphery—it is a deficit of recognition and circulation. This is a structural problem in feminist thought on a world scale. If the only versions of theory that circulate globally and hold authority are those that arise from the social experience of a regional minority, there is a drastic impoverishment of gender studies as a form of knowledge.

Decentring the dominant epistemic frame

Here is an example of what organisations working in the sector could do to support the decentring of the dominant epistemic frame and challenge the hegemony of whiteness in international development.

At the time of writing this chapter, the International Women's Development Agency (IWDA) is supporting a research project in Papua New Guinea. Since one of the IWDA's strategies is to support movement-building that contributes to gender equality, the project must fit within these parameters. Beyond this, the Papua New Guinean lead researcher, Dr Orovu Sepoe, has the licence to determine the research questions, the methodology and approach and to select steering committee and project team members. The entire team is Papua New Guinean. The research maps the ecosystem of organisations working on women's rights in Papua New Guinea and will provide recommendations on how to strengthen that ecosystem. The project has stimulated much interest in the country, not least for the IWDA's decolonising approach of trusting that locals know best their own context. In relation to the previous discussion, this project applies relational methodologies, acknowledges relational identities and the entire team possesses cultural fluency.

It is being able to support work such as this that enables me to continue working in a sector in which decolonisation is fast becoming a metaphor, and in which the hegemony of whiteness continues to subjugate Majority-World peoples.

Concluding thoughts

My opening to this chapter asked whose knowledge is privileged and whose knowledge is not privileged, and why that matters. And I asked what changes are possible for women in Papua New Guinea if whiteness via the coloniality of gender and the coloniality of knowledge that underpinned colonialism persists through developmentalism?

I argued that systemic changes towards greater gender equality in Papua New Guinea are possible only through a decolonial praxis that values the intellectual and experiential knowledge of locals and supports Indigenisation. I also argued that Indigenisation and cultural fluency are inextricably linked since without cultural fluency in a particular context there simply is no possibility of switching epistemic frames to enable the decentring of whiteness and the centring of Indigeneity.

I finished with an example of decentring whiteness in international development knowledge-creation. My final thoughts about whose knowledge matters acknowledges that many different people work in the space of knowledge production—some Indigenous to their context, many not. It may be impossible for some to switch epistemic frames since they lack even basic cross-cultural competencies, especially to do with relational thinking and execution. In this instance, the least that can be done is for knowledge and its production to be situated. Despite Donna Haraway's (1988) groundbreaking essay on the particularity of knowledge—now some 37 years since publication—white feminists still largely do not situate themselves and the knowledge they produce. White feminists often therefore practise epistemic injustice by contributing to normalising and maintaining the idea that the knowledge they produce is objective and that those of us who emplace ourselves do not and cannot produce knowledge. Thus, the Australian Volunteers International volunteer's belief that she was teaching agriculture to long-time agriculturalists. Thus, the invisibility of Dickson-Waiko and Sepoe in feminist and gender theory. Thus, the continued subjugation of Majority-World women in gender and development.

References

Alam, Shahidul. 2008. 'Majority World: Challenging the West's Rhetoric of Democracy.' *Amerasia Journal* 34 no. 1: 88–98. doi.org/10.17953/amer.34.1. l3176027k4q614v5.

Alcoff, Linda Martín. 2012. 'Enrique Dussel's Transmodernism.' *Transmodernity: Journal of Peripheral Cultural Production of the Luso-Hispanic World* 1, no. 3: 1, 60–68. doi.org/10.5070/T413012882.

Alcoff, Linda, and Elizabeth Potter, eds. 1993a. *Feminist Epistemologies*. London: Routledge.

Alcoff, Linda, and Elizabeth Potter. 1993b. 'Introduction: When Feminisms Intersect Epistemology.' In *Feminist Epistemologies*, edited by Linda Alcoff and Elizabeth Potter. London: Routledge.

Allen, Amy, and Eduardo Mendieta. 2021. *Decolonizing Ethics: The Critical Theory of Enrique Dussel*. University Park: Pennsylvania State University Press. doi.org/10.1515/9780271090320.

Bellwood, Peter. 2017. 'Early Agriculture in World Perspective.' In *Ten Thousand Years of Cultivation at Kuk Swamp in the Highlands of Papua New Guinea*, edited by Jack Golson, Tim Denham, Philip Hughes, Pamela Swadling, and John Muke, 29–37. Canberra: ANU Press. doi.org/10.22459/TA46.07.2017.02.

Connell, Raewyn. 2018. 'Meeting at the Edge of Fear: Theory on a World Scale.' In *Constructing the Pluriverse: The Geopolitics of Knowledge*, edited by Bernd Reiter. Durham: Duke University Press. doi.org/10.1215/9781478002017.

Dalmiya, Vrinda, and Linda Alcoff. 1993. 'Are "Old Wives" Tales' Justified?' In *Feminist Epistemologies*, edited by Linda Alcoff and Elizabeth Potter. London: Routledge.

Demian, Melissa. 2000. 'Longing for Completion: Toward an Aesthetics of Work in Suau.' *Oceania* 71: 94–109. doi.org/10.1002/j.1834-4461.2000.tb02729.x.

Demian, Melissa. 2006. '"Emptiness" and Complementarity in Suau Reproductive Strategies.' In *Population, Reproduction and Fertility in Melanesia*, edited by Stanley J. Ulijaszek. New York: Berghahn Books.

Denham, T.P., S.G. Haberle, C. Lentfer, R. Fullagar, J. Field, M. Therin, N. Porch, and B. Winsborough. 2003. 'Origins of Agriculture at Kuk Swamp in the Highlands of New Guinea.' *Science* 301, no. 5630: 189–93. doi.org/10.1126/science.1085255.

Dickson-Waiko, Anne. 2001. 'Women, Individual Human Rights, Community Rights: Tensions within the Papua New Guinea State.' In *Women's Rights and Human Rights: International Historical Perspectives*, edited by Marilyn Lake, Katie Holmes, and Patricia Grimshaw. Basingstoke: Palgrave. doi.org/10.1057/9780333977644_4.

Dickson-Waiko, Anne. 2003. 'The Missing Rib: Mobilizing Church Women for Change in Papua New Guinea.' *Oceania* 74: 98–119. doi.org/10.1002/j.1834-4461.2003.tb02838.x.

Dickson-Waiko, Anne. 2007. 'Colonial Enclaves and Domestic Spaces in British New Guinea.' In *Britishness Abroad: Transnational Movements and Imperial Cultures*, edited by Kate Darian-Smith, Patricia Grimshaw, and Stuart Macintyre. Melbourne: Melbourne University Press.

Dickson-Waiko, Anne. 2008. 'Finding Women in Colonial Papua: Gender, Race and Sex in Papua New Guinea History.' *South Pacific Journal of Philosophy and Culture* 10: 11–23.

Dickson-Waiko, Anne. 2009. 'Women, Policy Making and Development.' In *Policy Making and Implementation Studies from Papua New Guinea*, edited by R.J. May, 281–98. Canberra: ANU E Press. doi.org/10.22459/PMI.09.2009.15.

Dickson-Waiko, Anne. 2010. *Taking Over, of What and From Whom? Women and Independence, the Papua New Guinea Experience*. Alfred Deakin Research Institute Working Paper No. 10. Geelong: Alfred Deakin Research Institute, Deakin University.

Dickson-Waiko, Anne. 2013. 'Women, Nation and Decolonisation in Papua New Guinea.' *The Journal of Pacific History* 48, no. 2: 177–93. doi.org/10.1080/00223344.2013.802844.

Duituturga, Emele. 2017. 'Rethinking Development: Reshaping the Pacific We Want.' In *Relational Hermeneutics: Decolonising the Mindset and the Pacific Itulagi*, edited by Upolu Luma Va'ai and Aisake Casimira, 199–214. Suva: University of the South Pacific & Pacific Theological College.

Escobar, Arturo. 1992. 'Imagining a Post-Development Era? Critical Thought, Development and Social Movements.' In *Social Text: Third World and Post-Colonial Issues*, no. 31–32, 20–56. Durham: Duke University Press. doi.org/10.2307/466217.

Escobar, Arturo. 1995. *Encountering Development: The Making and Unmaking of the Third World*. Princeton: Princeton University Press.

Esty, Daniel C. 2002. 'The World Trade Organization's Legitimacy Crisis.' *World Trade Review* 1, no. 1: 7–22. doi.org/10.1017/S1474745601001021.

Fricker, Miranda. 2007. *Epistemic Injustice: Power and the Ethics of Knowing*. New York: Oxford University Press. doi.org/10.1093/acprof:oso/9780198237907.001.0001.

Godoy, Angelina Snodgrass. 2022. 'What Are We Trying to Do Here? Epistemic Racism in Human Rights Teaching.' *International Journal of Human Rights Education* 6, no. 1.

Grosfoguel, Ramón. 2002. 'Colonial Difference, Geopolitics of Knowledge, and Global Coloniality in the Modern/Colonial Capitalist World-System.' *Review (Fernand Braudel Center)* 25: 203–24.

Grosfoguel, Ramón. 2007. 'The Epistemic Decolonial Turn.' *Cultural Studies* 21, nos 2–3: 211–23. doi.org/10.1080/09502380601162514.

Haberle, Simon G., Carol Lentfer, Shawn O'Donnell, and Tim Denham. 2012. 'The Palaeoenvironments of Kuk Swamp from the Beginnings of Agriculture in the Highlands of Papua New Guinea.' *Quaternary International* 249: 129–39. doi.org/10.1016/j.quaint.2011.07.048.

Haraway, Donna. 1988. 'Situated Knowledges: The Science Question in Feminism and the Privilege of Partial Perspective.' *Feminist Studies* 14, no. 3: 575–99. doi.org/10.2307/3178066.

Harding, Sandra. 1993. 'Rethinking Standpoint Epistemology: "What Is Strong Objectivity"?' In *Feminist Epistemologies*, edited by Linda Alcoff and Elizabeth Potter. London: Routledge.

Hau'ofa, Epeli. 1994. 'Our Sea of Islands.' *The Contemporary Pacific* 6, no. 1: 148–61. hdl.handle.net/10125/12960.

Hau'ofa, Epeli. 2008. 'The Ocean in Us.' *We Are the Ocean: Selected Works*. Honolulu: University of Hawai'i Press.

Held, David. 2006. 'Reframing Global Governance: Apocalypse Soon or Reform!' *New Political Economy* 11, no. 2: 158–76. doi.org/10.1080/13563460600655516.

Hoekman, Bernard. 2002. 'Strengthening the Global Trade Architecture for Development: The Post Doha Agenda.' *World Trade Review* 1, no. 1: 23–45. doi.org/10.1017/S1474745601001008.

Lagi, Rosaina. 2017. 'Vanua Sauvi: Social Roles, Sustainability and Resilience.' In *Relational Hermeneutics: Decolonising the Mindset and the Pacific Itulagi*, edited by Upolu Luma Va'ai and Aisake Casimira, 187–98. Suva: University of the South Pacific & Pacific Theological College.

Lawrence, Salmah Eva-Lina. 2018. 'Speaking for Ourselves: Kwato Perspectives on Matriliny and Missionisation.' PhD diss., The Australian National University.

Lawrence, Salmah Eva-Lina. 2022. 'The Majority World: What's in a Phrase?' *News and Stories*, 4 November. Melbourne: Philanthropy Australia. www. philanthropy.org.au/news-and-stories/the-majority-world-whats-in-a-phrase/.

Lawrence, Salmah Eva-Lina. 2023. 'Challenging Power and Discrimination: A Letter to My Younger Self.' In *Dear Younger Me*, edited by Lee Wilson and Simon Milligan. London: Routledge.

Lawrence, Salmah Eva-Lina. Forthcoming. *Decolonising International Development: The View from the Majority World.* London: Bloomsbury.

Longino, Helen. 1993. 'Subjects, Power and Knowledge: Description and Prescription.' In *Feminist Epistemologies*, edited by Linda Alcoff and Elizabeth Potter. London: Routledge.

Lugones, María. 2007. 'Heterosexualism and the Colonial/Modern Gender System.' *Hypatia* 22, no. 1: 186–209. www.jstor.org/stable/4640051.

Lugones, María. 2008. 'The Coloniality of Gender.' *Worlds & Knowledges Otherwise* (Spring): 1–17.

Masta, Mercy Natalia. 2021. 'Pacific Masculinities: Exploring Men's Perspectives and Experiences of Masculinity, and Efforts to Engage Men and Boys in Preventing Violence in Papua New Guinea and Fiji.' PhD diss., RMIT University, Melbourne.

Mignolo, Walter. 1995. *The Darker Side of the Renaissance: Literacy, Territoriality, and Colonization.* Ann Arbor: University of Michigan Press.

Mignolo, Walter. 1998. 'Coloniality at Large: The Western Hemisphere in the Colonial Horizon of Modernity.' *CR: The New Centennial Review* 1, no. 2: 19–54. doi.org/10.1353/ncr.2003.0057.

Mignolo, Walter D. 1999. 'I Am Where I Think: Epistemology and the Colonial Difference.' *Journal of Latin American Cultural Studies: Travesia* 8, no. 2: 235–45. doi.org/10.1080/13569329909361962.

Mignolo, Walter D. 2002. 'The Geopolitics of Knowledge and the Colonial Difference.' *The South Atlantic Quarterly* 101, no. 1: 57–96. doi.org/10.1215/00382876-101-1-57.

Mignolo, Walter. 2009. 'Dispensable and Bare Lives: Coloniality and the Hidden Political/Economic Agenda of Modernity.' *Human Architecture: Journal of the Sociology of Self-Knowledge* 7: 69–87.

Mignolo, Walter D. 2011. *The Darker Side of Western Modernity: Global Futures, Decolonial Options*. Durham: Duke University Press. doi.org/10.2307/j.ctv125 jqbw.

Mills, Charles W. 1997. *The Racial Contract*. Ithaca: Cornell University Press.

Msimang, Sisonke. 2022. *Another Australia*. Melbourne: Affirm Press.

On, Bat-Ami Bar. 1993. 'Marginality and Epistemic Privilege.' In *Feminist Epistemologies*, edited by Linda Alcoff and Elizabeth Potter. London: Routledge.

Oyěwùmí, Oyèrónké. 1997. *The Invention of Women: Making an African Sense of Western Gender Discourses*. Minneapolis: University of Minnesota Press.

Pahuja, Sundhya. 2011. *Decolonising International Law: Development, Economic Growth, and the Politics of Universality*. Cambridge: Cambridge University Press. doi.org/10.1017/CBO9781139048200.

Pörtner, Hans-Otto, Debra C. Roberts, Melinda M.B. Tignor, Elvira Poloczanska, Katja Mintenbeck, Andrés Alegría, Marlie Craig, Stefanie Langsdorf, Sina Löschke, Vincent Möller, Andrew Okem, and Bardhyl Rama, eds. 2022. *Climate Change 2022—Impacts, Adaptation and Vulnerability: Working Group II Contribution to the Sixth Assessment Report of the Intergovernmental Panel on Climate Change*. Cambridge: Cambridge University Press. doi.org/10.1017/9781009325844.

Quijano, Aníbal. 1992. 'Colonialidad y Modernidad/Racionalidad [Coloniality and Modernity/Rationality].' *Peru Indigena* 13: 11–20.

Quijano, Aníbal. 1995. 'Raza, etnia y nación en Mariátegui: Cuestiones abiertas [Race, Ethnicity and Nation in Mariátegui: Open Issues].' *Estudios Latinoamericanos [Latin American Studies]* 2: 3–19. doi.org/10.22201/cela. 24484946e.1995.3.49720.

Quijano, Aníbal. 1999. 'Colonialidad del Poder, Cultura y Conocimiento en América Latina [Coloniality of Power, Culture and Knowledge in Latin America].' *Crítica Cultural en Latinoamérica: Paradigmas globales y enunicaciones locales [Cultural Criticism in Latin America: Global Paradigms and Local Communications]* 24: 137–48.

Quijano, Aníbal. 2000. 'Coloniality of Power and Eurocentrism in Latin America.' *International Sociology* 15, no. 2: 215–32. doi.org/10.1177/0268580900015 002005.

Quijano, Aníbal. 2007a. 'Coloniality and Modernity/Rationality.' *Cultural Studies* 21, nos 2–3: 168–78. doi.org/10.1080/09502380601164353.

Quijano, Aníbal. 2007b. 'Questioning "Race".' *Socialism and Democracy* 21, no. 1: 45–53. doi.org/10.1080/08854300601116704.

Santos, Boaventura de Sousa. 2013. *Epistemologies of the South: Justice Against Epistemicide*. Boulder: Paradigm Publishers.

Sepoe, Orovu V. 2000. *Changing Gender Relations in Papua New Guinea: The Role of Women's Organisations*. New Delhi: UBS Publishers Distributors Ltd.

Smith, Linda Tuhiwai. 2012. *Decolonizing Methodologies: Research and Indigenous Peoples*. London: Zed Books.

Stauffer, Robert H. 2003. *Kahana: How the Land Was Lost*. Honolulu: University of Hawai'i Press.

Stiglitz, Joseph E. 2003. *Globalization and its Discontents*. New York: W.W. Norton & Co.

Sullivan, Shannon. 2006. *Revealing Whiteness: The Unconscious Habits of Racial Privilege*. Bloomington: Indiana University Press.

Tuck, Eve, and K. Wayne Yang. 2012. 'Decolonization is Not a Metaphor.' *Decolonization: Indigeneity, Education & Society* 1: 1–40.

United Nations Population Fund (UNFPA). 2024. 'Papua New Guinea.' *World Population Dashboard*. [Online]. New York: UNFPA. www.unfpa.org/data/world-population/PG.

Va'ai, Upolu Luma. 2017. 'E ititi a lega mea—Less is more! A Pacific Relational Development Paradigm of Life.' In *Relational Hermeneutics: Decolonising the Mindset and the Pacific Itulagi*, edited by Upolu Luma Va'ai and Aisake Casimira, 215–31. Suva: University of the South Pacific & Pacific Theological College.

Wetherell, David. 1986. 'An Elite for A Nation? Reflections On a Missionary Group in Papua New Guinea, 1890–1986.' *Pacific Studies* 9: 1–40.

Wetherell, David. 2012. 'Creating an Indigenous Christian Leadership in Papua: Three Missions Compared.' *The Journal of Pacific History* 47, no. 2: 163–85. doi.org/10.1080/00223344.2012.684767.

Yunupingu, Galarrwuy, ed. 1997. *Our Land Is Our Life: Land Rights—Past, Present and Future*. Brisbane: University of Queensland Press.

6

Decolonial Disruptions: Feminist scholarship and practice across Oceania

Margaret Jolly[1]

Engendering politics in 'Our Sea of Islands'

The conference from which this volume emerges invited us to be nimble and imaginative in conceptualising gender and politics, challenging 'heteronormative, masculine, white political dominance' in Australia, Asia and the Pacific and eschewing an overreliance on Euro-American models and disciplinary parochialisms. In witnessing and promoting women's political agency in Oceania, we are confronted by pressing questions of cultural difference, reciprocal translation and historical relation—all embedded in perduring colonial relations and global geopolitics. Despite many programs and diverse schemes, women's representation in most national parliaments and political parties across the Pacific is still parlous (see Baker 2019), whereas women have been far more significant in other political spaces: in church groups, NGOs, regional organisations and activist movements.

1   Heartfelt thanks to Nayahamui Rooney, Katherine Lepani, Salmah Eva-Lina Lawrence, Kalpana Ram, Jonathan Ritchie, J. Kēhaulani Kauanui and Bob Foster for comments on earlier drafts, which occasioned significant revisions. Special thanks to my co-editor Tanya Jakimow for her close reading and valuable suggestions and for the overall inspiration for this volume and exemplary collaboration in what we have dubbed our 'dream team'. Thanks also to the anonymous reviewers for ANU Press.

In this chapter, I hope to refresh our thinking and practice by celebrating feminist scholarship and practice from a decolonial Oceanic perspective, highlighting the inspiring, creative work of three women, the late Anne Nealibo Dickson-Waiko of Papua New Guinea, J. Kēhaulani Kauanui, an Indigenous Hawaiian (Kanaka Maoli) scholar, and the late Teresia Teaiwa, who traced her ancestry to Banaba, Kiribati, Fiji and Afro-America.[2] Their feminist scholarship *and* their political practice are inspirational and disrupt dominant paradigms in compelling ways.

I develop three connected arguments. First, following Patricia Hill Collins (2012), I see their scholarship as social action, as an integral part of social change, but also consider how their scholarship translated into public political practices and alternative sites of knowledge production. Second, I distil the diversity of their feminist perspectives and how that relates to their own biographies, education and life trajectories. Third, I suggest that their approaches both appropriate and disrupt the canon of Euro-American theory, developing distinctly Oceanic decolonial perspectives that have a resonance beyond the region.

Considering this trio of remarkable scholar-activists blurs the foreign 'lines across the sea' that have divided Oceania between the three regions of Melanesia, Polynesia and Micronesia and, rather, emphasises their ancestral and contemporary Oceanic affinities (see Hau'ofa 1994, 2008;

---

2   I have had professional and personal relationships with each of these three extraordinary women. My relationship with Anne Dickson-Waiko dates from her time at The Australian National University, when I was an examiner of her PhD thesis, awarded in 1994. She contributed to several conferences and edited collections in Australia, including a special issue of *Oceania* on women's groups for which I wrote the epilogue (Jolly 2003). I have been a long-term admirer of her work and at times a mentor. I supported her for promotion at UPNG in the years before her death. We last had contact when she was a member of the PhD panel for her niece, Salmah Eva-Lina Lawrence. I first met J. Kēhaulani Kauanui when she was a Fulbright scholar in Māori Studies at the University of Auckland, in Aotearoa New Zealand, and invited her to Australia for the 'Migrating Feminisms' conference organised by Kalpana Ram and myself. This resulted in a special issue of *Women's Studies International Forum* (1998), which Kalpana and Kēhaulani co-edited. I regularly reviewed her work and supported her in professional promotions. I have shared this chapter and other recent writing about her work with her while she has been recovering from a long illness. I first met Teresia Teaiwa in the 1990s around our dinner table in Canberra when she was visiting for a conference. I engaged with her essay on bikini when she was a graduate student at the University of California at Santa Cruz and contributed to a conference and subsequent volume, *Native Cultural Studies on the Edge*, edited by Vicente Diaz and Kauanui for *The Contemporary Pacific* (in 2001). I last talked with her at a regional meeting in Suva and at the Pacific History Association conference in Guam, both in 2016, and attended her funeral in Wellington in 2017. I admired her writing, teaching, creativity and empathetic activism.

Jolly 2007).[3] Yet, in celebrating connections across this 'sea of islands', we must also acknowledge differences deriving from both Indigenous diversities and the differential effects of colonialism. These three women assume different positionalities, living and working in independent Pacific states (such as Papua New Guinea and Fiji) or in settler colonies (such as Hawai'i, the United States, Aotearoa New Zealand and Australia). Since their biographical trajectories profoundly influence their work, I offer brief vignettes of their lives as well as distilling their feminist scholarship and practice. I then compare their insights and situate them in broader projects of decoloniality and feminisms across borders. In conclusion, I consider how a better appreciation of their insights might inform the relationship between feminisms in Oceania and Australia.

My perspective derives from my own positionality in the settler colony of Australia, where Indigenous peoples have cared for Country for more than 65,000 years. I am of Anglo-Celtic ancestry: my mother's family migrated from Sheffield in England, my father's, from Glasgow in Scotland only a couple of generations ago. They were white settlers, albeit working-class families of Sydney's Inner West living on the lands of the Wangal and Gadigal peoples of the Eora Nation. I live, own a home and work in Canberra, the national capital, now as a Professor Emerita of The Australian National University on the Country of the Ngunnawal and Ngambri peoples. As a doctoral scholar in anthropology at the University of Sydney in the 1970s, I was passionately engaged with the second-wave feminist movement and with undoing the masculinism and coloniality of that discipline. While researching in Vanuatu (then the New Hebrides), I met Grace Mera Molisa, an inspiring nationalist leader and poet, who celebrated the independence of her country in 1980 but lamented that ni-Vanuatu women were still colonised by men (for example, Molisa 1983, 1987). We engaged in rich conversations about the politics of difference between women, between what Grace perceived as the individualism of women's liberation in Australia and the collectivist, relational values of ni-Vanuatu women (for example, Jolly 1991a, 1997b, 2005; Marsh 1998). I contended that individualism was far more characteristic of the liberal feminist stream than the socialist feminist stream in which I swam in the large second wave of feminism in Australia, which early on considered how gender intersected with class and

---

3   The division of these three regions dates to the French explorer and naval officer Jules-Sébastien-César Dumont d'Urville in 1832, though there were several precursors. The origin, racist character and significance of this tripartite division has been much debated. These names have been appropriated and their racist origins subverted by Pacific peoples in various ways (see Narokobi 1983; Kabutaulaka 2015).

race.[4] But, I also acknowledge that the values of feminist collectivity[5] that we espoused were different to Oceanic values of relationality and that we were struggling against the possessive individualism of an affluent capitalist country and a white settler colony.

Over decades since as a transdisciplinary scholar of gender and Pacific studies, I have been generously hosted in many parts of Oceania—especially Vanuatu, Fiji, Hawai'i and Aotearoa New Zealand. I have explored the gender politics of decolonisation and offered critiques of white feminists who adopt a matronising stance of 'saving our sisters' towards non-white women (Jolly 1991b, 1994a, 1994b, 2005; see also Abu-Lughod 2013). Although many Indigenous Australians and Oceanic peoples are supportive of decolonial alliances with white settlers like myself, there are still enormous challenges for me and those like me to forgo the presumptions of white privilege and scholarly hierarchy, to listen to and be led in projects of decolonisation by the experts—those who have intimate, personal experience of being colonised (see Moreton-Robinson 2020). The project of decolonisation is far more than the raising of the flags of new sovereign nations; it is profoundly cultural and fundamentally challenges the power of Euro-American systems of knowledge (see Banivanua Mar 2016; Lawrence, Chapter 5, this volume).[6]

Anne Nealibo Dickson-Waiko (1950–2018)

Anne was born in 1950 in Port Moresby, Papua New Guinea, a sovereign country since 1975, with more than 850 distinct sociolinguistic groups in a population currently estimated to be 9.3 million.[7] Her father worked as an advisor for the Australian colonial administration in Port Moresby but

---

4   I thank Kalpana Ram for reminding me of the collectivist character of feminist groups with whom we were engaged in Sydney in the 1970s and 1980s and the way in which groups of migrant 'Third World' and Indigenous women were also part of this 'second wave'.

5   See the discussion of the collective ethos of the women's liberation movement in the chapter by Elizabeth Reid in *Women and Whitlam* (Arrow 2023) and her consideration of Indigenous women such as Pat Eatock.

6   To quote Banivanua Mar's fine words: 'Like the enrichment of the Ocean, cultures of decolonisation in the Pacific were kept alive by processes of upwelling and downwelling that resemble the exchanges of water and oxygen between the surface and the deeper currents that keep the Ocean alive. This framework of exchange, enrichment and energy, characterises the ideas linking Indigenous networks of decolonisation as they surfaced and coalesced in expressive actions of protest, artistic and literary media, or written and spoken petitions, speeches and articles' (2016: 15).

7   This estimate has been recently challenged by the United Nations Population Fund, which considers the population may be much higher, even as high as 17 million (Randall 2022).

the family came from the Milne Bay region, where matrilineality prevails and where women still have a higher status in contrast to most other parts of Papua New Guinea, which are patrilineal and far more patriarchal (see Weiner 1976 Lepani 2012; Lawrence 2018).[8] Anne early reflected on the distinctive position of Milne Bay women and saw this as a creative creolisation of Indigenous structures and values with the early influences of Christianity, which afforded women entry into education and the professions of teaching and nursing (Kaniku 1989). Her own life trajectory exemplifies this conjunction. She was an outstanding student from her earliest years, as a boarder at the Kwato mission school,[9] where her parents had been educated, subsequently at Port Moresby High School (unusual then for both a Papuan and a girl) and at a secondary teachers' college in Goroka, where she again excelled and graduated as dux. With her then boyfriend and later husband, John Kaniku, she became a secondary schoolteacher and, after their first son was born, a writer of community education materials. Despite the demands of motherhood, she swiftly completed a degree in history at the University of Papua New Guinea (UPNG) in 1977 but declined a teaching fellowship there to pursue a master's program in political science in the United States as a Fulbright scholar. Despite the tragic loss of their firstborn son while in the United States, she graduated in 1981 and returned to UPNG to teach history. Declining elevated administrative roles for the most part, she continued as an inspiring teacher and mentor for generations of students over 45 years. Her teaching had a profound effect on the many cohorts of women whom she taught at UPNG and on those such as Elizabeth Taulegebo with whom she worked on the history of World War II in Milne Bay (see Plate 6.1).[10] She initiated courses on gender in Papua New Guinea, on colonialism and nationalism and South-East Asian history (Keimelo 2019). Like her second husband, John Waiko, she completed a PhD at The Australian National University, aptly titled '"A Woman's Place is in the Struggle": Feminism and Nationalism in the Philippines' (1994). During that period, while John often remained in Papua New Guinea, Anne was a single mother to her four children.

8   I am only sparsely citing a huge literature on gender in Papua New Guinea since I want to keep the focus firmly on Anne Dickson-Waiko and the period in which she was writing.
9   Kwato Mission, established by Charles Abel, was, as Dickson-Waiko observed, a 'colonial showpiece'. Young children were removed from their families and the 'contaminating' influence of culture—a process symbolised by children being thoroughly scrubbed on arrival (Dickson-Waiko 2013: 179). See also the analysis of Kwato and the Abel legacy by Salmah Eva-Lina Lawrence (2018), the niece of Anne Dickson-Waiko.
10   I thank Jonathan Ritchie for this insight and detail.

Plate 6.1: Anne Nealibo Dickson-Waiko (right) doing research with Baloni Douglas and other women into the Battle of Milne Bay, at Bou village in Milne Bay Province, Papua New Guinea, 12 April 2017
Source: Keimelo Gima.

Dickson-Waiko's comparative historical sensibility about gender laid the foundations of an original scholarly corpus of many published papers and reports (see Lawrence, Chapter 5, this volume). Her scholarly critiques and reflections were accompanied by a suite of activities as a feminist advocate at national, regional and global scales (see Keimelo 2019; Ritchie 2018). I focus on her scholarly creativity as it developed in a trio of three successive papers (Dickson-Waiko 2000, 2003, 2013). In the first of these she explored the relation between individual human rights and community rights, discerning gendered tensions and contradictions in the PNG state. These were grounded in the differences between 'traditional gender constructs' in diverse stateless polities and the character of an independent state based on Western principles (if not the reality) of democracy and liberalism. She observed that, although the founding Constitution of Papua New Guinea enshrined ideas of human rights for all, profound tensions persisted between these promised ideals and practices that regularly infringed on women's rights, including women being used as compensation to settle tribal conflicts, forced marriages and pervasive gender violence. She observed that 'sexual inequality is striking throughout the country, even in matrilineal societies' (Dickson-Waiko 2000: 50). But, she argued, this was the consequence not just of precolonial *kastom*, but also of the 'partial incorporation' of women into modern state structures since 1884. Indeed, the 'partiality' of the white masculinist state meant women were barely incorporated at all.

Successive colonial powers in the two territories of Papua and New Guinea (Britain, Germany, Australia), whose agents were almost exclusively male, engaged Indigenous men but not women in colonial enclaves, on plantations, in mines and in towns. The protectionist policies of successive British governors Sir William MacGregor (1888–98) and Sir Hubert Murray (1908–40)[11] and German Governor Albert Hahl (1901–14) restricted women to villages, even requiring that domestic servants be male, known as '*hausbois*'. Although Christian missions and especially women missionaries had more everyday contact with women, during the process of state formation, women were systematically excluded. Women remained embedded as daughters, mothers and sisters, 'representing collective clan and tribal identities', while 'their male compatriots have moved on to acquire individual human rights, attaining citizenship within the modern state' (Dickson-Waiko 2000: 54–55). Dickson-Waiko suggested that colonialism entailed the introduction of novel gendered binaries between domestic and public life and between women's productive and reproductive roles. In 'traditional society', women's productive and procreative labour were both highly valued and not separated.

In her view, the colonial exclusion of women from the state and the continuing perception of women as communal rather than individual subjects[12] laid the foundation for women's parlous representation in parliamentary politics. She noted that even in the celebrated Eight-Point Improvement Plan of the Pangu Pati, which formed both the first self-governing and then first fully independent government under Michael Somare, the equal participation of women was urged in 'all forms of economic and social activity', but not political activity—'an unconscious omission or a conscious decision'

---

11 Murray cited the risks of both female prostitution and depopulation if women were employed as labourers (Dickson-Waiko 2013: 178).

12 This relates to long debates about notions and values of personhood in Papua New Guinea, Melanesia and across Oceania. See Strathern's (1990) formulation of 'dividuals', partible persons in Melanesia, versus Western individuals, and critiques of this by Wardlow (2006, 2014), Jolly (1992) and Lepani (2012). Still in Papua New Guinea and across Oceania this contrast continues to be made, including by many Pacific peoples, celebrating collective values and relationality against Western individualism.

(Dickson-Waiko 2000: 55)?[13] Although women have become more visible in local and provincial politics, they remain at best a parlous minority in the national PNG Parliament. Despite several efforts to reserve seats for women in the national parliament, none has succeeded, while votes are still often cast based on kinship and collective identity (Sepoe 2002; Baker 2019).

So, Dickson-Waiko perceived a dissonance between secular, state-based schemes for women's empowerment—often urged or supported by the United Nations, international agencies, aid programs and NGOs—and the character of gender relations in PNG society. She observed that even middle-class educated women in Papua New Guinea were reluctant to call themselves 'feminist' and often depicted local gender relations as complementary rather than patriarchal (Dickson-Waiko 2000: 55). She argued that in Papua New Guinea, 'church women's groups are the missing link—the missing rib— of an evolving indigenous feminism' (Dickson-Waiko 2003: 99). She did not deny the patriarchal character of most Christian denominations, their clerical hierarchies, their masculinist messages and longstanding projects of 'domestication' dedicated to remaking women as loyal wives and mothers (Dickson-Waiko 2013: 178; see also Wardlow 2014).[14] But, she asserted, from the early work of foreign women missionaries with Indigenous women, women's fellowships had expanded their preoccupation with domestic, welfare and spiritual concerns to embrace 'wider social, political and human rights issues' (Dickson-Waiko 2003: 98), including reproductive health, literacy and gender violence. She provided abundant evidence that such fellowships had become increasingly politicised. Moreover, many women were drawn into politics that transcended the local scale, at provincial, national, regional and even global levels. Women's participation in such fellowships had proved empowering and liberating.

Dickson-Waiko (2003) also astutely highlighted the emergent class differentiation between women—too often denied with claims of 'Melanesian egalitarianism'. The differences between women are clearly articulated in Tok Pisin (the lingua franca of Papua New Guinea) as *ol grassroots mama*

---

13 Though in her later paper she acknowledges that in an earlier submission to constitutional development in 1970 Pangu Pati had proposed five seats be reserved for women, 30 years before the idea of temporary special measures 'became fashionable in the twenty-first century' (Dickson-Waiko 2013: 182). Kathy Lepani notes that the Eight Point Improvement Plan that Somare introduced to the House of Assembly in 1973 was endorsed by the Assembly and then formed the basis for the independence Constitution's Preamble and the National Goals and Directive (Pers. comm., 12 February 2023).
14 There is a large literature on this but see Jolly and Macintyre (1989) and Choi and Jolly (2014) for syntheses and diverse perspectives.

('grassroots mothers') versus *ol save meri* ('women who know/are educated'), used for women of the literate, urban middle classes. Although some women in the latter category found this term repugnant, Dickson-Waiko, a *save meri* herself, insisted on acknowledging this difference and the realities of hard physical labour and urban precarity for many women. She recounts the extraordinary events of June 1974 (Dickson-Waiko 2003: 113) when, alongside students, teachers and public servants, women from the suburbs of Port Moresby organised through the United Church Women's Fellowship to protest in the streets. They lamented their poor living conditions and the low wages for women who were employed. They vented anger at the wealth of not just the departing white colonisers but also their fellow Papua New Guineans, and especially the extravagance of male government ministers and their expensive overseas trips. They hurled stones, smashed windows, besieged government buildings, threatened police, invaded the airport and even shouted down chief minister Michael Somare.[15]

Thus, for Dickson-Waiko (2013: 193), despite national independence, 'male hegemony prevailed before and after decolonisation'. Colonial policies were 'brazenly gendered and racialised', reinforcing and institutionalising women's earlier subordinate position. Decolonisation for Papua New Guinean women meant colonisation by male compatriots (as for Grace Mera Molisa in Vanuatu). In other postcolonial states (such as the Philippines, the subject of Dickson-Waiko's PhD thesis), feminist movements emerged as part of anticolonial nationalist movements. There was no such broad movement in Papua New Guinea before independence in 1975. Most Australian women in Papua New Guinea were more interested in promoting women's clubs, welfare, nutrition and Girl Guides than the second-wave feminism of the West. Second-wave feminism did exert some influence on more educated urban women, but this was often seen as a foreign import grounded in Western individualism: groups such as the Women's Action Group eschewed identification as 'feminist'. Male public figures, poets and artists satirised 'modern women' as inauthentic figures of fun. Bernard Narokobi, reformist judge and influential author of *The Melanesian Way* (1983), though staunchly opposed to forced marriage, was part of this 'male backlash'. Dickson-Waiko saw this as an expression of male fears of changing gender relations and a nostalgic revival of a frozen figure of a precolonial

---

15 Dickson-Waiko (2003: 113–14) also notes how the fact that the United Church Women's Fellowship recruited Josephine Abaijah to their cause meant that their protests were incorrectly seen as a manifestation of the Papua Besena separatist movement.

Melanesian woman.[16] This culture war made it difficult for women entering national parliament; Josephine Aibaijah and Nahau Rooney were among the few in the period after independence. In its architecture and composition, it remained a 'men's house', modelled on a house from the Sepik region from which women were excluded (Rosi 1991). Since independence only nine women have ever been elected to the PNG Parliament, with no woman elected in 2017 and only two women among 118 members in 2022.[17]

The feminism that emerged in Papua New Guinea after 1975 was 'not spontaneous nor was it driven from below'; rather, it was 'imposed from above by the state apparatus' (Dickson-Waiko 2013: 192), primarily in response to pressure from the United Nations. This liberal feminist approach, though it had some supporters among urban educated women, did not have the same traction as the Indigenous feminism of women's groups based in Christian churches. Although the PNG National Council of Women was formalised by an Act of Parliament in 1979 as an umbrella group, it morphed into an NGO rather than a formal government body. Thus, Dickson-Waiko concluded: 'The critical link between post-colonial feminism and the nascent women's movement in PNG was stillborn' (2013: 192).

Despite this dismal conclusion, Dickson-Waiko sustained hope through a range of important political engagements, nationally and internationally, as a woman representative of her independent nation. This likely catalysed her sense of the disconnection between the secular state–based politics of gender equality and the grassroots 'Indigenous feminism' in women's church fellowships. Dickson-Waiko represented Papua New Guinea in New York in 1995 and 2004 at sessions of the UN Commission on the Status of Women. She was president of the UPNG Women's Association from 1998 to 2003, deputy chair of the PNG National AIDS Council (2003–06) and represented Papua New Guinea at the Special General Assembly on HIV/AIDS in 2001. Her scholarly insights were distilled not just in a series of scholarly articles but also in a suite of reports she wrote on gender for the World Bank, World Vision, the United Nations, the European Union, the United Nations Children's Fund (UNICEF), the Asian Development Bank and the Secretariat of the Pacific Community. She fought strongly

---

16 Dickson-Waiko quotes Narokobi satirising Western dress trends: 'The men folk chuckle at women, who paint their lips, shave their eyebrows, wear pants, put on large sunglasses and walk on high-heel shoes' (Dickson-Waiko 2013: 186, quoting Narokobi 1983: 37). See also the writings of Laura Zimmer-Tamakoshi (1993) on this backlash and women's responses.
17 Dr Nayahamui Rooney is writing a biography of her mother, Nahau Rooney, tentatively called 'Into the Men's House'.

for women's formal political representation and was especially important in incorporating women's representation into both provincial and local government, approved by the national Parliament in 1997.[18] According to UPNG colleague Cathy Keimelo: 'This was a turning point of women in politics. The Late Dr Anne was less of a talker and more of a doer' (2019).

J. Kēhaulani Kauanui (1968–)

J. Kēhaulani Kauanui has a rather different decolonial perspective on her homeland of Hawai'i. This archipelago had distinct polities in the precolonial period, but its Indigenous population (Kanaka Maoli) was much more culturally and linguistically homogeneous than Papua New Guinea's. Hawai'i was unified under King Kamehameha I in 1810 and was a sovereign constitutional monarchy for much of the nineteenth century until the overthrow of Queen Lili'uokalani in 1893 and ultimate annexation by the United States in 1898. It became a state of the United States of America in 1959, and thus Kanaka Maoli (Indigenous Hawaiians), like Native Americans, are the original inhabitants of what has become a settler colony. Despite the ongoing struggles of Indigenous Hawaiians for sovereignty, Hawai'i remains crucial to US military influence in the Pacific, especially with the contemporary intensification of geopolitical rivalry between the United States and China.

J. Kēhaulani Kauanui is Kanaka Maoli with ties to family in Anahola (in Hawaiian Homelands Territory) on the island of Kaua'i and throughout the archipelago. She was born and raised in California and, after studying at Irving Valley College, transferred to and graduated with a BA in women's studies from the University of California Berkeley in 1992 and then a PhD in the History of Consciousness Program at the University of California Santa Cruz, working with James Clifford, Donna Haraway and Neferti X.M. Tadiar. She has eschewed marriage and motherhood. She is currently Eric and Wendy Schmidt Chair of Indigenous Studies and Professor of Anthropology in the Effron Center for the Study of America at Princeton University (after 24 years as Professor of Anthropology and American Studies at Wesleyan University). A prolific scholar, she is the author of two books and the editor of several more volumes, together with a large corpus

---

18 This was through her involvement in the Review of the Organic Law on Provincial and Local Level Government led by Ben Micah from 1995.

of essays. Her interests are wide-ranging: Hawaiian history, Indigeneity, critical race theory, feminist theory, gender and sexuality, international law, anarchism. Her scholarship is articulated with a passionate activism, promoting Kanaka Maoli and Native American alliances and anarchist solutions beyond the state and its authoritarian abuses of power.

From her large corpus, I focus on two of her books, *Hawaiian Blood* (Kauanui 2008) and *Paradoxes of Hawaiian Sovereignty* (Kauanui 2018b), and two articles that consider the intersection of race, gender and sexuality in the history of Hawai'i. Kauanui (2005) offered a critical analysis of the notorious US 'blood quantum' rule used to categorise Kanaka Maoli. She showed how the insistence on the '50 per cent blood quantum' rule for authentic Hawaiian Indigeneity effectively alienates most Hawaiians from their land and how the search for Hawaiian 'purity' discriminates against the majority of Hawaiians, who are 'mixed'. She also revealed how racialised notions inherent in US bureaucratic practices are mirrored in the politics of the Hawaiian sovereignty movement. She analysed a telling ambiguity between two claims in the sovereignty movement: one an argument for Indigenous determination under US domestic law (decolonisation protocols) and the other that Hawai'i (and not just Kanaka Maoli) has a right to self-determination under international law (de-occupation) (Kauanui 2005).

Kauanui elaborated that critical analysis in her book *Hawaiian Blood*, arguing that 'blood quantum is a colonial project in the service of land alienation and dispossession' (2008: 194). It not only secures white privilege but also generates a divisive, genocidal logic dividing Kanaka Maoli between 'fifty percenters' and 'less than fifties' and between those who are on and off-island—divisions that fracture the Hawaiian movement for sovereignty. Legislative proposals that are seen to protect Hawaiians in fact make them 'racialised beneficiaries' of the United States, limit full sovereignty claims in international law and extinguish land rights. Kauanui proposed an alternative vision based on relatedness, nurture and genealogy rather than race and blood—'forms of identification that serve to connect people to one another, to place, and to land' and to their responsibility for descendants (Kauanui 2008: 196).

In her second book, Kauanui (2018b) focused on how colonialism profoundly transformed Indigenous relations of gender and sexuality. She witnessed the confluence of America's twin imperial interests in Hawai'i, where capitalism and Christianity were tightly conjoined (for an extended reflection, see Jolly 2024). The American families who developed lucrative sugar plantations in the nineteenth century were often kin or descendants of those who had first brought the Protestant gospel from Boston. In Kauanui's analysis, the laws that privatised land, dispossessing and displacing most ordinary Hawaiians, while benefiting high-ranking *ali'i nui* such as Hawaiian royals, were mirrored by the gendered enclosures enforced by new laws of heteronormative, monogamous Christian marriage. The gender and sexual fluidity of ancient Hawai'i, embracing same-sex relations and gender-crossing, were outlawed. Paradoxically, it was high-ranking women, the royals of the Hawaiian Kingdom, who were the most prominent in promoting these new Christian ideals. This meant that women were not only subject to New England's laws of coverture in marriage, whereby their legal personhood was eclipsed by their husbands, but also increasingly pushed out of broader political influence.

This book, again, explored the perduring tension between models of Hawaiian Indigeneity as either a 'tribe' or a 'kingdom'. US Government initiatives to federally recognise Kanaka Maoli would render them a dependent, encompassed entity like Native American tribes on the continental US (thus occluding the way in which the United States illegally occupied a sovereign nation and eventually incorporated it as the fiftieth state). On the other hand, part of the Hawaiian sovereignty movement, in insisting on the illegal overthrow of the Hawaiian monarchy in the late nineteenth century, is yoked to the project of reinstating the kingdom. Kauanui's alternative model seeks to go beyond a statist nationalism, which, in her view, disavows the salience of deeper Indigeneity in relation to land, gender and sexuality.

Core to her analysis is a feminist reclamation of the fluidity of Indigenous gender and sexuality. Although committed to queer politics, Kauanui opposed the same-sex marriage law introduced in 2013 in Hawai'i as perpetuating settler colonialism by assimilating same-sex relations to the terms of a patriarchal, proprietorial male–female marriage. She celebrates a form of relationality vis-a-vis the land and sexuality that is not proprietary, a reciprocity embracing the love (*aloha*) between people, the land, the ocean and more-than-human kin. Against processes that eliminate or assimilate the 'native', suck the land dry and extract from and pollute the oceans, she celebrates an Indigenous corporeal, cultural and spiritual presence. Her book offers a history deep with insights for the present and horizons for the future, stressing the importance of a deep decoloniality that relies not just on interrogating introduced juridical and political regimes but also reclaiming Indigenous epistemologies and ontologies against their subjugation by Euro-American regimes of knowledge.

I turn finally to Kauanui's very first publication (1998), which poignantly evoked her own positionality. This is a sophisticated analysis of the gendered politics of the Hawaiian sovereignty movement and of the sensitive relations between Hawaiians 'at home' and those 'off-island' (like herself). It argues that diasporic Hawaiians, many of whom have left Hawai'i for reasons of economic survival, should be seen as an integral part of the complex coalition of sovereignty politics and not dismissed as dubious 'absentees' unless they become 'transplants' and 'come home'. She discerns not just the prominence of women in some parts of the sovereignty movement (such as Ka Lāhui Hawai'i), but also the use of feminised notions of place (derived from colonial discourses and tourist images of hula girls). She also highlights gendered conceptions of familial nurture and heterosexual reproductive relations that place a particular burden on Hawaiian women to increase the 'full-blood' proportion of the Indigenous Hawaiian population. She offers a new view of 'ohana ('nurture') that might more generously relate Hawaiians on and off-island in a political coalition less defined by a sclerotic nationalism and ultimately reliant on racialised classifications of persons or primordialist notions of 'taro roots'. Her arguments thus brought a diasporic feminist sensibility to Hawaiian sovereignty politics.[19]

Kauanui has engaged a disruptive decolonial feminist presence not just in her homeland of Hawai'i, but also in the mainland United States, especially in relation to Native Americans. As well as her public engagement with sovereignty politics in Hawai'i, she has been heavily involved with the broader politics of decolonisation and Indigeneity. Her ideas have been brought to wider public audiences through radio. From 2007 to 2013, she hosted a public affairs program called *Indigenous Politics: From Native New England and Beyond*, which was broadcast across 12 states and syndicated by the Pacifica Radio Network. Selected interviews from that show were published in a book (Kauanui 2018c) and the full set is available online (www.indigenouspolitics.com). She has also taught and broadcast on anarchism, originally in a program called *Horizontal Power Hour*,[20] and later *Anarchy On Air*.[21] Kauanui has thus established a reputation as a decolonial feminist scholar and has extended her reach as a public intellectual, heard by a broad audience in the United States and elsewhere. An interview with 'Time Talks' reveals the depth and breadth of her public engagement (see Kauanui 2018a, see Plate 6.2).

---

19 Her work on ancestral Oceanic same-sex relations, the effects of Christianity on sexuality and the problematic relations between Oceanic models and Western lesbian identities was similarly astute, especially in the context of debates in Hawai'i and the mainland United States about same-sex marriage.
20 *Horizontal Power Hour* website: horizontalpowerhour.wordpress.com/.
21 *Anarchy On Air* website: anarchyonairwesu.tumblr.com/.

Plate 6.2: Portrait of J. Kēhaulani Kauanui, 2025
Source: J. Kēhaulani Kauanui.

Teresia Kieuea Teaiwa (1969–2017)

Teresia Kieuea Teaiwa was born in 1969 in Honolulu, Hawai'i, where her Afro-American mother, Joan, from Washington, DC, and her Banaban father, John, met on the campus of the University of Hawai'i at Mānoa (UHM). They moved to live in Suva, Fiji, to where people from Banaba (Ocean Island) had been forcibly displaced during World War II, settling on the island of Rabi.[22] Teresia's personal and professional connections were dispersed across many islands of Oceania and the mainland United States. Ancestrally connected to Banaba and Tabiteuea in Kiribati, she lived at various times in Suva, Washington, Honolulu, Santa Cruz and Wellington and was a regular guest in many islands across the vast expanse of Oceania. After undergraduate years at Trinity College Washington, she completed her master's in Pacific history at UHM and went on to pursue her PhD in the History of Consciousness Program at the University of California Santa Cruz. She became a lecturer at the University of the South Pacific in Suva and, in 2000, was appointed as the inaugural program director of Pacific studies at Victoria University Wellington in Aotearoa New Zealand. There she married Sean Mallon (curator of the Pacific Collection at Te Papa Tongarewa, the National Museum of New Zealand). She bore two sons, Mānoa and Vaitoa. She died suddenly and prematurely of pancreatic cancer in March 2017. She was just forty-eight (see Plate 6.3).

Plate 6.3: Teresia K. Teaiwa in 2014 with a Marshall Islands stick chart for navigation, a gift from her mother that she used to reflect on both ancient heritage and Pacific studies pedagogy

Source: Robert Cross, used with permission.

---

22 That story is told in the book by Teresia's younger sister Katerina Teaiwa, *Consuming Ocean Island* (2014).

Teresia has been widely celebrated as 'a voracious and sensitive learner …
[for] her ability to illuminate connections while demonstrating fundamental
respect for the particularities of peoples, places and histories' (Teaiwa 2021:
xv–xvi). She is one of the most cited Indigenous Pacific scholars but was
also an inspiring and prize-winning teacher and mentor, a charismatic
speaker, a poet and playwright and an activist, who worked with women's
organisations and NGOs on issues of gender, militarism and the liberation
of still-colonised territories such as West Papua. Her scholarly writing
was expansive, much of it directed towards decolonising the curriculum
in teaching Pacific studies and on notions of Indigeneity. I here focus on
a series of essays assembled under the rubric of militarism and gender in
her posthumous collection, *Sweat and Salt Water* (Teaiwa 2021). The title
derives from her widely circulated quote: 'We sweat and cry salt water, so we
know the ocean is really in our blood' (Teaiwa 2021: xv).[23]

Her very first publication, 'Microwomen' (in Teaiwa 2021), focused on the
relationships between US colonialism and Micronesian women activists in
the Marshall Islands, Chuuk (one of the Federated States of Micronesia)
and Belau (now Palau). The United States is but one of a suite of colonising
powers in Micronesia including the Spanish, German and Japanese
empires. Yet, since the bloody battles of World War II, American 'liberation'
of many islands from the Japanese, the granting of the 'Trust Territory of
the Pacific islands' to the United States by the United Nations and the
subsequent nuclear explosions in the Marshall Islands, the United States
is the most entrenched empire in the region. The political status of these
three territories—Marshall Islands, Chuuk and Palau—differs but there is
a broad commonality of experience.

So, Teaiwa suggests that pervasive male chauvinism was encouraged by a
male-dominated colonial experience. White men failed to recognise women's
power in islands where both descent and land tenure were traced through
mothers. They assumed that because men dominated public speaking,
women's voices were mute, when in fact they exercised influence in more
subtle ways. Yet, Teaiwa analysed louder articulations of women's voices:
against pervasive alcohol abuse on Chuuk from 1976 to 1977 (they secured
prohibition) and when Belau women protested nuclear testing before the
US Senate and the United Nations in 1988. Marshallese women's embodied
experience of irradiation inspired women's antinuclear activism in the

---

23 This was first coined as an epigraph for the essay by Epeli Hau'ofa 'The Ocean in Us' (1998,
republished in Hau'ofa 2008).

region and globally. Teaiwa declared that 'so-called cultural traditions that bind women are no longer viable in a world that has permitted male egoism to run amok in the form of neocolonialism and nuclear militarism' (2021: 91). She suggested that the relentless force of colonialism had profoundly distorted gender roles and Micronesian men were the beneficiaries of US colonial power and were downplaying women's relevance in political affairs. She saw Micronesian women activists as trying to balance the power 'not only between the sexes but between nations' (Teaiwa 2021: 106). And that meant highlighting the 'vitally political aspects' of what are too often diminished as domestic concerns: nutrition, health and substance abuse.

Teaiwa's brilliant 1994 essay on bikini continued her preoccupation with gender and militarism in provocative and creative ways. She asked: 'What does the word bikini evoke for you? A woman in a two-piece bathing suit, or a site for nuclear-weapons testing? A bikini-clad woman invigorated by solar radiation, or Bikini Islanders cancer ridden from nuclear radiation?' (Teaiwa 2021: 110). This perverse conjunction derives from the moment in 1946 when French designer Louis Réard launched a sensational two-piece bathing suit to celebrate the Allied victory in World War II. Christened the 'bikini' after Bikini Atoll in the Marshall Islands, it was cast as the epitome of freedom and heterosexual release—the 'atom bomb of fashion'. Bikini Atoll had been selected by the US military as a favoured testing site due to its remote location, its climatic stability, its small population and the crucial fact that it was under US control. The Bikinians (about 170 people), who had recently been experiencing a drought and food shortages, were persuaded to relocate to Rongerik Atoll by appeals to their sense of Christian duty. Their military governor said this was for the 'good of mankind and to end all world wars' (Teaiwa 2021: 112). Two nuclear tests conducted in July 1946 subjected Bikinians, many other Marshall Islanders, US personnel and the surrounding land, sea and air to radiation, with devastating, long-lasting effects. Twenty further tests in the vicinity of Bikini and Enewetak atolls were conducted between 1946 and 1958.[24] Teaiwa highlighted the tragic

---

24 Teaiwa notes that in 1980 the United Nations estimated that more than 200 nuclear bombs and devices had been detonated in the Pacific, by the United States in the Marshall Islands, by France at Mururoa and Fangataufa atolls in French Polynesia (Ma'ohi Nui) and by the United Kingdom on Johnston Atoll (and later at Montebello Islands, Emu Field and Maralinga in Australia; see Maclellan 2017). As she cogently points out, this does not include nuclear missiles launched into the Pacific by the United States, Soviet Union and China. Although both the United States and France agreed to suspend nuclear tests in the Pacific in 1993, nuclear-powered and armed vessels continue to patrol the ocean. And, as I write, Australia is projected to join this contingent through the AUKUS (Australia, United Kingdom, United States) alliance.

history of displacement and inept relocations, the failure of the United States to appreciate the enduring intergenerational effects of radiation on people, other species and the environment and the paltry compensation offered for the physical, emotional, social and spiritual devastation wrought on Marshallese peoples (2021: 112–13).

As well as protesting this wrong, Teaiwa (2021: 110) forensically analysed how the bikini swimsuit fitted into a longer, broader history of the eroticisation of the islands, from early European male explorers, who evoked a Pacific paradise akin to a Greek golden age, to the contemporary 'tourist trivialisation of Pacific Islanders' experience and existence'.[25] The sexualisation and objectification of the female body through 'excessive visibility' distract from violence and colonial power, rendering it invisible. The bikini both marginalises 's/pacific' bodies and genericises female bodies. To unravel the bikini, Teaiwa used a compelling synthesis of Edward Said's theories of Orientalism, a critical appropriation of Sigmund Freud's analysis of the fetish in traumatic amnesia, Julia Kristeva's ideas of women as inside/outside society and Emily Apter on the commodification of exotic others. She suggested that the bikini 'manifests both a celebration and forgetting of nuclear power (Teaiwa 2021: 110) and 'simultaneously transcribes and erases the dispossession of the Bikini Islanders onto millions of female bodies' (p. 117).[26]

Undoing these perverse conjunctions and decolonising 's/pacific bodies' were for her intimately woven into women's activism in the Pacific—against nuclear testing, for independence and sovereignty and around concerns about health, the environment, substance abuse and domestic violence. She charted the movement of the Nuclear Free and Independent Pacific from the late 1970s through the 1980s.[27] She acknowledged the salience of women in Christian organisations in such activism, as did Dickson-Waiko, but considered that 'Christianity's role in the Pacific has certainly been ambiguous' (Teaiwa 2021: 118).

---

25 See my dialogue with Teresia's paper in 'From Point Venus to Bali Ha'i' in the volume *Sites of Desire/Economies of Pleasure* (Jolly 1997a).

26 In a later section of the essay, she depicts these largely Eurocentric theories as 'ornamental' to decolonial narratives that interrupt or disrupt hegemonic colonial stories (Teaiwa 2021: 120). Yet, elsewhere, in talking about writing and teaching, she acknowledges 'The Ancestors We Get to Choose: White Influences I Won't Deny' (Teaiwa 2021: 223–34), claiming not just Banaban and Pacific ancestors, teachers and scholars (including several white men), but also Jean-Jacques Rousseau, Thomas Hobbes, Antonio Gramsci and John Berger, all of whom she used in her classes.

27 Talei Mangioni is currently completing a PhD in Pacific Studies at The Australian National University on the history of the Nuclear Free and Independent Pacific.

Teaiwa's critical analysis of gender and militarism also played out in Fiji, the country where she grew up and which she loved fiercely—'full speed, no brakes' (2021: xv). In twin essays, she analysed both the centrality of Indigenous masculinity in Fiji's military and the situation of women soldiers.[28] In 'Articulated Cultures' (2021: 127), Teaiwa pointed to how, although British colonial authorities had ended Indigenous warfare by the late nineteenth century, militarism thrives in Fiji. At the time of her writing, it was 'the most militarized independent nation in the Pacific' (Teaiwa 2021: 127), with a large army and navy, deploying forces internally and externally, in wars such as those in Iraq and in UN peacekeeping operations in the Middle East. But, she insisted, militarism extended far beyond military institutions. For her, this was materialised in the gigantic concrete replicas of Indigenous war clubs (*i wau*) that frame the entry to state-recognised Fijian villages along the highway from Nadi Airport to the capital, Suva. And it was palpable in how the military intervened in Fijian politics: the Sitiveni Rabuka coups of 1987, the putsch of George Speight in 2000 and, after the time of her writing, the long period of Frank Bainimarama's rule, from 2006 to 2014 as military commander, and then as elected prime minister (2014–22), when autocratic rule persisted, the media was controlled and dissent was squashed.

Teaiwa analysed how in Fiji there was an 'articulation' between different cultures of military masculinity. Historically, it was manifest in ideals of self-sacrifice and loyalty to the British Crown, especially on the part of Indigenous (iTaukei) Fijian men, who dominate the military forces. Indo-Fijians, primarily working as imported, indentured labourers, were segregated from Indigenous Fijians by colonial policy and developed a far more critical stance on British colonialism. Militarism is also articulated with notions of service and respect to the Indigenous hierarchy of male chiefs on the part of a warrior class (*bati*), who were urged to protect the chief and his interests. Christianity, and especially Methodism, also articulated with the military: '[T]he institution is unquestioningly invested with an aura of Christian mission' (Teaiwa 2021: 136). Rabuka, an ordained Methodist minister, who orchestrated the first ethno-nationalist coup of 1987, proclaimed it as a

---

28 Her second essay examining the situation of Fijian women soldiers argues that, in exploring how they make a career 'in such an entrenched domain of men and masculinity as the military', context matters (Teaiwa 2021: 147). She compares the experiences of women soldiers over three distinct periods—late colonial, nationalist and neocolonial—and between being employed by the British Army and the Fijian Military Forces, with different rhythms of desegregation by race and gender. The overwhelming concerns of contemporary Fijian women soldiers whom she interviewed were, like their male counterparts, economic issues and securing their livelihoods.

'mission' from God. Militarised masculinity also pervades popular culture and sports, especially rugby, which is seen as a national game and a battle engaging predominantly Indigenous men. Players in both the codes of original rugby union and the later rugby league are portrayed as 'warriors' for the nation, performing Indigenous war dances before their matches. Political leaders have been tightly enmeshed with rugby—inaugural prime minister of independent Fiji, Ratu Sir Kamisese Mara, with union, Rabuka with league—and military men with both. Teaiwa asks how all these tightly articulated cultures of military masculinity might be disarticulated to value a different kind of Fijian man.[29]

In a later essay, Teaiwa returned to this concept of 'articulation' and its origins in British cultural studies, in the work of Stuart Hall and others. Whereas some tended to view articulation through the image of an articulated truck or train, from which loads or carriages could be unhooked, where there is no necessary or determined connection, following Hall and Grossberg, Teaiwa argued for a connection that was more determined, through 'lines of tendential force'. She posits an alternative image of the articulation of a limb in a human body.[30] Catalysed by extraordinary photographs of male military veterans who had suffered amputations but who desired to celebrate their survival, strength and sexuality, she analysed the situation of both Guam and Fiji in relation to what former US president Dwight D. Eisenhower described as the 'military-industrial complex' (hereinafter MIC) (see Teaiwa 2021: 167–68). In her vision, the MIC is held together not simply by mechanistic linkages but also by tendential forces analogous to those surrounding an articulated limb. Again, she wondered about disarticulation:

> So if the lines of tendential force that bind Guam and Fiji, respectively, to the MIC make it impossible to simply unhook them, does this mean that disarticulation must be as violent as the severing of a limb

---

29 Since Teaiwa's analysis, further research on Fijian masculinities has been done by Geir Henning Presterudstuen (2019). Jope Tarai (2016) offered a compelling critique of Indigenous Fijian ideas of manhood grounded in his own experience of gender violence in a TEDx talk called 'Re-Thinking the Fijian Man'. Romitesh Kant is exploring masculinities in Fijian politics in his PhD in Pacific Studies at The Australian National University. Rabuka was returned as Prime Minister in 2022.

30 'The articulated limb thus provides a more appropriate illustration, an analogy of articulation's engineering, the difficulty and trauma of disarticulation, and the literal possibilities of rearticulation. For while the basic ball and socket of a hip or shoulder joint, the hinge of a knee, or the pivot and hinge of an elbow may share the fundamental mechanics of that joint between a lorry/truck and trailer, or between the caboose and cars of a train, the ligaments, tendons, nerves and blood vessels that grow around an articulated joint make the possibility of disarticulation inevitably violent and traumatizing' (Teaiwa 2021: 167).

> by something like a mine blast … In Fiji and Guam, women's and feminist groups have long maintained a commitment to seeking demilitarized solutions to their island economies' development challenges … But the economic logic and the lure of employment and social mobility through military or militarized service is as difficult to resist in Fiji as on Guam. (Teaiwa 2021: 178)

This disturbing dystopic vision of Pacific geopolitics came from a woman who was not just a scholar but also a creative poet and playwright. She early co-authored a satirical play with Vilsoni Hereniko, *Last Virgin in Paradise: A Serious Comedy* (1993), and throughout her life she created poetry, which was published in book form (Teaiwa 1995) and on CDs (Teaiwa with Figiel 2000, Teaiwa 2008) and through her publishing imprint, Fiery Canoe Productions. Her poetry was often forthright, often playful and sometimes offered more-than-human perspectives—for example, that of a flying fish, which can see two horizons at once. From her adolescent years, growing up amid the heady politics of Suva, Teaiwa was passionately engaged in politics in and beyond the academy—as president of the Pacific History Association, as a participant in the Nuclear-Free and Independent Pacific movement, in several women's organisations, publishing on her 'Microwomen' blog and in advocacy for West Papuan independence (Manson 2017). Her decolonial feminist scholarship and political practice were so deeply entangled as to be seamless.

Some comparative reflections

What do we see when we combine the perspectives of these three remarkable women? How might we adjudge their work as both decolonial and feminist?

They all see colonialism as profoundly changing Indigenous gender relations—diminishing the influence and political agency that women had precolonially (especially in matrilineal places) and increasing male dominance through the new regimes of masculinist state politics and modern militaries with global connections. They offer more diverse views on Christianity. Although highlighting the problematic Christian, colonial introduction of gendered domains of public and domestic life, Dickson-Waiko celebrates how Christian women's groups offered a foundation for women's empowerment. Kauanui, rather, sees the imposition of monogamous heterosexual marriage and ideals of a Christian home as ultimately sequestering women more firmly in family and outlawing the gender and sexual fluidity of precolonial

Hawai'i. Teaiwa celebrates the Christian dimension of women's activism against militarism and nuclear imperialism and for independence and better health and nutrition but suggests that Christianity's impact in the Pacific has 'certainly been ambiguous' (2021: 118).

There are, as earlier intimated, important differences between these three scholars in how they are situated in the geopolitics of the Pacific. This is not so much because they are associated with the three conventional subregions of Melanesia (Dickson-Waiko), Polynesia (Kauanui) and Micronesia (Teaiwa), but because they are differently situated in terms of the sovereignty of states and thus different parameters for decolonisation. Anne Dickson-Waiko, born of Milne Bay parents in Port Moresby, was working and writing in the period after Papua New Guinea became a sovereign state, although clearly neocolonial influences still permeate its politics—through the corrupt regimes of the extractive industries of mining and logging and through the practices of development agencies, especially from the erstwhile colonial *masta*,[31] Australia. Her activist engagement in women's issues extended to meetings of the United Nations and reports for many development institutions as a representative of an independent nation. Kauanui, an 'off-island' Hawaiian, born and raised in California, firmly identifies as Kanaka Maoli but eschews the rival models of state nationalism for her homeland. Her activist politics are directed to the legitimation of Indigenous gender and sexual fluidity in her ancestral home and to coalitions of Indigenous politics with Native Americans. Through public appearances and radio broadcasts, she promotes an anarchistic vision of politics outside and beyond the state. Teaiwa, born in Honolulu and raised in Suva, had wide diasporic experience as a displaced Banaban having lived in both an independent state (Fiji) and settler colonies (the United States and Aotearoa New Zealand). Her international feminist activism was with grassroots organisations and NGOs, rather than through the state-based UN system. Significantly, *all* the women express doubts about the role of the state in women's empowerment. They did not see the state as the sole engine of social change and equality but rather saw it as often inimical to women's interests, dissonant from grassroots women's movements and a major driver of enhancing masculinist and militarised power.

---

31 This is a Tok Pisin word for master or boss.

Importantly, the education of both Kauanui and Teaiwa in the United States and especially their graduate work at the prestigious History of Consciousness Program at the University of California Santa Cruz afforded access to radical scholars such as James Clifford, Donna Haraway and Angela Davis. They were significantly influenced by Euro-American theory. Teaiwa (2021: 223 ff.) expressly wrote about 'white influences I won't deny', including Jean-Jacques Rousseau and Antonio Gramsci, as well as white American feminists such as Haraway and Cynthia Enloe. She regularly spoke at international feminist conferences and published in feminist journals. Kauanui did her first degree in women's studies, publishes in feminist journals and is in conversation with white feminist anthropologists such as Sally Engle Merry and Haraway as well as Oceanic and Indigenous feminists. Teaiwa and Kauanui acknowledged their mutual influence and collaborated in publication. Given their education in the United States, they have had broader access to global networks to promote and publish their work. A generation earlier, Dickson-Waiko had graduate experience in both the United States and Australia but her work was more in tune with the empirical tone of much Pacific history and political science, although clearly influenced by the inspirational examples and analyses of feminist movements in the Philippines and beyond in what was then called the 'Third World'.

Significantly, more so than Dickson-Waiko, Kauanui and Teaiwa wrote within a genealogy of decolonial scholarship in Pacific studies, such as the pioneering work of Epeli Hau'ofa (1994, 2008) and Linda Tuhiwai Smith (2013). As such, they expressly challenged the historically sedimented structures of colonialism and how knowledge is a crucial part of colonial subjugation. They dismantled the imaginaries and conventional portrayals of region, race, gender and sexuality and celebrated alternative Indigenous ontologies, epistemologies and methodologies in research. None of these three scholars draws on the decolonial theories emanating from Latin America and the Caribbean propounded by Arturo Escobar (1995, for example), Walter Mignolo and Catherine Walsh (2018, for example) or even the feminist scholar Maria Lugones (2021). Lugones reconceptualises the intimate relations of race and gender and shows how a colonial gender regime based on a heterosexual and hierarchical binary between men and women was naturalised in diverse colonial formations in Africa and North America (2021). Their complex analyses distilled above suggest diverse Indigenous binaries of women and men across Oceania—some more diarchical, some more hierarchical—but reveal how Euro-American colonialism everywhere created far more hierarchical and heteropatriarchal regimes of power.

Moreover, their analyses resonate beyond Oceania, beyond the Pacific. The region is too often seen as irretrievably specific, as indelibly local in relation to human universals that are typically seen as emanating from the Global North. As Teaiwa (2021: 110 ff.) has dubbed it, with characteristic wit and perspicacity, 's/pacific'. There are important connections between the arguments advanced by these three women and the work of those committed to decolonising feminisms and developing Indigenous feminisms in settler colonies such as the United States and Australia (for example, Arvin et al. 2013; Anderson 2021).

Dickson-Waiko, Kauanui and Teaiwa were/are arguably feminist, but there are differences in their willing embrace of the 'f-word'. Given the way in which 'modern' women were lampooned in independent Papua New Guinea and second-wave feminism was portrayed as a white, foreign intrusion, Dickson-Waiko was more reticent in public about such an alignment in her home country. But, as we can see, her scholarly writing evinces a strong critique of patriarchy in Papua New Guinea—both before and after independence— and she expressly celebrates the 'Indigenous feminism' of grassroots women's Christian groups. Moreover, she lamented the disconnection between this and the state-based projects of gender equality in which she herself participated, both within Papua New Guinea and beyond, in meetings of the United Nations. Kauanui and Teaiwa are more avowedly feminist but both distance themselves from state-based solutions. Kauanui critiques the autocracy of state nationalisms and increasingly advances anarchist values and political projects. Teaiwa's feminism discerns a pervasive masculinist militarism in the formation of states across Oceania and, rather, engages feminist social movements working outside the state system. In Fiji, where she grew up, there was an early and easier embrace of the 'f-word', although in creating feminist coalitions, she espoused a politics of 'fluidarity' rather than solidarity, recognising profound differences and inequalities as well as commonalities between women.[32]

---

32 Nicole George (2012) offers a fine history of feminism in Fiji. At a meeting reviewing the Australian Department of Foreign Affairs and Trade's Pacific Women Shaping Pacific Development program held in Suva in 2016, which both Teresia Teaiwa and I attended, the differences between identification with the word 'feminist' by women delegates from Fiji and its rejection by those from Papua New Guinea was clear. In that year, the regional Pacific Feminist Forum was inaugurated in Suva—significantly, welcoming trans women. In November 2022, the West Papuan Feminist Forum was founded by Esther Haluk and others, which combines women's concerns with issues of structural violence, environmental destruction and the marginalisation of Indigenous Papuans in the context of Indonesian colonial occupation.

Although these authors do not allude to the notion of intersectionality (as developed by Kimberlé Crenshaw 1991; Collins and Bilge 2016; and others), although they were likely aware of it, all stress how women are divided by class and by race. Kauanui's history of Hawai'i reveals the profound differences between high-ranking and low-ranking women in the history of colonial Christianity in her ancestral archipelago. Dickson-Waiko talks directly of the emergent class differences created by colonialism and modern capitalist development in Papua New Guinea, through the gap between *ol grassroots mama* and *ol save meri*, implicating herself in that divide. Teaiwa is alert to the privileges that come with education and material wealth—between women in rural and urban Fiji, for instance—and how global inequalities structure the relations between Oceanic peoples living in the islands and Oceanic diasporas within rich countries such as the United States, Australia and Aotearoa New Zealand.

But the divisions of race loom larger for them and influence how they appraise 'feminism' where that carries a presumption of being 'white'.[33] There has been a decades-long discussion of whether and how far the 'f-word' is embraced by women across Oceania. In an early assessment, stellar scholar and poet Selina Tusitala Marsh (1998) wondered whether feminism was a 'maligned overstayer' or a 'model citizen' in Oceania. She concluded that

> for some women of the Pacific, feminism has become and is becoming a worthy seafarer and a knowledgeable traveller … [F]eminism can voyage the cultural and historical specificities of the 10,000 islands in the Pacific, travel through the veins of Pacific oppression without rendering blanket victim status and ignoring contradictions and potentially subversive strategies. (Marsh 1998: 677)

I suggest the scholarship and activist practice of Dickson-Waiko, Kauanui and Teaiwa bear witness to this prescient prophecy. Critical to its successful localisation was, Marsh argued, the acknowledgement of the predominantly collective or relational values of Oceanic peoples.

As we have seen, Dickson-Waiko sees the individualism of Western feminism[34] as inappropriate for the PNG context, where relational values perdure, especially for women, who, unlike men, are rarely seen as individual citizen-

---

33 Sara Ahmed, in her stellar book *Living a Feminist Life* (2017), challenges this travelling story of feminism as an imperial gift, suggesting that she absorbed feminist values from her Pakistani aunties.
34 As I observed earlier in this chapter, I do not totally accept this characterisation of Western feminism. It may be more accurate as a depiction of liberal feminism, but in other channels of 'whitestream feminism' there has been a celebration of relational values and collectivity in contrast to what is seen as expressly masculinist individualism. However, this is a recurring critique made by women across Oceania.

subjects. Kauanui celebrates the relational values of Kanaka Maoli culture, not just in living human relations but also in kinship with the cosmos, with ancestors and more-than-human kin, other species and the formations of land and ocean. In both her scholarly writing and her poetry, Teaiwa celebrates collective, ancestral values connecting humans to a wider world of kin and laments how nuclear geopolitics and the perverse conjunctions of mili-tourism have ravaged Oceania. Echoing others, all three see relational rather than individual values as fundamental to their Oceanic identity and thus divergent from hegemonic Western feminisms.

We might, then, better listen to and learn from nuanced gendered histories and decolonial feminist insights like those offered by Dickson-Waiko, Kauanui and Teaiwa. Too often Australians, including Australian feminists, have presumed they have the answers to make lives better for women in Oceania—by ensuring there are more women in parliaments and formal politics, by encouraging women's economic empowerment through entrepreneurial programs and through redressing the pervasive problems of gender violence. All these are noble aims. But, as those critically involved in aid and development programs know so well, improving women's lives in Oceania cannot simply follow a white, imperial script. We must eschew the perduring salvationism of white women 'saving our sisters'—albeit from the perils of paganism, of poverty, of gender and sexual violence or, most recently, of the climate crisis (see Jolly 2019). Celebrating women's agency and potential for political leadership in Oceania means respecting the values and priorities articulated by women themselves, in diverse and changing contexts. This entails a position of humility rather than the hubris that too often accompanies those of us from countries with greater material wealth and geopolitical influence, such as Australia. It also entails a recognition that Australian feminisms have not been so monolithically white and middle class as some histories suggest. From the 1970s, some Indigenous and migrant working women were engaged in feminist struggles in Australia and, over several decades, the influence of Black and Latina women in the United States and postcolonial scholars from Asia has profoundly shaped Australian feminist thought and practice. Today the ethos and practice of intersectionality suffuse Australian feminisms at home and hopefully are increasing in partnerships of practice with women across Oceania.

References

Abu-Lughod, Lila. 2013. *Do Muslim Women Need Saving?* Boston: Harvard University Press. doi.org/10.4159/9780674726338.

Ahmed, Sara. 2017. *Living a Feminist Life*. Durham: Duke University Press.

Anderson, Kim. 2021. 'Multi-Generational Indigenous Feminisms: From F Word to What IFs.' In *Routledge Handbook of Critical Indigenous Studies*, edited by Brendan Hokowhitu, Aileen Moreton-Robinson, Linda Tuhiwai-Smith, Chris Andersen, and Steve Larkin. London: Taylor & Francis.

Arrow, Michelle. 2023. *Women and Whitlam: Revisiting the Revolution*. Sydney: NewSouth Publishing.

Arvin, Maile, Eve Tuck, and Angie Morrill. 2013. 'Decolonizing Feminism: Challenging Connections between Settler Colonialism and Heteropatriarchy.' *Feminist Formations* 25, no. 1: 8–34. doi.org/10.1353/ff.2013.0006.

Baker, Kerryn. 2019. *Pacific Women in Politics: Gender Quota Campaigns in the Pacific Islands*. Honolulu: University of Hawai'i Press. doi.org/10.2307/j.ctv7r42qp.

Banivanua Mar, Tracey. 2016. *Decolonisation and the Pacific: Indigenous Globalisation and the Ends of Empire*. Cambridge: Cambridge University Press. doi.org/10.1017/CBO9781139794688.

Choi, Hyaeweol, and Margaret Jolly, eds. 2014. *Divine Domesticities: Christian Paradoxes in Asia and the Pacific*. Canberra: ANU Press. doi.org/10.22459/DD.10.2014.

Collins, Patricia Hill. 2012. *On Intellectual Activism*. Philadelphia: Temple University Press.

Collins, Patricia Hill, and Sirma Bilge. 2016. *Intersectionality*. Cambridge: Polity Press.

Crenshaw, Kimberlé. 1991. 'Mapping the Margins: Intersectionality, Identity Politics, and Violence Against Women of Colour.' *Stanford Law Review* 43, no. 6: 1241–99. doi.org/10.2307/1229039.

Dickson-Waiko, Anne. 1994. '"A Woman's Place is in the Struggle": Feminism and Nationalism in the Philippines.' PhD diss., The Australian National University.

Dickson-Waiko, Anne. 2000. 'Women, Individual Human Rights, Community Rights: Tensions within the Papua New Guinea State.' In *Women's Rights and Human Rights: International Historical Perspectives*, edited by Katie Holmes and Marilyn Lake, 49–70. Gordonsville: Palgrave Macmillan. doi.org/10.1057/9780333977644_4.

Dickson-Waiko, Anne. 2003. 'The Missing Rib: Mobilizing Church Women for Change in Papua New Guinea.' *Oceania* 74, nos 1–2 [SI]: 98–119. doi.org/10.1002/j.1834-4461.2003.tb02838.x.

Dickson-Waiko, Anne. 2013. 'Women, Nation and Decolonisation in Papua New Guinea.' *The Journal of Pacific History* 48, no. 2: 177–93. doi.org/10.1080/00223344.2013.802844.

Diaz, Vicente M., and J. Kēhaulani Kauanui. 2001. 'Native Pacific Cultural Studies on the Edge.' *The Contemporary Pacific* 13, no. 2: 315–41. scholarspace.manoa.hawaii.edu/server/api/core/bitstreams/7b37362e-31e4-444b-bf3d-12f9841ed864/content.

Escobar, Arturo. 1995. *Encountering Development: The Making and Unmaking of the Third World*. Princeton: Princeton University Press.

George, Nicole. 2012. *Situating Women: Gender Politics and Circumstance in Fiji*. Canberra: ANU E Press. doi.org/10.22459/SW.11.2012.

Hau'ofa, Epeli. 1994. 'Our Sea of Islands.' *The Contemporary Pacific* 6, no. 1: 148–61. hdl.handle.net/10125/12960.

Hau'ofa, Epeli. 2008. *We are the Ocean: Selected Works*. Honolulu: University of Hawai'i Press.

Jolly, Margaret. 1991a. 'The Politics of Difference: Feminism, Colonialism and Decolonisation in Vanuatu.' In *Intersexions: Gender/Class/Culture/Ethnicity*, edited by Gillian Bottomley, Marie de Lepervanche, and Jeannie Martin, 52–74. London: Routledge. doi.org/10.4324/9781003116165-4.

Jolly, Margaret. 1991b. '"To Save the Girls for Brighter and Better Lives": Presbyterian Missions and Women in the South of Vanuatu: 1848–1870.' *The Journal of Pacific History* 26, no. 1: 27–48. doi.org/10.1080/00223349108572645.

Jolly, Margaret. 1992. 'Partible Persons and Multiple Authors (Contribution to Book Review Forum on Marilyn Strathern's *The Gender of the Gift*).' *Pacific Studies* 15, no. 1: 137–49.

Jolly, Margaret. 1994a. 'Colonizing Women: The Maternal Body and Empire.' In *Feminism and the Politics of Difference*, edited by Sneja Gunew and Anna Yeatman, 103–27. London: Routledge. doi.org/10.4324/9780429039010-7.

Jolly, Margaret. 1994b. *Women of the Place: Kastom, Colonialism and Gender in Vanuatu.* Reading: Harwood Academic Publishers.

Jolly, Margaret. 1997a. 'From Point Venus to Bali Ha'i: Eroticism and Exoticism in Representations of the Pacific.' In *Sites of Desire/Economies of Pleasure: Sexualities in Asia and the Pacific*, edited by Lenore Manderson and Margaret Jolly, 99–122, 303–6. Chicago: University of Chicago Press.

Jolly, Margaret. 1997b. 'Woman–Nation–State in Vanuatu: Women as Signs and Subjects in the Discourses of *Kastom*, Modernity and Christianity.' In *Narratives of Nation in the South Pacific*, edited by Ton Otto and Nicholas Thomas, 133–62. Amsterdam: Harwood Academic Publishers.

Jolly, Margaret. 2003. 'Epilogue.' In *Women's Groups and Everyday Modernity in Melanesia*, edited by Bronwen Douglas. *Oceania* 74, nos 1–2 [SI]: 134–47.

Jolly, Margaret. 2005. 'Beyond the Horizon? Nationalisms, Feminisms, and Globalization in the Pacific.' In *Ethnohistory* 52, no. 1 [SI]: 137–66. doi.org/10.1215/00141801-52-1-137.

Jolly, Margaret. 2007. 'Imagining Oceania: Indigenous and Foreign Representations of a Sea of Islands.' *The Contemporary Pacific* 19, no. 2: 508–45. doi.org/10.1353/cp.2007.0054.

Jolly, Margaret. 2019. 'Engendering the Anthropocene in Oceania: Fatalism, Resilience, Resistance.' *Cultural Studies Review* 25, no. 2: 172–95. doi.org/10.5130/csr.v25i2.6888.

Jolly, Margaret. 2024. 'Oceanic Sexualities: Persistence, Change, Resistance.' In *The Cambridge World History of Sexualities*, edited by Merry E. Wiesner-Hanks and Mathew Kuefler, 201–27. Cambridge: Cambridge University Press. doi.org/10.1017/9781108896016.011.

Jolly, Margaret, and Martha Macintyre, eds. 1989. *Family and Gender in the Pacific: Domestic Contradictions and the Colonial Impact.* Cambridge: Cambridge University Press. doi.org/10.1017/CBO9781139084864.

Kabutaulaka, Tarcisius. 2015. 'Re-Presenting Melanesia: Ignoble Savages and Melanesian Alter-Natives.' *The Contemporary Pacific* 27, no. 1: 110–45. doi.org/10.1353/cp.2015.0027.

Kaniku, Anne Nealibo. 1989. 'Those Massim Women.' In *Papua New Guinea: A Century of Colonial Impact 1884–1984,* edited by Sione Latukefu, 357–76. Port Moresby: National Research Institute & University of Papua New Guinea Press.

Kauanui, J. Kēhaulani. 1998. 'Off-Island Hawaiians "Making" Ourselves at "Home": A (Gendered) Contradiction in Terms?' *Women's Studies International Forum* 21, no. 6: 681–93. doi.org/10.1016/S0277-5395(98)00081-8.

Kauanui, J. Kēhaulani. 2005. 'The Multiplicity of Hawaiian Sovereignty Claims and the Struggle for Meaningful Autonomy.' *Comparative American Studies* 3, no. 3: 283–99. doi.org/10.1177/1477570005055982.

Kauanui, J. Kēhaulani. 2007–13. *Indigenous Politics: From Native New England and Beyond.* Audio Archive. [Online]. www.indigenouspolitics.com.

Kauanui, J. Kēhaulani. 2008. *Hawaiian Blood: Colonialism and the Politics of Sovereignty and Indigeneity.* Durham: Duke University Press. doi.org/10.1215/9780822391494.

Kauanui, J. Kēhaulani. 2018a. 'J. Kēhaulani Kauanui on Hawaiian Sovereignty, Sexuality, Anarchism, and Decolonization.' *Time Talks: History, Politics, Music, and Art*, [Podcast], 16 December. timetalks.libsyn.com/j-khaulani-kauanui-on-hawaiian-sovereignty-sexuality-anarchism-and-decolonization.

Kauanui, J. Kēhaulani. 2018b. *Paradoxes of Hawaiian Sovereignty: Land, Sex and the Colonial Politics of State Nationalism.* Durham: Duke University Press. doi.org/10.1215/9780822371960.

Kauanui, J. Kēhaulani. 2018c. *Speaking of Indigenous Politics: Conversations with Activists, Scholars and Tribal Leaders.* Minneapolis: University of Minnesota Press. doi.org/10.5749/j.ctv8j71d.

Keimelo, Cathy. 2019. 'Anne Nealibo Dickson-Waiko: Pioneering Gender Academic.' *PNG Attitude: Keith Jackson and Friends*, [Blog], 30 March. Noosa. www.pngattitude.com/2019/03/anne-nealibo-dickson-waiko-pioneering-gender-academic.html.

Lawrence, Salmah Eva-Lina. 2018. 'Speaking for Ourselves: Kwato Perspectives on Matriliny and Missionisation.' PhD diss., The Australian National University.

Lepani, Katherine. 2012. *Islands of Love, Islands of Risk: Culture and HIV in the Trobriands.* Nashville: Vanderbilt University Press. doi.org/10.2307/j.ctv16759zt.

Lugones, Maria. 2021 [2005]. 'The Coloniality of Gender.' In *Decolonial Feminism in Abya Yala: Caribbean, Meso and South American Contributions and Challenges*, edited by Yuderkys Espinos Miñoso, Maria Lugones, and Nelson Maldonado Torres. Lanham: Rowman & Littlefield.

Maclellan, Nic. 2017. *Grappling with the Bomb: Britain's Pacific H-Bomb Tests.* Canberra: ANU Press. doi.org/10.22459/GB.09.2017.

Manson, Bess. 2017. 'A Life Story—Dr Teresia Teaiwa, "Leading Light" of the Pacific, Dies, 48.' *Stuff*, [New Zealand], 22 April. www.stuff.co.nz/national/education/91548606/a-life-story–dr-teresia-teaiwa-leading-light-of-the-pacific-dies-48.

Marsh, Selina Tusitala. 1998. 'Migrating Feminisms: Maligned Overstayer or Model Citizen?' *Women's Studies International Forum* 21, no. 6: 665–80. doi.org/10.1016/S0277-5395(98)00080-6.

Mignolo, Walter D., and Catherine E. Walsh. 2018. *On Decoloniality: Concepts, Analytics, Praxis*. Durham: Duke University Press. doi.org/10.1215/9780822371779.

Molisa, Grace Mera. 1983. *Black Stone*. Port Vila: Black Stone Publications.

Molisa, Grace Mera. 1987. *Colonised People*. Port Vila: Black Stone Publications.

Moreton-Robinson, Aileen. 2020. *Talkin' Up to the White Woman: Aboriginal Women and Feminism*. 20th anniversary edn. Brisbane: University of Queensland Press.

Narokobi, Bernard. 1983 [1980]. *The Melanesian Way*. Boroko: Institute of Papua New Guinea Studies.

Presterudstuen, Geir Henning. 2019. *Performing Masculinity: Body, Self and Identity in Modern Fiji*. London: Bloomsbury Academic. doi.org/10.5040/9781350043367.

Randall, Angus. 2022. 'Papua New Guinea Population Could Hit 17 Million.' *The World Today*, [ABC Radio], 5 December. www.abc.net.au/radio/programs/worldtoday/papua-new-guinea-population-could-hit-17-million/101734306.

Ritchie, Jonathan. 2018. 'Anne Nealibo Dickson-Waiko (1950–2018).' *The Journal of Pacific History* 53, no. 3: 330–33. doi.org/10.1080/00223344.2018.1505213.

Rosi, Pamela. 1991. 'Papua New Guinea's New Parliament House: A Contested National Symbol.' *The Contemporary Pacific* 3, no. 2: 289–324.

Sepoe, Orovu. 2002. 'To Make a Difference: Realities of Women's Participation in Papua New Guinea Politics.' *Development Bulletin* 59: 39–42.

Smith, Linda Tuhiwai. 2013. *Decolonizing Methodologies: Research and Indigenous Peoples*. London: Zed Books.

Strathern, Marilyn. 1990. *The Gender of the Gift: Problems with Women and Problems with Society in Melanesia*. Oakland: University of California Press.

Tarai, Jope. 2016. 'Re-Thinking the Fijian Man.' *TEDx Talks*, 31 May. www.youtube.com/watch?v=qh_ClbaSVTs.

Teaiwa, Katerina Martina. 2014. *Consuming Ocean Island: Stories of People and Phosphate from Banaba*. Bloomington: Indiana University Press.

Teaiwa, Teresia K. 1995. *Searching for Nei Nim'anoa*. Suva: Mana Publications.

Teaiwa, Teresia K. 2008. *I Can See Fiji: Poetry and Sound*. [CD]. Wellington: Fiery Canoe Productions.

Teaiwa, Teresia Kieuea. 2021. *Sweat and Salt Water: Selected Works*. Compiled and edited by Katerina Teaiwa, April K. Henderson, and Terence Wesley-Smith. Honolulu: University of Hawai'i Press.

Teaiwa, Teresia K., with Sia Figiel. 2000. *Terenesia: Amplified Poetry and Songs by Teresia Teaiwa and Sia Figiel*. [CD]. Honolulu: Hawai'i Dub Machine and 'Elepaio Press.

Wardlow, Holly. 2006. *Wayward Women: Sexuality and Agency in a New Guinea Society*. Oakland: University of California Press. doi.org/10.1525/978052093 8977.

Wardlow, Holly. 2014. 'Paradoxical Intimacies: The Christian Creation of the Huli Domestic Sphere.' In *Divine Domesticities: Christian Paradoxes in Asia and the Pacific*, edited by Hyaeweol Choi and Margaret Jolly, 325–44. Canberra: ANU Press. doi.org/10.22459/DD.10.2014.12.

Weiner, Annette. 1976. *Women of Value, Men of Renown: New Perspectives on Trobriand Exchange*. Austin: University of Texas Press.

West Papua Daily. 2022. 'Papuan Women Talk About Papuan Women at the West Papua Feminist Forum.' *West Papua Daily*, 29 November. en.jubi.id/papuan-women-talk-about-papuan-women-at-the-west-papua-feminist-forum/.

Zimmer-Tamakoshi, Laura. 1993. 'Nationalism and Sexuality in Papua New Guinea.' *Pacific Studies* 16, no. 4: 61–97.

7

Decolonising the Stories of Women Political Leaders in Asia and the Pacific

Camilla Batalibasi, Chandy Eng, Donna Makini,
Vani Nailumu and Geraldine Valei, with Sonia Palmieri
and Melissa MacLean[1]

Since the United Nations' First World Conference on Women in 1975, the situation of women in political leadership around the world has been carefully monitored, researched and championed. With increasingly powerful normative intent, international organisations have made publicly available databases of a limited range of indicators, including the number of seats in national parliaments held by women and the numbers of women heads of state/government, speakers and ministers.

Academic and practitioner researchers use these data as a starting point in the discussion of women's contribution to political leadership at global, regional and national levels. These data have allowed a community of researchers to explain the progress and setbacks of women—on an aggregate scale—in the political sphere, and they have allowed for international comparisons. A key insight from these data has been that while women have increased their share of seats in various decision-making forums such as parliaments

---

1   The authors gratefully acknowledge the generous and instructive comments of Tanya Jakimow.

and executive governments,[2] the pace of change has been incredibly slow,[3] and women's presence at the decision-making table cannot yet be taken for granted in most countries around the world.

These insights apply to the relatively under-researched regions of Asia and the Pacific. These regions have seen extremely limited change in the proportion of women in political leadership: both have remained in the bottom half of the Inter-Parliamentary Union (IPU) regional classification of women in national parliament,[4] and the rate of increase over the past 10 years is significantly slower than in other world regions. That said, less research has focused on the *experience* of women political leaders in Pacific Island countries (see Baker et al. 2020) and in some parts of Asia. Of course, this relates to the fact that there are simply fewer women *to research* (Vijeyarasa 2022). Yet, the much slower rate of progress in these regions raises interesting questions about not only why progress is so incremental, but also how to capture—in culturally meaningful ways—the lived experience of the few women who reach the high echelons of political power.

On this, we consider that the way research is undertaken—that is, the research process itself—can contribute to social change. An increasingly prominent cohort of researchers has suggested that a decolonialist feminist approach to research design and practice has the potential for significant emancipatory impact (Smith 1999; Leavy and Harris 2018; Tickner 2014; Harding 1987). Specifically, research partnerships between academics and practitioners across the majority and minority worlds can support a more nuanced understanding of critical problems in context and can suggest culturally appropriate solutions to address them (Greenwood and Levin 2007). Underpinning this approach is a commitment to certain forms of collaboration. In development contexts, collaborative research has been explained as 'a way of working that provides the greatest potential to create

---

2 The global average of women in national parliaments has more than doubled in the past 25 years, from almost 12 per cent in 1997 (when the Inter-Parliamentary Union began publishing monthly data on its website) to just under 27 per cent in 2023 (IPU 2023).

3 The IPU's yearly analysis of women in national parliaments has reported the annual rate of change since 2004. The past few years have seen minimal change in women's share of seats in national parliaments. Indeed, in 2015, the headline of the analysis referred to a 'plateau' in the numbers (IPU 2015).

4 After a decade of being the region with the lowest proportion of women in national parliaments, the Pacific was replaced with the Middle East and North Africa in July 2022, following a general election in Australia that resulted in an increase of women MPs in both houses. Without the inclusion of Australia and Aotearoa New Zealand in the regional classification, however, the Pacific has the fewest women MPs in the world (IPU 2023).

real changes ... [and] generate evidence which is usable and contributes to development effectiveness, and to inform future development of policy and practice' (Winterford 2017: 4).

While there is considerable promise of positive outcomes, this kind of research can also be fraught with challenges and risks. These include hurdles in execution, resource limitations and, importantly, challenges related to colonialist frames of inquiry and analysis that may be built into traditional research practices (Jakimow 2020; Winterford 2017; Leege and McMillan 2016; Roche and Kelly 2014; Schaaf 2015; Thom and Cope 2016). For this reason, we suggest it is worth reflecting on the experiences of those involved in research that explicitly aims to decolonialise knowledge generation and understanding.

This chapter is structured as follows. First, we outline our approach to researching women's lived experience of political leadership. We describe the research projects on which we have worked and the process by which we collectively reflected on this experience for this chapter—that is, our autoethnography. We present our reflections on whom we were able to research, how we undertook our research, what we researched, who we are in the research relationship and why we do this research. We find that women political leaders, and particularly the most senior women leaders in our countries, are hard to access for both institutional and personal reasons. They can be suspicious of researchers—and potentially more suspicious of local researchers—when they feel they will be judged harshly or placed in particularly vulnerable situations. We consider that where we can find physically and emotionally safe spaces in which to interview women politicians, we can deftly navigate the cultural cues that non-local researchers might not pick up on. We can see the 'masks' that women wear in their political settings—masks that aim to deflect from the constant sense of being observed. We also noticed that we could elicit new stories from women political leaders, sometimes divulged in the culturally appropriate silences that we maintained—stories of discomfort that tell us different answers to those of the usual questions asked of these women, and which have not yet filled the pages of history. We are not passive in these storytelling processes; we are conscious of our own positions of power in relation to these women and our responsibility, within our own communities, to keep the momentum towards gender equality alive.

Decolonising research through practice and voice

While women are underrepresented in political leadership globally, there are serious gaps in data collection that make it difficult to understand comprehensively women's experience in leadership, particularly in some of the countries of Asia and the Pacific (Buvinic et al. 2014). Numerical data on women's participation at local and subnational levels, for example, are extremely difficult to find for Pacific Island countries and are therefore notoriously underreported.[5] These data collection gaps point to two things: first, there has been an overreliance on the numbers of women elected representatives to tell the story of women's political leadership; and second, the true extent of women's leadership has not yet been captured.

Accepting that the full story of women's political leadership in Asia and the Pacific has not yet been told, we suggest that there is also a need to consider new approaches to capturing that story. Moreover, alternative approaches must be mindful of the complex and often culturally and historically informed gendered barriers to women's election and political appointment. In our view, decolonising the stories of women's political leadership involves two things: first, feminist collaborative research practice; and second, privileging local experience and usually unheard voices.

Collaborations between local and non-local researchers

On our first approach, we are mindful that feminist collaborative research is not yet ubiquitous across all the social sciences (see Jenkins et al. 2020). It represents an 'innovative' methodology in political science, but even in development studies, we still hear calls for more research that uncovers new stories and contributes to the strengthening of all partners' research and analysis skills to improve understanding of varied contexts. The work of J. Ann Tickner (2014: 92) in defining feminist research has been a useful starting point for us. Tickner identifies four main elements: a deep concern with *which research questions are asked and why*; the production of research

---

5   In 2023, UN Women's 'Women in Local Government' website, dedicated to women's representation in local government (localgov.unwomen.org/), had no data for more than half the Pacific Island countries listed in its database.

that is *useful to women* (and men); a commitment to reflexivity and an acknowledgement of the *subjectivity of the researcher*; and a commitment to *knowledge as emancipation*.

Since 2017, we have been involved in various projects that aim to align research with feminist, accountable, collaborative and transformative principles. More specifically, we have established research partnerships that privilege local researchers and facilitate their active participation in the design, implementation and analysis components of research.

The first project was part of a broader program supported by an Australia-based NGO with funding from the Government of the Kingdom of the Netherlands.[6] This research project intended to generate new and deeper understandings of women's leadership pathways that would inform programs and advocacy, as well as contribute to research discourses on leadership. Camilla, Donna, Geraldine and Chandy, along with several other researchers from the region, used their personal and organisational networks in their own local contexts to reach out to women whom they knew to be political, economic and social leaders, and asked them to tell their stories. Sonia and Melissa supported the local researchers for the duration of the project (2017–20), primarily remotely from their home bases in Australia and Canada, respectively, although there were some in-person workshops held to hone research and analysis skills.

At the time this research was undertaken, none of us was employed by an academic institution: Camilla and Donna worked for the Women's Rights Action Movement NGO in Solomon Islands; Geraldine worked for the Bougainville Women's Federation; Chandy worked (and still works) for the Gender and Development Cambodia NGO; Sonia and Melissa were consultants. All of us had extensive experience in advocating for, and developing programs in, gender equality, but of course acknowledged significantly different levels of privilege among us, not least due to differing education opportunities. At the beginning of 2017, none of us had ever worked together; by 2022, we had maintained relationships of mutual trust and admiration through irregular but positive interactions, even after our initial project had ended (in 2020).

---

6   More information about this project, including its final report (IWDA 2020), are available from the website of the International Women's Development Agency, at: iwda.org.au/resource/wpl/.

This project easily aligns with Tickner's criteria of feminist research. First, the questions we asked were explicitly—and exclusively—related to the experience of women leaders across Asia and the Pacific. Second, the knowledge we produced has been used, and will continue to be used, by our organisations to support more programming on women's leadership in our own countries. Third, through these mutually supportive relationships, we continually reflected on and acknowledged our own positionalities. Finally, we undertook this research because we wanted to improve—and expand—the pathways available to women becoming leaders.

The second project, still in its data collection and sense-making phase at the time of writing, is a collaboration between Vani and Sonia and is concerned with the effective implementation of a gender-sensitive rule introduced into the Fijian Parliament in 2014. It is connected to wider practitioner and academic scholarship on the gender sensitivity of parliaments around the world that has underpinned advocacy for cultural and policy changes in historically male-dominated and masculinised institutions (Palmieri 2019). Vani and Sonia have known each other since 2020, having regularly worked together on this and other projects. Therefore, they describe their relationship as both professional and personal. Vani conducted most of the in-person interviews in Suva, while Sonia conducted a few interviews remotely via Zoom. This research is undertaken under a more formal framework: it was granted approval by the Speaker of the Fijian Parliament and ethical clearance from an Australian university. It is expected to produce both academic and practitioner-focused outputs.

Like the Women's Pathways to Leadership (WLP) project, the methodology is underpinned by a feminist lens and reflects the principles outlined by Tickner. First, the research takes a women-centric approach to the question of parliamentary reform, asking how gender-sensitive rules are applied in this institutional context. Second, the research topic is of direct use to women given that the gender analysis required in the parliamentary rule aims to identify any intended or unintended, advantageous or disadvantageous gendered impacts of policies, laws or draft bills. Third, the data collection process has required an explicit acknowledgement of, and reflection on, researcher positionalities and power dynamics given the division of labour in undertaking interviews and traditional/colonialist framings of 'research experience'. Finally, because the process will bring together both policy designers and end users to identify, analyse and solve problems with the current process, the research explicitly aims to emancipate various groups of women (policymakers, voters, activists) in Fiji.

Privileging local experience and unheard voices

A second approach to decolonising the stories of women political leaders is to actively 'grab the space' in which the experiences of local researchers are broadcast. Previous research has suggested that elite interviews are among the most widespread research methods in the social sciences but are also 'emotionally exhausting' and 'fraught with uncertainties and anxieties' (Jakimow 2020: 150). An interesting body of research—primarily focused on experiences in Africa—has shone a spotlight on the challenges to local researchers in conducting elite interviews (Ntienjom Mbohou and Tomkinson 2022; Sowatey and Tankebe 2019; Gokah 2006).

In Pacific contexts, calls for Indigenous knowledge creation are longstanding but still far from mainstreamed. Perhaps not surprisingly, women have been at the forefront of change movements, eloquently articulating both the problems and the solutions to colonialist knowledge practices. Māori scholar Linda Tuhiwai Smith first argued for decolonialist approaches to research over two decades ago, noting:

> [I]t is surely difficult to discuss research methodology and indigenous peoples together, in the same breath, without an analysis of imperialism, without understanding the complex ways in which the pursuit of knowledge is deeply embedded in the multiple layers of imperial colonial practices. (1999: 2)

In similar tones, Hawaiian scholar Haunani-Kay Trask identified the local practices that would serve her in reclaiming Indigenous knowledge:

> To know my history, I had to put away my books and return to the land. I had to plant *taro* in the earth before I could understand the inseparable bond between people and *aina*. I had to feel again the spirits of nature and take gifts of plants and fish to the ancient alters. I had to begin to speak my language with our elders and leave long silences for wisdom to grow. (1999: 118)

These calls inspire us to take seriously what we know and what we have learned in conducting elite interviews in our own country contexts. We appreciate Winduo's challenge to us 'to return to our roots to learn the culture that our people have transmitted orally without the dependence on writing' (2009: 2). For this reason, this chapter deliberately privileges the voices of local researchers; our voices are the data of this research.

Autoethnography—a qualitative method that 'uses personal experience to describe and interpret cultural texts, experiences, beliefs and practices' (Adams et al. 2017; but see also Holman Jones 2005)—allows us to reflect on our methodological practice, but it also gives us a platform from which we establish our experience, our thoughts and our practice as legitimate knowledge. We held a series of conversations via email, Zoom and WhatsApp between January and June 2022. Transcripts of our discussions were shared among the whole group by email, and Sonia created a Google document outlining emerging themes. We then added to these at our own pace. We crystallised some of the key findings in the process of presenting a paper at a conference held at The Australian National University in July 2022, for which we created a video. While Sonia and Melissa facilitated these conversations—and captured our reflections in writing—they did not contribute their reflections to these discussions. This chapter is not about their experience of researching in minority-world contexts, although we are happy to contribute to a longer reflective journey on some of our collaborations (see Palmieri and MacLean 2021).

We now turn to our lessons in relation to the access to, conduct and purpose of interviewing women.

Access, hierarchy and connections: *Whom* we research

While self-evident, it is worth noting that women's relative absence from key political institutions in Asia and the Pacific makes it more difficult to study them than, say, men political leaders or women leaders in other fields (such as economic or community leaders). We noticed this difficulty in accessing women political leaders in several ways. First, we discovered that some aspiring women leaders did not wish to be part of research projects when they had not been successful in their political pursuits. Donna and Camilla shared their experience of interviewing a woman who contested a provincial election but, having lost, declined to participate further in the WLP project. Again, it may be obvious, but when unsuccessful women candidates decline to be involved in research, the sample of 'women political leaders' decreases still further, given that the pool of women candidates is always larger than the pool of elected or appointed representatives.

We consider that there are additional consequences of the 'lost numbers'. This finding also speaks to the emotional and reputational cost of running for election and losing. It is worth reflecting on the emotional state of women who are unsuccessful in their electoral campaigns: might they be worried that the research team will be critical of them personally, or concerned they have little to share with researchers that can be used for wider lesson learning? Might these women be ashamed of having put their hands up for leadership? There is room for us to think through how we approach women who have expended enormous emotional energy and been defeated. 'Research' in this instance may not be a sufficient calling card; there may simply be a need to lend emotional support (see also Jakimow 2020).

Access issues also arise in relation to women who have been successful in their electoral campaigns. We noted that research opportunities are impacted by women's elevation (or not) to positions of parliamentary leadership (such as committee chairs) and membership across all committee portfolios (including, for example, finance, public accounts, defence). Vani and Sonia noticed that in the Fijian Parliament project, none of the committee chairs was a woman and some committees had no women members. As researchers interested in generating more inclusive data, Vani and Sonia deliberately broadened their sample of Members of Parliament (MPs)—from just committee chairs and deputy chairs—to ensure that women politicians could have their say. While women's absence from these leadership positions is a factor of numbers, it also speaks to the institutional norms and cultural assumptions about the capacity and skill of women to take on certain roles. A recent study of Pacific Islander students found that perceptions of leadership legitimacy are higher for women in the portfolios of health and women's issues than in the portfolios of defence and foreign affairs (Nailumu et al. 2023).

We found it more difficult to access the most senior women politicians in our countries. In Bougainville, Geraldine was able to interview the relatively newer MPs for the WLP project, although the former deputy speaker and longest-serving of the women MPs could not be reached, despite repeated attempts. While this could be attributed to women MPs' already crowded schedules, or a sense of being 'over-researched', it is also perhaps about the more limited connections local researchers have to women in political power. Donna, Camilla, Chandy and Geraldine had personal relationships with women leaders in the community and business sectors in their own countries but did not have these personal connections with senior women politicians. They were, then, less able to rely on their own networks to reach women political leaders. In our collective reflections, we wonder whether this is an indication that the more senior women become, the stronger are their ties to the political establishment; the more entrenched they are in the system, the less freedom they have in speaking even to local researchers.

While personal relationships seemed less helpful in securing interviews with women political leaders, Vani's personal connection to an *institutional interview organiser* proved instrumental in facilitating access. Vani had an existing relationship, through her university networks, with a staffer in the parliament, who arranged all her meetings with MPs, including some that were conducted online. In fact, Vani's connection set up an entire interview schedule in consultation with the Speaker of Parliament and the secretar-general:

> If it wasn't for them, I wouldn't have been able to interview all the women as we had planned ... [W]ith research work, [access] is a really important thing. Especially with research work here in the Pacific because ... we are relational people. Especially when we're talking about sensitive issues—like gender equality—it's still a very sensitive topic to talk about, given our cultural context, so having a relationship with someone to help you gain access, based on your relations, is a very instrumental way of interviewing and collecting data. (Vani)

Vani's point is that local knowledge and understanding of the local context in terms of knowing the political landscape and political party dynamics and structure are important when reaching out. Interviewing women political leaders is also easier when a recognisable institution (such as a university) makes a formal request. In the case of the Fijian Parliament project, a 'formal' letter of request to participate in the project drafted on academic letterhead was sent to the Speaker of the House, outlining the research objectives and methods and providing a biography of the researchers. While a similar template was prepared for the WLP project, individual researchers were responsible for preparing the letter—on NGO letterhead—and sharing this with their intended research participants. In Geraldine's case, this approach was less effective in securing access:

> My initial approach was drafting [each woman MP] a letter explaining the research work and time frame. It didn't really work for Honourable Francesca as she was always busy and I never found the time to interview her ... [T]he letter and knowing Honourable Francesca personally didn't really work for her ... I sensed that [she thought] I was trying to be political by trying to find out about her [experience]. (Geraldine)

The paucity of women political leaders to interview in our regions and specific challenges inherent in accessing the most senior women speak to the nature of the job women sign up to when they become politicians. It tells us—unsurprisingly—that the high demands on their time for research purposes exacerbate women leaders' existing time poverty. In some of our countries, where the community is particularly tightly knit and elites are well known, research requests can also appear to be nosy to women who are already in the spotlight (and often face harsh criticism), rather than serving a more noble purpose of knowledge generation and sharing.

Respect, safety and vulnerability: *How* we research

We found that women political leaders need to feel physically (as well as emotionally) safe in the research relationship. Through trial and error—and sometimes by chance—we came to realise that the physical space in which the interview is conducted affects the kind of information women political leaders share, as do the initial set of questions and the language in which we conducted (and organised) the interview. We worked hard to establish a comfort zone, both physically and emotionally.

The location of the interview set its tone. Geraldine's chance encounter with two women MPs while all were travelling meant that an interview could be held in a relaxed and comfortable environment:

> I happened to meet them in the same guesthouse that I was transiting through at that time. When I had a chat with them during dinner time, both women MPs were willing to share their stories with me. That was when I started to interview them. (Geraldine)

Chandy deliberately relocated some of her interviews away from the office to elicit different kinds of information and stories:

> I normally [interviewed them] in their office, but on some [issues], they didn't want to speak in their office, so I said maybe we could talk later at your home, or private coffee shop room, and then they agreed, and … they were hungry to tell the story. So, they felt like I understood about them sharing the info that is confidential and that they didn't want to talk about it in the working space, so I chose different locations for them. (Chandy)

Conversely, parliamentary settings established a more formal and, at times, intimidating interaction:

> [T]he environment I was in [made a difference]. We were inside the conference room at the parliament, one of the highest policymaking institutions in the land. I had only heard about these women in the news. And to sit across from them [in that room], I would say that I was intimidated. I was like, 'Oh, my gosh, I'm going to interview this MP!' (Vani)

In this more formal environment, Vani had the sense that MPs were keen to answer questions 'correctly'. The Fijian women MPs always requested that a research officer be present for their interviews and regularly looked to them when giving their answers as a way of ensuring they gave accurate information. Reflecting on this experience, Vani considered that the interviews would have been quite different had they been conducted in less formal settings, as had been Geraldine's and Chandy's experience.

We also created that sense of safety by communicating with women in our local languages:

> In the Melanesian context, such as Bougainville and PNG, speaking the local Tok Pisin language and local dialect where appropriate can be key to enabling a researcher to collect the information we are seeking from the women leaders. (Geraldine)

But this also imposed some challenges on us as researchers when we needed to translate back and forth from English because the common language of the projects on which we were working—and of shared project tools such as questionnaires—was English.

> I admit that I lost some interest in speaking with older women political leaders who cannot read or write well or cannot understand English, because I had to spend so much energy to get to know them in the interview. During the interview they keep asking me again and again about a question, and it was hard for me to frame it [in Khmer language] and make them understand. (Chandy)

There is significant potential for misunderstanding questions and for increasing the administrative burdens on researchers when interview formats are developed in a foreign language (that is, English), and this can be detrimental to data collection and systematic analysis (see also Palmieri and MacLean 2021).

These experiences demonstrate the dexterity of local researchers in understanding and acting on social cues and cultural nuances that non-local researchers may miss or misunderstand. The finding that women can be more circumspect in their parliamentary environments speaks to the political cultures in which we live, some of which can be characterised as more authoritarian than democratic. In these cultures, women may feel observed in formal settings, prompting the wearing of 'masks', particularly while they are 'on duty'.

Lost stories, comfort and discomfort: *What* we research

In our interviews with political leaders, we discovered that we needed to demonstrate a sense of openness—that is, we had to be ready to listen and respond appropriately. We tried to create a safer space by sharing our own positionality: who we are and where we are from (for example, our province and family name). We asked them for a little personal background or what Donna and Camilla referred to as 'starting to *stori stori* to make them comfortable'. Chandy had a similar strategy to encourage a more familiar interview conversation:

> The first two political women leaders I interviewed, I felt this [awkwardness]. Then later I learned how to get away from that feeling by starting with [their] personal interests, not jumping straight into the interview questions, but starting with questions like, 'How are you? How is your family? Did you go anywhere during holiday? Do you know any good places to go? If you could travel, what country would you want to go [to]?' When you talk about food, going into personal interest, they feel good. Some of the women knew the director of my organisation, who is the same age as them, and I would talk about her, because they feel the same, and I would tell them, 'She really misses you, too. I will tell her to call you.' (Chandy)

These accidental personal stories were some of the most interesting of the entire research process:

> It was an enjoyable experience interviewing these two women MPs as I learned a lot from them, especially on their personal leadership journeys … I was inspired by the way these women overcame those challenges in bringing about change in their communities. 'From a village woman entering the Bougainville House of Representative

Parliament' is how I can describe Honourable Marcelline Kokiai. She had the heart of her people because of the Bougainville crisis and ensured help was sought for the displaced mothers, children and loved ones when it was needed the most. It was an act of courage and bravery. (Geraldine)

While important, these stories were also hard to hear:

One interview [went for] three hours; I just listened to their painful moments. [She told me about] some women in the Khmer Rouge region who had difficulty when they had their period—none of that kind of information is ever mentioned in the history that was written, there is no publication about that. When I interviewed her, I was so interested and kept asking about all these issues, the kind of secret moments. They told me that some women cried and talked about abandoned kids. They had to escape as a group into the forest, and suddenly the baby cried. They feared a Khmer Rouge soldier would follow and kill the whole group, so they had to choose so many different ways to deal with that: some had to abandon the kid; some even left the kid with someone to kill them. Those painful moments, I don't think they were used to sharing them with others; they are political leaders, meaning they have to keep some secrets that might affect their life and position. [Sharing these stories meant] they spent so much time, a longer time [with me] because they had to pause to cry, not speak, think about their past. But I said nothing; I just kept silent, looking at them, giving them a tissue, and left it as a moment for them to feel that I was there and they could talk to me, confident that the information would [not be used against them]. (Chandy)

Women political leaders have more to tell us than their responses to predefined questions. These are the lost stories that have not yet been captured in the history books; the stories that fill the gaps in our understanding of women's leadership. In part, this speaks to what we consider to be 'knowledge'. Traditional narratives of women's political leadership commonly invite women to talk about their pathways to politics and their parliamentary impact. In our majority-world contexts, however, these narratives may have less resonance to women leaders themselves. Their personal stories of discomfort keep them motivated as politicians and as change-makers. As local researchers, our role must be to find—and hold—the moments in which these difficult stories can be shared. Otherwise, we risk losing these stories forever.

Power, patience and responsibility: *Who* we are in the research

As researchers, practitioners and activists, we have found that engaging women political leaders as research subjects comes with significant power imbalances, perhaps more so than with other women. In our conversations, we all reflected on the power dynamics inherent in interviewing women political leaders. Geraldine considered that navigating power imbalances was a core part of the research process itself: 'First, one has to understand the local power dynamics that exist between individuals in trying to strike up a conversation.'

Power imbalances had various consequences. Perhaps most obviously, by virtue of their elected position, political leaders command a certain degree of social and cultural respect. In the Fijian context, Vani related that MPs with a chiefly background commanded even greater respect:

> [I]t was a bit intimidating and challenging talking to women MPs who were from a certain social standing—like, had a chiefly background. With our culture, our iTaukei culture, that's what I had in the back of my mind. I had to reinforce my thinking— 'remember, she is a *marama*' [a *marama* is like a chief]—and I still had to act accordingly. So ... I would say, I had to ask questions in a very respectful way. Just because of that dynamic. I was still very mindful of that dynamic. (Vani)

For Chandy, the power imbalance had a different and potentially more serious consequence: navigating, and indeed accepting, the power inequality was necessary not only for the data collection process, but also to sustain an institutional relationship between her organisation and the political leader: 'I felt the power imbalance: they are older, richer, more powerful, and I know if I did something wrong or said something, it would affect the relationship of my organisation with the government.'

In our reflections on these interviews, it became clear that we often felt responsible for managing these power dynamics, even though we were the more disempowered party. Vani, for example, explicitly put herself in the shoes of a woman political leader:

> I [understood] to an extent these women—they are in a male-dominated space—they have to put up those barriers. They would be like, 'Who is this person coming in to interview me?'

Chandy was critical of herself in the way she managed some of the women she interviewed, while Geraldine gave some thought as to how she would do this differently in the future:

> I felt scared somehow, and I had that moment of thinking, 'Oh, my God, can I just finish this interview right now?' And that's bad because the skills to listen to people, my skills of listening to people of different ages and views, are not yet fully ... [I]t's very, very important for local researchers to be patient enough to get away from the power imbalance. (Chandy)

> If I were to do another interview with women political leaders, I would bring them together in a panel video interview. (Geraldine)

Women political leaders are not always free to share everything, and we sometimes felt that we were not getting the full story. We felt that there were double standards between community expectations and 'keeping them accountable':

> I interviewed a young woman political leader, and she started to tell me something and then stopped. I didn't know if it was enough, but then later I realised she might have something more to tell me. And she told me how she got there in her position because of the network of her father—so, I guess it is like nepotism—but it was also because she's skilled and knowledgeable. She got there, not only because of her father, but because she's also smart, that's why she's there ... It's very hard when talking with women political leaders. I always had the feeling of needing to be cautious, making sure they are okay, [especially] with problems in their political party or [with] their party leader. (Chandy)

The finding that local researchers feel responsible for managing power dynamics in which they are inherently disadvantaged requires further consideration. Specifically, discussion is warranted about the kinds of supportive tools and processes required to navigate power dynamics so that researchers are not placed in vulnerable situations, and about the perception that their behaviour could jeopardise a research project, development program or an entire organisation.

Yet, the finding also speaks to the often precarious nature of the leadership positions women hold, and their dependence on others—usually men—to keep those positions. Women can feel, as Puwar (2004) eloquently phrased it, like 'space invaders', working in institutions that traditionally have not welcomed their inclusion. In our countries, this experience is muddied by the perception that women have achieved their positions of leadership through non-meritorious processes: the 'nepotism' implied in Chandy's example, but also the common framing of temporary special measures as 'discriminatory against men' (Palmieri and Zetlin 2020). In these cases, job precarity mixes with a special kind of imposter syndrome, resulting in another set of emotions for the local researcher to manage.

Gender and sensitivity: *Why* we research

On reflection, we consider that the research topic of gender equality itself can be very sensitive in our local contexts, particularly if it is being researched by individuals in NGOs that have an advocacy role. In the WLP project, for example, Camilla and Donna had been asked to try to interview women ministers with whom they had had separate interactions on temporary special measures (TSMs) to increase the representation of women in parliament. As staff of a feminist NGO, Donna and Camilla were expected to engage with women who they knew would not consider themselves feminist and who had publicly rejected calls for TSMs for women in politics. This history immediately established a difficult position from which to undertake research, especially since that research was also interested in understanding women's gendered pathways to leadership in politics:

> When you're trying to share information, they say, 'You're bringing in a foreign concept.' You know, it's issues we face every day. They should know: as duty bearers, that's their role; we are here to hold them accountable. It's not like we are putting the blame on them. (Donna)

> Political will. This is the biggest thing, the non-sensitisation of people around gender. This needs to be strengthened, because when you throw it on the table … it's already seen as something like, 'What are these people doing against the cultural mindset?' (Camilla)

Vani also noticed that addressing the topic of gender equality can be a barrier to eliciting women political leaders' lived experience:

> I would also attribute it to the fact that they have to put up their guard; they are always in the limelight. They are not afraid of me! But it's more about the nature of the topic—gender equality—yes, it's the subject matter. Women MPs who are more conservative, I would say they were … more reluctant, more guarded—yes, guarded about some of those questions. Other women MPs who are bit more easygoing and approachable, they didn't hold back, they

explained that this is their reality, and we should do more. Those women who are a bit more conservative and formal, they were a bit more diplomatic in how they responded to our questions. (Vani)

In part, this challenges the assumption that women political leaders are inherently interested in promoting gender equality. We found in our local contexts this is not always the case. For us as gender equality advocates, however, it remains *our* fundamental driver for further research on and with women leaders. This suggests that there is a space between us that we still need to bridge. We must build that bridge.

Conclusion

The numerical focus on men's overrepresentation in formal political institutions, particularly in Asia and the Pacific, has eclipsed a more nuanced appreciation of the lived experience of the women who do succeed in politics. Yet, as we have argued in this chapter, authentically capturing this lived experience requires research partnerships that privilege the experience and contextual understanding of local researchers.

Our collective experience in interviewing women political leaders paints a valuable picture. Their limited numbers mean that they are in high demand, exacerbating their existing time poverty, but also potentially exacerbating their sense of vulnerability. Women are already subject to harsh criticism and, without a clear sense of what they will be able to contribute to the research, they may be suspicious of us. When we can connect and find emotionally and physically safe spaces in which to speak with them, women politicians share new—and sometimes difficult—stories with us.

We reflected that in these moments, we have taken on the emotional labour of ensuring women MPs' safety in the research relationship. We find strategies to keep women at ease, whether by personalising the initial moments of an interview or securing a location that will encourage a sense of security. Our finding that gender equality as a research topic can sometimes heighten tension between researchers and research subjects also suggests that we may be asking more of these research relationships than we had perhaps previously envisaged. When emerging local researchers engage in research about or with women leaders, in places where this leadership is especially contested and tenuous, the research itself becomes a site for or process of intersecting power dynamics. Both the researcher and the research subject are powerful and vulnerable in different ways—in relation to each other and in relation to the structures and gatekeepers that influence or constrain them, including Western academic and development funding structures, patriarchal political institutions (parties and legislatures) and social norms and voter perceptions.

We find that both researchers and research subjects put themselves on the line in this process—in personal, political and professional ways. This becomes particularly problematic when there is no shared ideology or value system to support the research relationship—specifically, when not all women leaders are in favour of promoting gender equality or identify as feminists. Yet, we often premise effective research in local contexts on the ability of researchers to create connections and establish safety and security, to elicit the lived experiences of women politicians. This ultimately suggests that research projects must consider and manage the conditions required for both the researchers and the subjects to be motivated and feel safe so that the requisite openness can occur, without unintended consequences to the individuals involved or their institutions and wider communities. There is significant scope to consider these conditions much further.

References

Adams, Tony E., Carolyn Ellis, and Stacy Holman Jones. 2017. 'Autoethnography.' In *The International Encyclopedia of Communication Research Methods*, edited by J. Matthes, C.S. Davis, and R.F. Potter. New York: John Wiley & Sons. doi.org/10.1002/9781118901731.iecrm0011.

Baker, Kerryn, Roannie Ng Shiu, and Jack Corbett. 2020. 'Gender, Politics and Development in the Small States of the Pacific.' *Small States and Territories* 3, no. 2: 261–66.

Buvinic, Mayra, Rebecca Furst-Nichols, and Gayatri Koolwal. 2014. *Mapping Gender Data Gaps*. [Report], March. Washington, DC: Data2x. data2x.org/resource-center/mapping-gender-data-gaps/.

Gokah, Theophilus. 2006. 'The Naïve Researcher: Doing Social Research in Africa.' *International Journal of Social Research Methodology* 9, no. 1: 61–73. doi.org/10.1080/13645570500436163.

Greenwood, Davydd J., and Morten Levin. 2007. *Introduction to Action Research: Social Research for Social Change*. Thousand Oaks: SAGE.

Harding, Sandra. 1987. *Feminism and Methodology*. Bloomington: Indiana University Press.

Holman Jones, Stacy. 2005. 'Autoethnography: Making the Personal Political.' In *Handbook of Qualitative Research*, edited by N.K. Denzin and Y.S. Lincoln, 763–91. Thousand Oaks: SAGE.

Inter-Parliamentary Union (IPU). 2015. *Women in Parliament in 2015: The Year in Review*. Geneva: IPU.

IPU. 2023. 'Global and Regional Averages of Women in National Parliaments.' *IPU Parline*. [Online]. Geneva: IPU.

International Women's Development Agency (IWDA). 2020. *Women's Pathways to Leadership: Our Pathways, Our Voice*. Melbourne: IWDA.

Jakimow, Tanya. 2020. 'Rethinking the Self: Vulnerability and its Uses in Research.' In *Navigating Fieldwork in the Social Sciences: Stories of Danger, Risk and Reward*, edited by Philip Wadds, Nicholas Apoifis, Susanne Schmeidl, and Kim Spurway, 147–62. Cham: Palgrave Macmillan.

Jenkins, Fiona, Marian Sawer, and Karen Downing. 2020. 'Introduction: The Gender Lens and Innovation in the Social Sciences.' In *How Gender Can Transform the Social Sciences: Innovation and Impact*, edited by Marian Sawer, Fiona Jenkins, and Karen Downing, 3–15. Cham: Palgrave Pivot. doi.org/10.1007/978-3-030-43236-2_1.

Leavy, Patricia, and Daniel X. Harris. 2018. *Contemporary Feminist Research from Theory to Practice*. New York: Guilford Press.

Leege, David, and Della McMillan. 2016. 'Building More Robust NGO–University Partnerships in Development: Lessons Learned from Catholic Relief Services.' *Journal of Poverty Alleviation and International Development* 7, no. 2: 68–119.

Nailumu, Vani, Epeli Tinivata, and Sonia Palmieri. 2023. *Student Perceptions of Women's Political Leadership in the Pacific*. Suva: Balance of Power Program.

Ntienjom Mbohou, Leger Felix, and Sule Tomkinson. 2022. 'Rethinking Elite Interviews Through Moments of Discomfort: The Role of Information and Power.' *International Journal of Qualitative Methods* 21: 1–10. doi.org/10.1177/16094069221095312.

Palmieri, Sonia. 2019. 'Feminist Institutionalism and Gender-Sensitive Parliaments: Relating Theory and Practice.' In *Gender Innovation in Political Science: New Norms, New Knowledge*, edited by Marian Sawer and Karen Baker, 173–94. Cham: Palgrave Macmillan. doi.org/10.1007/978-3-319-75850-3_9.

Palmieri, Sonia, and Melissa MacLean. 2021. 'Critical Reflection as Feminist Pedagogy: Teaching Feminist Research in the Field.' *International Feminist Journal of Politics* 24, no. 3: 439–59. doi.org/10.1080/14616742.2021.1907206.

Palmieri, Sonia, and Diane Zetlin. 2020. 'Alternative Strategies to Support Women as Political Actors in the Pacific: Building the House of Peace.' *Women's Studies International Forum* 82: 102404. doi.org/10.1016/j.wsif.2020.102404.

Puwar, Nirmal. 2004. *Space Invaders: Race, Gender and Bodies Out of Place*. New York: Berg.

Roche, Chris, and Linda Kelly. 2014. *Partnerships for Effective Development*. Canberra: Australian Council for International Development.

Schaaf, Rebecca. 2015. 'The Rhetoric and Reality of Partnerships for International Development.' *Geography Compass* 9, no. 2: 68–80. doi.org/10.1111/gec3.12198.

Smith, Linda Tuhiwai. 1999. *Decolonizing Methodologies: Research and Indigenous Peoples*. Dunedin: Otago University Press.

Sowatey, Emmanuel Addo, and Justice Tankebe. 2019. 'Doing Research with Police Elites in Ghana.' *Criminology & Criminal Justice* 19, no. 5: 537–53. doi.org/10.1177/1748895818787022.

Thom, Victoria, and Alice Cope. 2016. *Partnering for Sustainable Development: Challenges and Pathways for Building Cross-Sector Partnerships*. Issues Paper. Melbourne: UN Global Compact Network Australia. unglobalcompact.org.au/wp-content/uploads/2016/10/Issues-Paper-Cross-Sector-Partnering-for-Sustainable-Development-FINAL.pdf.

Tickner, J. Ann. 2014. *A Feminist Voyage through International Relations*. New York: Oxford University Press. doi.org/10.1093/acprof:oso/9780199951246.001.0001.

Trask, Haunani-Kay. 1999. *From a Native Daughter: Colonialism and Sovereignty in Hawai'i*. Revised ed. Honolulu: University of Hawai'i Press. doi.org/10.1515/9780824847029.

Vijeyarasa, Ramona. 2022. *The Woman President: Leadership, Law and Legacy for Women Based on Experiences from South and Southeast Asia*. Oxford: Oxford University Press.

Winduo, Steven Edmund. 2009. 'Reframing Indigenous Knowledge, Research Methodologies and Indigenous Pedagogies.' In *Reframing Indigenous Knowledge: Cultural Knowledge and Practices in Papua New Guinea*, edited by Steven Edmund Winduo. Port Moresby: Melanesian and Pacific Studies Centre, University of Papua New Guinea.

Winterford, Karen. 2017. *How to Partner for Development Research*. Canberra: Research for Development Impact Network.

Part III: Reframing the Narrative, Reclaiming the Space

Introduction

Margaret Jolly

What does it mean to reframe the narrative, to reclaim the space for women in politics? The four chapters in this section show how the stories we tell are grounded in place, and how reconceptualising how we think about place is fundamental to reclaiming the space for women's political agency and telling different stories about women and leadership at several scales.

Ramona Vijeyarasa's Chapter 8 provocatively asks what is 'Asian' and what is 'global' in conventional stories about the many women who have led Asian nations. This builds on her book *The Woman President* (2022), which interrogated what women who assumed executive office did for other women and revealed how some synergised with powerful women's movements while others did not. She asks whether what has been seen as distinctively 'Asian' is so different to elsewhere (for example, dynastic politics whereby daughters, wives or widows of male leaders assume power). Growing up in a politically engaged family everywhere confers advantages, she suggests. Moreover, she shows how similar presumptions pertain globally, naturalising male and denaturalising female power and privileging a woman's appearance and clothing over her intellectual acuity and policies. So, Vijeyarasa argues, we must erase the boundaries of conventional thought and what characterises a region such as 'Asia'. Still, insights from Asia can contribute by offering exemplary case studies of what difference women leaders make to women's lives, by helping to strengthen global solidarities among women presidents and prime ministers and by offering Asian lessons for global practice and theory—still utterly dominated by examples and authors from the minority world. In exploring the depths of gender in politics, we must transcend Asian exceptionalism as well as the alleged universalism of the minority world.

Mema Motusaga and Elise Howard's compelling Chapter 9 moves to a more intimate scale in analysing gender and politics in Samoa, where, by contrast with Asia, the first woman Prime Minister, Afioga Fiamē Naomi Mata'afa, assumed power only in 2021. In re-storying the narrative of gender and politics, they point to contests about whether there is gender equality in Samoa. In Samoan gender ideology, the balance between women and men is celebrated, especially in that the sister is seen to have a complementary power in relation to her brother, according her a spiritual power in contrast to his temporal authority. But this has not translated into gender equality in parliamentary politics—a fact that most foreign observers and development agents privilege. Motusaga and Howard reveal how the brother–sister relation (the *feagaiga*) was radically transformed by Christianisation. This sacred covenant and women's spiritual power passed to the male pastor while Christian missions celebrated the husband–wife relation in a novel monogamous marriage. Moreover, the introduced Westminster parliamentary system privileged masculine rather than feminine sources of power and rank and thus parliament became gendered in a way that excluded women. The authors suggest that the Samoan concept of *vā*— a sacred space between people or other entities, which celebrates respectful relations across difference—offers an ideal from which to further enable women's political participation. They advocate seeing politics as more than contest and conquest and through a different ontological lens, which values relationality and reciprocal responsibility, spiritual as well as secular authority and the long-term life of all creatures over generations.

Longgina Novadona Bayo consummately reframes conventional narratives about women and politics in Malaka, West Timor, in Chapter 10. She suggests that domesticity, rather than being a sequestered, apolitical space for women, is in fact full of political potential for creating affective bonds. She reveals how Indigenous ideologies of gender were diarchic, balancing power between outer masculine and inner feminine realms. Women were 'housemasters', wielding strong divine authority over the flow of life in expansive matrilineal clans. The combined effects of foreign colonial rule, missionary maternalism and Indonesian state *ibuism* ('motherism') promoted a gender hierarchy in which women were ideally selfless housewives not interested in pursuing public power. Timorese women adeptly navigate these divergent ideologies. Women political leaders, and especially those of noble rank, consummately use domestic spaces and communal cooking to create and sustain affective ties to constituents and win elections.

Deepak K. Mishra and Aparimita Mishra in Chapter 11 take us to Arunachal Pradesh, a frontier state in northern India. They show how women have been marginalised in both 'traditional' and 'modern' governance structures, which, alike, have been overwhelmingly patriarchal. They observe how the political economy of the contemporary state creates ethnicised forms of belonging and political alliances. Women are increasingly finding a place in grassroots governance, in *Panchayati raj* institutions, but in so doing must be mindful of several interconnected frontiers—that of the state itself, the frontiers separating different ethnic territories and the everyday frontiers created between their domestic and public political lives. The ecology and colonial and postcolonial history of this state are distinctive while its remoteness on the border with China makes for an anxious security situation. Ethnic differences, including some inhabitants who are seen as outsiders and cannot elect representatives, mitigate against a sense of shared citizenship, although there are some signs of pan-tribal civic movements emerging. Women are subject to pervasive ideals of feminine domesticity. And, although women are finding a place in grassroots governance, partly through special measures such as reserved seats, they are often only included in nominal or patronising ways; they are thought to be less capable than men, their voices are not heeded and they are often seen as proxies for their husbands. Thus, the authors develop the concept of 'exclusionary inclusion'.

All four chapters highlight the importance of challenging hegemonic ideas of gendered space in reframing narratives of women in politics. Two chapters show the importance of reclaiming Indigenous gender ideologies that often differed from those promoted during colonisation and the formation of nation-states, such as the gendering of the domestic as feminine and the public as masculine. The authors occupy diverse subject positions in their research, offering fertile dialogues between insider and outsider perspectives.

8

Erasing the Boundaries: Situating the 'Asian' among the world's women leaders

Ramona Vijeyarasa

In 2018, I found myself in Sri Lanka's capital, Colombo. I had the privilege of interviewing activists and politicians about former president Chandrika Bandaranaike Kumaratunga (1994–2005), often referred to as CBK, the nation's first woman president and second woman head of government. My visit to Sri Lanka was the start of a long journey to better understand whether women leaders are necessarily better for fellow women and, if so, in what ways these leaders shape the enactment of laws that impact women's lives. What better place to start than the country that boasts having had the world's first elected woman leader, CBK's mother, Sirimavo Bandaranaike, whose party won a landslide victory that saw her named prime minister of what was then Ceylon, as well as its Minister of Defence and External Affairs, back in 1960.

I sat in the office of the director of a Sri Lankan women's rights NGO, Prisha.[1] Prisha and I discussed the patriarchal and multi-religious ideologies that continue to buttress women's underrepresentation in the Sri Lankan Parliament (Jayasuriya 2011). Despite high measures of social development

---

1   Name changed for anonymity. My interview with Prisha was one of 50 conducted in Indonesia, the Philippines and Sri Lanka. Ethics approval was obtained from the University of Technology Sydney (UTS HREC ETH17-1449). All interviews were transcribed and coded using grounded theory (Corbin and Strauss 2008).

in areas such as health and education—what some have called a 'façade of a progressive nation' (Yatawara 2016: 10)—Sri Lankan women still face a severe absence from politics at all levels of government. This is despite a local government quota introduced in February 2019. While the quota helped to raise the percentage of women from 1.9 per cent to about 25 per cent of elected officials in local government (Election Commission of Sri Lanka 2019; Vijeyarasa 2020), the quota failed to truly diversify politics or enhance respect for the right of women to participate in politics in the first place.

Prisha, like many of my informants, commented on what a remarkable time it was in the mid-1990s in Sri Lanka to have a mother–daughter duo leading the nation: 'At one point, there was both Sirimavo and Chandrika on stage. It was an amazing time, when Chandrika was President and the mother was Prime Minister' (Vijeyarasa 2022: 100). This image of women's leadership presents a stark contrast to Sri Lanka's political landscape in recent times. Mass protests, beginning in March 2022—known as Aragalaya ('Struggle')—ended with Sri Lankan president Gotabaya Rajapaksa fleeing the nation to Singapore via the Maldives, leaving the country economically devastated after a failure of governance: a balance of payments crisis, a bloated public sector and wasteful companies layered with corruption that 'seemed to flourish' under Rajapaksa's leadership (DeVotta 2022: 92). Indeed, the juxtaposition of women leaders Sirimavo and Chandrika Bandaranaike with brothers Mahinda and Gotabaya Rajapaksa would be comical if not so tragic when one is asking what difference presidential leaders make in people's lives. The tide has, however, perhaps turned with the swearing in of Harini Amarasuriya, female activist and academic, as Sri Lanka's seventeenth prime minister.

This comparison of female and male leaders reminds us, too, of an overarching assumption that appears to sustain men's dominance in politics—a notion that leadership is innate to men while women must prove their place. Conversing about Kumaratunga, Prisha recalled the president's change of hairstyle:

> And then she cut her hair. No female politicians can cut their hair. The woman decided to cut her hair and that became a big issue because she had stopped being the image of the strong, South Asian woman. (Vijeyarasa 2022: 106)

As an Australian scholar who lived through the prime ministership of Julia Gillard (2010–13) and the excess attention the press paid to the short hair and other superficial characteristics of Australia's first and only woman prime minister, it triggered an immediate reflection: Prisha's observation could have been validly made about a woman leader almost anywhere in the world. The comment was characteristically Asian but also 'global'. Prisha's remarks about president Kumaratunga reflected a common burden experienced by women leaders, whose bodies are too often privileged and 'the mind ignored', as remarked of former Aotearoa New Zealand prime minister Helen Clark (1999–2008) (Motion 1996: 111). The 'revamping' of Clark's political image was considered newsworthy: women leaders' physical appearance becomes a political commodity.[2] When president Kumaratunga formed a coalition with the Sri Lankan Muslim Congress, the media published cartoons that were replete with 'sexual undertones' (Vijeyarasa 2022: 106). Such experiences of women leaders becoming the objects of political discussion and not subjects of political processes are clearly not uniquely Asian. Disgruntled constituents in Sri Lanka were unhappy that president Kumaratunga eschewed social norms with her French-educated ways, short hair and free will as a widow. Her badge as a female president both delighted the crowds—especially some women activists—and confounded many.

At this juncture in the scholarship, we have nearly three decades of comparative multi-country research on women's leadership in the region (starting as early as Richter's 1990 theories of female leadership in South and South-East Asia). This academic literature has dissected the pathways into politics of Asia's women leaders and studied their experiences of executive office as one example of women's political agency. Yet, perhaps this is precisely the moment to ask whether these experiences have been so starkly different from those of women leaders from other nations and other regions of the world? Have scholars of 'Asia'—as though there can really be such a thing as 'Asia' (for earlier work, see Dirlik 1992; and for a more recent discussion, Khoo 2019)—who have been, rightly, so focused on carving a space for ourselves in the scholarship to amplify what is distinct about the region been at the same time blind to the commonalities that might enable us to build not just a regional but a global theory?

In this chapter, I grapple with these questions to reach one main conclusion. We have categorised and named these experiences as 'Asian' to the detriment of our analysis, our understanding and our ability to value these 'Asian'

---

2   At the same time, it is incorrect to argue that this is a problem unique to female politicians: the same media scrutiny of male politicians' physical appearances is documented, for instance, in the case of Australia's male executives (Campbell 2003: 17), albeit this is rarely based on a male leader's body (Sinclair 2013: 239).

women for Asian studies but also for global knowledge. By contrast, I suggest that rather than constructing small categories, in which nothing neatly fits and everything spills over, we should take down the walls and erase some of the lines that we naturally draw as scholars of particular disciplines, particular regions and particular subject matter. With those walls down, an Asian view may serve a fundamental purpose of offering insights that benefit the global community.

I begin this chapter by examining the tendency in the political sciences scholarship to 'theorise from Asia'. I seek to better understand the dynamic that drags us towards seeing a particularism in the experiences of women in Asia instead of understanding such experiences as a manifestation of global experiences and challenges that are common across postcolonial nations. Indeed, in a collection that calls on us to decolonise our approaches (see Eva-Lina Lawrence, Chapter 5, and Jolly, Chapter 6, in this volume), a global standpoint reminds us of the historical origins of women's marginalisation from political institutions, whereby women—and non-white people—were sidelined in seemingly masculinist, so-called democratic colonial institutions. My chapter then turns to the central goal of trying to find the global in the local. In doing this, I identify three potential advantages, discussed in the second half of the chapter, to removing the boundaries to offer a global perspective of women's experiences of executive office.

First, with such a dearth of women making it to executive office, a global perspective enables a stronger narrative of what difference women's presence as political agents makes in women's lives. Second, we often and rightly value solidarity among women leaders at other levels of political leadership, including the grassroots, local and national levels (Vanniasinkam and Gunasekera 2022). Here, I argue that a global perspective on women's leadership may strengthen what are presently very weak institutional structures at the global level for solidarity among the world's female presidents and prime ministers. Third and finally, a global picture can enable us to theorise from an Asian standpoint and extract lessons for global gain. Here, I focus on the ways in which a global approach to understanding women's leadership in the region can advance regional and global human rights advocacy, law and policy reform. In short, rather than trying to see Asia as distinct, I aim to emphasise what would be lost in the struggle for women-centred law reform if these 'Asian lessons' were viewed as being of little significance to other parts of the world.

Theorising from Asia: Why we do it and what is the cost?

In this section, I discuss the gravitation of scholars of Asia to the region's women leaders. I seek to offer some reasons for an apparent drive to particularise their experiences but also begin to unpack what is lost in framing these experiences as distinctly and uniquely Asian.

The relatively high number of women who have occupied executive office in Asia is sufficiently stark to be a 'phenomenon'. Naturally, the academy has responded. In turn, scholarship about women in executive office in the region has proliferated in order to understand the 'Asian' nature of their rise. In many respects, we could be forgiven. It is natural that the reproduction of power among political elites in Asia would lead scholars to frame these experiences as a form of Asian exceptionalism (see, for example, Derichs and Thompson 2013; Fleschenberg 2013; Labonne et al. 2015). Presidents such as Corazon Aquino (1986–92), Megawati Sukarnoputri (2001–4) and Kumaratunga (1996–2005) were the 'suffering martyrs who clung to the threads of patriarchal lineage' when confronted with the death of a husband or father (Vijeyarasa 2022: 98; see also Rajasingham-Senanyake 2004; Weiner 1995).

Indeed, this is the very narrative I studied as a student of Asian gender studies. Being a housewife is seen as a 'good' and natural thing—from the Philippines to Indonesia's state *ibuism* ('motherism')—enabling these leaders to present themselves as a humble alternative to the male opposition candidate while being not *too* great an affront to societal expectations. Yet, the 'housewife' label permitted the suggestion that these women were unprepared for politics, allowing disgruntled male party elites to overlook the political apprenticeship that so many of these 'housewives' had undergone by growing up or living in political homes as members of political families (Jakimow et al. 2023). A mother is someone to be trusted but the role leaves many women juggling an incredibly heavy burden of expectations across the blurred terrain of the personal and political, as the 'martyr' and 'mother of the nation' who will lead the country out of dictatorship or civil war—clear Asian narratives (Derichs and Thompson 2013; Gerlach 2013; Rajasingham-Senanyake 2004; Thompson 2013; Vijeyarasa 2022: 22). This Asian exceptionalism is so strongly embedded in the literature that it takes a shift in thinking to challenge the 'Asian' and seek global commonalities.

Moreover, scholars are vying for space in response to a Global North–driven framework in this field. Somewhat ironically, given the sheer number of women who have held the office of president or prime minister in Asia, efforts to narrate an 'Asian story' are partly a response to the neglect of the Asian woman leader. A study written by former Australian prime minister Julia Gillard and Ngozi Okonjo-Iweala, former Nigerian Minister of Foreign Affairs and the World Trade Organization's seventh director-general, *Women and Leadership: Real Lives, Real Lessons*, did not include a single account of a woman leader from Asia or the Pacific (Gillard and Okonjo-Iweala 2020). Minna Cowper-Coles' review of the state of play of literature on women in politics concludes that the Western and Eurocentric perspectives of women's rise to and experiences of executive office, and their contributions as national leaders, are undeniably more visible (Cowper-Coles 2020: 13).

Yet, with due respect to the scope of the work undertaken in Cowper-Coles' review, a literature review can be as biased as the literature itself, as my co-editor Tanya Jakimow highlights in Chapter 1 of this volume. Indeed, this bias in what literature is accessed, studied and included is acknowledged in Peace Medie and Alice Kang's critique (2018), in which they challenge the dominance of English-language literature in this field and the 'severe' underrepresentation of Global South scholars in some of the leading journals addressing women, gender and politics. A literature review can only speak to the literature found and read, creating a demand on Asian and non-Asian scholars to play our part in making more visible scholarship that may be less accessible or simply deliberately not read and valued by other scholars.

Indeed, as Shim demonstrates in this collection (Chapter 2), when one looks at the nationality of authors and the countries that are the subject of 219 studies published between 1991 and 2022 in the Web of Science and Scopus databases, the domination of developed Western democracies in general (making up 80 per cent) and English-speaking ones in particular (making up 45 per cent) is undeniable. Partly this is explained by the fact that these are English-language databases. Nonetheless, literature concerning Hillary Clinton, former US First Lady (1993–2001) and Secretary of State (2009–13) and former US presidential candidate, is probably the most telling. The 32 studies of Clinton between 1996 and 2020 (14.6 per cent of the total) are equivalent to the total number of studies covering 28 countries in the sample. The inclusion of other languages—for instance, Spanish and French—and a study of a different database may have yielded a different result. Shim's study is revealing of a tendency for research on Global North leaders and using Global North frameworks to be more prominent.

This is not to overstate the absence of Asia's women leaders in the literature. Global comparative studies have been attempted. While seemingly a very ambitious project, they have been possible precisely because of how few women have risen to the lofty heights of executive office. Gretchen Bauer and Manon Tremblay's (2011) study of women as heads of state and government (and in cabinet) is the closest attempt: nine regional chapters, including South and South-East Asia in one and 'Oceania' in another. The latter acknowledges that Oceania is a highly diverse region, but erroneously and to its detriment focuses on Australia and Aotearoa New Zealand (Bauer and Tremblay 2011). Farida Jalalzai's (2013) global study of women executives is a second example.[3] Unsurprisingly, Asia's leaders find a place in these global collections.

Often, however, the experiences of women leaders from the region are elucidated in chapters and articles offering an Asia-region perspective. Andrea Fleschenberg (2011: 24) has described a comparative study of women in executive office in Asia as 'at first glance' an 'impossible task given the diversity and heterogeneity of the region, its political systems and cultures, gender ideologies and political developments', but nonetheless attempts this in a chapter in a global book. Even if Asia ends up a little hidden, these comparative studies offer value. The observed patterns and trends enable scholars to extract highly relevant lessons. Scholars of Asia—'Asianists'—have, for instance, noted the remarkable similarities between the Philippines and Indonesia, where the 'media, money and machine politics' dominate (Aspinall 2005: 117).[4] Yet, too often these are the only places where Asia's women leaders are made visible.

In short, there are three key circumstances at play. Women leaders, globally, are a minority but the relatively high number of women leaders in Asia over the past half-century has led scholars to frame their leadership as a form of Asian exceptionalism, thereby carving out a narrative in Asian gender

---

3   For another example, see the valuable edited collection by Janet Martin and MaryAnne Borrelli (2016), which contains some chapters that are comparative but the majority of which are single-country case studies, with a particular focus on the United States.

4   In making this argument, Edward Aspinall (2005: 119) refers to the power held in the hands of a few—'former bureaucrats, political fixers and politically connected business interests'—arguably in stark opposition to the 'rowdy, student-led popular protest movement alongside mass rioting among the urban poor' that 'drove the political crisis that ended the Suharto regime' (p. 120). In Indonesia today, in contrast to such free and somewhat disorganised politics of protest, 'machine politics' has seen a rise in the 'professional political stratum, modern campaigning techniques and big money' (p. 120). The Philippines, too, Aspinall argues, is characterised by systematic vote-buying and political corruption. One important distinction to make, which has proved particularly relevant to understanding women's movements in Indonesia, is that Indonesia is dominated by 'mass-based political forces that derive sustenance from resilient socioreligious identities' (p. 122).

studies. Second and perhaps as a result, in global studies, Asia's leaders may be entirely absent. Finally, the scholarship that does exist on a global scale tends to be largely comparative studies of Asia, with few lines drawn across regions.

What is Asian? A personal perspective

I am an Australia-born child of migrant parents. My parents were born in Malaysia and migrated to Australia in the mid-1970s. Late in my life, I found out that my grandmother, who had migrated from Sri Lanka, was brought to Malaysia as a teenager to marry my grandfather. In other words, she was what most Global North institutions term a 'child bride'. My grandmother wore white for more than 30 years after my grandfather died. The role played by my grandmother as a Hindu widow was what most human rights institutions—which I value significantly in my own scholarship—would consider being the 'subject of the patriarchy'.[5] Even later in life I found out that my grandmother's sister was married into a polygamous relationship.

As the daughter of Malaysia-born parents, I recall studying the role of Wan Azizah Wan Ismail, the wife of Malaysia's current Prime Minister, Anwar Ibrahim, after he had spent half a century in politics in government and opposition. Perhaps it was during my undergraduate days that my fascination with the place of women in politics began. I recall a persistent sense that surely there must have been more to the remarkable women across Asia who have occupied influential roles in difficult times and in complex sociopolitical contexts than is explained merely by the 'wives and widows' syndrome. Since I was first introduced to Wan Azizah, she has been Deputy Prime Minister of Malaysia and Minister of Women, Family and Community Development (2018–20), evidently demonstrating the significant roles women hold as political 'counterparts'.

---

5   The *Convention on the Elimination of All Forms of Discrimination against Women* (CEDAW) has been the subject of much of my scholarship in recent years (Vijeyarasa 2021a). While the CEDAW does not explicitly refer to the 'patriarchy', in softer terms, it seeks the elimination of 'prejudices and customary and all other practices which are based on the idea of the inferiority or the superiority of either of the sexes or on stereotyped roles for men and women' (UNGA 1979: Art. 5). By virtue of being a global human rights treaty, it tends to adopt a singular approach to issues, including the role of religion in shaping women's lives, unable to sufficiently value the importance of religion for some individuals while critiquing the limits religion may impose on women's lives.

I have been preoccupied ever since those early days with the question of women's leadership. Despite spending time, particularly as a lawyer and human rights activist, reflecting on women's leadership roles in other spaces, including as judges and community leaders of women's development and human rights organisations, my attention has always been drawn to executive office. Indeed, in my own lifetime, while I have seen shifts in women's occupation of leadership positions in other challenging spaces— from CEOs of Fortune 500 companies to the benches of international and regional courts—the ground has hardly shifted when it comes to women presidents and prime ministers around the world.

It is with this background that I found myself sitting at the dining table of a former female MP in Colombo who had been a member of president Kumaratunga's cabinet, when I went to Sri Lanka for that fieldtrip back in 2018. I entered her warm home, grateful for the invitation, and the first thing I saw was a wall-sized portrait of her husband, who had led the Sri Lankan Muslim Congress. This photo was probably put up after he died. He was explicitly and unquestionably the reason she had decided to enter politics in the first place. That male familial stepping stone for a woman entering politics is a story that has global relevance, as will be discussed in this chapter.

She spoke openly and happily of being a Muslim woman in politics, despite how unacceptable that initially was. She remarked how she was 'all wrapped up, as a good Muslim woman should be' and therefore eventually it was forgotten that she was a woman and breaking the norm and commentators let her be. What I also remember was being chastised by her for not speaking Tamil and encouraged, to say the least, to make sure I teach my two girls some of my 'mother tongue'. My mother tongue *is* English, but I perfectly understood what she meant. That chastising, of not being 'Asian enough', has been a common experience for me from my childhood right through to where I am today.

My personal context in writing this chapter naturally leads me to ask whether the kind of patriarchal family values described here are present in many families who migrate to economically advanced countries from other parts of the world. Is the idea of honouring your local language and tradition that different from what you see among migrants living in Europe and in other parts of the world who speak European minority languages, about which plenty has been said (Lonardi 2022; Pérez-Izaguirre et al. 2022)?

In the same ways that regional borders must be blurred in these personal experiences of migration, so must the regional borders in politics. In short, there is too much at risk and much to lose if a blanket label is thrown over everything 'Asian' without nuance, without distinctions and without giving visibility to complexities. It calls for a rethink of the experiences of Asia's women executives to determine whether there is something distinctly Asian about their leadership or whether the experiences of these leaders from South and South Asia are not so distinct from others across the globe. While acknowledging the non-monolithic nature of the category 'women', of women leaders and of women leaders from Asia, here I seek to explain both what is universal in their experiences and perhaps, more importantly, what we gain from a global lens.

Finding the global in the local

Women leaders in Asia, despite being relatively high in number, have struggled to find a place in the global narrative. Where their presence is acknowledged and attributed value, it is largely through a lens of Asian exceptionalism. In the second half of this chapter, I offer my views on what are the advantages of instead viewing these experiences as part of a global picture and a global contribution.

Asian women leaders: A foundational piece of the global narrative

Asian experiences of leadership are an important part of a holistic story of women's leadership that must be told. In other words, there are far too few women who defy barriers and reach the apex of leadership in their nations to allow the global narrative to ignore the stories of their leadership or for these stories to be framed as distinctly Asian and of lesser relevance to the global account.

As of October 2022, there were 32 women presidents and prime ministers worldwide. When women have led, it is sometimes for very short periods, including in Canada, for four months; Ecuador and Madagascar, for two days each; and South Africa, for 14 hours (although she previously briefly served as acting president). In October 2022, Liz Truss became the UK Prime Minister with the shortest tenure in history. Most women leaders are, or have been, their countries' first and only woman executive (Geiger and Kent 2017), while only a handful of countries—Iceland, Denmark, Aotearoa New Zealand and the United Kingdom—have reached three or four female leaders in their histories.

The dominance of men in executive-level leadership has shaped the practice of politics as well as the narrative. An expectation that leaders adopt so-called masculine leadership styles has fostered a derisive approach to female leadership, which is frequently associated with emotionality, weakness and even hysteria (Jamieson 1995; Wright and Holland 2014: 456). We are at the point where some still consider a *woman* president or prime minister a gender incongruity comparable with *women* police chiefs and *men* nurses (Meeks 2012: 177). While this analogy was drawn some years ago, coincidentally, a domestic battle ensued in Sri Lanka in February 2021 as the Women Parliamentarians' Caucus, among others, defended the appointment of Bimshani Jasin Arachchi as Sri Lanka's first and, to date, only female Deputy Inspector General of Police.

In sum, women presidents and prime ministers are hard to come by. With so few women having reached this apex, there is more than ample justification to approach women's occupation of executive office expansively. By contrast, there is potentially much lost in terms of a platform from which to theorise and extract lessons if Asia's many experiences are seen as distinct or standalone.

There are indeed many experiences. Even non-experts are familiar with just how many women have risen to leadership in the region: Thailand's Yingluck Shinawatra (2011–14); the very romanticised rise to power and fall of Myanmar's Aung San Suu Kyi (2016–21); India's former prime minister Indira Gandhi (1980–84); Pakistan's Benazir Bhutto (1988–90 and 1993–96); and the alternating tenures of prime ministers Khaleda Zia (1991–96, 2001–06) and Sheikh Hasina (1996–2001, 2009–24) in Bangladesh. In fact, Bangladesh is the only country in the world where a woman has been head of government for more years than a man during the past half-century (WEF 2020: 24). The rarity of women outnumbering men in the global landscape more than justifies inclusion rather than exclusion in the global narrative, both for the 'good' stories and the 'bad'.

It is important, too, to draw attention to how often these Asian women leader's stories are overlooked even by scholars of Asia. In other words, it is not the Global North framing alone that is to blame. President Megawati presents an excellent example of the erasure of her leadership from four years of Indonesia's history. This is particularly remarkable given that some describe her as still the most powerful woman in Indonesian politics, as the first and current leader of the Indonesian Democratic Party of Struggle (Partai Demokrasi Indonesia Perjuangan) and whose daughter, Puan Maharani, is also a key political figure today.

For instance, in the work of highly regarded scholar Tim Lindsey (whose writing has also benefited me), his analysis of reform to the legal infrastructure and governance in post-crisis Indonesia appears to show a rather broad disregard for the significance of Indonesia having had a woman hold executive office (2007: 14). By contrast, Lindsey refers to other actors—all male—who were considered significant players *during* Megawati's era. This example is used here to illustrate the fact that if women leaders in Asia struggle to find a place in the scholarship among 'Asianists', we cannot risk erasure altogether by encouraging an approach to women's experiences of politics in the region that further justifies minimal attention or exclusion altogether.

Importantly, the arguments presented here remain as true for women in executive office in Asia as in the Pacific region. The inclusion of the experiences of women leaders from Pacific Island countries is perhaps particularly necessary because of the very low levels of female representation in most parts of the region. Pacific women have risen to executive office *despite* the general exclusion of women from state political institutions. Dr Hilda Heine was the first woman to head the Republic of the Marshall Islands (2016–20); Afioga Fiamē Naomi Mata'afa was the first woman to serve as the Prime Minister of Samoa (2021–25). I separately note that Aotearoa New Zealand has had three women prime ministers in its history—Jenny Shipley (1997–99), Helen Clark (1999–2008) and Jacinda Ardern (2017–22)—not wanting to merge the Australian and New Zealand experiences with those of Pacific Island nations, which too often risks presenting a false picture of the Oceanic experiences of women's political participation in global statistics.

In short, Asia's women leaders make up a notable portion of the few women who have risen to these high ranks. With such a small sample from which to draw and renarrate an alternative story of what happens when women are present in executive office—for good and bad—we must see Asia's leaders as part of a bigger whole, rather than an exception.

Deconstructing the narrative to identify the global

Scholars are hesitant to undertake regional comparisons of women leaders across Asia (Fleschenberg 2011: 24). This hesitancy escalates when it comes to multiregional or even global comparisons. Yet, the similarities in the experiences of women leaders globally invite such a comparison. I suggest that the failure to see the potential in such comparative analysis, and to identify commonalities, has hindered the creation and effectiveness of solidarity-building platforms for women leaders worldwide.

I am hardly the first scholar to identify the similarities in the experiences of women presidents and prime ministers. Numerous examples on a global scale illustrate the 'double bind' of which Kathleen Hall Jamieson (1995: 16) spoke many years ago in offering a 'feminine' leadership yet still fitting masculine moulds. There is an impossible juggling act in pursuing the public's desire for a woman leader who is feminine, but not too feminine, while avoiding being seen as 'playing the gender card' (see, for example, Donaghue 2015; McLean and Maalsen 2017). This double bind is as much a reality in Asia as elsewhere. While president Kumaratunga eschewed those gendered norms (Vijeyarasa 2022: 255), the Philippines' Corazon Aquino called on these narratives to aid her rise to power and her anticorruption agenda as a 'crusading housewife let loose in a den of world-class thieves' (Vijeyarasa 2022: 108). It is a constant back and forth with which female leaders must wrestle.

Yet, many world leaders outside the region have evidently also struggled with this 'double bind'. Britain's 'Iron Lady', Margaret Thatcher (1979– 90), was photographed in the kitchen of 10 Downing Street while she was prime minister, while Liberian supporters of Ellen Johnson Sirleaf, former president of Liberia (2006–18) and the first elected woman head of state in Africa, waved signs at rallies stating, 'Ellen, she's our man' (Thomas and Adams 2010: 118). One Sri Lankan scholar drew positive parallels between president Kumaratunga's leadership style and that of Thatcher, saying, 'Chandrika played with that hypermasculinity in her peace agenda'— a woman leader tough enough to contest the civil war and promise what no leader before her had achieved (Vijeyarasa 2022: 105). Again, we can move beyond borders and beyond regions to identify this common leadership style. The parallels envisaged between Sri Lanka's Kumaratunga and Britain's Thatcher worked as much in Thatcher's favour as against her (Pilcher 1995: 494) when she was seen as compromising her femininity for power (Whitehead 2007: 238). This same gender paradox was noted by one Sri Lankan informant critical of both president Kumaratunga and her mother, saying they demonstrated a 'total insensitivity to women's issues' (Vijeyarasa 2022: 108); despite turning up, they were often late to meetings of the Sri Lankan Mothers' Front and the first to leave.

Widowhood is worn as a badge among Asia's women leaders. In fact, the successful presidential election campaign of Kumaratunga in 1994 was dubbed the 'Battle of the Widows' when she (widowed after her husband's 1988 assassination) ran against Srima Dissanayake, the spouse of the opposition candidate, who had been killed shortly before the election in a suicide-bomb attack and whose candidacy she replaced (Weiner 1995). This is just one example of the stepping stones into politics in Asia that are dependent on male connections and amplified in scholarship about Asia.

Yet, the parallels with Latin America, where a pathway dependent on male lineage is also common, are stark. Argentina's Isabel Martínez de Perón (president, 1974–76), Panama's Mireya Moscoso Rodríguez de Arias (president, 1999–2004), Guyana's Janet Jagan (prime minister, March–December 1997; president, 1997–99) and Argentina's Cristina Fernández de Kirchner (president, 2007–15; Vice-President 2019–present) were all married to male leaders of their countries (Jalalzai 2010: 150). In Africa, too, the husband of Malawi's Joyce Banda (vice-president, 2009–12; president, 2012–14) was the country's former chief justice. Meanwhile, Hillary Clinton's path as, first, US First Lady (1993–2001) and, later, presidential candidate is well known worldwide. What is so commonly described as an 'Asian' phenomenon of wives and widows is indeed a global commonality.

Most countries have never gone beyond one woman leader. Being the 'female first' is another reality that unites women leaders beyond cultural and geographic limits. How that manifests may be country specific but the manipulation of one's gender to characterise women as unsuitable for such leadership roles is unifying. The response to Indonesia's first and only female leader, Megawati, announcing that she would run as a candidate for the 1999 presidential election says much about what it means to be a 'female first' and its significance for the Islamic community, but also for Indonesian society in general (Dewi 2015: 61). The Congress of Indonesian Muslims (Kongres Umat Islam Indonesia) in November 1998 recommended that the Indonesian Ulema Council (Majelis Ulama Indonesia) publish a fatwa challenging female leadership, titled 'Perempuan Untuk Sementara Tidak Dibenarkan Jadi Presiden' (loosely translated as 'For the time being, women are not allowed to be president') (Dewi 2015: 61).

What subsequently unfolded was the manipulation of Megawati's gender by those around her, foremost among them Abdurrahman Wahid, long-time president of the Nahdlatul Ulama religious organisation, founder of the National Awakening Party and the presidential alternative to Megawati. The 1999 election campaign in Indonesia saw the use of banners by the United Development Party's youth wing pronouncing, 'A Woman President— No Way!' (Suryakusuma and Johnson 2001: 11), while the Indonesian Islamic Party of Liberation (Hizbut Tahrir Indonesia) cited an infamous Hadith: 'A nation which makes a woman its ruler will never succeed' (Dewi 2015: 62). Yet, if one were to draw comparisons more critically across the region, these challenges for a woman stepping up to be a nation's first female leader are not common. Pakistan and Bangladesh, despite being Muslim-majority nations, did not see the same backlash as Indonesia. The sufferings of president Megawati when she first raised her hand to contest may be more similar to, for example, Liberia's Sirleaf, Malawi's Banda or even Italy's Prime Minister, Giorgia Meloni, and Australia's Gillard.

If we are to acknowledge and draw new lines and connections between past and present female leaders across countries and regions, we may also see heightened success in attempts to build solidarity among such leaders. In 1996, an independent, self-governing network, the Council of Women World Leaders, was established by Vigdís Finnbogadóttir, President of Iceland (1980–96), Mary Robinson, President of Ireland (1990–97), and Laura Liswood, who became the council's secretary-general (Council of Women World Leaders 2021). It has received minimal scholarly attention. What has been said acknowledges the importance of women world leaders having a space for solidarity (Hoogensen and Solheim 2006: 109), but again, questions its value by asking whether the voice of women world leaders can be collectivised. It is worth noting that rarely are such critiques directed at 'male leader' collectives and only in recent times has a spattering of voices—mine among them—sought to point out the loss for the world when far too few women have a seat in global decision-making spaces like the G7 or G20. Despite the need for such female-centred spaces, the critiques go on. By finding greater dissimilarity than commonality, scholars have described the work of the Council of Women World Leaders as a 'monolithic corporate rhetoric' that attempts to speak on behalf of what is a highly diverse group of women from highly diverse geopolitical contexts (Richards and Dingo 2014: 43). In this scant scholarship, the council has been critiqued as fraught for its masculinised language and for obscuring differences between members (Richards and Dingo 2014: 116).

These harsh evaluations—while valid in part—overlook the significant potential of this assembly of women leaders to illustrate why women's leadership matters, to offer such leaders mutual support, to provide a platform for further research and to possibly build a collective consciousness among the world's women leaders of their capacity and, arguably, their responsibility to make visible women's issues. Its virtual meetings in recent years have been dedicated to gender-based violence and what a diversity of leadership can mean for advancing gender equality globally (Council of Women World Leaders 2021).

The sixty-sixth US Secretary of State, Condoleezza Rice, launched another such group, a collaboration that included the tenure of Philippines president Gloria Macapagal Arroyo. Like the council, the Women Leaders' Working Group was explicit in seeking 'to ensure that women's empowerment issues such as education, political and economic empowerment, and access to justice are international priorities' (Department of State 2008). It was at one Women Leaders' Working Group meeting that president Macapagal Arroyo declared:

> So, as women leaders, we must be champions of women in this special hour of need. It is now, more than ever, that we need women's voices to be heard to fight for the rights and opportunities of women both in our respective nations and in the whole world. (Macapagal Arroyo 2008)

President Macapagal Arroyo was hardly a voice for women and yet here we must acknowledge her attempt to rise above the singularity of the Philippines and place greater value on a collective of global women leaders.

Learning from what makes Asia distinct for global gain

What does 'Asia' have to offer the world? In this final section, I acknowledge that there are attributes to women's leadership that are distinct to the region, but I seek to do so in a way that amplifies what lessons can be extracted for global gain due to their applicability beyond Asia. Rather than contradicting my argument against Asian specificity, I seek to demonstrate that Asia does have something particular to offer. Yet, it is, in many respects, the flip side of the coin: there is a problem in excluding Asian experiences from the global narrative, as noted earlier, but we must also understand what global value can be drawn from these Asian experiences, rather than diminishing or devaluing Asia by assuming their relevance is only to the region. These 'Asian' lessons, if seen as part of a bigger, global picture, allow us to theorise and learn from the Asian platform.

All three women whom I studied for my monograph *The Woman President* led in a distinctive political atmosphere (Vijeyarasa 2022). I have witnessed at first hand the vibrancy of women's movements in the region and in the Philippines and Sri Lanka in particular, and the collectivisation of women's struggles in a way that articulates a demand for change well ahead of global women's movements. I will never forget the feeling of joining a sea of women activists in Manila to protest gender-based violence in December 2004. There is also something seemingly unique in the small but notable numbers of women who manage a transition from movement activism to politics in the region. Here, I think about the Philippine's Risa Hontiveros, a serving senator since 2016, and Indonesia's Nursyahbani Katjasungkana, elected as an MP for the Islam-based People's Awakening Party (2004–09), although without suggesting that the pathway for either was easy. I have had the privilege of interviewing both women during my research.

There are many lessons to extract from how women's movements in Asia make the most of the presence of a woman leader to push through reforms to laws on gender-based violence, equality and non-discrimination at work. These lessons can be of global benefit. Women's movements in the region use the votes of women as a negotiating tool to achieve significant law reform, *specifically when women lead*. Collaboration among feminist activists, women in the legislature and, to borrow an Australian term, 'femocrats' or inside agitators (Sawer 1996, 2007) in 'triangles of empowerment' (Holli 2008: 169) was accelerated when these women were president. From a gender lens being applied to the Philippines Development Plan (1989), gender-based violence laws enacted in the Philippines (2004), Indonesia (2004) and Sri Lanka (2005), and Indonesia's introduction of a quota for gender equality in parliament (2004), many lessons can be extracted for how women in government can collaborate with women's groups to use the 'women's vote' to achieve feminist goals when women occupy executive office (Vijeyarasa 2021b). In fact, these nations are in many ways global leaders. The Philippines introduced 10 days of paid leave from work for victims of gender-based violence before any other nation in the world (Republic of the Philippines 2004: S. 43).

There is equally much for the global community to learn from their struggles, including the less successful fights of Filipino women whose reproductive rights were most supressed under the country's two female presidents. The Aquino administration offered the Catholic Church reassurance that abortion would remain illegal even as foreign aid flowed into the Philippines, while president Macapagal Arroyo rejected all forms of modern contraceptive as forms of abortion, limited government support for family planning to natural methods for married couples and restricted access to emergency contraception (Austria 2004: 96). Both Aquino and Macapagal Arroyo demonstrate that women presidents, too, 'can become captives of the gender ideology' (Son 2005). If Asia is seen within this global setting, the struggles and strategies developed in response to these events can aid activists seeking to advance reproductive rights in parts of the Americas, Africa and Europe, in countries with or without women leaders.

Meanwhile, when the Tsunami struck at the tail end of president Kumaratunga's leadership on 26 December 2004, she was able to bring a gender lens to the government's response. In May 2005, the *Disaster Management Act* was passed by parliament and a disaster management centre was operational by September of that year (Parliament of the Democratic Socialist Republic of Sri Lanka 2005a). The Kumaratunga government brought into effect the *Tsunami (Special Provisions) Act* (Parliament of the Democratic Socialist Republic of Sri Lanka 2005b) and approved the National Committee on Women to mainstream gender in the post-tsunami recovery and reconstruction, with a specific focus on widows, livelihood assistance for women, the appointment of women to disaster management committees at all levels and providing land rights and ensuring joint ownership for women. The policy, like many, was not perfect but nonetheless shows global leadership from which other nations have much to gain.

Conclusion

Asia's women leaders are a phenomenon—because they are relatively high in number. They have also risen to leadership in a region often characterised as particularly patriarchal, although, in my view, patriarchy is truly a global phenomenon even if its manifestation may be more or less overt in some places than others. Asia's women leaders stand out because they have been framed as living a very particular Asian experience of leadership.

This chapter has sought to challenge this view, finding a place for Asia's leaders in the global narrative but also illustrating what is to be gained for global knowledge about women leaders when we see these Asian experiences as more than just 'Asian'. This is not to diminish or discount what is unique to the region, or devalue what is culturally significant. Rather, my goal has been to draw new lines across the global map that stretch us from Asia to Africa, or Europe to Africa, as well as across South and South-East Asia, where the lines have been etched by several decades of scholarship.

We are left with a narrative that is more open. Borders offer contained stories, silos and chapters in which to put various leaders and their experiences. Yet, this chapter has also demonstrated that there is more to lose by creating silos than by seeking some degree of erasure of these boundaries. Hopefully, the result is a narrative in which the region's female leaders always find a place, where overlaps in their experiences of leadership with those of other women leaders around the world are visible and yet the distinct achievements, successes and strategies of women leaders in the region, as well as Asia's movements, legislators and 'femocrats', are valued for what they can teach the rest of the world.

References

Aspinall, Edward. 2005. 'Elections and the Normalization of Politics in Indonesia.' *South East Asia Research* 13, no. 2: 117–56. doi.org/10.5367/0000000054604515.

Austria, Carolina S. Ruiz. 2004. 'The Church, the State and Women's Bodies in the Context of Religious Fundamentalism in the Philippines.' *Reproductive Health Matters* 12, no. 24: 96–103. doi.org/10.1016/S0968-8080(04)24152-0.

Bauer, Gretchen, and Manon Tremblay, eds. 2011. *Women in Executive Power: A Global Overview.* New York: Routledge. doi.org/10.4324/9780203829981.

Campbell, Andrew. 2003. 'John Howard: Leadership and Character; Peter Costello, "the Hollow Man".' *National Observer*, no. 58: 12–21.

Corbin, Juliet, and Anselm Strauss. 2008. 'Analyzing Data for Concepts.' In *Basics of Qualitative Research: Techniques and Procedures for Developing Grounded Theory*. 3rd edn. Thousand Oaks: SAGE. doi.org/10.4135/9781452230153.

Council of Women World Leaders. 2021. *Council of Women World Leaders Newsletter—March 2021*. us13.campaign-archive.com/home/?u=6d0e0f41c3f0 80faa26e03822&id=c2512fa97a.

Cowper-Coles, Minna. 2020. *Women Political Leaders: The Impact of Gender on Democracy*. London: Global Institute for Women's Leadership, King's College London, and Westminster Foundation for Democracy. www.kcl.ac.uk/giwl/assets/women-political-leaders.pdf.

Department of State. 2008. 'Women Leaders' Working Group.' [Online]. Washington, DC: US Department of State. 2001-2009.state.gov/s/we/c25293.htm.

Derichs, Claudia, and Mark R. Thompson, eds. 2013. *Dynasties and Female Political Leaders in Asia: Gender, Power and Pedigree*. Hamburg: LIT Verlag.

DeVotta, Neil. 2022. 'Sri Lanka's Agony.' *Journal of Democracy* 33, no. 3: 92–99. doi.org/10.1353/jod.2022.0042.

Dewi, Kurniawati Hastuti. 2015. 'The Normative Expectation of Javanese Muslim Women and Islamic Perspectives on Female Leadership.' In *Indonesian Women and Local Politics: Islam, Gender and Networks in Post-Suharto Indonesia*, 50–63. Singapore: NUS Press.

Dirlik, Arif. 1992. 'The Asia-Pacific Idea: Reality and Representation in the Invention of a Regional Structure.' *Journal of World History* 3, no. 1: 55–79.

Donaghue, Ngaire. 2015. 'Who Gets Played By "The Gender Card"?' *Australian Feminist Studies* 30, no. 84: 161–78. doi.org/10.1080/08164649.2015.1038118.

Election Commission of Sri Lanka. 2019. 'Women's Representation.' [Online]. Colombo: Election Commission of Sri Lanka. elections.gov.lk/en/all_inclusive_election/all_inclusive_women_representation_E.html.

Fleschenberg, Andrea. 2011. 'South and Southeast Asia.' In *Women in Executive Power: A Global Overview*, edited by Gretchen Bauer and Manon Tremblay, 23–44. New York: Routledge.

Fleschenberg, Andrea. 2013. 'Benazir Bhutto: Her People's Sister? A Contextual Analysis of Female Islamic Government.' In *Dynasties and Female Political Leaders in Asia: Gender, Power and Pedigree*, edited by Claudia Derichs and Mark R. Thompson, 63–112. Hamburg: LIT Verlag.

Geiger, Abigail, and Lauren Kent. 2017. 'Number of Women Leaders around the World Has Grown, but They're Still a Small Group.' Fact sheet, 8 March. Washington, DC: Pew Research Center.

Gerlach, Ricarda. 2013. '"Mega" Expectations: Indonesia's Democratic Transition and First Female President.' In *Dynasties and Female Political Leaders in Asia: Gender, Power and Pedigree*, edited by Claudia Derichs and Mark R. Thompson. Hamburg: LIT Verlag.

Gillard, Julia, and Ngozi Okonjo-Iweala. 2020. *Women and Leadership: Real Lives, Real Lessons*. Sydney: Random House Australia.

Holli, Anne Maria. 2008. 'Feminist Triangles: A Conceptual Analysis.' *Representation* 44, no. 2: 169–85. doi.org/10.1080/00344890802080407.

Hoogensen, Gunhild, and Bruce Olav Solheim. 2006. *Women in Power: World Leaders Since 1960*. Westport: Greenwood Publishing Group. doi.org/10.5040/9798216037255.

Jakimow, Tanya, Mario Gomez, Viyanga Gunasekera, Aida Fitri Harahap, Asima Yanty Siahaan, Nadine Vanniasinkam, Ramona Vijeyarasa, and Yumasdaleni. 2023. 'Broken Pathways to Politics: Clearing a Path from Grassroots to Representative Politics.' *Journal of Women, Politics & Policy* 44, no. 3: 336–53. doi.org/10.1080/1554477X.2023.2174367.

Jalalzai, Farida. 2010. 'Madam President: Gender, Power, and the Comparative Presidency.' *Journal of Women, Politics & Policy* 31, no. 2: 132–65. doi.org/10.1080/15544771003697643.

Jalalzai, Farida. 2013. *Shattered, Cracked, or Firmly Intact? Women and the Executive Glass Ceiling Worldwide*. New York: Oxford University Press. doi.org/10.1093/acprof:oso/9780199943531.001.0001.

Jamieson, Kathleen Hall. 1995. *Beyond the Double Bind: Women and Leadership*. Oxford: Oxford University Press. doi.org/10.1093/oso/9780195089400.001.0001.

Jayasuriya, Dharmasoka Laksiri. 2011. 'Post–Civil War Sri Lankan Electoral Politics and the Future of Liberal Democracy.' *Asia Pacific World* 2, no. 1: 25–53.

Khoo, Olivia. 2019. 'Diaspora as Method: Inter-Asia Cultural Studies and the Asian Australian Studies Research Network.' *Inter-Asia Cultural Studies* 20, no. 2: 290–301. doi.org/10.1080/14649373.2019.1613731.

Labonne, Julien, Sahar Parsa, and Pablo Querubin. 2015. 'Political Dynasties, Term Limits and Female Political Empowerment: Evidence from the Philippines.' Mimeo. New York University.

Lindsey, Timothy. 2007. 'Legal Infrastructure and Governance Reform in Post-Crisis Asia: The Case of Indonesia.' In *Law Reform in Developing and Transitional States*, 3–41. London: Routledge.

Lonardi, Serena. 2022. 'Minority Languages and Tourism: A Literature Review.' *Journal of Heritage Tourism* 17, no. 3: 342–56. doi.org/10.1080/1743873X.2021.2012183.

Macapagal Arroyo, Gloria. 2008. 'Statement of President Gloria Macapagal-Arroyo during the Session of the Women Leaders' Working Group.' Presented to Women Leaders' Working Group, New York, 25 September. Manila: Official Gazette, Republic of the Philippines. www.officialgazette.gov.ph/2008/09/25/statement-president-arroyo-during-the-session-of-the-women-leaders-working-group/.

Martin, Janet M., and MaryAnne Borrelli. 2016. *The Gendered Executive: A Comparative Analysis of Presidents, Prime Ministers, and Chief Executives.* Philadelphia: Temple University Press. doi.org/10.2307/j.ctvrdf3zm.

McLean, Jessica, and Sophia Maalsen. 2017. '"We Don't Want It to Be Like That for Her Again": Gendered Leadership and Online Feminism in Australian Politics and Planning.' *Australian Planner* 54, no. 1: 24–32. doi.org/10.1080/07293682.2017.1297316.

Medie, Peace A., and Alice J. Kang. 2018. 'Power, Knowledge and the Politics of Gender in the Global South.' *European Journal of Politics and Gender* 1, nos 1–2: 37–53. doi.org/10.1332/251510818X15272520831157.

Meeks, Lindsey. 2012. 'Is She "Man Enough"? Women Candidates, Executive Political Offices, and News Coverage.' *Journal of Communication* 62, no. 1: 175–93. doi.org/10.1111/j.1460-2466.2011.01621.x.

Motion, Judy M. 1996. 'Women Politicians: Media Objects or Political Subjects?' *Media International Australia* 80, no. 1: 110–17. doi.org/10.1177/1329878X9608000117.

Parliament of the Democratic Socialist Republic of Sri Lanka. 2005a. *Sri Lanka Disaster Management Act No. 13 of 2005.* Colombo: Department of Government Printing. www.dmc.gov.lk/images/DM_Act_English.pdf.

Parliament of the Democratic Socialist Republic of Sri Lanka. 2005b. *Tsunami (Special Provisions) Act No. 16 of 2005.* Colombo: Department of Government Printing. childprotection.gov.lk/images/pdfs/acts-guidelines/Tsunami%20Act%20No%2016%20of%202005.pdf.

Pérez-Izaguirre, Elizabeth, Gorka Roman, and María Orcasitas-Vicandi. 2022. 'Immigrant Minority Languages and Multilingual Education in Europe: A Literature Review.' *International Journal of Multilingualism* 21, no. 2: 932–52. doi.org/10.1080/14790718.2022.2121401.

Pilcher, Jane. 1995. 'The Gender Significance of Women in Power: British Women Talking about Margaret Thatcher.' *European Journal of Women's Studies* 2, no. 4: 493–508. doi.org/10.1177/135050689500200405.

Rajasingham-Senanyake, Darini. 2004. 'Between Reality and Representation: Women's Agency in War and Post-Conflict Sri Lanka.' *Cultural Dynamics* 16, nos 2–3: 141–68. doi.org/10.1177/0921374004047741.

Republic of the Philippines. 2004. *Republic Act No. 9262; An Act Defining Violence against Women and Their Children, Providing for Protective Measures for Victims, Prescribing Penalties Therefore, and for Other Purposes*. 8 March. Manila: Congress of the Philippines.

Richards, Rebecca S., and Rebecca Dingo. 2014. *Transnational Feminist Rhetorics and Gendered Leadership in Global Politics: From Daughters of Destiny to Iron Ladies*. Blue Ridge Summit: Lexington Books.

Richter, Linda K. 1990. 'Exploring Theories of Female Leadership in South and Southeast Asia.' *Pacific Affairs* 63, no. 4: 524. doi.org/10.2307/2759914.

Sawer, Marian. 1996. *Femocrats and Ecorats: Women's Policy Machinery in Australia, Canada and New Zealand*. UNRISD Occasional Paper No. 6. Geneva: United Nations Research Institute for Social Development. www.econstor.eu/handle/10419/148823.

Sawer, Marian. 2007. 'Australia: The Fall of the Femocrat.' In *Changing State Feminism*, edited by Joyce Outshoorn and Johanna Kantola, 20–40. London: Palgrave Macmillan. doi.org/10.1057/9780230591424_2.

Sinclair, Amanda. 2013. 'Essay: Can I Really Be Me? The Challenges for Women Leaders Constructing Authenticity.' In *Authentic Leadership: Clashes, Convergences and Coalescences*, edited by Donna Ladkin and Chellie Spiller, 239–51. Cheltenham: Edward Elgar Publishing. doi.org/10.4337/9781781006382.00029.

Son, Johanna. 2005. 'PHILIPPINES: Church, a Goliath Against Reproductive Health.' *Inter Press Service*, [Rome], 20 November. www.ipsnews.net/2005/11/philippines-church-a-goliath-against-reproductive-health/.

Suryakusuma, Julia, and Paige Johnson. 2001. 'Creating *Indonesia Baru*: The Political Parties and Views of Women in Contemporary Indonesia.' Paper presented to 2nd International Symposium of *Journal Antropologi Indonesia*: Globalization and Local Culture: A Dialectic towards the New Indonesia, Padang, 18–21 July. simposiumjai.ui.ac.id/wp-content/uploads/20/2020/03/17.3.3-Julia-Suryakusuma.pdf.

Thomas, Gwynn, and Melinda Adams. 2010. 'Breaking the Final Glass Ceiling: The Influence of Gender in the Elections of Ellen Johnson-Sirleaf and Michelle Bachelet.' *Journal of Women, Politics & Policy* 31, no. 2: 105–31. doi.org/10.1080/15544771003697270.

Thompson, Mark R. 2013. 'Presidents and "People Power" in the Philippines: Corazon C. Aquino and Gloria Macapagal-Arroyo.' In *Dynasties and Female Political Leaders in Asia: Gender, Power and Pedigree*, edited by Claudia Derichs and Mark Thompson, 151–89. Hamburg: LIT Verlag.

United Nations General Assembly (UNGA). 1979. *Convention on the Elimination of All Forms of Discrimination against Women*. UN Doc. A/34/46 (1979), Opened for signature 1 March 1980, Entered into force 3 September 1981. New York: UNGA.

Vanniasinkam, Nadine, and Viyanga Gunasekera. 2022. 'Solidarity among Women in Politics in Sri Lanka: Potentials and Challenges.' *Polity* 10, no. 2: 58–63. polity.lk/wp-content/uploads/2024/06/Polity_10.2_12Nadine_Viyanga.pdf.

Vijeyarasa, Ramona. 2020. 'Women's Absence in Sri Lankan Politics: Lessons on the Effectiveness and Limitations of Quotas to Address Under-Representation.' *Women's Studies International Forum* 81, no. 102371. doi.org/10.1016/j.wsif.2020.102371.

Vijeyarasa, Ramona. 2021a. 'Quantifying CEDAW: Concrete Tools for Enhancing Accountability for Women's Human Rights.' *Harvard Human Rights Journal* 34, no. 1: 37–80.

Vijeyarasa, Ramona. 2021b. 'Women's Movements under Women Presidents: Bringing a Gender Perspective to the Legal System.' *Gender & Development* 29, nos 2–3: 569–91. doi.org/10.1080/13552074.2021.1978736.

Vijeyarasa, Ramona. 2022. *The Woman President: Leadership, Law and Legacy for Women Based on Experiences from South and Southeast Asia*. Oxford: Oxford University Press. doi.org/10.1093/oso/9780192848918.001.0001.

Weiner, Eric. 1995. 'Where Women Rule, They Leave a Genderless Legacy Behind.' *Christian Science Monitor*, 10 May. www.csmonitor.com/1995/0510/10011.html.

Whitehead, Stephen. 2007. 'Metrosexuality! Cameron, Brown and the Politics of "New Masculinity".' *Public Policy Research* 14, no. 4: 234–39. doi.org/10.1111/j.1744-540X.2008.00495.x.

World Economic Forum (WEF). 2020. *The Global Gender Gap Report 2020*. Insight Report. Geneva: World Economic Forum. www3.weforum.org/docs/WEF_GGGR_2020.pdf.

Wright, K.A.M., and Jack Holland. 2014. 'Leadership and the Media: Gendered Framings of Julia Gillard's "Sexism and Misogyny" Speech.' *Australian Journal of Political Science* 49, no. 3: 455–68. doi.org/10.1080/10361146.2014.929089.

Yatawara, Dhaneshi. 2016. 'In Their Own Words.' *Options* 56: 10–11.

9

Weaving a Pacific Narrative into Understanding Women's Underrepresentation in Politics in Samoa

Mema Motusaga and Elise Howard

In 2021, after 35 years of political stability, Samoa[1] elected its first woman to serve as Prime Minister, the Honourable Afioga Fiamē Naomi Mata'afa. Alongside Mata'afa, six women are serving in Samoa's Parliament, the highest number since independence, with only 21 women becoming an MP since 1962. Samoa is the first country in the Pacific which has actively sought to address women's underrepresentation in politics through temporary special measures (TSMs). The TSMs operate as a safety net to ensure a minimum of 10 per cent of parliamentarians are women (Baker 2019). The 2021 elections were only the second national elections since the introduction of the TSMs and reignited significant public debate about women's place in politics. After a 35-year uninterrupted reign by the Human Rights Protection Party, early election results hung in the balance, and the TSMs had the potential to alter a close election result.[2] Designed at a time of political stability, the quota system suddenly offered potential for political gain and led to the unusual sight of public protests about

---

1   Samoa in this chapter refers to Western Samoa, which was first under German and then New Zealand administration.

2   For the full story on the potential influence of the quota system on the outcome of the 2021 election, please see Motusaga (2021).

women's representation. Events reached a pinnacle when Mata'afa was sworn in as first woman prime minister inside a tent outside the doors of a locked Parliament House (Motusaga 2021). While Mata'afa carried herself calmly throughout the controversy, it was clear by the end of 2021 that her patience had been tested. During a budget debate to secure funding for gender-based violence programs, Mata'afa called on opposition members to 'stop politicising women' (Feagaimaali'i 2021). Her comments highlighted the fact that, while Samoa has improved women's representation in politics, efforts to promote women's inclusion still have potential to be tokenistic and politicised.

A common refrain in Samoa is that there is no gender inequality, that '*o Samoa ua uma ona tofi*' ('Samoa's stratification is very clear') and men and women are equal based on inheritance. In Samoan culture, women hold the highest status, called *saotamaitai*, and are traditionally the wealth-producers, the main fundraisers and supporters of the church, well educated and economically active. Inherited brother–sister relationships based on complementary and relational power, known as the *feagaiga* or *tamasa*, are the evidence that Samoan women hold equal status to men. Yet, the gender equality narrative is a product of homogenised ideas about what constitutes Samoan culture or the *fa'asamoa* ('the Samoan way') when, in reality, culture is constantly shifting, contested and untidy (Merry 2003; Zetlin 2014). Gender relations are complex and vary in different spaces between different family relations and have been complicated by colonial and contemporary influences.

The requirement for all political candidates to take up a masculine *matai* (or 'chiefly') title is quite rightly regarded as the main barrier to women's participation in politics, and a 'cultural' barrier at that (Meleisea et al. 2015). Taking up a *matai* title requires women to become more like men and compete for power to participate in politics rather than draw on women's traditional and complementary sources of power. The problem with women's underrepresentation in politics, then, lies not in 'cultural barriers' themselves, but in how selectively and incompletely aspects of culture have been transmitted through narratives and reified in the Samoan Constitution. We also argue that the perpetuation of the gender equality narrative and the source of this narrative, the *feagaiga*, are based on an incomplete story and constrain efforts to discuss, debate and promote women's place in politics.

Studies of women's participation in politics have favoured Western ontologies, particularly to consider how power can be claimed, controlled or divided through changes to electoral systems, improving women's educational levels, strengthening women's movements or endorsing frameworks such as the *Convention on the Elimination of All Forms of Discrimination against Women* (CEDAW) (Viterna et al. 2008). This conceptualisation of power comes from a conflict perspective to analyse who has control and power in a given context (Slatter 2012; Brigg et al. 2019). Key concepts in Samoan culture, however, offer a different potential—for power to be conceived as complementary, relational and balanced due to *feagaiga* ('complementary brother–sister relationships') and *tausi le vā* ('respectful and relational space'). These key cultural concepts are currently used to exclude rather than include women from political spaces.

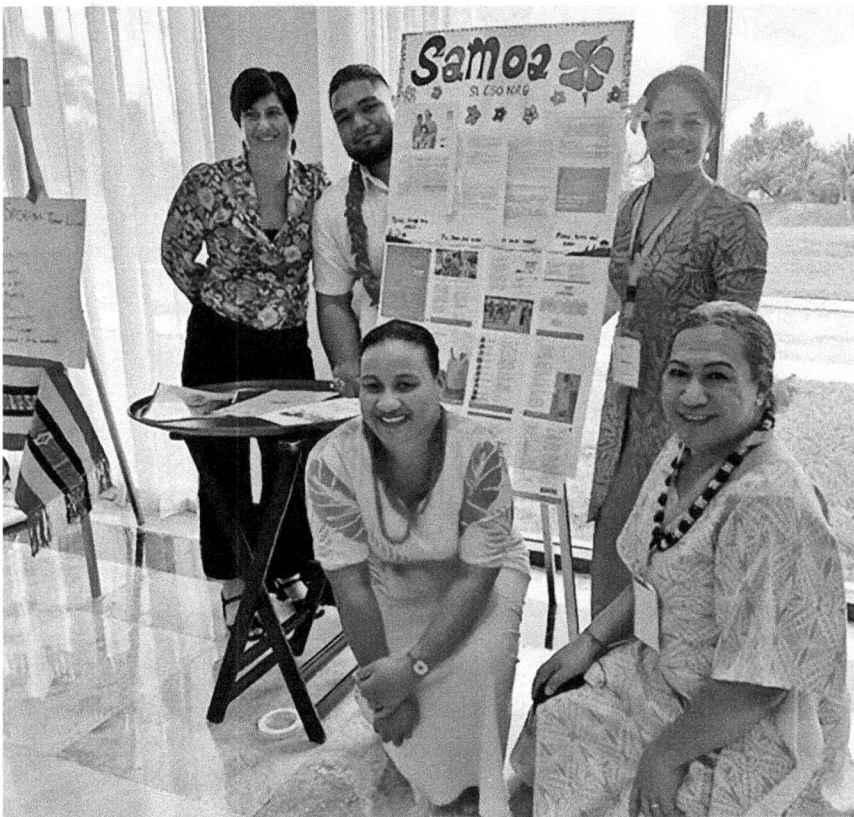

Plate 9.1: The Samoan delegation to the Ending Violence Against Women and Girls Reflection Summit in Cancun, Mexico, 2022

Note: Left to right: Abby Erikson, Gutu Faasau, Mema Motusaga, Gabrielle Apelu and Fagalima Tuatagaloa.

Source: Mema Motusaga.

Plate 9.2: The Samoan community coming together to support gender equity at all levels

Note: Taken during the Ministry of Women, Community and Social Development's 16 Days of Activism campaign that was held from 25 November to 10 December 2022.

Source: Mema Motusaga.

This chapter explores the contradictions between beliefs that there is no gender inequality in Samoa and the fact that women can be politicised and treated as tokens. We seek to reclaim women's traditional sources of power to ensure their participation in politics, where women are not politicised or treated as tokens, as was seen in the recent election in Samoa, but rather valued and offered equal reverence to men. We explore the duality of unchanging narratives and constitutions alongside significant cultural shifts, to consider how this affects women's participation in politics. We focus on the shift in the *feagaiga* relationship due to the arrival of missionaries from the 1830s in Samoa and the design of the Westminster system by colonial and *matai* actors. We take a view of culture as contested and dynamic, constructed by many factors: institutions, domestic and external actors, political arrangements, legal structures *and* historical trajectories (Merry 2003; Jolly 1992). This view requires us to consider 'spaces of change, contestation and to analyse the links between power, practice and values', and the interplay of institutional changes with gender roles and representation (Merry 2003: 71; Zetlin 2014). The chapter concludes by considering how to shift popular narratives by drawing on the concept of *vā* or relational, respectful and sacred space, to reconstruct political spaces to enable women's participation. Given women's underrepresentation is not unique to Samoa, the chapter will consider the implications for other locations, by floating the possibility of rethinking ontologies to re-story politics as a relational and respectful rather than combative site of power.

Re-storying: Our perspectives

Writing from the perspectives of a Samoan and a non-Indigenous Australian author, this chapter draws on the authors' academic research, practitioner experiences and many conversations to develop shared understandings from insider and outsider perspectives. These conversations explored the entanglement of Indigenous, missionary and colonial influences that privileged some master narratives over others and reinforced women's political underrepresentation today. The first author, Dr Mema Motusaga, holds a powerful position as the CEO of the Ministry of Women, Community and Social Development in Samoa and is a well-known advocate for women's leadership and the prevention of violence against women. Samoa is a place where power, sourced through familial ties and status, comes with great obligations and actions, which reflect not just on individuals but also on extended families. The second author, Elise Howard, is a non-academic staff member at The Australian National University, an institution still working to dismantle its patriarchal and discriminatory structures. The two authors' relationship started online in 2020 during Covid-19 lockdowns. At that time, Dr Motusaga had just published an article about gender quotas in Samoa and shared how, by putting herself out there, she was subject to much scrutiny and criticism within Samoa, as an insider commenting on her own country, especially when her ideas pushed gender boundaries. Elise naively expressed surprise at this and highlighted how the conversations in Canberra were so focused on decolonisation and questioning by others and herself as to whether she was 'the right person' as a white Australian woman to be doing research with Pacific women. Mema and Elise laughed together about how women are criticised and scrutinised, regardless of their insider or outsider status, not always by men, but many times by other women, too. We noticed how there are ways to discount our words through one justification or another. It is clear though that for Mema as an insider the stakes are higher. Mema suggested the way to overcome this was to collaborate, as together our voices could be stronger, so our working relationship was born with the intent to increase each other's power. Our working relationship has since evolved into friendship, as we were able to visit each other post-Covid restrictions.

We draw on a counselling and social work practice known as 're-storying'. Re-storying has two stages. The first requires revisiting and deconstructing common narratives to understand how they create dominant beliefs and the consequences of those narratives. The second stage is to reframe narratives by drawing out new meanings from old stories, to identify beneficial pathways forward (White and Epston 1990). While re-storying is used as an individual therapy practice, the concept has been applied to decolonise the history curriculum (Ragoonaden et al. 2020), as a pedagogical practice (Clandinin and Connelly 2000) and in narrative inquiry (Ollerenshaw and Creswell 2002). We draw on this idea for the possibility of re-storying master narratives not just to derive new meanings, but also to reclaim the narratives that could contribute to the construction of gender-equal political spaces. Given relationality is strongly valued in Samoa, this will require much public deliberation and debate to contest and reframe shared narratives. In this context, we propose re-storying as a relational and respectful process of reclamation and restitution that celebrates story-holders as the experts with the power to revisit and reframe women as agentic political subjects.

Re-storying gender equality narratives

Narratives are politically important. Narratives construct gendered political subjects, shape individual and collective identities, reinforce common beliefs and limit notions of what is possible (Patterson and Monroe 1998). Narratives shift over time, are selective and can be used to justify the way things are done (Frederick 2013). Political leaders employ narratives of a universally accepted culture as a tool to build support and legitimacy, or for unifying diverse groups in nation-building (Merry 2003; Jolly 1992). Resisting outsider influence is a popular political strategy to build constituency support by demonstrating strength against threats to nationhood (Merry 2003). For example, initiatives to promote gender equality across the Pacific are often resisted as a Western threat to the Pacific way of life (Slatter 2012). This is regularly enforced through speech acts by leaders who reify culture in ways that privilege masculine power sources while ignoring the possibilities that culture offers for women's empowerment. Narratives are a key means of transmitting knowledge and maintaining understanding of key cultural concepts in Samoa. Narratives also underpin approaches to improving women's participation in politics that emphasise 'cultural barriers' as a problem.

As Zetlin (2014) has pointed out, while narratives that position culture as the key barrier to women's political participation are widely shared, they can also be contested and can shift each time they are revisited. In Samoa, some key changes had political consequences for women, particularly the arrival of missionaries in the early 1800s and the shift in 1962 to independence from New Zealand administration, which had been in place since 1914. These periods led to significant transformations in women's power, yet the master narrative that there is no gender inequality in Samoa largely remains. At the same time, neocolonial development actors have had much influence on gender policy in Samoa, often bringing models that butt up against rather than embrace key aspects of Samoan culture: Christian values and the *fa'asamoa*. For example, while the *fa'asamoa* and Christian values are part of the guiding principles in the national strategy on gender equality and are enshrined in the national Constitution,[3] in 2018, the UN Human Rights Council identified the meaning that is ascribed to the Samoan way as the 'root cause' of gender inequality (OHCHR 2018: 18). In 2020, the CEDAW expert committee, in its review of Samoa, described the constitutional amendment to recognise Samoa as a Christian country as a 'step backwards' for human rights (OHCHR 2018: para. 20).

Narratives, linguistic practices and cosmologies can also construct gendered political spaces. In our discussion of space, we draw on Samoan concepts of *vā* ('space') and *vā fealoai* ('spatial relations') as the core of the *fa'asamoa* and key to determining who can be seen as a leader. *Vā fealoai* determines the way that individuals and groups can relate to one another and informs how language should be used to respect and confirm relations (Koya Vaka'uta 2017). *Vā* also dictates sociocultural roles and responsibilities, and the closer the *vā*, the greater are the responsibilities and obligations (Koya Vaka'uta 2017). Space can be physical but also intangible, spiritual and cosmological, meaning that space can be embodied, felt, believed and/ or perceived. We also draw on the concept of gendered space employed in sociology, anthropology and feminist political ecology that centralises the role of space (whether human-constructed architecture or landscapes and natural environments) and the cultural rules (informal or formal) that create

---

3   See *Constitution of the Independent State of Samoa*: Preamble, p. 7, and Part 1, Clause 3: www. refworld.org/legal/legislation/natlegbod/1960/en/39855.

gendered boundaries around those spaces. Gendered spaces organise gender relations, particular ways of being a man or a woman and influence access to different resources and 'socially valued' knowledge (Phillips and Ilcan 2000; Rocheleau et al. 1996; Spain 1993: 137). In Samoa, women's status and ways of operating are fluid and shift depending on their relations to others (Latai 2014). Women's roles and status depend on whether they are wives or sisters, chiefly or untitled, and this dictates which spaces women and men may occupy in the *fale* ('house'), *aiga* ('extended family') and *fono* ('village council') (Latai 2014). Missionaries sought to introduce distinctions between domestic (feminine) spaces and public (masculine) roles based on ideas of nuclear rather than extended families (Latai 2014). However, as the following sections illustrate, distinctions between feminine and masculine spaces have mainly been taken up in local and national-level governance.

The source of the equality narrative: The *feagaiga*

The *feagaiga* is the foundation of narratives in Samoa that there is no gender inequality. While *feagaiga* is often referred to as a covenant[4] or sacred relationship between brother and sister, this is deeper than a reciprocal dyadic relationship and part of the *fa'asamoa* system of organising social life, underpinned by the belief that secular governance and action require moral or spiritual support (Latai 2015; Schoeffel 1995).

The *fa'amatai*, or chiefly system, and *fa'asamoa* established structures and processes that prescribe a way of life and being. The *fa'asamoa* helps each person know where they are positioned as a Samoan and how they should relate to one another (Fairbairn-Dunlop 1991; So'o 2008). *Matai* hold secular power (*pule*) and are responsible for governance and action, while *tamatai* or *tamasa* ('sacred offspring') hold and transmit spiritual power (*mana*) and are responsible for spiritual guidance or support (Fairbairn-Dunlop 1991; Latai 2014; Tagaloa 1997). The *tamatai* hold *saotamaitai* titles. These sacred spiritual powers were considered equal, offered equal opportunities for

---

4   Missionaries likened the *feagaiga* relationship to the term 'covenant' used in the Bible to describe taboos, processes or obligations that must be followed by two parties, yet this relationship was hierarchical and did not truly capture the meaning of the *feagaiga* relationship, which is based on complementary power (for more details, see Latai 2015; Schoeffel 1995).

status enhancement (Fairbairn-Dunlop 1991) and underpinned the belief that women held high and sacred status and occupied an important place within the *fa'asamoa*.

Matai are also expected to mentor and encourage women to take up leadership positions within the community, including chiefly titles. Women who descend from *matai* lineages may take on the title of *taupou* (or ceremonial virgin), which is equivalent to the chiefly titles bestowed upon the brothers. These ascribed statuses come with assigned responsibilities, under which women, according to Tagaloa (1997), are known as the healers, teachers, priestesses, makers of wealth and peacemakers. In contrast, men are the sister's protector, the decision-makers and the spokesperson for the family and are given responsibility for all the heavy duties such as cultivating the land, building and being warriors. While this is a complementary relation, an important distinction is that women's power lies in spiritual and moral authority in contrast to the secular authority and action required of her brother (Schoeffel 1995).

Before missionary contact, brother–sister relationships could extend to all offspring of *matai* within a village, or 'circle of chiefs made as one' (Tcherkézoff 2015: 167), or beyond a village, due to polygamous practices designed to create powerful dynasties (Schoeffel 1995). Brothers must ensure that their sisters are fully satisfied with his service, because of the belief that the sister, as the sacred child, has the power to curse him if she is not pleased. Brothers must also refer to sisters for final approval before any decision is enacted (Latai 2014; Tagaloa 1997).

Polygamous practices were central to the *feagaiga* relationship and *matai* sources of power. Marriage to high-ranking virgins was used to establish alliances and maximise connections with genealogically well-established families (Schoeffel 1995). Missionaries regarded such practices as immoral and sought to improve women's status through monogamous stable marriage and emphasised dutiful wifehood and domestic life. However, wives were the lowest status group within a village (Tcherkézoff 2015) and ceremonial rather than domestic roles were the key means for women to acquire status (Schoeffel 1995). In promoting monogamy and encouraging domesticity, missionaries effectively wiped out pathways for women to gain status through the *feagaiga* relationship. Missionaries, misunderstanding that women's power came only through rank rather than also through gendered roles, emphasised women as wives, while Samoan culture had emphasised women as sisters.

In addition, the interpretation of *feagaiga* as a covenant led to the pastor replacing the sister as the closest spiritual connection to God, while the *matai* source of secular power remained unchanged (Schoeffel 1995). Early Bibles created by missionaries also referred to women as *fafine* ('female' or 'wife') *rather* than *tamaitai* ('lady') (Motusaga 2016). The distinction is important because *tamaitai* were thought to hold equal status to the *matai*, while *fafine* has several negative connotations. '*Fafine*' refers to a woman who is either a wife from outside the village without chiefly lineage (and therefore low status) or no longer a virgin (and therefore a potential source of shame) (Tcherkézoff 2015). The term can therefore be used to deliver an insult, particularly to a high-ranking woman or a *tamaitai* (Schoeffel 1995; Tcherkézoff 2015). As a participant in Mema's research explains:

> [I]f you have a look at how the bible was translated the word '*tamaitai*' was not used at all. The missionaries used the word '*fafine*' all throughout the bible. Why? Because they didn't want the word *tamaitai* to be kept because to the Samoans the use of the word *tamaitai* associates not only with the female's responsibilities within the family and society but also promotes the status of the sister as *feagaiga*. (Motusaga 2016: 87)

Tamaitai may bear chiefly titles, however, they inherit the *saotamaitai* title, which is the equivalent of the chiefly title. While this is less established in contemporary times, *tamaitai* are still given greater status than outsider wives, undertake ceremonial duties and have obligations to their village and for maintaining founding titles (Tcherkézoff 2015).

In contemporary practices, the secular and spiritual power division has translated into women's secondary status in decision-making. *Matai* councils or the *fono* at local levels have responsibility for community-level governance—a role now enshrined in the Constitution. Decision-making meetings are held by *matai* first, followed by consultations with the women's council in the village (Motusaga 2016). In some locations, women reported that 'this is how we have done it all along' (Interview participant in Motusaga 2016). Yet, this practice is now more token than substantial and not reflective of the *feagaiga* relationship in which a brother is beholden to his sister's decisions. Yet, pride in the equality narrative grounded in the value of *feagaiga* offers powerful perceptions that these practices are the substantive and the right way that things are done.

Political systems that require women to become more like men

The Samoan legislature is celebrated as a successful hybrid model of traditional Westminster governance (Meleisea et al. 2015; So'o 2008). A democratic unitary national legislature (the *Fono*) is complemented by local-level village councils (*fono*) comprising *matai* ('chiefly') titleholders, with political candidacy limited to *matai* titleholders only. Initially, suffrage was also limited to *matai* titleholders, however, a constitutional amendment in the leadup to the 1991 elections means that all Samoan citizens over the age of 21 may vote in national elections (So'o 2008).

The Samoan Constitution incorporates the *matai* system as a key element of governance while other aspects of 'tradition', particularly women's spiritual power, are missing. In the leadup to independence from New Zealand administration in 1962, the constitutional design process was dominated by men. An executive committee on self-government, with advice from constitutional lawyers from Aotearoa New Zealand and Australia, drafted the Constitution, which was then endorsed by a 174-member constitutional convention comprising 159 *matai* titleholders and 15 European[5] members (So'o 2008).

However, women played a part in endorsing the Constitution. In 1961, the Constitution was put to a vote in a national plebiscite conducted under UN supervision with universal suffrage and was endorsed by 83 per cent of voters (Meleisea et al. 2015; So'o 2008). The priority at that time, for women and men, was to preserve the *fa'asamoa* and to seek independence from outside influences (Meleiseā et al. 2015; So'o 2008). In addition, because Samoa is a relational culture that places great weight on spiritual as well as political forms of authority, this impacts who can make claims or who will want to claim to belong to state power structures (Kantola 2016). In this context, it is understandable that women voted in favour of a political system that preserved the *fa'asamoa*, yet restricted their own political rights (see Palmieri et al. 2023). This can also explain why many women lack the

---

5   At that time a legal distinction existed between 'native' and 'European' (or 'part-Samoan') status, and enabled Samoans who were classified as Europeans with additional legal privileges in political status access to English-language schools and secondary education in Aotearoa New Zealand, but to enjoy such rights required forgoing the rights of a *matai* title (Meleisea et al. 1987).

aspiration to participate in politics and instead celebrate their powers as the backbone of a church system that provides the alternative space for spiritual forms of authority (Motusaga 2016).

Analysis of gendered barriers to participation in politics in Samoa quite rightly places firm emphasis on the requirement for aspiring candidates to hold a *matai* or chiefly title as the key limitation on women (Meleisea et al. 2015). Women hold approximately 12 per cent of *matai* titles (Samoa Bureau of Statistics 2018) and, while the number is growing, some villages still prohibit or strongly discourage women from becoming *matai* (Haley et al. 2017; Baker 2018). Women are therefore regularly encouraged to take up *matai* titles to enter politics, yet this requires working through gendered notions of who is the right person to take up a *matai* title and who is the right person to serve. To secure political candidacy, *matai* must receive signed endorsement from the near-exclusively male *fono* about their service or *monotaga* to their village (Meleisea et al. 2015). To enter the space of the *fono* in the first place requires significant courage to push through gendered boundaries (Tuuau and Howard 2019). While many women have sought to improve their status with secular and political forms of authority through the *matai* titles, many have resisted this domain as being outside women's interests and aspirations. Encouraging women to stand for politics therefore is not a simple matter of improving women's political aspirations, but rather of understanding that there are deep ideological foundations to the distinctions between political, secular and spiritual service for families and communities.

Women taking up *matai* titles has gendered consequences. While women may take up *matai* titles and go on to gain political office, this requires them to forgo their spiritual and sacred status. The devaluing of women's sacred forms of status and lack of integration into the political system mean that women must behave more like men and take on the masculine tasks of serving the family to become a political actor. The effect is that, by taking up *matai*, women are changing the meaning of the title by having some influence on the gendered space of politics. However, the greatest consequence is that the equivalent feminine title, the *saotamaitai*—a revered part of Samoan society—has been devalued in the realm of political institutions. This is a result of adopting a Westminster system without thoroughly investigating the gender context in Samoa.

While independence in Samoa is seen as a time when traditional customs were reconciled with introduced political institutions, notions of custom were entangled with missionary influences. Constitutional limits on political candidacy to *matai* titleholders only recognises the secular powers of the *matai* and reinforces their role as political authorities, yet there is no equivalent recognition for the *saotamaitai* titles for Samoan women. The Constitution was important in preserving the *fa'asamao*, but this occurred in an unbalanced way. Now, the problem remains that culture and gender roles are constantly shifting and being reinterpreted, yet the Constitution authorises this incomplete understanding of Samoan culture as ultimate and unchanging.

Entrenching masculine power by creating gendered political spaces

Space in the *fono* or meeting house is used deliberately as a means of enacting rank, hierarchy and power. Participants are seated according to their status, with high ranking at the front and low at the back (Keating and Duranti 2006). Lower-status *matai* are expected to serve their political apprenticeship at the back to learn the pathway to leadership and to 'understand what it is like to be "in the back"' (Huffer and So'o 2005: 318). Many women who hold *matai* titles are hesitant to enter the masculine space of the *fono*, yet this is the only pathway to becoming a national-level political subject.

Demonstrated mastery of the oratorical language in the *fono* is also a key means of enacting status or validating others' rank (Holmes 1969; Milner 1961; Kruse Va'ai 2011). Given that Samoa is primarily an oral culture, speechmaking and deliberation are key elements of the system: 'a *matai* is someone who knows how to speak the *proper language*, someone who is strong, someone who is not a follower, someone who is not just a yes person' (Tuuau and Howard 2019: 6).

The 'proper language' is the oratorical language, a register used for speechmaking that can only be heard and learned within the masculine space of the *fono*, meaning most women, whether *matai* or not, will be unfamiliar with this language. Oratory is a masculine source of power and the knowledge and skill required to execute this language are 'jealously guarded' because of the level of power its usage can confer (Milner 1961). Oratorical language is used in the Parliament in opening and closing ceremonies and in formal speeches, and the honour of closing Parliament is only settled after deliberation on who may 'take the honour of displaying their oratorical skills in addressing all of Samoa' (Kruse Va'ai 2011: 60).

While the oratorical register is used in formal proceedings and is effectively a means of constructing both the national-level *Fono* and the local-level *fono* as gendered spaces, the Samoan term *tala tau sua* ('men jesting') is used to describe another style of communication in politics. The connotation of this term is that politics is dirty (Meleisea et al. 2015). Given the requirement for respect and taboo relationships between brother and sister or the *feagaiga*, concerns arise from women entering this space and experiencing disrespect from their brothers. For example:

> I believe that women should not be in politics because of the brother and sister covenant. There is great emphasis in protecting the value and obligations of this relationship. The men believe that women are their *feagaiga* and when it comes to everyday political life there are times where [the] language used will go overboard and that is not appropriate when their sisters are in there, while they discuss taboo issues or when they swear for instance … So the men strongly feel that women should not be in politics. (Participant in Motusaga 2016: Interviewed 16 January 2013)

Linguistic practices, whether high-level oratorical displays or low-level jesting, in both the local-level *fono* and the national-level *Fono* are a significant constructor of gendered boundaries (Tuuau and Howard 2019) and underpin narratives that women have no place in politics, ultimately constructing politics as a gendered space. Ironically, the concept of *vā* or relational and respectful space that exists between people or between spaces excludes women from politics as a means of 'protecting' the *feagaiga*. We propose to change the emphasis by using *vā* to include rather than exclude women, by developing respectful political spaces.

Using *vā* to create gendered space, including through taboos, has been key to maintaining respectful relational spaces within and between families within a community, particularly through brother–sister relations (Koya Vaka'uta 2017). The *feagaiga* relationship is founded on the values of *fa'aaloalo* ('respect'), *vā* ('relational space between people'), *vā fealoai* ('respectful space'), *vā fesootai* ('connecting space'), *vā fetufaai* ('sharing space'), *vā tapuia* ('sacred space') and *vā fefaasoaai* ('consultative space'). These core values form the foundation of all matters for discussion of the welfare of the family. *Vā* ('space') is the core of the *fa'asamoa* and crucial in the everyday life of every individual, determining people's actions and behaviour towards other people and the environment. *Vā* tames relations to keep peace and stability within Samoan families, villages and society as a whole. *Vā* establishes personal boundaries through several cultural values: *fa'aaloalo* ('respect'), *alofa* ('love'), *lotofoai* ('giving heart') and *fa'autauta* ('carefulness'). All Samoans, from leaders to children, know and understand their place, their responsibilities and their roles in keeping society together (Motusaga 2016).

Vā is integral to respect in the *feagaiga* relationship, but it is also used to exclude women from politics through claims that politics perforce entails dirty talk or jesting. What would happen, then, if we re-story politics as a site of respect and relationality, where *vā* is integral to political practice? When we enable *vā* in all its forms, would this construct political spaces that can be inclusive of both women and men?

Re-storying from gendered to respectful spaces: Integrating *vā* in politics

So far, this chapter has addressed the first step of re-storying, to understand how the narrative that there is no gender inequality in Samoa has come about through the *feagaiga*. We have also considered the consequences of this narrative for the construction of politics as a gendered space. Dirty politics somehow preserves the *fa'asamoa*, while high linguistic practices render women as outsiders.

The second step to re-storying is to reframe narratives, to draw out new meanings from old stories and to identity the way forward. Narratives are difficult to shift, they reinforce perceptions that there is really no problem and, even if there is, this is the way that we have always done things. Yet, narratives can be contested. In Samoa's oral culture, families hand down stories that can be reframed and retold. The gender equality narrative can be reframed to recognise, first, that women's power has been changing because of missionisation, and second, that the Westminster system only incorporated masculine and secular forms of power. To move forward, we propose making use of the blurring between state, church and traditional means of authority by engaging with the concept of *teu le vā* to re-story politics as a safe and respectful, rather than dirty, space. *Teu le vā* means ensuring that, in any context, respectful and polite communication is adhered to by all. For example, when at an event where people of higher rank or status are present, it is deemed respectful to ensure they are treated in accordance with their nobility. The same can be said of the respectful relationship between a brother and sister or, in a nonfamilial context, males and females (Ponton 2018). *Vā* provides an opportunity to promote politics, governance and secular authority as a respectful and relational space.

At this point we turn to Australia and take inspiration from Aboriginal elder, academic and author Mary Graham and her colleagues, not to compare Aboriginal world views with Samoan ontologies, but because of their paradigm-shifting work that challenges all of us to consider the limitations of political science theory and analysis. Political science is biased towards colonial-settler logics that privilege the state and individuals, where political authority is claimed through land possession and material progress. Rights, power, authority, regulation, administration, service delivery and law are all based on a naturalised focus on the state and the individual. Political science takes for granted competitive power and conquest as the basis of sovereignty and its ensuing political relations (Brigg et al. 2019). Such a paradigm cannot simply incorporate Indigenous notions of ecological and sociopolitical ordering that include moral obligations to others[6] through relations in space and place (Brigg et al. 2019). Finding a way for diverse world views to work alongside and in dialogue with each other therefore requires re-storying or 'knowing and unknowing' political science itself (Brigg et al. 2019: 425).

In Samoa the incorporation of the *matai* into the Westminster system to the exclusion of the *saotamaitai* titles has led to a system that introduces competition into what was once a complementary power relation. If we instead focus on cultural values and processes that enable relational power, what would a Pacific model for women's participation in politics look like? If political power was understood and practised as relational (based on obligation) rather than competitive (based on conquest), what would this require us to change or reconsider? With conquest comes potential for retaliation and therefore insecurity and tactics to maintain power bases. With relationality comes regard for others, obligations, mutuality and practices to maintain respectful relationships (Brigg et al. 2021). Relationality also encompasses intergenerational and cosmological relations; those making decisions and acting are accountable not just to others in the here and now, but also to past and future generations and to animals, the planet and spiritual beings. These ontologies are likely to be what are needed to underpin politics on a planet facing significant climate challenges and intergenerational injustices.

---

6   Note that relations to others include Country and non-human living or spiritual beings. For a short explanation, see Brigg and Graham (2020).

There are risks, however, that this will be interpreted in simplistic ways, as just being more polite and respectful to one another. Instead, we must look at the foundations that shape politics to re-story language, governance, architectures and recognition in terms of relationality, to enable conflict to be navigated through dialogue and negotiation, through grounding in relations and accountability to others in the past, present and future, rather than through combat (Brigg and Graham 2020).

This requires shifting taken-for-granted notions such as *balance of power* to instead conceive of governance as 'balanced sets of paired responsibilities' of which no part of the balance intends to destroy another (Brigg and Graham 2020: para. 5). It requires re-storying who may be seen as a political actor (Graham 2014) by revisiting not just political but also spiritual authority, by reclaiming feminine spiritual power and requiring political actors to be relationally embedded within community and obligations to the planet, and to past, present and future generations (Brigg et al. 2021).

We can interpret this in the Samoan space to consider which practices, artefacts or other tools would enable *vā* or connections of obligation and responsibility to others in political spaces. What systems would enable respectful political orders that truly reflect the *feagaiga* relationship, in which brothers must please their sisters and seek their final authority and guidance on decisions? What legislative and political architectures would enable governance through paired rather than tiered sets of responsibilities? This requires an understanding of inclusion beyond direct and physical participation, to inclusion of past wisdom from elders, spiritual authority and the pleas of future generations.

Conclusion

In this chapter, we proposed re-storying to enable women's political participation. Revisiting and reclaiming narratives that enable women's substantive forms of power drawn from feminine sources, rather than requiring women to behave more like men, are important to cease normalising political institutions that legitimise only masculine and competitive sources of power. We also proposed that re-storying is a relational and respectful process of reclamation and restitution, which places story-holders as the experts with the power to revisit and reframe women as agentic political subjects. Rather than accepting that this is the way things have always been done, we propose asking why this is the way this has always been told? This implies that change requires public discussion and deliberation to unpack the past, to reconsider what worked well and to consider how power can be shared rather than protected, to propose meaningful pathways forward. This will require some confidence by story-holders to discard colonial mindsets and be open to reclaiming and redesigning political systems that truly reflect the *fa'asamoa*. Samoa's political systems have long been entangled with missionary and colonial influences, and now gender equality initiatives are driven by neocolonial development actors. Snapping back to the past, therefore, is not a possibility. However, moving forward for new forms of governance that can meet contemporary challenges can draw on past systems to create future wisdoms.

This chapter demonstrates that women's power sources are temporal, spatial and relational, and were reshaped in post-missionisation periods. The colonial shaping of political spaces valued masculine sources of status and power while maintaining a fundamental blindness to feminine forms of status and power, effectively sidelining women from the 'political' process. The next step is to revisit narratives and develop more popular understandings of how the gendered space is effectively excluding women from politics. Women's participation will continue to be problematic within structures influenced by colonial and patriarchal values. By reclaiming women's legitimate place as authorities, leaders and advisors who work through complementary power relationships with men, the question should be *why* are political spaces designed based on masculine sources of power and what do we lose when we exclude feminine power?

There is a need to redesign political systems to encompass the cultural values of both women and men. These models are already available to Samoans at the local level through the *feagaiga* relationship and could be trialled to influence change at the national level. There is also a need to challenge conceptions of power as combative rather than relational. Proposals for change could be actioned in the form of popular discussion and debates, policies, enabling access to funding, grants, improved outcomes and moral support towards adopting *teu le vā* methodologies. In addition, there is a need for partnerships with Pacific researchers as they are culturally competent to implement appropriate approaches for Pacific participants (Anae 2010; Mila-Schaaf 2006). Using Pacific methods and weaving Pacific narratives into the existing research and literature with recommended models that are informed by the reality of Pacific practices such as the Samoan model discussed in this chapter are highly recommended.

References

Anae, Melani, and Airini Airini. 2010. *Teu Le Va: Relationships Across Research and Policy: A Collective Approach to Knowledge Generation and Policy Development for Action Towards Pasifika Education Success*. Wellington: Ministry of Education, New Zealand. www.researchgate.net/publication/259043753.

Baker, Kerryn. 2018. 'Gender and Candidate Selection in a Weakly Institutionalised Party System: The Case of Samoa.' *Australian Journal of Political Science* 53, no. 1: 57–72. doi.org/10.1080/10361146.2017.1416582.

Baker, Kerryn. 2019. *Pacific Women in Politics: Gender Quota Campaigns in the Pacific Islands*. Honolulu: University of Hawai'i Press. doi.org/10.2307/j.ctv7r42qp.

Brigg, Morgan, and Mary Graham. 2020. 'The Relevance of Aboriginal Political Concepts (6): Relationalism, Not Sovereignty.' *Religion & Ethics*, [ABC], 5 December [Updated 27 July 2021]. www.abc.net.au/religion/aboriginal-political-philosophy-relationalism/12954274.

Brigg, Morgan, Mary Graham, and Lyndon Murphy. 2019. 'Toward the Dialogical Study of Politics: Hunting at the Fringes of Australian Political Science.' *Australian Journal of Political Science* 54, no. 3: 423–37. doi.org/10.1080/10361146.2019.1625863.

Brigg, Morgan, Mary Graham, and Martin Weber. 2021. 'Relational Indigenous Systems: Aboriginal Australian Political Ordering and Reconfiguring IR.' *Review of International Studies* 48, no. 5: 891–909. doi.org/10.1017/S02602 10521000425.

Clandinin, D. Jean, and F. Michael Connelly. 2000. *Narrative Inquiry: Experience and Story in Qualitative Research*. San Francisco: Jossey-Bass.

Fairbairn-Dunlop, Peggy. 1991. '*E au le inailau a tamaitai*: Women, Education and Development in Western Samoa.' Unpublished thesis, Macquarie University, Sydney.

Feagaimaali'i, Joyetter. 2021. '"Stop Politicising Women": Fiame Tells Opposition.' *Samoa Observer*, 21 September. www.samoaobserver.ws/category/samoa/91875.

Frederick, Angela. 2013. 'Bringing Narrative In: Race–Gender Storytelling, Political Ambition, and Women's Paths to Public Office.' *Journal of Women, Politics & Policy* 34, no. 2: 113–37. doi.org/10.1080/1554477X.2013.776379.

Graham, Mary. 2014. 'Aboriginal Notions of Relationality and Positionalism.' *Global Discourse: An Interdisciplinary Journal of Current Affairs* 4, no. 1: 17–22. doi.org/10.1080/23269995.2014.895931.

Haley, Nicole, Roannie Ng Shiu, Kerryn Baker, Kerry Zubrinich, and Sala George Carter. 2017. *2016 Samoa General Election Domestic Observation Report*. Canberra: The Australian National University.

Holmes, John W. 1969. 'The American Problem.' *International Journal: Canada's Journal of Global Policy Analysis* 24, no. 2 (June): 229–45. doi.org/10.2307/40200045.

Huffer, Elise, and Asofu So'o. 2005. 'Beyond Governance in Samoa: Understanding Samoan Political Thought.' *The Contemporary Pacific* 17, no. 2: 311–33. doi.org/10.1353/cp.2005.0054.

Jolly, Margaret. 1992. 'Specters of Inauthenticity.' *The Contemporary Pacific* 4, no. 1: 49–72.

Kantola, Johanna. 2016. 'The Gendered Reproduction of the State in International Relations.' In *Handbook of Gender in World Politics*, edited by Jill Steans and Daniela Tepe-Belfrage, 77–85. Cheltenham: Edward Elgar Publishing.

Keating, Elizabeth, and Alessandro Duranti. 2006. 'Honorific Resources for the Construction of Hierarchy in Samoan and Pohnpeian.' *The Journal of the Polynesian Society* 115, no. 2: 145–72.

Koya Vaka'uta, Cresantia. 2017. 'The Digital Va: Negotiating Socio-Spatial Relations in Cyberspace, Place and Time.' In *The Relational Self: Decolonising Personhood in the Pacific*, edited by Upolu Lumā Vaai and Unaisi Nabobo-Baba, 61–78. Suva: University of the South Pacific & Pacific Theological College.

Kruse Va'ai, Emma. 2011. *Producing the Text of Culture: The Appropriation of English in Contemporary Samoa*. Apia: National University of Samoa.

Latai, Latu. 2014. 'From Open *Fale* to Mission Houses: Negotiating the Boundaries of "Domesticity" in Samoa.' In *Divine Domesticities: Christian Paradoxes in Asia and the Pacific*, edited by Hyaeweol Choi and Margaret Jolly, 299–323. Canberra: ANU Press. doi.org/10.22459/DD.10.2014.11.

Latai, Latu. 2015. 'Changing Covenants in Samoa? From Brothers and Sisters to Husbands and Wives.' *Oceania* 85, no. 1: 92–104. doi.org/10.1002/ocea.5076.

Meleisea, Leasiolagi Malama, Measina Meredith, Muagututi'a Ioana Chan Mow, Penelope Schoeffel, Semau Ausage Lauano, Hobert Sasa, Ramona Boodoosingh, and Mohammed Sahib. 2015. *Political Representation and Women's Empowerment in Samoa. Volume 1: Findings and Recommendations*. Apia: Centre for Samoan Studies, National University of Samoa. www.dfat.gov.au/sites/default/files/samoa-overcoming-barriers-womens-participation-local-government-final-report.pdf.

Merry, Sally Engle. 2003. 'Human Rights Law and the Demonization of Culture (And Anthropology Along the Way).' *Political and Legal Anthropology Review* 26, no. 1: 55–76. doi.org/10.1525/pol.2003.26.1.55.

Mila-Schaaf, Karlo. 2006. 'Vā-Centred Social Work: Possibilities for a Pacific Approach to Social Work Practice.' *Social Work Review* 18, no. 1: 8–13.

Milner, G.B. 1961. 'The Samoan Vocabulary of Respect.' *Journal of the Royal Anthropological Institute* 91, no. 2: 296–317. doi.org/10.2307/2844417.

Motusaga, Mema. 2016. 'Women in Decision Making in Samoa.' PhD diss., Victoria University, Melbourne.

Motusaga, Mema. 2021. *The Controversial Use of the Gender Quota in the 2021 Samoan General Election: A Personal Perspective—Part 1*. In Brief 2021/16, 1 June. Canberra: Department of Pacific Affairs, The Australian National University. www.pacwip.org/wp-content/uploads/2022/02/DPA-controversial_use_of_Samoa_genderPart1.pdf.

Office of the High Commissioner for Human Rights (OHCHR). 2018. *CEDAW/C/WSM/CO/6: Concluding Observations on the Sixth Periodic Report of Samoa*. 14 November. Geneva: OHCHR. www.ohchr.org/en/documents/concluding-observations/cedawcwsmco6-concluding-observations-sixth-periodic-report-samoa.

Ollerenshaw, Jo Anne, and John W. Creswell. 2002. 'Narrative Research: A Comparison of Two Restorying Data Analysis Approaches.' *Qualitative Inquiry* 8, no. 3: 329–47. doi.org/10.1177/10778004008003008.

Palmieri, Sonia, Elise Howard, and Kerryn Baker. 2023. 'Reframing Suffrage Narratives: Pacific Women, Political Voice, and Collective Empowerment.' *The Journal of Pacific History* 58, no. 4: 392–411. doi.org/10.1080/00223344.2023.2247348.

Patterson, Molly, and Kirsten Renwick Monroe. 1998. 'Narrative in Political Science.' *Annual Review of Political Science* 1: 315–31. doi.org/10.1146/annurev.polisci.1.1.315.

Phillips, Lynne, and Suzan Ilcan. 2000. 'Domesticating Spaces in Transition: Politics and Practices in the Gender and Development Literature, 1970–99.' *Anthropologica* 42, no. 2: 205–15.

Ponton, Vaoiva. 2018. 'Utilizing Pacific Methodologies as Inclusive Practice.' *SAGE Open* 8, no. 3: 1–8. doi.org/10.1177/2158244018792962.

Ragoonaden, Karen, Margaret Macintyre Latta, Kelly Hanson, Rhonda Draper, and Jordan Coble. 2020. 'Storying and Re-Storying Indigenous Content, Perspectives and Histories in an Elementary Arts Based Curricular Experience.' *Alberta Journal of Educational Research* 66, no. 1: 32–49. doi.org/10.55016/ojs/ajer.v66i1.61667.

Rocheleau, Dianne, Barbara Thomas-Slayter, and Esther Wangari, eds. 1996. *Feminist Political Ecology: Global Issues and Local Experiences*. New York: Routledge.

Samoa Bureau of Statistics. 2018. *Statistical Abstract 2017*. Apia: Social Statistics Division, Samoa Bureau of Statistics.

Schoeffel, Penelope. 1995. 'The Samoan Concept of *Feagaiga* and its Transformation.' In *Tonga and Samoa: Images of Gender and Polity*, edited by Judith Huntsman, 85–109. Christchurch: Macmillan Brown Centre for Pacific Studies.

Slatter, Claire. 2012. 'Gender and Custom in the South Pacific.' *Yearbook of New Zealand Jurisprudence* 13–14: 89–111.

So'o, Asofu. 2008. *Democracy and Custom in Samoa: An Uneasy Alliance*. Suva: IPS Publications, University of the South Pacific.

Spain, Daphne. 1993. 'Gendered Spaces and Women's Status.' *Sociological Theory* 11, no. 2: 137–51. doi.org/10.2307/202139.

Tagaloa, Aiono Fanaafi Le. 1997. *O le Faasinomaga: le tagata ma lona Faasinomaga*. Alafua, Samoa: Lolomi e le Lamepa Press.

Tcherkézoff, Serge. 2015. 'Sister or Wife? You've Got to Choose. A Solution to the Puzzle of Village Exogamy in Samoa.' In *Living Kinship in the Pacific*, edited by Christina Toren and Simonne Pauwels. New York: Berghahn Books. doi.org/10.3167/9781782385776.

Tuuau, Ali'imalemanu Alofa, and Elise Howard. 2019. *The Long Road to Becoming a Parliamentarian in Samoa: Political Apprenticeship, Learning New Language and Pushing Gender Boundaries*. DPA Discussion Paper 2019/04. Canberra: Department of Pacific Affairs, The Australian National University.

Viterna, Jocelyn, Kathleen M. Fallon, and Jason Beckfield. 2008. 'How Development Matters: A Research Note on the Relationship between Development, Democracy and Women's Political Representation.' *International Journal of Comparative Sociology* 49, no. 6: 455–77. doi.org/10.1177/0020715208097789.

White, Michael, and David Epston. 1990. *Narrative Means to Therapeutic Ends*. New York: W.W. Norton & Co.

Zetlin, Diane. 2014. 'Women in Parliaments in the Pacific Region.' *Australian Journal of Political Science* 49, no. 2: 252–66. doi.org/10.1080/10361146.2014.895796.

10

Cooking as Activism: Affective journeys and the politics of being a housewife in Malaka, West Timor

Longgina Novadona Bayo

Vignette one

One fine day, I embarked on an extraordinary adventure following a group of women and their husbands to the estuary, where the sea and river converged, in a fishing village in Malaka, East Nusa Tenggara Province, Indonesia. With [low tide set for] 3 pm, the women set out on their fishing expedition to catch the fish that would later grace the market (Plate 10.1). With the clock nearing 1 pm, I trudged alongside them through the muddy ground, uncovering the glistening white grains of sea salt as the terrain dried. Upon arriving at the estuary, the women skilfully fashioned a barrier of bamboo, a curtain demarcating the boundary between the sea and the river. This bamboo curtain, their creation, served as barricade, ensuring that the fish entering the river would not slip back into the vast sea again. The water at that moment reached waist-high, and they began to cross gracefully.

As the late afternoon descended, around 3 pm, the tide began its gentle retreat, reducing in height to a mere adult's calf. During this opportune time the village fishermen and women harvested a bountiful catch of fish and shrimp, their hands deftly manoeuvring amidst the flowing currents. Around 5 pm, just before the high tide could reclaim its territory, we hastened back to the village. The local fishpond offered us solace, where we cleansed ourselves from the day's daring exploits. Amidst the friendship of conversation, I found myself engrossed in the experiences of these women. Suddenly, one of the men who had joined our entourage, offered an insight, 'Here, the housewives are not confined to domestic roles of cooking and childcare alone. They are untiring beings, diligently engaging in activities like this to earn their livelihood. Tonight, the women will persevere, venturing out to sell the fruits of their labour—the fish and shrimps.' (Fieldnotes, 21 August 2021)

In Malaka, more women have been elected village head than in any other part of East Nusa Tenggara (Nusa Tenggara Timur, NTT) Province. In the simultaneous village elections (*pilkades serentak*) on 9 December 2022, 19 of 119 participating villages elected a woman as village head (almost 16 per cent). This was an increase from 13 women heads among 127 villages (approximately 10 per cent). At the district level, Malaka also boasts three female MPs, who were elected in 2019. Interestingly, most of the women village heads are housewives with no prior political experience. Of the 13 women village heads, seven were housewives, four were development workers, one ran a small livestock business and only one had experience as an activist or social worker.

The comparative literature highlights the potential of NGOs as breeding grounds for women's grassroots leadership and promising candidates for elections (Kabeer 2011). State-led development has also been recognised for creating opportunities for people to engage in development and encouraging women to become grassroots leaders (Jakimow 2017, 2020). However, beyond these, I propose that domestic spaces can also serve as fertile ground for nurturing grassroots leadership in rural areas. Through my research, I demonstrate how years of cooking activism have shaped women's affective experiences and empowered their political agency. This leads me to explore how housewives primarily engaged in domestic roles can emerge as leaders in their communities. My observations in Malaka reveal that women adeptly harness the affective resources cultivated within domestic spaces, particularly when they assume dominant roles in cooking activities within their extended families and the community's social life. These affective experiences are then transformed into valuable political resources.

Plate 10.1: A woman fishing in the estuary, Malaka, Indonesia, 4 October 2021

Source: Longgina Novadona Bayo.

During my time living with people in a remote village in Malaka, I was captivated by the statement about the role of a housewife described in the opening vignette. It challenges the prevailing notion of Indonesian women portrayed in the literature that is often associated with the Indonesian state's *ibuism* ('motherism') ideology (Suryakusuma 2011). In the agrarian context of Timorese society, where the family serves as a productive unit, housewives are actively engaged in roles such as cultivation, fishing and livestock rearing. This reality contrasts with the function of households in industrialised societies, where they have shifted from being centres of production to centres of consumption. The statement about a housewife's tasks reflects the impact of capitalism, which has diminished the family's pre-industrial role and consequently eroded the economic independence once enjoyed by housewives.

In nineteenth-century Europe, the experiences of wives underscored the influence of capitalism, leading to the emergence of new values that ideally rendered wives, especially in middle-class families, domesticated beings, passive and dependent (Malos 1980). Although working-class women in certain European and industrially based developing countries continued to engage in productive waged labour, the context in NTT is different. Despite still greatly relying on the agricultural sector, in which women are heavily engaged, the state has perpetuated a gender ideology that envisions housewives as serving men, families, communities and the country (Suryakusuma 2011: 11). Women are expected to give their energy selflessly, without seeking prestige or power. This conception, foundational to the state's gender ideology, permeates the way women are perceived in Indonesia's broader social framework.

Yet, in the context of my research on women village heads and politicians in the Malaka region, I found that women can effectively utilise domestic spaces, particularly through cooking activities, to accumulate affective resources, transforming these spaces into political sites. As village heads and local politicians, women actively participate in cooking activities for the betterment of their communities. I have coined this process 'public domesticity', whereby domestic practices extend beyond private spheres and intersect with public life, thus offering an alternative dimension to politics. These women use the transformation of domestic spaces to their advantage, turning them into communal gathering spots for discussions, information-sharing and deliberation on public and political matters.

Cooking together frequently in village, clan and extended family settings—tasks typically overseen by women—nurtures a strong sense of affectionate bonding among women. Even after assuming leadership roles, be it as village heads or politicians, these women maintain a feeling of connection through cooking activities, recognising them as essential reservoirs of affective resources crucial to sustaining their political careers. The blending of public and domestic realms within 'public domesticity' is a unique way for women to wield political influence while keeping true to their roots and nurturing the social fabric of their communities.

Inspired by Jakimow (2017, 2018, 2020), I argue that affective resources can be transformed into resources in formal politics. In Indian elections, according to Jakimow (2020: 15), women politicians rely not only on financial capital, but also on affective investments. Before participating in elections, they often work as social workers (made possible by women's empowerment programs) and help others, and thus are loved by their communities. It is through such social work that affective investments between social workers and communities are formed, thereby becoming the basis for women's political capital when participating in elections. This shows that the relationship between broader grassroots empowerment and formal politics is facilitated by affective relationships. However, while Jakimow (2020) shows that affective investment is formed due to the interaction of communities with social workers, my study demonstrates that affective investment experienced in the domestic sphere—the cooking space—can also be effectively expanded into the political realm. Hence, I challenge any conception of the domestic realm as being apolitical.

The transformation of affective resources from domestic spaces into resources for formal politics exemplifies how intimate connections and emotional investments play a crucial role in shaping the dynamics of political engagement. By recognising the potency of affective bonds in both grassroots empowerment and political arenas, we gain a greater understanding of the interplay between affect and politics, illuminating the significance of the domestic as fertile ground for political agency.

While many works critique the notion of separate spheres of the domestic and public domains, few studies explore the political potential of domestic spaces. Rita Segato's (2018) article stands out as an example, suggesting that domesticity can indeed be political. Women transform the traditionally marginalised and depoliticised domestic sphere into a site of political action by harnessing the politics of nearness and the power of affective experiences.

Following Segato (2018), I call this phenomenon 'housewife politics', challenging the perception of domesticity as apolitical and embracing the significance of cultural processes in shaping women's political leadership. Housewife politics thus embodies a politics of local rootedness (Segato 2018), highlighting a specific mode of political engagement connected to local practices and customs, which give meaning to their communities. In this light, the transformative capacity of everyday life and collective experiences takes centre-stage in shaping political realities.

In my research, I delved into the development of the housewife concept within Timorese society, while seeking a comprehensive understanding of women's status and position in the matrilineal society of the South Tetun in Malaka. I discovered that the housewife concept originated with German women missionaries who arrived in the region in the early twentieth century. Their mission was to restructure family life and redefine gender relations, introducing a Christian perspective that depicted women as auxiliary figures, fulfilling roles as wives and mothers, promoting a novel ideal of domesticity for Timorese women. Consequently, this ideology promoted hierarchical gender dynamics within the family that deviate from the Indigenous diarchic principles. By tracing the origins of the housewife concept, I aim to shed light on its influence on the gender dynamics of Timorese society, considering its impact on women's roles and identities.

The South Tetun people have a distinct perspective on women's roles that transcends the conventional notion of a housewife. Rather, they regard women as housemasters (Therik 2004), signifying a more authoritative position within the household. This unique perspective arises from the gender-based spatial division inside the house (*uma* in Tetun language), which designates separate feminine and masculine spaces (Plate 10.2). As housemasters, women hold authority over domestic tasks, including responsibilities such as food-work. It is crucial to emphasise that Timorese familial structures encompass extended kin, considering the family as an interconnected part of the larger community rather than an isolated, independent entity. Consequently, women's authority not only extends over their immediate household but also encompasses the domestic spheres of the clan and village, further contributing to their significant roles and influences in various communal settings.

Plate 10.2: An *uma* or traditional house in Malaka, Indonesia, 14 August 2021

Source: Longgina Novadona Bayo.

Contrary to perspectives suggesting that the kitchen symbolises women's oppression (Charles and Kerr 1988; DeVault 1991; Giard 1998), this study illuminates the potential empowerment that domestic cooking spaces hold for women. Drawing inspiration from Abarca (2006: 19), who views the kitchen as a dynamic space, not merely a physical place, we can see how it becomes a realm with increasing degrees of freedom, self-awareness, subjectivity and agency. The significance of the kitchen lies in the social interactions unfolding within it. Moreover, this chapter aims to contribute to the literature on kinship and women's political leadership by showcasing a positive correlation between matrilineality and gendered political space. I argue that kinship systems influence gender dynamics. Matrilineality not only grants women access to social and material resources but also gives them affective resources. Consequently, matrilineal societies foster common expectations of increased female influence and thus sustain more progressive gender roles (Robinson and Gottlieb 2021: 70).

In this chapter, I embrace a mixed methodology, combining insights from colonial archives with ethnographic fieldwork and life histories shared through interviews with women political leaders in Malaka, West Timor. Working alongside a local assistant, I interviewed all 13 women village heads in Malaka. My ethnographic fieldwork spanned 10 months, from August 2021 to May 2022, encompassing several villages in Malaka, Belu, South Central Timor and North Central Timor. In this chapter, my focus is on the politics of women village heads and women politicians in the matrilineal society of the South Tetun. Before delving into my fieldwork findings, I explore the gender transformations in Timor driven by colonial institutions and Indonesia's 'New Order' state formation. By providing this historical context, I shed light on the conception of the housewife in Timor.

Indigenous gender ideology: A diarchal system

In Timor, the construction of Indigenous gender ideology revolves around the notions of spatiality, fixity and mobility. Timorese cultural imaginaries adhere to a diarchic principle,[1] attributing gender symbolism to the

---

1   Fox (1982: 25) describes the Wehali system as a classic form of diarchy—a rigorous division between spiritual authority and temporal power predicated on a conceptual opposition between female and male. Here, metaphors based on this analogy abound: the coastal plains of Wehali form the female centre, while the domains in the surrounding hills constitute the male periphery.

political structure. According to Hoskins (1988: 51), diarchic societies are characterised by a pervasive system of gender dualisms—an 'ideology of balanced powers' wherein the male/female pair is organised based on difference and interdependence, rather than dominance and subjugation. This results in the female domain being perceived as the centre (inside), requiring protection from males in the peripheral domain (outside). Hence, the concept of leadership in Timor becomes gendered, aligning with binaries of female/male, inside/outside, centre/periphery (Kammen 2012; Hägerdal 2013) and feminine spiritual/ritual authority, which is typically held by an older man exhibiting performative feminine characteristics, and masculine political/temporal power, which is spearheaded by a man. The male domain, synonymous with 'outside' (the Tetun word for male is *mane*), is characterised as active and aggressive, while the female domain (*feto*) embodies a dark, silent superiority, representing an invisible yet potent power (Fox 1982).

Given Timor's gender-based Indigenous leadership, the ideological construction of the centre/periphery holds deep significance, as expressed in the myth of Wehali[2] (see Ormeling 1955; Schulte Nordholt 1971;

---

2   In the construction of polity in Timor, Wehali positioned itself as the centrum/navel of all the kingdoms in Timor, which then formed a centre–periphery ideology with Wehali as the centre. This historical narrative was built by Wehali and inseparable from the arrival of the Sina Mutin Malaka group, for it is from them that the Tetun people were descended. According to several historical documents (see Ormeling 1957; Nordholt 1981; Fox 1982; Parera 1994; Francillon 1967; Therik 2004), there were four subgroups of Sina Mutin Malaka, all of whom were brothers, and who landed on the southern coast of Malaka. In the Wehali cosmology, these four kingdoms—Wehali, Wewiku, Haitimuk and Fatuaruin—formed the inner area or 'centre' of Wehali, while the area outside these domains was categorised as the exterior or periphery. To conquer all of Timor, *Maromak Oan*, the supreme spiritual leader who reigned in Wehali (later, during Dutch and Portuguese colonialism, *Maromak Oan* was positioned as emperor or *Keizer*), delegated three of his sons to become *Liurai*—the political powerholders who represent *Maromak Oan*. Because *Maromak Oan* is the supreme spiritual leader, he is not allowed to be involved in worldly affairs such as politics and government. *Liurai* are thus *Maromak Oan*'s representatives for public and political affairs outside Wehali (Parera 1994). The first *Liurai* is *Liurai Wewiku*, which is based in Wewiku-Wehali, and serves as a direct representation of *Maromak Oan* for the Wehali region. *Liurai Wewiku-Wehali* ruled in central Timor—essentially the western part of Tetun territory. Since the Timorese only know two axes, based on the direction of the sun—namely, East and West—the appointment of the other two *Liurai* is based on these directions. In the east or the domain towards the sunrise, *Liurai Loro Sae* (who was later replaced with *Liurai Suai-Kamanasa* because he rebelled against *Maromak Oan*) was appointed as the ruler. *Liurai Suai-Kamanasa* ruled the eastern parts of Timor (now Timor-Leste). In the western part, *Liurai Sonbay* (*Liurai Loro Toba*) was appointed as the ruler of the domains towards the sunset. *Liurai Sonbay* ruled the Atoni/Dawan territory in western Timor. Before the arrival of the Sina Mutin Malaka in Timor, several groups were already recorded as existing, including Atoni or Dawan people. Currently, Dawan refers to people who inhabit the western part of Timor Island, particularly Ambenu District (East Timor, Oecusse), North Central Timor District, South Central Timor District and Kupang District. All these *liurai* were represented as male. The relationship between the Wehali (*Maromak Oan*) and these *liurai* confirms the diarchy and gendered Indigenous polities mentioned by Fox (1982) and Francillon (1967). Following this analogy, the coastal plains of Wehali form the female centre, with the surrounding domains constituting the male periphery.

Fox 1982; Parera 1994; Francillon 1967; Therik 2004). Throughout Timor's political history, Wehali has consistently stood as a paramount ritual centre and the sacred palace of *Maromak Oan*. The King of Wehali was titled either *Maromak Oan* ('Son of God') or *Nai Bot* ('Great Master'). *Maromak Oan*, often referred to as the Female Lord, was recognised as the ultimate authority in Wehali, overseeing spiritual matters and agricultural rituals. However, the primary duty of the Female Lord was not to rule but rather existence (Fox 1982). At present, Wehali resides in the Malaka district, specifically, in the subdistrict of Central Malaka. For the Tetun people, the Wehali myth transcends time, serving as a sacred charter, a structural injunction and a testament to history (Therik 2004: 79). Yet, in its essence, this myth also embodies the elemental gendered dualism that permeates social organisation (Wouden 1968).

In the cosmic realm of Wehali's symbolism, the elder sons were cast as denizens of the gardens, dwelling in the 'outside domain'. Their cultural role entailed tilling the land, nurturing sustenance to feed their mother and father residing in the centre, whom they shielded. Embracing the mantle of male children within the family, these elder sons, known as protectors (*makdakar*), held elevated status as executive rulers and revered central authorities, bestowed with the titles of *loro* (literally, 'sun') or *liurai* (literally, 'above the earth') (Therik 2004: 75–76). Meanwhile, the younger sons remaining in Wehali, bestowed with the status of the last-born, were deemed 'insiders', akin to 'females', and were perceived as physically vulnerable. Thus, those deemed first-born (outsiders, male) were ritually deemed their guardians, often likened to doors, fences and posts. Fox (1982: 23) illuminates this connection, viewing the centre as 'a kind of receptive powerlessness that left it open to protection and vulnerable to intrusion'. Notably, several researchers, including Wouden (1968: 114–15), Cunningham (1962: 63–67) and Schulte Nordholt (1971: 236–39), have discerned the foundation of this origin myth in the division of spiritual and temporal authorities in Timor.

This myth reflects a curious reversal of the flow of life and wealth. By relinquishing their elder sons to the periphery, the Wehali envision a return of prosperity to the centre, thus resulting in a juxtaposition of life's flow with the flow of wealth. The periphery, in the context of life's origin, becomes both the life-taker and the wealth-giver (Therik 2004: 76). In this cultural spatiality, the *Maromak Oan*, reigning over Wehali, exhibits gender ambiguity. Although male in essence, *Maromak Oan* is designated as female, entrusted solely with the functions of eating, drinking and sleeping ('he eats reclining, drinks reclining [*mahaa toba*/*mahemu toba*]') (Therik 2004: 62). This portrayal stems from *Maromak Oan*'s role as a spiritual authority, a silent and immobile figure dwelling inside the house—resembling the concept of the female in the Wehali cultural narrative. This delineation of the female diverges from the notion of the male, who has the right to speak and remains active and mobile outside the home. Hence, being masculine in Timorese society means having every right to speak in public (Therik 2004: 76). The personification of *Maromak Oan*, existing as both male and female, illuminates the Timorese perspective that gender is not rigidly confined to fixed constructs or even secure binaries. Such tenets of the Wehali myth shape Timorese people's perception of women, echoing their belief in women's silent, superior essence, revered and safeguarded to preserve the wellspring of life.[3]

Resonating with the realm of the Wehali myth, the depiction of women as 'insiders' finds expression in the spatial arrangement of the *uma* ('house' in Tetun). For the Timorese, the *uma* transcends a mere household status, emerging as the very nucleus of society, a crucial social and political entity. Beyond its role as a ritual centre, the *uma* symbolises Timorese political organisation. As elucidated by Therik (2004: 172), the 'mother', who occupies the inner house, and the 'father', positioned on the platform, become emblems of power and authority. The highest authority is entrusted to the 'mother'; she embodies the wellspring of life and fertility, while the 'father', positioned at the periphery, assumes the role of protector of the centre, providing material wealth and security. In this spatial configuration, the Indigenous ideology of gender diarchy comes into focus, with women central to the source of life and men entrusted with material wellbeing and protective responsibilities.

In the Indigenous ideology of gender diarchy, the spatial organisation of the *uma* materialises the concept of the house and its significance. Commonly, South Tetun has two types of *uma*, called *uma roman*[4] (literally, 'bright

---

3   Interview with Father Rosindus Tae, senior Catholic priest in Timor, 20 January 2022.

4   The *uma roman* is designed as a residential unit and comes in two varieties. One, a 'named house' (*uma maho naran*), also known as an ancestral/lineage house, contains ancestral relics passed through the female line and guarded by women and a man from that line. The other are houses that have no ancestral relics, known as an 'unnamed house' (*uma maho naran ha'i*). While an 'unnamed house' is a residence for other members of lineages, a 'named house' is lived in by a female guardian of the lineage (Therik 2004: 150–51).

house'), which serves as a residential unit, and *uma kukun*[5] (literally, 'dark house'), which represents the clan's house because it is used to store ancestral relics (Therik 2004). Although they have different functions, both types of house have a spatial arrangement reflecting the Wehali cosmology that recognises the gender division. The *uma* is typically divided into two distinct spaces: the inner house (*uma laran*) is the core living space reserved for women, children and parents, and the outer platform or verandah (*labis*, 'layer') is attached to the living area (Therik 2004). This division guides the roles of household members. The inner space, exclusive to women, serves as their domain. On the other hand, the platform is designated for men, primarily serving as their sleeping quarters. Only male guests are permitted to enter this section of the house. When sons reach adulthood, which is signified by their ability to carry betel-nut pouches, they join their fathers in the platform area. Similarly, the *mane foun* ('son-in-law') has limited access to join his wife in the inner house. The platform area (*labis*) being a male space designates men as *labis na'in* or 'platform masters', while wives (and their children) are known as *uma na'in* or 'housemasters' (Therik 2004: 167). This spatial arrangement of the *uma* signifies balanced gender power.

Today, these spatial protocols have faded with the Indonesian Government's promotion of a new style of house to meet health standards (Therik 2004), known as the *rumah malae/Malay* (Therik 2004: 150). *Uma roman* as a residential dwelling unit has been largely replaced with the *malae/Malay* house, while *uma kukun* is well preserved despite some now being built with materials such as concrete. In terms of both structure and materials, the *Malay* house lacks any necessary rituals for its construction, unlike the *uma*.

Colonial institutions and maternalism

In the sixteenth century, Portuguese colonial forces arrived in the Indonesian archipelago, pursuing both profit and the conversion of souls. Accompanying these colonial officials were Catholic missionaries, who established a significant religious influence in the region. Unlike many parts of Indonesia that embraced Islam, Timor and the eastern Indonesian islands

---

5   The *uma kukun* is not designed as a residence and also comes in two varieties. The first is 'the forbidden house' (*uma lulik*) or 'the black house' (*uma metan*), which represents the clan because the clan's ancestral relics are kept inside. The second is the 'amulet house' (*uma kakaluk*), named for the *kakaluk* pouch carried by a man wherever he goes. The *uma kakaluk* is categorically a male house because originally it was constructed as a place where men came to seek strength and immunity in times of warfare (Therik 2004: 150–51).

were predominantly Christian. Timor, in particular, saw the emergence of Catholicism in the seventeenth century, introduced by Dominican missionaries.

Later, the mission was passed into the hands of the Society of Jesus or Jesuit congregation, who established a mission centre in Atapupu, Belu District. The Jesuit congregation had already taken charge of the mission in what was then known as the Dutch East Indies, including Timor, in 1865. After serving for 47 years in Timor, the Jesuits eventually transferred the Catholic mission to Society of Divine Word (SVD) missionaries,[6] on 1 March 1913. This marked a pivotal moment as the mission centre relocated from Atapupu to Lahurus, in the foothills of Lakaa'an. The legacy of these religious missions played a profound role in shaping the religious landscape of Timor and the surrounding region.

The arrival of the SVD signalled a new chapter for the Catholic Church in Timor, ushering in the establishment of modern schools aimed at advancing projects of civilisation for Indigenous men and women. However, a gendered mission became evident as the SVD focused on educating men, while the Servants of the Holy Spirit (SSpS) were tasked with educating women's groups. This gendered division of roles mirrors the prevailing gender ideologies of late-nineteenth-century Germany (and elsewhere in Europe and America), which upheld a 'polarisation of the character of the sexes', assigning men to work in the world and relegating women to work at home (Hausen 1981: 63). The roles envisioned for women missionaries by the SVD's founder and the SSpS were aligned with these gender ideologies. Consequently, the presence of the SSpS in Timor, beginning in 1921, about eight years after the SVD's arrival, marked the beginning of Timorese encounters with missionary maternalism.

I adopt the definition of maternalism introduced by Lutkehaus (1999), which was used to describe the dominant character of gender ideology fashioned by women missionaries in Timor. The term 'maternal' signifies a strong commitment to 'caregiving and nurturance' and a focus 'on the

---

6   The Society of the Divine Word (SVD) emerged as one of several Catholic mission-sending societies established in Europe during the revival of Catholic foreign mission work in the latter half of the nineteenth century (Schmidlin 1933, cited in Huber and Lutkehaus 1999: 182). Founded in 1875 as a seminary with the purpose of training German priests for mission endeavours, the institute's statutes subsequently underwent revision, and it evolved into a comprehensive religious congregation encompassing priests, brothers and a related order of dedicated sisters. Their collective mission involved serving and staffing Catholic missions in foreign territories (Bornemann 1975: 166–75, cited in Huber and Lutkehaus 1999: 182).

upbringing and socialisation of children, and on the development of "inner" qualities of morality and spirituality, all pursued in a compassionate manner' (Lutkehaus 1999: 208). The approach of missionary maternalism was practised by women missionaries to craft the model of the exemplary wife and mother, aligning with the principles of Catholicism. They introduced the domestic ideals that centred on the concept of sphere separation that places women in the domestic sphere and men in the public sphere (Boardman 2000). So, the separate sphere paradigm was introduced to Timor by women missionaries, signalling an encounter between the gendered diarchy of inside/outside and a gendered hierarchy of domestic/ public. However, it is essential to clarify that the term 'maternalism' goes beyond merely serving as a female-centred substitute for the male-centred concept of paternalism or a contrast between domestic/public in orientation and demeanour. Rather, it signifies the interplay of race, class and gender for European women, particularly those of the SSpS, who were embedded within the patriarchal structure of the Catholic Church and the German SDV (Lutkehaus 1999: 217).

In Timor, the introduction of Indigenous women to Christian morality and domestic ideals was achieved through schools for girls. A year after the SSpS arrived in Lahurus, in 1922, the first primary school was established there. The pioneering efforts in the mission centre of Lahurus were undertaken by four dedicated SSpS sisters: Sister Gonzagina Van Lunssen, Sister Jolenta Miltenburg, Sister Blanda Dorr and Sister Antonie de Leeuw.[7] These remarkable women were brought from Lela, Flores Island, and were part of the first SSpS mission in NTT since 1917. Alongside providing religious teachings to mothers and young women in the villages, the SSpS mission took the initiative to educate Indigenous girls in the primary school. Moreover, older girls were offered places in boarding schools, where they were taught valuable work and domestic skills. In short, their mission primarily focused on educating women through multiple avenues: 1) young girls in primary schools; 2) older girls in boarding schools, where they received instruction in various work and 'domestic skills' (*kerajinan rumah tangga*); and 3) religious teachings to mothers and young women in the villages.[8] This marked the beginning of a significant chapter in the history of Timorese engagement with missionary maternalism and its educational initiatives.

---

7   See the SSpS Timor website: sspstimor.org/sejarah/.
8   See 'History' on the SSpS Timor website: sspstimor.org/sejarah/.

The girl's boarding school was known as *sekolah kepandaian putri* ('school for girls' skills') or *kerajinan rumah tangga* (KRT; 'school for domestic skills'). The KRT curriculum focused primarily on equipping women with domestic skills, preparing them for marriage by teaching sewing, cooking and handicrafts.[9] During its establishment, the KRT was accessible only to those from noble backgrounds. This exclusivity was due to the importance of maintaining relations between the Catholic missions as foreigners or outsiders and the local rulers. This relationship was crucial in securing land for the establishment of mission stations, which was granted by the local rulers. Thus, the women missionaries were the ones who introduced literacy and concepts of the modern housewife to Timorese women. Women became pivotal in the civilisation project that began within the household, introducing the concept of the ideal housewife: the modern wife and mother.

During the tenure of the first Bishop of Atambua, Monsignor Theodorus Fransiskus Maria van den Tillaart, SVD (known as Monsignor Theodorus Sulama in Indonesia), who served from 1961 to 1984, the initiative to enhance women's capacity continued. In this period, a junior high school for girls was established in Timor with the primary objective of providing education to Timorese women, enabling them to manage modern households adeptly. The commitment to maternalism was further evident when Monsignor Sulama established the first *sekolah pendidikan guru* (SPG, 'teacher education school') at the high school level, in Belu. Bishop Sulama's education-focused policies extended to encouraging the Catholic sisters to send daughters from noble families to schools outside Timor, thereby facilitating their access to quality education. When Indonesia declared independence in 1945, the scope of education broadened to encompass not only the nobility but also non-noble groups, who received substantial attention from the missions. For instance, access to the SPG was opened to all segments of Timorese society—a significant shift in the education landscape.[10]

The presence of missions in Timor, which introduced new gender relations within the family, challenged the Indigenous gender ideology that recognised the mother as the housemaster. Beyond a merely dominant role, the housemaster concept conveys a connection between women/mothers and the household. Being a master of the house signifies that a mother

---

9   Interview with Father Rosindus Tae, 20 January 2022.
10   ibid.

embodies the essence of the home—body, soul and spirit. In Timorese tradition, women are nurtured to reside within the house, ensuring their safety and that of all household members. Inside the house, women exude strength as the home stands as a repository of knowledge as much as security. It is within the house that women wield power and gather the wisdom that shapes the foundation of their world.

However, when the principle of gender diarchy encountered the forces of coloniality, it was confronted with the weight of a patriarchal gender ideology. In terms of political leadership, colonial rulers did not recognise the Timorese ideology of gender diarchy. The significant changes introduced by Dutch colonial rule included the failure to recognise the superior spiritual power of women, instead valuing only the active masculine power as the sole political power. Colonial authorities failed to comprehend the Indigenous political ideology of gender diarchy of the Timorese, opting instead to impose a gendered hierarchy. This transformation had far-reaching implications for the status and role of women in Timorese society.

Women's primary spiritual authority was undermined, relegating their political position to a secondary role. When the colonial powers established the hierarchical structure of modern governance in Timor, they exclusively relied on Indigenous men to assume leadership positions. For example, at the village level, the Dutch colonists created the *temukung* structure (equivalent to the rank of village head) and appointed noble Indigenous men to fill these positions. Meanwhile, even noble Indigenous women were excluded from colonial society, confined to supporting missionary maternalism by assuming roles as teachers, nurses and engaging in domestic work for pastoral activities. This gendered division of labour further reinforced a dichotomy of public/political and domestic/non-political spaces, effectively confining women to the realm of domesticity, stripped of authority.

The transformation of the gender order from diarchy to hierarchy reverberated throughout Timorese society, significantly impacting the status and roles of women. This becomes particularly evident when contemplating the influence of the maternalism of colonial institutions, which sought to reshape gender dynamics within family life. This cannot be detached from Mary Taylor Huber and Nancy C. Lutkehaus' insightful observation that 'imperialism was a manly act, the missionary enterprise was gendered as "feminine"' (1999: 12). The ideology of the mission, while promoting broader colonial endeavours, embraced a maternal focus, emphasising the care and nurturing of children, the education of girls and women and the creation of morally upright Christian families (Lutkehaus 1999: 227).

The mission of Catholicism thus held a gendered intention to transform Indigenous women into 'new women', shifting them from being housemasters to housewives. This transformation challenged the sacred power of women's status as the centre of spiritual knowledge within the Timorese diarchic system. The melding of Indigenous diarchy with the concept of gendered hierarchy introduced a novel notion of domestic space or feminine domesticity, contrasting it with the public space, which was characterised as masculine in nature. Consequently, the public space, which was perceived as superior, overshadowed the domestic sphere, which was designated as a woman's space. As a result, Christian missionaries played a role in facilitating the domestication of Timorese women. The shift from housemasters to housewives represented a significant transformation of gender roles in Timor under the influence of colonial and Christian ideologies.

This experience resonates with Segato's (2018) assertion that coloniality has transformed the gender structure of Indigenous communities, elevating the masculine figure as the ideal human model and the quintessential subject of public discourse—the one possessing political agency. Simultaneously, the women's domain and all aspects related to the domestic sphere were stripped of their political significance. They were rendered marginal and disconnected from the political sphere.

Ibuism as state gender ideology

The colonial legacy of maternalism was carefully cultivated and perpetuated by Indonesia's New Order regime (1966–98), which continued to prioritise the roles of wifehood and motherhood in contemporary Indonesian society. Embracing developmentalism as a state-led ideology, the New Order regime introduced and promoted 'state *ibuism*' as the official gender ideology (Suryakusuma 2011). The term *ibu* not only denotes respect for older women but also means 'mother' in Indonesian. According to Suryakusuma (1996), this ideology led to the reduction of Indonesian women to dependent wives, existing solely for their husbands, families and the state. It defined women as extensions of their husbands, companions in marriage, procreators of the nation, mothers, educators of children, housekeepers and members of society—in that order.

Suryakusuma (1996) perceptively draws parallels between state *ibuism* and the notions of 'housewifisation' (Mies 1988) and *'priyayi ibuism'*, as coined by Djajadiningrat-Nieuwenhuis (1992). 'Housewifisation', as defined by Mies (1988), entails the social categorisation of women as housewives, regardless of whether they fulfil that role, rendering them dependent on their husbands' income for survival. Meanwhile, *priyayi ibuism* represents an ideology that endorses a mother's dedication to caring for her family, community, class, company or nation without seeking power or prestige in return (Djajadiningrat-Nieuwenhuis 1992: 44). In both concepts, women are expected to provide their labour selflessly, without aspiring to recognition or influence. Similarly, state *ibuism* prescribes women's service to men, children, families, communities and the country (Suryakusuma 2011: 11), emphasising that women should contribute their energy without anticipating prestige or power in exchange.

The patriarchal grip of state *ibuism* extends its influence across all realms, from intimate family dynamics (micropolitics) to the level of government (macropolitics), permeating daily life and power structures alike, effectively limiting women's autonomy and agency (Tickamyer and Kusujiarti 2012). This gender ideology stands as the foundation on which Indonesian gender relations were shaped, strategically promoting a more nuclear form of family. Within such nuclear households, a clear demarcation emerged, casting the male household head as the representative and provider, while the female housewife and mother assumed the role of the husband's supporter, the children's nurturer and society's guardian of morals and culture (Saptari 2000: 18). In this way, state *ibuism* entrenched a hierarchical framework, perpetuating colonial gender roles and leaving women with limited avenues to attain self-determination.

The historical context I present unveils a contrast between the Indigenous diarchic ideology, celebrating feminine principles and women's spiritual authority, and the gendered hierarchy and maternalism imposed by colonial institutions advancing the ideal of the domestication of Timorese women. The intrusion of state *ibuism* as an Indonesian gender ideology fortified the patriarchal nature of the gender order promoted by colonialism in Timorese society. While the Indigenous ideology acknowledges gender diarchy, envisioning relations rooted in difference and interdependence rather than dominance and subjugation, the separate sphere paradigm introduced through coloniality and amplified by state gender ideology has significantly impacted contemporary Timorese women. Through this historical lens, I reveal the interplay of ideologies shaping the multifaceted roles of women in Timorese society. Today, some Timorese women are negotiating these apparently incommensurable ideologies of housewives and housemasters to make domestic spaces into sites for creating affective bonds and resources for political office.

The politics of the housewife: *Tanam kaki* and social presence as affective investment

In this section, I examine the realm of domestic politics, unravelling how affective experiences metamorphose into political resources within electoral politics. My focus remains on the narratives of women village heads and politicians who, before assuming their political positions, filled the role of housewives. To weave this narrative, I started on a journey of participant observation, conducting interviews and crafting in-depth profiles. I present two women political leaders here: Mama Rosinda, village head of Mandala, and Mama Retha, a woman MP of Malaka. Mindful of preserving their identities, I assign pseudonyms to safeguard their names and the villages they lead.[11]

Mama Rosinda

During my conversation with Mama Rosinda, the village head of Mandala, she consistently emphasised the core concept of *tanam kaki* ('grounded feet' or 'planting the feet') as her strategic political investment during the 2017 village head election. In a tightly knit community of approximately 1,500 people, the bonds among villagers grow stronger through their active participation in various social gatherings held within the village. Mama Rosinda shared:

> Before assuming the role of village head, I was not actively involved in village governance as I preferred not to be managed by others. However, whenever there was a social event like a wedding, funeral or any other village celebration, I would wholeheartedly partake in what is known as *tanam kaki* ... Through *tanam kaki*, we extend our assistance and support during family gatherings, diligently contributing to household chores, such as food preparation, cooking in the kitchen and ensuring everything is well taken care of until the completion of the event.

---

11 Pseudonyms have also been assigned to my esteemed research assistants, protecting their invaluable contributions.

Mama Rosinda believes that the community values her presence more than material or monetary contributions. She continued: 'It is the essence of being present that matters most to them … The villagers here may not forget the service I provided and the genuine presence I offered.'[12]

The affective investment made by Mama Rosinda was a result of her long-term dedication and effort. She had cultivated bonds with women in the community long before her tenure as the village head. Mama Rosinda, in her eloquent expression, revealed that despite not actively participating in official village meetings, she consistently favoured social gatherings with her presence. This commitment was further affirmed and supported by her elder brother, who holds a distinguished position as a senior Catholic priest in Timor. He shared his observations, stating:

> [*T*]*anam kaki* is not something that happens automatically, meaning you don't just show up if you want to run as a candidate. Mama Rosinda has been consistently engaging in *tanam kaki* within the community for a significant period. For instance, at a wedding celebration, she would attend and offer her assistance from the background, often lending her support in the kitchen.[13]

Mama Rosinda's genuine involvement and compassionate contributions have made a lasting impact on the community and serve as a testament to her commitment to the wellbeing of her fellow villagers.

With her lineage as a descendant of the noble family in her village, Mama Rosinda wielded the power to rally other village women to actively participate in these social gatherings. This form of Indigenous political leadership is encapsulated in the term *tai* (or *tei*) *manu'ak* (literally, 'her stomach is very wide'), which metaphorically suggests that food barns are open to all who come, symbolising the duty of a noble leader to ensure that food is prepared for everyone. By generously providing food to the people, leaders are held in high regard and, in return, their people replenish their barns with bountiful crops. Thus, the essence of *tai manu'ak* is that a leader must embrace the practice of living and dining with their people while wholeheartedly serving them. *Tanam kaki*, therefore, embodies the exemplary characteristics that nobles should embody in their leadership role.

---

12 Interview with Mama Rosinda, 6 September 2021.
13 Interview with Father Rosindus Tae, 20 January 2022.

Mama Rosinda's noble background is reinforced by her eldest brother being a respected Catholic priest, which holds great significance in her community. With a Catholic family background and such influential familial ties, Mama Rosinda's candidacy as the village head was undoubtedly strengthened. Interestingly, before Mama Rosinda decided to run for the village head position, her husband had stood for election as village head, but he narrowly lost to another candidate. When he ran for the legislative candidacy in Malaka district, he was similarly defeated.

When I was talking with one of the research assistants who accompanied me to Mandala village, and who has a kinship connection with Mama Rosinda's family, he shared this insight about the consecutive defeats experienced by Mama Rosinda's husband:

> Being a son-in-law [*mane foun*] makes it difficult to win in his wife's village. However, people in Mandala always think ahead and consider preserving Mama Rosinda's husband's feelings. For example, during village events, they wouldn't allow a member of the Regional People's Representative Council [*Dewan Perwakilan Rakyat Daerah*, DPRD] to sit on a mat on the ground. According to the tradition here, due to his position as a *mane foun*, he is not entitled to sit on the platform.[14]

This explanation reinforces the significance of Mama Rosinda's husband's defeat, highlighting the enduring influence of the matrilineal kinship system on the political behaviour of the villagers in Malaka. The matrilineality of South Tetun is accompanied by uxorilocality in postmarital residence—that is, the man leaves his natal house after marriage and resides in his wife's house. This transition bestows on him the status of a 'new man' (*mane foun*; known as *anak mantu* ['son-in-law'] in Indonesian), while the bride assumes the role of a 'new woman' (*feto foun*). As a *mane foun*, he is considered a 'guest' in his wife's house This guest status becomes particularly apparent during social gatherings, when house members have the privilege of sitting on the platform, while the *mane foun* (those residing in their wives' houses) sit on mats spread on the ground (see Therik 2004). Moreover, *mane foun* are also involved in domestic activities, including cooking during social gatherings of their wives' clan.

Due to his status as *mane foun* in Mandala village, Mama Rosinda's husband faced challenges running for election as village head and as a legislative member in Malaka. In the villagers' view, they would feel uneasy seeing their

---

14 Interview with Tobius, 17 September 2021.

leader sitting on mats spread on the ground due to his *mane foun* status, while ordinary villagers who were his wife's brothers occupied the upper platform. This sophisticated cultural feeling made it difficult for Mama Rosinda's husband to succeed in electoral contests. However, the situation changed when Mama Rosinda herself ran for village head. In the context of South Tetun's matrilineality, women hold the role of guardians of the village and house, as all property, land and houses are passed from one generation of women to the next. Hence, women's position is valued over men's. Within Mama Rosinda, a convergence of three significant social aspects takes place: *tanam kaki*, her noble background and her status as a daughter in an uxorilocal, matrilineal system—all of which played a crucial role in her successful election as the village head in Mandala.

Mama Retha

Steeped in the traditions of Malaka that celebrate motherhood, cooking holds a central place in the daily rhythms of mothers. Mama Retha, raised in a noble, middle-class family, was immersed from a tender age in the knowledge and skills required to proficiently manage household chores. Her passion for cookery is deeply cherished among her extended family, becoming an integral part of their memories. Kanisius, Mama Retha's cousin, told me: 'Mama Retha has been selling cakes since she was a child because they live near the dormitories, such as the parish dormitories, [the] Teacher Education School and high schools, where her cakes are kept.'[15] From her earliest years, Mama Retha cultivated a profound love for cooking and actively participated in the kitchen during familial and customary gatherings organised by her family or the members of her *uma*. Even after her marriage, Mama Retha pursued her cooking passion, establishing a successful catering business in her own home. In 1996, Mama Retha married Bapak Theodorus, who is currently serving as the head of a government agency in Malaka district. Hailing from a local aristocratic group in Malaka, some of Bapak's close relatives have emerged as prominent politicians in the region, including former *bupati* ('heads of district') of Malaka.

When Mama Retha's husband embarked on his civil service career in Malaka, he encouraged Mama Retha to venture into politics. In 1999, she officially joined the Golkar Party at the subdistrict level and decided to run as a legislative candidate representing Golkar in the 1999 elections.

---

15 Interview with Kanisius, 26 September 2021.

Unfortunately, Mama Retha fell short of securing a seat in that election. In 2014, she left Golkar to join the People's Conscience Party (Partai Hati Nurani Rakyat, or Hanura). It was through Hanura that Mama Retha achieved success, securing a seat in the Malaka DPRD for two consecutive terms, 2014 to 2019 and 2019 to 2024.

Mama Retha attributes her success as a female MP to the strong support of her extended family and her significant position as a daughter within the matrilineal system of Malaka. Embracing her role as 'guardian of the *uma*', she upholds a sense of responsibility for the wellbeing and prosperity of her clan, surpassing the role typically granted to her male counterparts. The cultural practice of uxorilocal marriage is viewed with disfavour in political terms as it tends to diminish a man's authority within his wife's clan. Mama Retha expressed her appreciation for this integral aspect of her identity as a woman in Malaka: 'It is preferable for our daughters to become MPs, as they will be able to care for us … If a son becomes an MP, he may prioritise his wife's family instead.'

Beyond the strength of her familial bonds, Mama Retha's expertise in the culinary arts within her clan and her village significantly strengthens the support and votes of villagers from her electoral district. Within the clan, Mama Retha's dedication to kitchen duties is revered by all members of her extended family. She actively engages in nearly every cooking event within her familial circle. Similarly, at the community level, her emotional closeness with the villagers developed through her initiative to establish a catering group with fellow mothers in Bakiruk, where she currently lives. Mama Retha's popularity in her neighbourhood flourished as she contributed to and coordinated cooking activities during village gatherings. 'Her active involvement in community cooking activities in Bakiruk led to Mama Retha receiving 400 votes during the first term. Bakiruk is the most populous village,' shared Kanisius.

In her second legislative term, Mama Retha experienced a significant increase, earning 1,952 votes in the 2019 election (Jenahas 2019). According to Mama Retha, the increase in votes was partly because she continued to maintain social intimacy with her constituents, which involves nurturing socially affective ties. Mama Retha believes the essence of her support lies in her devoted presence during the momentous social gatherings of her constituents, safeguarding her support base. She told me: 'After being elected as a legislative member, we must strive to retain that position. So, I take great care of the people who have chosen me. I make every effort to fulfil their needs related to their wellbeing.' Along with the social affect that Mama Retha developed in maintaining relationships with her constituents, placing witnesses at each polling station (*tempat pengumuman suara*) was one of her tactics for victory in the 2019 elections. This strategy differed from her approach in the previous term, as she recognised the importance of both familial support and financial capital to ensure the presence of witnesses at every polling station.

Through her cooking competency, Mama Retha has gained an appreciation of the underlying costs entailed in family gatherings, be they weddings, funerals or *sambut baru*[16] ceremonies. As a result, whenever her constituents extend invitations to such events, Mama Retha ensures that attending and offering her support take precedence, whether in the form of financial contributions or material assistance. Accepting this duty, she shoulders the responsibility of providing aid to ease the financial strain accompanying these momentous family occasions. She explained:

> If there is a funeral ceremony, I must be present. I always help in various forms, such as contributing towards the coffin, providing livestock for slaughter, giving rice or money. Whether or not the person has a direct familial relationship with me is not a concern if they are my constituents. I must take care of my constituents because they are the ones who voted for me. It's important. By doing so, if we run as candidates again, they will surely vote for us. Wherever my constituents hold a ceremony, I will be there, no matter the circumstances. If I am unable to attend due to being away on duty, my husband or relatives will attend.

With a robust social presence, Mama Retha adeptly practised patronage politics by actively assisting her constituents in resolving various personal matters. Her support extended across a wide spectrum, from aiding with national identity card issues and facilitating bank transactions to settling fines and contributing construction materials for housing projects. Additionally, she endeavoured to secure 'decent' employment opportunities for her constituents. Mama Retha's commitment to providing comprehensive support has earned her trust within her community. She observed:

---

16 *Sambut baru* is the local phrase used to commemorate the joyous occasion of receiving the Sacrament of Holy Communion.

We are roughly like their servants. We must take care of administrative stuff such as KTP [National Identity Card] as they surely do not want to queue at the office but ask Mama to help them. Even when the motorbike is ticketed by the police, they will call Mama to ask for help to talk to the police or pay the ticket fine. One day, I was even phoned by one of my constituents to help him disburse his loan at the bank. So, I then had to contact the bank so that the loan could be disbursed immediately.

Mama Retha's experiences in meeting the needs of her constituents speak to the blurred boundaries between the public and private domains, revealing how the notion of separate spheres is messy.

Fascinatingly, despite her esteemed position as a legislative member, Mama Retha takes pride in actively engaging in food-work during social gatherings arranged by her relatives or affiliated clans. According to Kanisius:

In Kamanasa, she always took charge of the back of the house [that is, kitchen]. Even after becoming a legislative member, she still commands the kitchen … When there are family gatherings, she brings all the kitchen equipment … She has always been like that.

Mama Retha's unwavering commitment to overseeing cooking activities exemplifies the status of women as housemasters, retaining their authority over domestic tasks. It suggests that the process of domestication of Timorese women has not been entirely successful. The idealised notion of a Timorese woman as housemaster remains ingrained in Mama Retha's thinking. One of my interviewees, Father Rosindus Tae, emphasised the significance of being a woman in Malaka:

If you want to give something, every time you visit someone's house, you should not enter from the front but go straight to the back. By entering from the back, your position will be 'higher'. So, even if our social status is high, we must go straight to the back [that is, the kitchen] to help them cook. By doing so, your name will be etched in their memory.[17]

The political strategies employed by Mama Retha have garnered widespread recognition from many villagers, particularly the women whom I had the privilege of meeting during my fieldwork. In one of the villages that falls within Mama Retha's electoral district, I found that many women with whom

---

17 Interview with Father Rosindus Tae, 27 January 2022.

I spoke were acquainted with her name and contributions. As a testament to Mama Retha's significant impact, Mama Fidelia, for instance, revealed that she came to know Mama Retha through the care and involvement she displayed in various social gatherings within the community:

> If there is an event here, whether it's a joyous occasion like a wedding or a mournful event like a funeral, if Mama Retha hears about it in advance, she will immediately send equipment such as chairs, tables or tents. Even if Mama Retha only learns about the event over the phone, she still sends the necessary supplies. On the contrary, if we have an event but we don't inform her, she might get a little upset, especially if she hears about the event from someone else. She can get angry about it.[18]

In the realm of women such as Mama Retha, the affective experiences intertwined with cooking activities and social presence encapsulates the core concept of *tanam kaki*. For Mama Retha, the kitchen is not merely a physical space; it embodies an affective space—a realm where emotions are awakened and connections with the world are felt. These domestic spaces become arenas of affective investment, where household activities transcend the mundane, influencing the fabric of public life. For Mama Retha, cooking not only serves as a means of sustenance; it also becomes a powerful form of activism, from which the affective investments during electoral moments manifest into tangible support in the form of votes.

Conclusion

Historically, the Indigenous political system's gender diarchy faced erosion under the influence of colonial maternalism and the state's gender ideology, advocating state *ibuism*—all seeking to reshape family-based gender relations. The colonial missions, as maternalistic institutions, introduced the novel concept of the 'housewife', which was previously unknown to local people, who instead conceived of women as housemasters. This fostered the emergence of a paradigm of separate spheres, emphasising women's position and status as confined to the domestic realm. Consequently, the gender order transitioned towards a hierarchical framework, with masculinity assuming a superordinate role over femininity. The shift orchestrated by

---

18 Interview with Mama Fidelia, 24 October 2021.

colonial institutions and Indonesian state formation effectively reversed the Indigenous system of gender relations, favouring a patriarchal gender hierarchy.

However, in my observations of daily life, I discovered that the domestication of women in Timor has been only partial. Despite the deep distinctions between gender diarchy/hierarchy and housemaster/housewife ideologies, women exhibit skill in adeptly navigating these differences to continue matriliny and the authority of being a housemaster. By maintaining control and power inside the house, women leverage their domestic expertise, particularly in the realm of cooking, as a significant resource for advancing their political agency. These women leaders harness the power of domesticity, with cooking as their form of political activism. They nurture affective connections with other women through their cooking activism, and converting these affective investments into votes during elections. Thus, I propose that domestic spaces serve as a realm where women can acquire political leadership skills. Within these spaces lies the potential for empowerment, fostering the cultivation of affective networks. Therefore, we must not underestimate the role of housewives, as it opens diverse possibilities and opportunities for women.

However, affective relations are not the sole determinant of success in political contests. Connections to the local nobility also hold significant influence over women's electability. The two women I have presented, despite having a strong social identity as housewives, belong to the dominant clan in their respective villages and hail from the noble group of Malaka. Nevertheless, even as noblewomen, they must still engage in the practices of *tanam kaki* and demonstrate their politics of being present. Therefore, the noble position of women must be complemented by affective relations in their pursuit of political agency. Thus, while the position of Timorese women has partially transitioned from housemasters to housewives, they retain the ability to leverage this status by transforming the domestic space into a political realm, thereby converting it into a political resource.

References

Abarca, M. 2006. *Voices in the Kitchen: Views of Food and the World from Working-Class Mexican and Mexican-American Women.* College Station: Texas A&M University Press.

Boardman, Kay. 2000. 'The Ideology of Domesticity: The Regulation of Household Economy in Victorian Women's Magazines.' *Victorian Periodicals Review* 33, no. 2: 150–64.

Charles, Nickie, and Marion Kerr. 1988. *Women, Food and Families*. Manchester: Manchester University Press.

Cunningham, Clark. 1962. 'People of the Dry Land.' Unpublished D.Phil. thesis, Oxford University.

DeVault, Marjorie L. 1991. *Feeding the Family: The Social Organization of Caring as Gendered Work*. Chicago: University of Chicago Press.

Djajadiningrat-Nieuwenhuis, Madelon. 1992. '*Ibuism* and *Priyayization*: Path to Power?' In *Indonesian Women in Focus*, edited by E. Locher-Scholten and A. Niehof, 43–51. Leiden: KITLV Press. doi.org/10.1163/9789004488816_005.

Fox, James J. 1982. 'The Great Lord Rests at the Centre: The Paradox of Powerlessness in European–Timorese Relations.' *Canberra Anthropology* 5, no. 2: 22–33. doi.org/10.1080/03149098209508552.

Francillon, Gerard. 1967. 'Some Matriarchic Aspects of the Social Structure of the Southern Tetun of Middle Timor.' PhD diss., The Australian National University.

Giard, Luce. 1998. 'Doing Cooking.' In *The Practice of Everyday Life. Volume 2: Living and Cooking*, edited by Michel de Certeau, Luce Giard, and Pierre Mayoll, 149–247. Minneapolis: University of Minnesota Press.

Hägerdal, H. 2013. 'Cycles of Queenship on Timor: A Response to Douglas Kammen.' *Archipel* 85, no. 1: 237–51. doi.org/10.3406/arch.2013.4394.

Hausen, Karin. 1981. 'Family and Role-Division: The Polarisation of Sexual Stereotypes in the Nineteenth Century—An Aspect of the Dissociation of Work and Family Life.' In *The German Family: Essays on the Social History of the Family in Nineteenth- and Twentieth-Century Germany*, edited by Richard J. Evans and W.R. Lee, 51–83. Totowa: Barnes & Noble Books.

Hoskins, Janet. 1988. 'Matriarchy and Diarchy: Indonesian Variations on the Domestication of the Savage Woman.' In *Myths of Matriarchy Reconsidered*, edited by Deborah B. Gewertz, 34–56. Sydney: University of Sydney.

Huber, Mary Taylor, and Nancy C. Lutkehaus. 1999. *Gendered Mission: Women and Men in Missionary Discourse and Practice*. Ann Arbor: University of Michigan Press. doi.org/10.3998/mpub.16332.

Jakimow, Tanya. 2017. 'Becoming a Developer: Processes of Personhood in Urban Community-Driven Development, Indonesia.' *Anthropological Forum* 27, no. 3: 256–76. doi.org/10.1080/00664677.2017.1379005.

Jakimow, Tanya. 2018. 'Beyond "State Ibuism": Empowerment Effects in State-Led Development in Indonesia.' *Development and Change* 49, no. 5: 1143–65. doi.org/10.1111/dech.12374.

Jakimow, Tanya. 2020. *Susceptibility in Development: Micropolitics of Local Development in India and Indonesia.* Oxford: Oxford University Press. doi.org/10.1093/oso/9780198854739.001.0001.

Jenahas, Teni. 2019. 'Ini Data Terbaru Perolehan Kursi DPRD Malaka Periode 2019-2024 masing-masing Partai [This is the Latest Data on the Acquisition of Seats in the Malaka DPRD for the 2019–2024 Period for Each Party].' *Kupang Post*, 8 May. kupang.tribunnews.com/2019/05/08/ini-data-terbaru-perolehan-kursi-dprd-malaka-periode-2019-2024-masing-masing-partai?page=1.

Kabeer, Naila. 2011. 'Between Affiliation and Autonomy: Navigating Pathways of Women's Empowerment and Gender Justice in Rural Bangladesh.' *Development and Change* 42, no. 2: 499–528. doi.org/10.1111/j.1467-7660.2011.01703.x.

Kammen, D.A. 2012. 'Queens of Timor.' *Archipel* 84, no. 1: 149–73. doi.org/10.3406/arch.2012.4367.

Lutkehaus, Nancy C. 1999. 'Missionary Maternalism: Gendered Images of the Holy Spirit Sisters in Colonial New Guinea.' In *Gendered Mission: Women and Men in Missionary Discourse and Practice*, edited by Mary Taylor Huber and Nancy C. Lutkehaus, 207–35. Ann Arbor: University of Michigan Press.

Malos, Ellen. 1980. *The Politics of Housework.* London: Allison & Busby Ltd.

Mies, Maria. 1988. *Women: The Last Colony.* London: Zed Books.

Ormeling, Ferdinand Jan. 1955. *The Timor Problem: A Geographical Interpretation of an Underdeveloped Island.* Djakarta: J.B. Wolters.

Parera, A.D.M. 1994. *Sejarah Pemerintahan Raja-Raja Timor* [History of the Reign of the Kings of Timor]. Jakarta: Pustaka Sinar Harapan.

Robinson, Amanda Lea, and Jessica Gottlieb. 2021. 'How to Close the Gender Gap in Political Participation: Lessons from Matrilineal Societies in Africa.' *British Journal of Political Science* 51, no. 1: 68–92. doi.org/10.1017/S0007123418000650.

Saptari, Ratna. 2000. 'Women, Family and Household: Tension in Culture and Practice.' In *Women and Households in Indonesia: Cultural Notions and Practices*, edited by J. Koning, M. Nolten, J. Rodenburg, and R. Saptaripp, 10–25. London: Taylor & Francis.

Schulte Nordholt, Henk G. 1971. *The Political System of the Atoni of Timor*. The Hague: Nijhoff. doi.org/10.26530/OAPEN_613379.

Segato, Rita Laura. 2018. 'A Manifesto in Four Themes.' Translated by Ramsey McGlazer. *Critical Times* 1, no. 1: 198–211. doi.org/10.1215/26410478-1.1.198.

Suryakusuma, Julia. 1996. 'The State and Sexuality in New Order Indonesia.' In *Fantasizing the Feminine in Indonesia*, edited by L.J. Sears, 92–119. Durham: Duke University Press. doi.org/10.2307/j.ctv1134ctq.7.

Suryakusuma, Julia. 2011. *State Ibuism: The Social Construction of Womanhood in New Order Indonesia*. East Beji: Komunitas Bambu.

Therik, Tom. 2004. *Wehali: The Female Land—Traditions of a Timorese Ritual Centre*. Canberra: Pandanus Books.

Tickamyer, Ann R., and Siti Kusujiarti. 2012. *Power, Change, and Gender Relations in Rural Java: A Tale of Two Villages*. Columbus: Ohio University Press. doi.org/10.2307/j.ctt1j7x7w5.

Wouden, F.A.E. 1968. *Types of Social Structure in Eastern Indonesia*. Dordrecht: Springer. doi.org/10.1007/978-94-015-1076-9.

11

Territories and Frontiers: Exclusionary inclusion of women in grassroots governance in Arunachal Pradesh, India

Deepak K. Mishra and Aparimita Mishra[1]

The participation of women in grassroots governance through the special reservation of seats in local body elections was expected to be a major step towards gender empowerment in India (Nassbaum et al. 2003). The outcomes of this intervention have been found to be regionally uneven and contingent on a variety of enabling factors (Kudva 2003; Jayal 2006). Despite the significant challenges elected women representatives faced initially, in many instances, they tried to reduce corruption, pursued an independent vision and felt empowered (Kudva 2003). Many studies also documented the limitations of empowerment through participation in grassroots governance and, while highlighting the diversity of experiences of women from different socioeconomic backgrounds, called for supportive changes in governance and wider sociopolitical structures (Mohanty 1995; Devika and Thampi 2012). Caste and class differences among women limited the scope of gender solidarity (Vyasulu and Vyasulu 1999) and women from marginalised social groups faced additional constraints (Chatterjee 2010).

---

1   The authors would like to thank Dr Tashi Phuntso, Dr M.A. Salam and Prem Droima for their help and support during the field survey.

The 'frequent derailing of local democracy by social inequality' (Drèze and Sen 2002: 17) meant that the context of the marginalised group's interactions with the local power structures is critical. This chapter presents the case of Arunachal Pradesh, where participation in grassroots governance has created a 'new political space' for women from tribal communities. While the state is well known for its long-enduring community institutions at the village level, women were marginalised in both the 'traditional' and 'modern' institutional spaces.

First, the chapter examines how women's economic and political rights are being reconfigured against the backdrop of rapid and complex institutional transformation involving state, market and community institutions. The specificities of a borderland are key constitutive elements in this uneven and layered transition. Second, by analysing the day-to-day negotiations of women *Panchayat* (municipality and village council) representatives through multiple rounds of field surveys, we argue that in the context of an ethnicised political economy that has entrenched a framework of ethnic political patronage, and inadequate devolution of financial powers to the *Panchayati Raj* institutions (PRIs),[2] women's participation through legislative change can be seen as a form of 'exclusionary inclusion'.[3] Finally, the chapter argues that the multipronged struggles of women representatives in Arunachal Pradesh provide a useful starting point to reconceptualise grassroots political space as a contested domain in which structural inequalities of various kinds are challenged, even when the overwhelming dominance of ethnic politics is rarely questioned. The chapter attempts to demonstrate the blurred boundaries between the state, market and community institutions in understanding the processes that empower and disempower women.

This study is based on multiple rounds of field surveys in West Kameng District, Arunachal Pradesh, conducted in 2010, 2015–16 and 2019. The selection of the PRI representatives was made to represent the well-connected and remote areas of the district. In the initial round of the field survey, 20 *Panchayati Raj* (PR) representatives (14 women and six men) and 15 bureaucrats and government officials were interviewed. Among the women PRI members, one *Zilla Parishad* ('district council') member, four *Anchal Samiti* ('zonal committee') members and nine *Gram Panchayat* ('village council')

---

2   *Panchayati Raj* is the system of local self-government for villages in rural India.
3   The term 'exclusionary inclusion' has been used in diverse contexts in the literature to signify the differential treatment and exclusion of some individuals and groups in seemingly inclusive contexts, or unfavourable inclusion. For example, see Gubrium et al. (2017); Kneebone (2005).

members (GPM) were interviewed.[4] An additional 105 individuals from the three selected villages were interviewed to learn about their perceptions of *Panchayati Raj* institutions and representatives. Three villages in the West Kameng District were selected. One was a newly settled, multi-ethnic village; the second was an old village where most of the inhabitants were Monpa, the numerically dominant tribe of the district; while in the third village, the Bugun tribe dominated. During the study, the three-tier system was changed to a two-tier PR system. In subsequent rounds, an attempt was made to contact the same PRI members (irrespective of their current position), and it was supplemented by informal discussions with new PRI members. During 2022–23, we continued these interactions through telephone interviews.[5]

With our early training as economists, both authors have investigated multiple dimensions of economic development in Arunachal Pradesh from a broad political economy perspective. In the previous rounds of our field research, we focused on agrarian change and livelihood diversification (for the first author) and the impact of deforestation on women's work burden (for the second author). One of the insights from this work was that compared with other dimensions of social and economic life, the gender gap in political participation is relatively high in the state, which prompted us to undertake this current research. We moved from our quantitative, structured, questionnaire-based field research to a qualitative approach. Having spent nearly nine years in the state during the late 1990s and early 2000s, four of which were spent in West Kameng, the district under study, we had developed a network of friends and acquaintances in the area. Through these, we made initial contact with the respondents, which helped establish a level of trust. In the multi-ethnic social context of Arunachal Pradesh, the distinction between ethnic communities Indigenous to the state (officially known as Arunachal Pradesh Scheduled Tribes) and outsiders (those who have come from other states of India) is stark. Still, such differences do not normally lead to hostile attitudes. Thus, our identities as outsiders were known to our respondents. The other identity of the authors, as the 'educated folk' who know of official processes and rules and who have 'come all the way from Delhi', the national capital, was also mentioned and commented upon a few times during our interactions. While there is a possibility that these distinctions influenced some of the responses, we believe that the impact on the key findings of our research was minimal.

---

4   We were accompanied by local interpreters, generally not from the same villages, during the interviews. Most of the conversations were in Hindi, the language spoken by people from Arunachal Pradesh, while communicating with people from other tribes and states.

5   All names have been changed to protect the identity of the respondents.

The political economy of ethnicised development

Arunachal Pradesh, in north-eastern India, borders Bhutan, China, Myanmar and the Indian states of Assam and Nagaland. Known as the North-Eastern Frontier Agency (NEFA) until 1972, the state has been the site of a border dispute between China and India. Recent studies on the political economy of development in the state refer to its many specificities that have had a decisive influence on its polity and economy. The first set of such specificities includes the mountain ecology of this large Himalayan state, which is often expressed through its ecological diversity and fragility; the limited scope and high cost of much industrialisation and economic diversification because of its topography; and its perceived and actual 'remoteness', leading to its political and economic marginalisation (Jodha 1992).

The second set of specificities emerges from the encounters of the region with the colonial and postcolonial states. Present-day Arunachal Pradesh was 'unadministered' during the colonial period; it was treated as a buffer zone between an external and inner line demarcating borders. The colonial state restricted movements beyond the inner line—a practice that has continued with minor alterations. An important implication of this colonial legacy was that unlike in other parts of the country, here, the postcolonial Indian state had to build the administrative and political infrastructure from scratch. The Indian state followed a gradualist approach towards developing its bureaucratic infrastructure in this sensitive border area, partly under the influence of anthropologist Verrier Elwin, who was appointed by Jawaharlal Nehru, India's first prime minister, as an advisor on the NEFA. The 'Nehru–Elwin' policy guarded against sudden and massive changes imposed from above and advocated the integration of the Indigenous community institutions into the formal governance structures (Elwin 1988). This helped the state to gain legitimacy among the Indigenous population, but the policy was criticised as 'isolationist', particularly after the Sino-Indian War in 1962 (Haokip 2010). Yet, the recognition of village-level community institutions, oral community laws and community rights over land, even though done in an ad hoc and ambiguous manner, was a significant development, particularly when compared with the tribal-dominated areas of central and eastern India.

The Indigenous community institutions of Arunachal Pradesh were diverse, ranging from chieftainship to loosely republican structures. Though termed 'traditional', many of these institutions carried the legacy of colonial interventions. These administrative innovations meant incorporating tribal elites into the 'new' governance structures and reconfiguring the roles of community institutions under the new, postcolonial dispensation. The diverse and uncodified community laws, customs and norms significantly impacted the gendered transformation of the economy and society.[6] In political economy terms, it meant that the state emerged as the prime mover of economic transformation, virtually establishing 'markets' for goods, services and labour, both in the physical and the economic senses, in a remote region. The resultant institutional political economy resulted in the co-evolution of state, market and community institutions—something that continues to shape the development trajectory and capitalist transition in the state (Harriss-White et al. 2009, 2022), with profound implications for gender disparities and other forms of inequality.

The third set of specificities are those of a borderland. In a profound sense, the redrawing of boundaries by the 'modern' postcolonial state changed the spatial economy of the region, where the movements of people, goods, domesticated animals, crafts and cultures had a much longer and more vibrant history than that suggested by relatively recent narratives of isolation and remoteness from the (new) centres of power (Misra 2013; Cederlöf 2013: 3–6). The new administrative, political and economic architecture of present-day Arunachal Pradesh, with international borders with three different countries, was anchored to security concerns (Mishra 2013). At a general level, the political and economic governance of the region often invoke the logic of exceptionalism, which is premised on the uniqueness of being and governing a borderland.

Partly because of these developments, a durable structure of ethnicised governance has emerged in the state (Harriss-White et al. 2009), in which competition, concessions and collaborations among tribal communities

---

6   Recognition of uncodified community law had several implications for women as access to resources and opportunities was mediated through community norms. The community laws marginalised women in several ways. In 2021, the state government attempted to pass a law, the Arunachal Pradesh Marriage and Inheritance of Property Bill, to regulate divorce, alimony payments and marriage registration. Apart from making polygamy illegal, it has provisions for securing women's right to inherit immovable assets. The Bill was criticised as 'anti-tribal' because it had a provision that said: 'An APST [Arunachal Pradesh Scheduled Tribes] woman married to a non-APST man shall enjoy the legal right over any immovable properties acquired or inherited from her family in her lifetime.' Considering the significant opposition to the Bill, the government decided not to table it (for a discussion, see Kundu 2022).

replace the principles of civic governance (Baruah 2003b). Outsiders cannot own land, immovable property and business establishments in the state. Labour from other states of India cannot move into Arunachal without securing an Inner Line Permit (Harriss-White et al. 2017). However, migration of outside labour has continued, and this has been a cause of concern for the state's Indigenous communities.

Despite the low productive base of the economy, capitalism has made inroads into the region, leading to a limited and uneven differentiation of the peasantry, a massive inflow of consumer goods and rising economic inequality. The emergence of a new class of elites from among the educated professionals, government officers, politicians and businessperson/'contractors' class has sharpened ethnic competition. Rental income is extracted from agricultural land, residential and commercial buildings by renting business licences to others and through private extraction from state and common properties (Harriss-White et al. 2009, 2017, 2022). The state remains the most important sector of the economy.[7] Hence, access to the state's resources is central to the accumulation strategies of the elites. Political patronage through personalised ethnic networks is the primary process through which ethnic politics is articulated. A significant aspect of ethnicised governance is competition and collaboration among the elites claiming to represent their communities to access state power and its resources, which, in turn, has established ethnic patronage networks. To the extent that women were absent or marginalised in these structures of accumulation and patronage, they remain marginal in this new economic and political order.

In the neoliberal phase (since the early 1990s), emphasis on big-ticket development projects, including transport and communications infrastructure, mining and hydropower projects and public–private partnerships, has increased substantially.[8] Grassroots politics and the entry of women into political governance at the lowest level, discussed in the subsequent sections, must be viewed in the broader context described in this section.

---

7   In a framework of asymmetric federalism, Arunachal Pradesh has been granted the status of a 'special category state'. Contributions from the central government, in the form of grants and aid, rather than the state government's revenue, have been the primary source of funds for the government (Roy 2020). It has resulted in perpetual dependence on the central government, *en masse* switching of loyalty by the state-level political representatives to join the party in power at the centre and a disproportionately high degree of control by the central government, which has been described as 'cosmetic federalism' (Baruah 2003a).

8   The overall implications of this 'neoliberal' development model in Arunachal Pradesh are hard to gauge based on the scant information available. Such restructuring is known to have uneven impacts across communities, gender and classes (Harriss-White et al. 2022).

The rapid transformation of the economy has been a gendered process. The informal but pervasive process of transition from collective to private property has often meant that women peasants, who were active participants in the traditional *jhum* ('shifting') cultivation, are being turned into a class of 'disinherited peasants' (Krishna 2005). As forest products are being commercialised, women, despite spending much time collecting forest products, for both domestic and commercial use, are being pushed out of the marketing process. The occupational structure of the state has changed with greater significance placed on the services sector. Still, women with relatively lower levels of educational attainment tend to be concentrated in agriculture and allied activities, as well as the lower rungs of government jobs (Planning Commission 2009). Given the context of ethnic competition and intratribal conflicts and contestations, the issue of gender rights is often pushed onto the backburner. Against the backdrop of land acquisition for neoliberal development projects, the government has enacted new laws partially recognising private property rights over land, but the rights of women over land have not yet been recognised.

Women in grassroots governance

In Arunachal Pradesh, the experimentation with grassroots democracy had a different and unique trajectory compared with other states of India. Self-governed community institutions for natural resource management and conflict resolution had a long history in Arunachal Pradesh (Elwin 1965). In line with the Nehru–Elwin policy towards tribal development, the Indigenous institutions of the tribes, called village councils, were treated as legitimate structures of grassroots governance in the early post-independence period. *Panchayati Raj*, or decentralised governance structures, were formalised through the implementation of the *Panchayati Raj* Regulations in 1967 (Luthra 1971). When a need for local representation in governance was felt, an agency council was created by nominating members from the village councils to the apex body. Only at a later stage were members of the legislative assembly elected. A new phase of decentralisation was introduced through the *Arunachal Pradesh Panchayat Raj Act 1997*.

The seventy-third and seventy-fourth amendments to the Indian Constitution in 1992 paved the way for establishing a three-tier *Panchayati Raj* system in India. These amendments had provisions for the reservation of 33 per cent of seats for women, along with similar reservations for marginalised social groups, constitutionally identified as Scheduled Castes and Scheduled Tribes.[9] After some delay, the *Panchayati Raj* system based on the universal adult franchise was introduced in the state, providing 33 per cent reservations for women candidates. The new system, however, did not completely replace 'traditional' community institutions.[10] Separation of functions among the two kinds of institutions was envisaged— that is, community institutions for conflict resolution and *Panchayats* for developmental activities. However, in practice, this distinction was fuzzy. The reservation for women candidates was a genuine watershed in the state's politics, as it was in the rest of India. However, the devolution of financial and administrative power to the grassroots was not as significant as desired. A report on decentralisation in Indian states in 2015–16 placed Arunachal Pradesh as one of the worst performers (Government of India 2016). There has been some devolution of functions to the *Panchayats* but, without adequate devolution of financial power, it has resulted in little scope for decision-making at the grassroots level.

While looking for possible outcomes of the selective inclusion of women in the structures of grassroots governance, it is important to note the overall context of decentralisation. Democratic decentralisation is supposed to work through a process of greater autonomy for the lower rungs of the governance mechanisms and their democratic functioning. The reality of the devolution of power to the *Panchayats* in Arunachal Pradesh and many other parts of India is better described as a process of institutional decentralisation without effective autonomy, financial devolution or decision-making power. From the point of view of the *Panchayat* representatives, their main task is to implement programs. These programs are designed at the top, with stringent guidelines, and are often executed under the supervision of the district-level administration. A special discretionary grant called Local

9   The Constitution of India has enabling provisions, such as reservations in parliament and assemblies (state-level legislature), higher educational institutions, government jobs and municipal and village councils (*Panchayats*) for disadvantaged social groups who are economically backward and historically subjected to discrimination. Articles 341 and 342 of the Constitution list the castes and tribes entitled to such benefits. Scheduled Castes include formerly untouchable castes and Scheduled Tribes include tribal communities.

10   Arunachal Pradesh is home to nearly 26 major and 100 minor tribes. Most tribes have their distinctive community institutions for conflict resolution. These 'traditional' community institutions in Arunachal Pradesh varied from plebian village councils to chieftainships. Some of these structures and their chiefs were recognised during colonial rule and subsequently by the Government of India. Though they were termed 'traditional' village councils, the process of recognition and interactions with the colonial (and postcolonial) orders and subsequent socioeconomic changes have altered these institutions. Although Elwin (1965) emphasised the democratic nature of the councils, women, by and large, were not part of the decision-making process of these institutions.

Area Development (LAD) funds, earmarked for MPs[11] and Members of the Legislative Assembly (MLAs), was the other source of funding available to the *Panchayats*. Insofar as the *Panchayats* depend on the goodwill of the MPs or MLAs of the area for fund mobilisation, decentralisation strengthened politicians' hold on local governance. The elected representatives, particularly the MLAs, represent not just their constituencies but also their tribes. Therefore, grassroots politics remains embedded in the ethnic politics we have already outlined. We do not, however, imply that *Panchayat* politics is simply a derivative of politics at the upper levels.

Panchayat elections are fought with great enthusiasm in the state. Given the small size of the electorate and the low population density of the state (16 people per square kilometre in 2011), *Panchayat* elections are personalised affairs. Candidates from different national and regional political parties contest elections with their respective party symbols. Yet, a noticeable tendency is the share of posts that go uncontested (Mishra and Mishra 2016), most of which go to candidates aligning with the ruling party in the state. The phenomenon of winning without contests generally results from the ruling parties' overwhelming political and economic dominance. However, the culture of consensus-building found in the community institutions and bargaining among the prospective candidates also play a role. Ethnic considerations are more important for local body elections than for the assembly or the parliament. *Panchayat* elections are seen as contests between clans and not between individual candidates (Bath 2021: 201). These elections are 'costly' from the candidates' perspective.

The hilly, tribal-dominated states of north-eastern India have consistently performed better than the more populous states on indicators of women's empowerment and gender equality (Kishor and Gupta 2004; Singh et al. 2021). In comparison with the region's neighbouring states, which also have a high share of the tribal population, Arunachal Pradesh has an unimpressive performance. Women do not have inheritance rights over land and other immovable property among any of the tribes (Mishra and Upadhyay 2012). They were excluded from 'traditional' community institutions. Women's political marginalisation has continued. At the state level, the share of women members in the legislative assembly has never exceeded 6 per cent. As far as the state's representation in the national

---

11 Under this scheme, each MP has the choice to suggest to the district collector works worth up to INR5 *crores* (10 million) per annum (nearly A$909,000) to be undertaken in his/her constituency. Similarly, MLAs can also suggest development works, subject to some guidelines.

parliament is concerned, none of the elected members has been a woman. Against this backdrop, the emergence of women leaders at the bottom, through the reservation system, was a watershed.

Most female PRI members are from 'political' families—that is, those with a history of other, typically male, members holding public office or being active in political parties. In multi-ethnic areas, these families are most likely from the numerically dominant tribes. They are the relatives of *gaon burahs*[12] ('village chiefs'), former members of the PRIs, local politicians or government officials, and are viewed as 'proxy' candidates representing their male relatives.

As one of our respondents confided, it was her family who took the decision to register her as a candidate when they found out that the seat had been reserved for women. She was elected unopposed. During the entire period, she was in Bhutan for her business selling craft products. Many women said they were hesitant to nominate, primarily because of their unfamiliarity with bureaucratic procedures. 'I did not want to contest, as I had no experience' was the initial reaction of many women *Panchayat* representatives. The only exceptions were the relatively young and educated women from established political families, who were happy to join public life as PRI members. This pattern of 'proxy' candidates has been noticed in the early phase in most Indian states. However, studies also note the increasing assertiveness of women members once their participation becomes the norm (Mohanty and Das 2022).

Politics in Arunachal Pradesh has a distinctly regional character. Politicians depend more on personalised patronage, informal transactions and contacts through family, clan and community networks than on impersonal mobilisations such as large rallies, although the latter are organised during elections for the assembly and the parliament. Patronage networks that operate through ethnic and clan connections are a noticeable feature of politics. National and regional political parties are, consequently, less significant than political leaders and their networks. Women representatives understand this and opt for strategies to be part of a network of patronage rather than challenging the structure. Given that they are new entrants

---

12   *Gaon burahs* or village chiefs (literally, 'the village old man') were 'selected' by the villagers and were recognised by the colonial government—a practice that continues. The mechanism for selection varies across tribes. In the study region, selection is largely through consensus. The post is not hereditary. Conflicts over nomination of *gaon burahs* were reported in few villages. In a few cases, women have been appointed as village chiefs or *gaon burhis*.

trying to negotiate the established but fluid institutional matrix of local ethnic patronage, it is hardly surprising that women PRI members also depend on the resources of their family and relatives.

Inclusion does not necessarily imply equality of opportunities. Inclusive policies are often portrayed as a solution to social exclusion but may better be conceived as the first step towards social inclusion. Exclusionary inclusion is a process whereby inclusion in one dimension or of one kind coexists with exclusion of a different type. Women's formal inclusion in decision-making, for example, does not result in their effective participation when patriarchal social norms restrict their ability to play leadership roles in the public sphere. At times, inclusion is premised on such grounds that it simultaneously results in exclusion. For example, women's participation in the *Panchayats* is embedded within the overall framework of ethnicised patronage, limiting their control over the outcomes. In a more substantive sense, inclusion might mean entry without the preconditions or opportunity for effective participation or the power to set the agenda or alter the outcomes. Scholars of inclusive policies typically point to the limitations that arise from structural constraints that differentiate the conditions of participation among those included (Raju 2005; Jayal 2006; Chatterjee 2010). The specific intersections of caste, class, religion and gender might lead to quite differentiated outcomes. Exclusion might result from systematic biases that mere inclusion cannot address. In other words, exclusionary practices could be higher-order determinants external to the practices of inclusion. Often, exclusion from state or governance structures is seen as a form of powerlessness that may be the cause of many other types of exclusion.

Women's participation in grassroots democracy could address several deficiencies—some because of the advantages of decentralised governance itself and others because of the participation of women, a previously marginalised group, in decision-making. There are interconnections between these two processes as well; precisely because grassroots governance is more personalised, localised and informal, it allows women to draw on their social and familial connections, their intimate knowledge of the local environment and the economic conditions of different households and individuals to participate in the decision-making process. During our focus group discussions with women voters, repeated references were made to the perceived 'personal characteristics' of the women representatives, such as their being friendly, accessible, fun-loving or otherwise. One of our respondents, when asked whether she could communicate her grievances to the woman representative from her village, said: 'I don't know about meetings. I don't go there. But I know her [the PRI representative] well. We meet at her home. We talk a lot about all sorts of things. She knows all about my problems.'

Gram sabha, the village-level meetings that are supposed to be held regularly, rarely occur. Even when they do, few women participate or raise questions. Villagers, particularly women voters, referred to informal meetings and casual chats during social and religious functions as occasions when they share their concerns with women representatives. Thus, the ordinary women (and men) of the village do not necessarily see their absence or exclusion from formal meetings as a serious hindrance. This can also be seen as an alternative, less visible sphere of politics, where women build informal support networks through everyday interactions and transactions. Such engagements transcend the binaries of public and private spheres and those of formal and informal institutional rules.

The 'informality', however, may be part of a shared notion of hierarchy that structures the interactions. Descriptions such as 'fixers' (Berenschot 2010), intermediaries in transactional politics, *malkins* ('landladies') aggressively creating their support networks (Bedi 2016) or 'servants/*naukaranis* of the ward' (Jakimow 2019) can not be used unproblematically to describe the position of the women representatives whom we interviewed. The selection of beneficiaries for different government schemes is made informally in meetings in which *gaon burahs*, other influential male elders or local politicians are present. Informality, of course, is premised on notions of a shared community space, with its own circles of exclusion and inclusion. Such an approach sometimes is a practical necessity.

Although the selection of beneficiaries, as per the official procedures, is the responsibility of the elected PRI representative, consultations with the village elders and the *gaon burahs* help minimise conflicts. In a context in which property rights are not well defined, any alterations to land use, such as the construction of a community hall or boundary wall, can potentially lead to conflict. Another source of conflict arises when the community owns the resource (such as land), but the schemes (such as horticulture development) can be implemented only through individual beneficiaries. For example, if the scheme involves allocation or modification of land, or even construction of a boundary wall or concrete steps, as per community norms, it requires the consent of the *gaon burah*.

Most representatives, however, see this as 'an exercise in consensus-building' so that the traditional village institutions and the *Panchayati Raj* can work together. '*Sab ko saath leke chalna hai*' ('we need to take everybody along') was a common refrain among representatives. Describing her role in the selection of beneficiaries, a woman *Panchayat* member said:

> In the village, there are all kinds of people. If I select any one person for the scheme, others will object. I cannot satisfy everyone. It is a headache for me. So, I talk to the *gaon burah*, and other people. I try to take everyone along. That helps.

At times, this has meant that the female representatives also follow the traditional hierarchies built into the community institutions. Newly settled households, households belonging to neighbouring tribal groups, women married outside the community and migrants often receive less priority in a graded and differentiated manner. In this way, the hierarchical membership structure of the community is extended to the domain of welfare governance. This does not, however, mean that such people are excluded from the general welfare schemes (such as primary education and health care), though they might face differential treatment in those that involve selection of a limited number of beneficiaries (Mishra 2018).

The 'non-tribal population', most of whom are daily wage labourers, tenants and shopkeepers, are not seen as part of the 'local' population or 'villagers'. They are rarely selected as beneficiaries of the schemes implemented by the *Panchayats*. Most of the representatives whom we interviewed did not realise or accept that this was a form of exclusion. Rather, they saw it as an acceptable part of the 'boundary rules' that define the 'community'. 'The schemes are not for the outsiders,' one of our respondents stated. The inclusion of a section of the marginalised, of course, does not automatically lead to the inclusion of other marginalised sections. But the systematic exclusion of the poor and disadvantaged among the non-tribal population is a characteristic of the broader ethnicised politics of the state rather than an exclusive feature of grassroots politics.

Several initiatives over the past decades to train women PRI members have been launched by government agencies such as the State Institute of Rural Development and *Panchayati Raj* and various NGOs. In parallel, self-help groups have been formed and entrepreneurship among women has been promoted.[13] Independent women's organisations, such as the Arunachal Pradesh Women's Welfare Society (APWWS 2016), have pointed out that the 'customary practices ... related to women and children are in conflict with modern laws' and, hence, codification of customary laws is necessary, with suitable modifications wherever these are in conflict with the welfare of women and children. Apart from that, there are demands for reservation of seats for women in the legislative assembly and parliamentary elections, repeal of the *Armed Forces Special Power Act*, which has been in force in parts of the state, and the establishment of a state human rights commission (APWWS n.d.). In the past, the APWWS has successfully campaigned against a bill that sought to legalise customary laws that were perceived to be against women's interests (Ete 1996). Despite their marginalisation in the state's politics, women's organisations are trying hard to create a space within civil society. However, insights from our field survey suggest that the connection between *Panchayati Raj* institutions and the wider political mobilisation of women remains weak. Also, the space that has been created for women *Panchayat* representatives, on the one hand, allows them to enter a hitherto inaccessible space and includes them in the governance process, but the terms of engagement, shaped through the mutually reinforcing interactions of the state, market and community institutions, leave them very little room to challenge the entrenched patriarchal bias.

Redefining territories, negotiating boundaries

Women representatives experience borders as they cross frontiers to move into public life. 'Public life' and the rules of engagement that shape their interactions with others are defined through institutional frameworks, bureaucratic procedures, rules and guidelines and the local cultures of public engagement. They are sometimes treated as 'special invitees'—participants who have come through a special provision—as a deviation of some kind. It is important to note here that reservations in jobs, government supply orders and business licences for the Arunachal Pradesh Scheduled Tribes are widely seen as a legitimate administrative mechanism to safeguard the

---

13   Self-help groups (SHGs) in Changlang District, a government blog reports, have started floriculture as an income-generating activity. During the Covid-19 pandemic, SHGs were actively involved in producing gloves, masks and hand sanitisers. A supermarket has been constructed in Seppa, a district headquarters, for facilitating the sale of craft and other items by the SHGs. See Arunachal Pradesh MyGov (2022).

interests of the local population. Even when reservation as a mechanism for social inclusion is accepted in principle, doubts are expressed about the efficacy of reservation for women in the PRIs. A senior district-level officer articulated his disapproval in clear terms: 'Reservation is good for women. But actual participation is low because of the low literacy rate of women. The reservation policy is rather spoiling the situation.'

Women's ability to perform their duties is questioned by officers, co-workers and occasionally by the female PRIs themselves. At times they are treated kindly but in a patronising way. 'My two fellow female GPMs are illiterate. I work on their behalf. They remain present, but *their presence hardly matters*,' said a male *Gram Panchayat* chairperson (emphasis added). He was convinced that women representatives do not have the agency to make a difference of any kind. Such negative perceptions about the ability of the women representatives—shared by the officials in the local administration, political activists, villagers and even by some elected male representatives— have the potential to become self-fulfilling prophecies. The biased attitude against women representatives creates significant barriers for them, which ultimately result in their being less effective (Mishra and Mishra 2016).

In our conversations with women representatives, the unwelcoming attitudes of the offices and officers and discomfort around meetings and interactions were often mentioned. They are made deeply aware that while moving from the private to the public spheres, they are moving into a different territory— not entirely unfamiliar and hostile, but potentially challenging.

The educational attainment of the women representatives makes a huge difference in the way they negotiate such 'border-crossing'. Educated *Panchayat* representatives felt that others respected them. Women in Arunachal Pradesh, as in many other states of the north-eastern region, are visible in the marketplaces as entrepreneurs, particularly engaged in petty trading. Increasingly, they are also present in government offices, mostly at the bottom of the job hierarchy. A familiar face from the village, an officer from one's own tribe speaking their language or the presence of male relatives could be significant markers of reassurance in these difficult transactions. When asked about her difficulties in negotiating the official procedures, a female *Panchayat Samiti* member said:

> I was a little scared when I visited the DC office at Bomdila. Then I met Pema. She works in that office. She took me to the *bara babu* [head clerk] and asked him to help me. It was difficult initially. It was easy for me after some years when Sangey was posted as an

officer in the same office. I have known him and his family for a long time. He also helped. Later, even others would approach me to get their files moved.

The institutional context of these interactions demands adherence to certain rituals, hierarchies and segregated roles and functions, performative obligations and temporality of certain kinds (namely, at group or one-to-one meetings or training sessions at specific hours). These mark the office setting as a different territory from life at home or in the village. These repeated meetings with the concerned line departments, officers at various levels in the administrative hierarchy, ritualised adherence to bureaucratic norms (seating arrangements, the order and manner in which one is to speak and the numbers and other information that are exchanged) and the primacy of the written word (annual operating plans, sanction letters, lists, reports, forms) over conversations act as the insignia of this new territory. We do not wish to imply that informality, laughter and intimacy are entirely absent from this space. Still, the underlying power relations of the office are too explicit and important to miss. It is here that women representatives face their gravest challenge. In sharp contrast to the opinions of those around them, women representatives do not see themselves as incompetent. They complain of unfamiliarity with the procedures as the reason behind their difficulties. Many of them, while articulating the problems that they face in dealing with the procedures, also talked about their learning, progress and strategies to negotiate this (partially) unfamiliar territory. A middle-aged *Gram Panchayat* member said:

> It is not an easy job. They [the officers] tell us about many rules. 'You cannot do this.' 'This is not allowed.' '[The] Bill will not be passed if you do this.' I had no previous experience of all these things. I take help from others. My husband and other *Gram Panchayat* members help me with the paperwork. I even went to a training program.

While acknowledging the help of the male *Anchal Samiti* member in visiting the subdivisional headquarters, a female member added: 'But in the village, I do not work under anybody's pressure. I perform my duties on my own.' A young, educated PR representative, who claimed she helped other women representatives complete paperwork, said 'they are gradually learning'. A female *Anchal Samiti* member described how she overcame the difficulties of having money sanctioned for a project:

> My village had no steps to reach the *Gompa* [monastery], situated at the hilltop. Villagers were facing difficulties in reaching the *Gompa*. They were demanding funds to construct concrete steps. The *Panchayat* finally got the funds to construct the steps, but it was used for personal expenses by the leaders at that time. So, when we approached the block officer, he refused to sanction any money for the same purpose. We kept on trying. After repeated attempts, finally, money was sanctioned under another scheme. All the members of the *Gram Panchayat* agreed, and we could build the steps and a boundary wall for the school.

She described as an accomplishment the fact that she could bend the rules by diverting funds from another program to build the steps.

The formal bureaucratic space may be unfamiliar to the women representatives, but they were not alone. Their male relatives and friends were there with them to guide and supervise them and to speak on their behalf. In our observations during such interactions, we did notice that officers and superiors also recognised these informal practices, such as the presence of relatives and others in formal meetings, as part of routine office culture.

The spatial context of these interactions is an important dimension, particularly in a sparsely populated mountain context with unreliable public transport:

> I cannot manage to reach the meetings at Bomdila [district headquarters] or Dirang [subdivisional headquarters] without someone's help. If I have to visit more than one office, I need someone with a car or a two-wheeler to be with me. Mostly it is my husband who takes me to the meetings.

The people accompanying them also become part of the conversations, transactions and negotiations. 'In winter, finishing the work and returning home is challenging. If I cannot finish the work, I stay with my sister-in-law. At times, I bring my kids with me.' Those members who stayed near the administrative centres did not face such problems, but for others, time and transport posed significant challenges.

The notion of spaces and boundaries entered our conversations in other contexts as well. The moral economy of the villages and communities does not correspond to the administrative divisions of space and its moral and ethical underpinnings. This is a difficult negotiation for the

PRI representatives, both male and female. To perform their duties and obligations, as representatives of a formalised institutional structure as well as people's *political* leaders at the grassroots, PRI representatives must be mindful of any transgressions on their part pertaining to two very different moral constructs.

The *gaon burah* and the community institutions do not represent just an alternative form of authority; they are also seen as custodians of tradition, customs and social norms. Such 'traditional' community norms are, of course, at times subject to negotiation. There is an inbuilt flexibility to the structures of the traditional institutions that opens scope for women to 'manoeuvre, re-invent and transform received forms of power and prestige' (Taylor 2009: 316). Women representatives are both part of these social norms as members of the community and outsiders in the sense of their unconventional role as leaders and representatives of an external, more powerful authority. Not many women representatives see this conflict as a critical one, perhaps because they come from the families who control the village-level community institutions. But almost all representatives emphasised the need to 'take everybody along' for 'getting the work done'. We found that in a few cases, the village elders are the ones who make the decisions even in the absence of women representatives. By and large, women representatives consult with *gaon burahs* and others, and they try to build a consensus that is mindful of the borders that divide the 'community' and the 'others'. They respect the hierarchical order within the community. They must also be mindful of the official rules, selection criteria for projects and beneficiaries, budget limits and other similar stipulations.

Criss-crossing both these spaces are the supporters of the political leaders and those who represent local MLAs and others. This is, generally, a transactional space in which patronage is distributed through open and concealed transfers, and loyalty is expected and displayed. The larger framework may be one of ethnic politics discussed before, but in day-to-day negotiations, many other factors count, such as the social prestige, political connections and economic position of the individuals and households concerned. The implication for grassroots politics is that supporters of the MLAs and politicians who control the flow of funds interfere in the activities of the *Panchayats*. Sometimes women representatives welcome such 'interference', which provides scope for them to negotiate with and be members of the local political elite. As one of the representatives said: 'I now know all the leaders, even the honourable MLA personally. I am invited to meetings. I go there and ask for more funds. If I face any problems, I call them.' At times, they feel that they are not being allowed to perform their duties because of such 'pressures'. Both male and female *Panchayat* members mentioned one of their challenges was balancing the demands of the villagers with those of the leaders who are close to the MLA.

Another significant aspect was the boundary between the domestic and the public spheres. Most women representatives talked about the challenge of managing their domestic responsibilities as well as the demands of their public life. All women representatives who have young children raised the issue of their domestic work burden. Regular meetings, visits to offices and supervision of projects mean extra demands on top of their domestic care burden. Support from husbands and in-laws is considered crucial.[14] In particular, the support of other women (relatives, occasionally paid domestic help) in the household was a critical element of support.

Does this opportunity to step into the 'public' sphere create the scope to change the life trajectories of women representatives by preparing them for a larger role in public life? Almost all women representatives saw their selection as a significant step, but the possibility of continuing with their career as politicians, according to the representatives, depended on many other factors. The young, educated women from politically well-connected families were clearly hoping to be in public life for longer periods. After interviewing one such woman seven years ago, we contacted her again recently and she said she is now active in a local NGO. Although her chances of gaining a party ticket in the legislative assembly elections are negligible, she thinks she has a 'future in politics/social service'. However, others were not equally enthusiastic about their political careers. Sonam, a 48-year-old woman who was once elected unopposed as a *Panchayat* member, is currently busy with her shop selling handicrafts to tourists. The rotation of reserved seats meant that the same seat was not reserved for women in subsequent rounds. Thus, she was no longer involved in politics of any kind: 'It [politics] is demanding and very time-consuming. I am happy with my business.' Yet others have continued with their public engagements. 'I am no longer a member. Still, I am called to the meetings by the honourable MLA. I go to these meetings. Sometimes, people come to me for help, and

---

14 In most cases, married women representatives described their husbands as very supportive. In one case, where the husband was described as unsupportive, the father-in-law's support was crucial. In another case, the elected member described her husband as 'indifferent', 'someone who doesn't interfere in my work'. She, however, described the support from her women relatives.

I try to help them as much as I can,' said another woman. While entry to politics through the reservation system has opened political space for some women, their continuation and rise within the political structures are contingent on a range of factors.

Concluding observations

The participation of women in the PRIs was a watershed in the politics of Arunachal Pradesh. Undoubtedly, it was an intervention from above and it did create a rupture in the traditional norms of the communities. Notwithstanding the initial reservations about the participation of women in grassroots politics, the reservation system has created a new space hitherto unavailable for women. However, women representatives who have been formally included in the *Panchayati Raj* institutions face several constraints on effectively performing their role as PRI functionaries. We have termed this '*exclusionary* inclusion' because the terms of inclusion, structured through everyday bureaucratic and formal practices and gendered norms of the community, limit their effective participation and control over decision-making.

In this chapter, we have documented the strategic choices of women representatives in different spaces through their reliance on family and community networks to facilitate their role as representatives, the choice of consensus-building and alliance through informal arrangements with the existing power structures of the community, through maintaining informal communication channels with the electorate and through building and utilising informal networks in the formal spaces of governance. As elsewhere, the women representatives, while trying to gain a toehold in a male-dominated space, are making the strategic choice to align with the existing ethnic political order, which in turn is limiting the scope for socially inclusive, transformative politics for gender justice. Yet, their day-to-day and microlevel negotiations with the political and bureaucratic establishment are rooted in the politics of a practical agenda (Jayal 2006). The grammar and articulation of that micropolitics follow the dominant narratives of ethnicity and difference.

At the same time, through protests against violence against women, corruption in recruitment and new hydropower dams, a new pan-tribal civic space is gradually taking shape.[15] Taylor describes the process with much optimism: 'At their best, emerging Arunachali civic life is articulating civic practices that *arise from, and are embedded in*, tribal identities, with pan-tribal, national, and transnational forms of imagination and action' (2009: 311; emphasis in original). This process has been described as '*tranversalizing* of particular into collective identity rather than the *universalizing* of collective identities that are so basic to liberal Western political traditions' (Reid and Taylor 2009, cited in Taylor 2009: 311; emphasis in original). The politics of difference that often accompanies an ethnic political order constantly reproduces and reimagines boundaries between 'us' and 'them', even while arguing for the collective rights of the community.

The evidence presented here suggests that formal political institutions are embedded in the informal landscape of societal norms. While the distinction between formal and informal is important to an extent, the interpenetrating nature of these spheres holds the key to understanding ethnopolitics. As the state and the economy remain embedded in society, access to the state by citizens is mediated through social networks, the 'political (and also often financial) success' of which 'depends on their capacity to manipulate the implementation of the state's policies and legislation' (Berenschot 2010: 885). In Arunachal Pradesh, patronage and manipulation of access to the state operate through ethnic networks. Women representatives in *Panchayats*, while relying on such networks, attempt to overcome the barriers set by exclusionary processes embedded in state, community and market institutions.

Decentralisation may not be enough for democratisation. Similarly, inclusion may be accompanied by effective 'exclusion' in such a way that the formal inclusion of women in governance does not challenge the discriminatory foundations of governance. The informal politics of the community, friends and family plays a crucial role as spaces of familiarity and solidarity for the marginalised—more so because, even when formal structures are modified to include the excluded, exclusionary inclusion persists.

---

15 Since the early 2000s, popular protests against hydro-power development projects have created solidarity networks across student and activist groups within and beyond Arunachal Pradesh. Similarly, a protest against alleged corruption in recruitment for government jobs has brought together people from diverse backgrounds. For a discussion of the protests and politics of dam construction, see Mishra (2019).

References

Arunachal Pradesh MyGov. 2022. 'Role of SHGs in Empowering the State of Arunachal Pradesh.' *MyGov Blog*, 21 January. Government of India. blog. mygov.in/role-of-shgs-in-empowering-the-state-of-arunachal-pradesh/.

Arunachal Pradesh Women's Welfare Society (APWWS). n.d. 'Memorandum on Behalf of Women of Arunachal Pradesh to Sri Kiren Rijiju, Hon'ble Union Minister of State, Ministry of Home Affairs, Govt. of India, New Delhi.' Itanagar: APWWS. www.apwws1979.org/sites/default/files/rep-homemin.pdf.

Arunachal Pradesh Women's Welfare Society (APWWS). 2016. 'Memorandum on Behalf of Women of Arunachal Pradesh Submitted to Hon'ble Chief Minister, Shri Pema Khandu, on 37th Foundation Day of APWWS.' 10 October. Naharlagun: APWWS. www.apwws1979.org/sites/default/files/letter-cm1.pdf.

Baruah, Sanjib. 2003a. 'Nationalizing Space: Cosmetic Federalism and the Politics of Development in Northeast India.' *Development and Change* 34, no. 5: 915–39. doi.org/10.1111/j.1467-7660.2003.00334.x.

Baruah, Sanjib. 2003b. 'Protective Discrimination and Crisis of Citizenship in North-East India.' *Economic and Political Weekly* 38, no. 17: 1624–26. www.jstor.org/stable/4413479.

Bath, Nani. 2021. 'Democracy with a Difference: Tribal Politics in Arunachal Pradesh.' In *Handbook of Tribal Politics in India*, edited by Jagannath Ambagudia and Virginius Xaxa, 190–209. New Delhi: SAGE. doi.org/10.4135/9789353884581.n11.

Bedi, Tarini. 2016. '"Network Not Paperwork": Political Parties, the Malkin, and Political Matronage in Western India.' *Politics & Gender* 12, no. 1: 107–42. doi.org/10.1017/S1743923X15000549.

Berenschot, Ward. 2010. 'Everyday Mediation: The Politics of Public Service Delivery in Gujarat, India.' *Development and Change* 41, no. 5: 883–905. doi.org/10.1111/j.1467-7660.2010.01660.x.

Cederlöf, Gunnel. 2013. *Founding an Empire on India's North-Eastern Frontiers, 1790–1840: Climate, Commerce, Polity*. Delhi: Oxford University Press. doi.org/10.1093/acprof:oso/9780198090571.001.0001.

Chatterjee, Baishali. 2010. 'Political Theory and Citizenship Discourses: Cast(e) in the Periphery—Understanding Representation of Dalit Women and Politics in India.' *Asien* 114, no. 115: 50–67.

Devika, Jayakumari, and Binitha V. Thampi. 2012. *New Lamps for Old? Gender Paradoxes of Political Decentralisation in Kerala*. Delhi: Zubaan.

Drèze, Jean, and Amartya Sen. 2002. 'Democratic Practice and Social Inequality in India.' *Journal of Asian and African Studies* 37, no. 2: 6–37. doi.org/10.1177/002190960203700202.

Elwin, Verrier. 1988 [1957]. *A Philosophy for NEFA*. Itanagar: Directorate of Research, Government of Arunachal Pradesh.

Elwin, Verrier. 1965. *Democracy in NEFA*. Shillong: North-East Frontier Agency.

Ete, Jarjum. 1996. 'Empowering Women.' *Seminar* 441: 44–45.

Government of India. 2016. *Devolution Report 2015–16: Where Local Democracy and Devolution in India is Heading Towards?* New Delhi: Department of Panchayati Raj, Government of India. cdnbbsr.s3waas.gov.in/s316026d60ff9 b54410b3435b403afd226/uploads/2023/02/2023021667.pdf.

Gubrium, Erika K., Bettina Leibetseder, Danielle Dierckx, and Peter Raeymaeckers. 2017. 'Investing in Work: Exclusionary Inclusion in Austria, Belgium and Norway.' *International Journal of Sociology and Social Policy* 37, nos 9–10: 605–22. doi.org/10.1108/IJSSP-01-2017-0001.

Haokip, Thongkholal. 2010. 'India's Northeast Policy: Continuity and Change.' *Man and Society: A Journal of North East Studies* 7: 86–99.

Harriss-White, Barbara, Deepak K. Mishra, and Aseem Prakash. 2017. 'Inclusive Development, Citizenship and Globalisation: The Case of Arunachal Pradesh.' In *Rethinking Economic Development in Northeast India: The Emerging Dynamics*, edited by Deepak K. Mishra and Vandana Upadhyay, 136–50. New Delhi: Routledge. doi.org/10.4324/9781315278490-7.

Harriss-White, Barbara, Deepak K. Mishra, and Vandana Upadhyay. 2009. 'Institutional Diversity and Capitalist Transition: The Political Economy of Agrarian Change in Arunachal Pradesh, India.' *Journal of Agrarian Change* 9, no. 4: 512–47. doi.org/10.1111/j.1471-0366.2009.00230.x.

Harriss-White, Barbara, Deepak K. Mishra, and Vandana Upadhyay. 2022. 'Capitalist Trajectories in Agrarian Mountain Societies of East and South-East Arunachal, India.' *Journal of Agrarian Change* 22, no. 2: 223–53. doi.org/10.1111/joac.12454.

Jakimow, Tanya. 2019. 'The "Servants" of Dehradun: A Changing Relationship Between Municipal Councillors and Voters in India.' *Journal of Contemporary Asia* 49, no. 3: 389–409. doi.org/10.1080/00472336.2018.1527388.

Jayal, Niraja Gopal. 2006. 'Engendering Local Democracy: The Impact of Quotas for Women in India's *Panchayats*.' *Democratisation* 13, no. 1: 15–35. doi.org/10.1080/13510340500378225.

Jodha, Narpat S. 1992. 'Mountain Perspective and Sustainability: A Framework for Development Strategies.' In *Sustainable Mountain Agriculture. Volume 1: Perspectives and Issues*, edited by N.S. Jodha, M. Banskota, and T. Pratap, 41–82. Kathmandu: International Centre for Integrated Mountain Development.

Kishor, Sunita, and Kamla Gupta. 2004. 'Women's Empowerment in India and Its States: Evidence from the NFHS.' *Economic and Political Weekly* 39, no. 7: 694–712.

Kneebone, Susan. 2005. 'Women within the Refugee Construct: "Exclusionary Inclusion" in Policy and Practice—The Australian Experience.' *International Journal of Refugee Law* 17, no. 1: 7–42. doi.org/10.1093/ijrl/eei002.

Krishna, Sumi. 2005. 'Gendered Price of Rice in North-Eastern India.' *Economic and Political Weekly* 40, no. 25: 2555–62.

Kudva, Neema. 2003. 'Engineering Elections: The Experiences of Women in "Panchayati Raj" in Karnataka, India.' *International Journal of Politics, Culture, and Society* 16, no. 3: 445–63. doi.org/10.1023/A:1022312613488.

Kundu, Bipasha. 2022. 'Why Criticism Against Arunachal Pradesh Draft Bill on Marriage and Inheritance of Property is Misplaced.' *The Leaflet*, [Mumbai, India], 1 February. www.theleaflet.in/why-criticism-against-arunachal-pradesh-draft-bill-on-marriage-and-inheritance-of-property-is-misplaced/.

Luthra, Pran Nath. 1971. *Constitutional and Administrative Growth of Arunachal Pradesh*. Itanagar: Department of Cultural Affairs, Directorate of Research, Government of Arunachal Pradesh.

Mishra, Aparimita. 2018. 'Multiple Marginalities: A Study of Participation of Women in Panchayati Raj Institutions in Arunachal Pradesh.' *Social Change* 48, no. 4: 558–74. doi.org/10.1177/0049085718801444.

Mishra, Aparimita, and Deepak K. Mishra. 2016. 'Gender, Ethnicity, and Grassroots Governance in Arunachal Pradesh, India.' *Asian Journal of Women's Studies* 22, no. 2: 147–64. doi.org/10.1080/12259276.2016.1182306.

Mishra, Deepak K. 2013. 'Developing the Border: The State and the Political Economy of Development in Arunachal Pradesh.' In *Borderland Lives in Northern South Asia*, edited by David N. Gellner, 141–62. Durham: Duke University Press. doi.org/10.1215/9780822377306-007.

Mishra, Deepak K. 2019. 'Himalayan "Hydro-Criminality"? Dams, Development and Politics in Arunachal Pradesh, India.' In *The Wild East: Criminal Political Economies in South Asia*, edited by Barbara Harriss-White and Lucia Michelutti, 115–39. London: UCL Press. doi.org/10.2307/j.ctvfrxr41.12.

Mishra, Deepak K., and Vandana Upadhyay. 2012. 'The Difficult Transition: Economic Development and Gender Relations in Arunachal Pradesh.' *Indian Journal of Gender Studies* 19, no. 1: 93–126. doi.org/10.1177/09715215110 1900105.

Misra, Sanghamitra. 2013. *Becoming a Borderland: The Politics of Space and Identity in Colonial Northeastern India*. New Delhi: Routledge. doi.org/10.4324/9780203085301.

Mohanty, Bidyut. 1995. 'Panchayati Raj, 73rd Constitutional Amendment and Women.' *Economic and Political Weekly* 30, no. 52: 3346–50.

Mohanty, Bidyut, and Sibabrata Das. 2022. 'Regional Disparity and Women in Local Government: Implications for Sustainable Development.' In *Women Reinventing Development*, edited by Asha Hans, Amrita Patel, Bidyut Mohanty, and Swarnamayee Tripathy, 207–33. New Delhi: Routledge.

Nassbaum, Martha, Amrita Basu, Yasmin Tambiah, and Nirja Gopal-Jayal. 2003. *Essays on Gender and Governance*. New Delhi: HDRC, UNDP India.

Planning Commission. 2009. *State Development Report of Arunachal Pradesh*. New Delhi: Academic Publishers.

Raju, Saraswati. 2005. 'Gender and Empowerment: Creating "Thus Far and No Further" Supportive Structures. A Case from India.' In *A Companion to Feminist Geography*, edited by Lise Nelson and Joni Seager, 194–207. Oxford: Blackwell. doi.org/10.1002/9780470996898.ch14.

Reid, Herbert G., and Betsy Taylor. 2009. *Democracy's Portals: Ecology, Justice and Democratic Space*. Champaign: University of Illinois Press.

Roy, Nirod C. 2020. *Impact of Central Funds on the Economic Development of Arunachal Pradesh*. Working Paper No. CDS/05/2020. Itanagar: Centre for Development Studies, Rajiv Gandhi University.

Singh, Abhishek, Praveen Chokhandre, Ajeet Kumar Singh, Kathryn M. Barker, Kaushalendra Kumar, Lotus McDougal, K.S. James, and Anita Raj. 2021. 'Development of the India Patriarchy Index: Validation and Testing of Temporal and Spatial Patterning.' *Social Indicators Research* 159: 1–27. doi.org/10.1007/s11205-021-02752-1.

Taylor, Betsy. 2009. 'Grounds for Democratic Hope in Arunachal Pradesh: Emerging Civic Geographies and the Reinvention of Gender and Tribal Identities.' In *Beyond Counter-Insurgency: Breaking the Impasse in Northeast India*, edited by Sanjib Baruah, 308–28. Delhi: Oxford University Press.

Vyasulu, Poornima, and Vinod Vyasulu. 1999. 'Women in Panchayati Raj: Grass Roots Democracy in Malgudi.' *Economic and Political Weekly* 34, no. 52: 3677–86.

Part IV: Disruption, Solidarity and Resistance

Introduction

Ramona Vijeyarasa

Can a diversity of women find a way to come together in collective resistance to state oppression? When is a challenge sufficiently provocative to count as 'disruption'? Moreover, in a context in which 'solidarity' is perhaps now a timeworn term but 'disruption' is a little too *in vogue*, how can we revisit and reconceptualise the role of women and their collectives in rising against the state?

The three chapters in this section present to readers the various struggles of women's movements—from Japan, Hong Kong and Indonesia—in promoting feminist agendas and confronting patriarchal norms that continue to marginalise, exclude and oppress. The chapters have a common starting point: acknowledging the existence of a diversity and plurality of women's groups participating in the struggles for change in Asia, whether they comprise missionaries or elites, marginalised or grassroots organisations or state-affiliated women's groups. The task at hand is to find common ground in the pursuit of women's rights and wellbeing.

Ruby Y.S. Lai takes us on a journey to Hong Kong. Set in the context of the political reintegration of Hong Kong into China, in Lai's Chapter 12, we begin to understand the role of non–state-affiliated feminist activism in negotiating space with pro-China women's rights groups. As Lai— a feminist scholar, journalist and sociologist—explains, many of these non–state-affiliated groups were forced to reposition themselves and develop new strategies in the face of political change. Hong Kong's feminist activists offer the region lessons on how to allow a more conventional women's rights agenda to persist alongside the pursuit of much more progressive discourses related to sexual rights and marginalised minority groups. The author lays on the table strategies that range from diversifying the agenda through to careful choices about when to ally with state agents and political parties.

In Chapter 13, Rachael Diprose, Bronwyn Anne Beech Jones and Ken M.P. Setiawan take us to village governance in Indonesia's Gresik District as they urge us to move our focus away from more traditional forms of collective action such as electoral politics to more localised forms. Here, we see how solidarity in the form of grassroots women's community organisations, known as Women's Schools, can be a powerful way for individual women and their groups to obstruct and resist, particularly in the face of deeply entrenched cultural norms concerning women's place in society at the village level. The Women's Schools offer women who might otherwise be excluded from activism a platform for growing their power at this level.

Serena Eleonora Ford in Chapter 14 takes us to Japan, where the euphemistically named Technical Intern Training Program has seen the harrowing exploitation of migrant workers, largely but not only from Vietnam. Ford's lens is one of 'depletion through social reproduction', helping readers to understand the ways in which these workers' existence is drained through both inadequate help and wellbeing alongside little regard for the socially reproductive roles of these predominantly female workers, both in Japan and at home. While a more vocal opposition to the work program has existed for more than 30 years, Ford's chapter turns to a softer coalition of activists based in Japan and in sending communities in their home country. Their contribution is to replenish and care and not necessarily demand an overhaul of the program itself. In notable parallels to Lai's analysis of Hong Kong, again, we see division—between those who challenge and those who supplement—as Ford seeks to frame and understand how both can sit in solidarity and even amplify the cause.

Together, these three chapters offer rich lessons from the experiences of very diverse women's groups who have built solidarity from the opposition camp. Having spent a decade working as an activist alongside women from across the globe, I was taken back in time by these authors as I remembered the weight borne by groups of women, not wanting their own internal struggles for coherence, energy and voice to undermine the ability of a broader agenda to push through. Hierarchies within movements are inevitable, while goals must be negotiated and agreed upon. We are left wanting to praise these collectives for what they have achieved in the face of such oppression and resistance but also acknowledge the realities of diversity within.

Yet, we may also want to ask how much these women's groups have managed to succeed because their agendas—although in some contexts controversial—are by and large politically palatable and socially acceptable, as the groups themselves have constrained their own demands for change. Ultimately, readers may perceive these quieter, more localised and negotiated forms of opposition as amounting to disruption; perhaps it is the notion of 'disruption' that needs a rethink.

12

Towards a Self-Limiting Movement? Feminist advocacy in times of political uncertainty

Ruby Y.S. Lai

The women's movement in Hong Kong—an affluent financial centre in Asia and a former colony of Britain, which returned to China's control in 1997—has a long history. In the past century, the territory has witnessed substantive progress in women's rights across political, economic and sociocultural domains. For example, gender mainstreaming—a form of political and policy practice that aims to advance gender equality by reforming all mainstream policy areas (Walby 2005: 453–54; for a critique of gender mainstreaming, see Caglar 2013)—was institutionalised within the government's bureaucratic structure as a priority and was considered a cross-sector consensus that was affirmed by the government, commercial sector, civil society and the general public (Cheung and Holroyd 2009). As antidiscrimination legislation[1] and institutions have been put in place to combat gender discrimination in various arenas, women's access to higher education has continued to surpass men's in recent years (Census and Statistics Department 2022); and the gender attitudes held by the young and the educated have become more liberal overall (EOC 2009).

---

1 This legislation refers to the Sex Discrimination Ordinance and the Family Status Discrimination Ordinance. The statutory body, the Equal Opportunities Commission (EOC), was founded in 1996 to enforce the antidiscrimination ordinances.

This progress in gender equality is also reflected in various global indexes. In 2021, Hong Kong ranked fourth in the Human Development Index and scored a 0.976 in the Gender Development Index, which was higher than the score of developed countries such as Australia, the Netherlands and Japan (UNDP 2022).

Nevertheless, the goal of gender equality is far from fulfilled. In 2020, women in Hong Kong, excluding foreign domestic workers, still had a lower labour force participation rate (49.6 per cent) than men (66.2 per cent); in 2021, women were earning 15 per cent less than men, and only 14.2 per cent of all listed companies' directors in Hong Kong were women. In the political arena, women made up only 30.3 per cent (1,843) of the 6,088 non-official members serving on public sector advisory and statutory bodies in 2020, and the number of male directorate officers was higher than the number of women; last, sexual violence and harassment are still common threats predominantly faced by women (ACSVAW 2022; EOC 2021). In recent years, new challenges have emerged and hampered feminist advocacy, particularly in the non–state-affiliated feminist movement. These challenges, including the emergence of right-leaning nativism, the expansion of authoritarian governance and aggravating socioeconomic inequalities, have threatened not only the work but also the survival of progressive feminist activism in the city.

There is hardly a well-defined classification of women's and feminist movements in Hong Kong. In the early days of colonial history, participants of women's movements ranged from missionaries, expatriates, foreign politicians and Chinese elites to local Chinese women who formed concerned groups or organisations with religious or political affiliations (Hoe 1991; Wong 2000). In the postwar era, local women founded groups that sought to advance women's rights and wellbeing through social and institutional reforms. Since the 1950s, Hong Kong has witnessed the development of women's and feminist movements varying across the political spectrum. At one end, there is the pro-China or state government–affiliated faction; at the other end is the prodemocracy or progressive feminist faction, and there are also politically neutral concerned groups that promote gender equality and women's empowerment (Lee 2000; Lim 2015; Wong 2000). This chapter focuses primarily on the non–state-affiliated progressive feminist movement.

I have been a keen observer of feminist movements in Hong Kong as a journalist and a sociologist, who has researched and written widely about gender issues in the past decade. Historically, academia and the media have been important sites for feminist scholars and journalists to proactively advocate feminist agendas and confront patriarchal culture by various means, such as action research, policy studies, investigative reporting and collaboration with concerned groups (Chan 2002; Chan and Wong 2004; Cheung 1989; Kong 2018; Kong et al. 2015; Lai et al. 1997; Luqiu 2022). Following this tradition, I see myself at the intersection of academia, journalism and the feminist movement. This standpoint enables my access to in-depth knowledge of the developmental trajectories of feminist activism and allows me to retain a relatively independent position to reflect on the movement's internal dissonances and constraints. My past research on Hong Kong and Chinese society also equips me with the necessary knowledge to analyse the emergent challenges faced by feminists from within the opposition camp and the political regimes corresponding to the sociopolitical and economic transfigurations of the territory since the 2010s (Choi and Lai 2021; Choi et al. 2020; Lai 2021, 2023). Rather than providing a systematic historical account of the full spectrum of feminist or women's movements in Hong Kong, my objective is specific: to highlight and elucidate the most pressing challenges faced by progressive feminist activism in post-handover Hong Kong.

Sharing a drastically different fate from the pro-China faction within the women's movement (see Fischler 2003; Lee 2000; Lim 2010), non–state-affiliated feminist activism has established itself as one of the indispensable parts of civil society since the colonial era (Chiu and Lui 2000). For years, the movement has played a pivotal role in fostering the democratisation of the city (Choi and Cheung 2012; Lee 2000; Lim 2010, 2015). Despite tensions, it has been a close ally of the pan-democracy camp,[2] which strives for universal suffrage and social reforms through negotiation and other peaceful means and has dominated the city's political opposition and civil society since the 1980s (Cho et al. 2020; Ma 2007). After the handover, the territory witnessed the development of new political pursuits and activism. First, in the 2000s, was the emergence of the progressive left, which advocated for social justice and the preservation of grassroots communities and local heritage, posing direct challenges to the city's neoliberal governance

---

2   The pan-democracy camp, also known as the prodemocracy camp, was constituted by the liberal and left-leaning political parties and groups, such as the Democratic Party, Civic Party, League of Social Democrats and Labour Party.

through contentious actions (Chen and Szeto 2015). In the 2010s, the sociopolitical tensions created by rapid regional integration between China and Hong Kong, as well as the Chinese Government's increased political interventions, provided the circumstances for the rise of the right-leaning nativist[3] movement. Claiming itself to be rooted in the interests of local Hong Kong citizens, the movement demanded the expulsion of mainland Chinese immigrants and demarcation between China and Hong Kong through militant tactics (Choi et al. 2020; Veg 2017; Lam and Cooper 2018). The discord in ideologies and movement tactics led to unresolvable hostility and divided the opposition camp: the liberal and progressive left was heavily criticised by the nativists as a failure, while the moderates also condemned the xenophobic agenda and violent actions of the nativists (Lee 2020). Due to its ideological proximity to and historical alliance with the liberal progressive left, the feminist movement in Hong Kong inevitably faced intensified confrontations and criticisms from the nativists (Choi et al. 2020; Ho and Li 2021). In the aftermath of the 2019 anti–Extradition Bill protests, progressive feminists faced unprecedented challenges under democratic backsliding—a process in which the state eliminated all kinds of political institutions that sustain a democracy (Bermeo 2016; Lee and Chan 2022). Against this backdrop, this chapter intends to unravel the challenges, contributing insights into the strategies and repositioning of feminist activism in the context of social movement abeyance and political reconfiguration.

This chapter begins with a summary of the background of the women's and feminist movements in Hong Kong. It then delineates the sector's development and identifies the structural challenges that threaten the sustainability of the non–state-affiliated progressive feminist movement. After that, the chapter critically examines the idea of a self-limiting movement as an epistemological and political strategy and discusses its applications in the context of Hong Kong feminist advocacy. It concludes by drawing inspiration from the strategies of resistance used by activists from different localities in response to local and global challenges to gender equality.

---

3   The nativists are often called localists, while both are referred to as *bún tóu pāai* in Cantonese. The two terms are used interchangeably. For a more nuanced classification, see Lam (2018).

A concise history of feminist advocacy in Hong Kong

Because Hong Kong was a colony of Britain for more than 100 years, the colonial legacy was ingrained in virtually every aspect of society. The history of colonisation also structured the formation and development of the city's women's movement. In the early days of colonisation, the British controlled almost all forms of political power, while the Chinese, except for the elites, were positioned as inferior (Carroll 2007). Chinese women, especially at the grassroots, were invisible in the eyes of the colonial government. This negligence was reflected in the coloniser's condoning of the trading of maids (*mui tsai* in Cantonese) even after the enforcement of the *Slavery Abolition Act* in 1833, which abolished slavery in most British colonies (see Sinn 1994). A Western-inspired women's movement slowly emerged in the late nineteenth century. In the earliest stage of the colony's women's movement, local British feminists and women's groups in the United Kingdom played a vital role in campaigning for social reforms, such as the abolition of child labour, licensed prostitution and the *mui tsai* system (Hoe 1991; Wong 2000). Between the 1920s and 1930s, Chinese women began to mobilise themselves and organise women's groups, some of them affiliated with the Chinese Communist Party and the Nationalist Party of the Republic of China, which focused on social reforms and promoted nationalistic agendas (see Wong 2000).

Between the 1950s and 1980s, Hong Kong society rapidly industrialised and transformed into a business and financial centre for Asia. This economic take-off set the stage for the development of the burgeoning women's movement. Challenging the patriarchal economic and sociocultural structures, the movement put forward diverse agendas to advance the interests of women in various domains, including marriage reform,[4] equal pay for equal work, legalisation of abortion,[5] maternity policy, a 'war on rape' and sexual violence, and land inheritance rights for women[6] (Cheung and Holroyd 2009; Lee 2000). Apart from the diversification of agendas, these were the founding concerns of various prominent pressure groups

---

4　The campaign, which was active between the 1940s and the 1970s, sought to abolish concubinage and legalise monogamous marriage. In 1971, monogamous marriage was finally recognised as the only legal marriage form.

5　Abortion was legalised in Hong Kong in 1981.

6　This campaign was mostly concerned with women's equal rights to inherit land in the New Territories, which were regarded as the rural part of Hong Kong.

and NGOs, such as the Hong Kong Council of Women (HKCW),[7] the Association for the Advancement of Feminism,[8] the Hong Kong Women Christian Council[9] and the Hong Kong Women Workers' Association.[10] Choi (2012) describes a process of localisation of the women's movement in terms of agenda setting and the composition of participants. Many of the campaigns focused on the rights of local women—in particular, the working class and the grassroots—and sought to counteract the patriarchal structure that systematically marginalised women. Likewise, most of the members of the newly founded NGOs and pressure groups were local Chinese women, many of whom were educated workers, university students, social workers or community organisers determined to promote social justice and gender equality.

As Lee (2000) observed, this period also reflected a discursive shift from the advancement of women's interests and protection, such as the equal pay agenda or the 'war on rape' campaign, to advocacy of gender equality and women's rights in all arenas. This shift validated the collective identity and subjectivity of women and affirmed their status as independent citizens in society, rather than dependants or victims of crime who needed protection (Lee 2000). Nevertheless, subtle ideological dissonances were ingrained within the movement, particularly between the elites and the grassroots. For example, the HKCW, which comprised female elites, was hesitant to identify with feminist standpoints on various issues, such as the 'war on rape' in the 1980s, which reinforced women's victim identity, as it demanded more community services but refused to directly confront conservative patriarchal ideologies (Cho et al. 2020; Lim 2015). Meanwhile, political factors started to become a source of division within the women's movement. The founding of the Hong Kong Federation of Women in 1981 signified the beginning of the divide between the pro–Communist China women's organisations and the independent feminist NGOs and pressure groups. In contrast to the prodemocracy stance of the independent feminist groups, the pro-China women's groups concentrated on service delivery and opposed demands for greater political rights (Fischler 2003; Lee 2000; Lim 2015). This political divide thus created long-lasting tensions and competition among different factions within the women's movement.

---

7   Founded in 1947.
8   Founded in 1984.
9   Founded in 1987.
10 Founded in 1989.

The local feminist movement gradually expanded from the 1990s and took a 'sexual and cultural turn' (Choi 2012), which some scholars have described as a 'paradigm shift' (Wong and Choi 2015). This shift signified an evolution from the reformative approach that problematised the class and patriarchal structures of society to a radical approach that affirmed women's sexual autonomy and recognised diverse gender identities. For instance, three prominent NGOs—Action for Reach Out (AFRO),[11] Ziteng[12] and Midnight Blue[13]—were founded in the early 1990s and the 2000s to fight for sex workers' rights. Their agendas, such as the legalisation of sex work, often raised controversy within the movement. Nevertheless, the liberal discourses around sexual issues popularised by their campaigns laid the foundation for demands for greater sexual rights and autonomy and created discursive opportunities that defied conservatism in the public sphere. Meanwhile, the LGBTQI+ movement began to take the stage. NGOs and pressure groups including Queer Sisters,[14] Rainbow of Hong Kong[15] and Women Coalition of HKSAR (Hong Kong Special Administrative Region)[16] put forward agendas for antidiscrimination legislation, the legalisation of same-sex marriage and protection of the human rights of sexual minorities, who had long suffered stigmatisation and invisibility in the territory. These new campaigns challenged the heterosexism inherent in Hong Kong society and prompted many feminist groups to reflect on their gender beliefs, thus broadening feminist ideologies and formulating a more inclusive agenda (Cho et al. 2020; Choi 2012).

In the meantime, there was also continuation and progression of the conventional feminist movement. This included the demand for equal opportunities for women, especially in tackling problems of the glass ceiling and precarious employment; the persistent concerns about equal pay and minimum wage protection; the setting up of women-led cooperatives to achieve economic autonomy; the promotion of a universal retirement protection scheme; and successive campaigns against sexual violence, such as the founding of the Association Concerning Sexual Violence Against Women (ACSVAW) in 1997, which concentrated on combating sexual violence, paving the way for the #MeToo movement in 2017 (Lai 2021).

11　Founded in 1993.
12　Founded in 1996.
13　Founded in 2006, it focuses on the rights of male sex workers.
14　Founded in 1995, it is mostly concerned with the rights of queer women in Hong Kong.
15　Founded in 1998, it is a non-profit gay community group that advocates for the rights of sexual minorities in Hong Kong.
16　Founded in 2003, the coalition works for the advancement of gay women's rights in the territory.

In addition, feminists opened new political and sociocultural spaces for the exploration of intersectional agendas. For example, the application of eco-feminist principles to organising women in grassroots communities has empowered women by realising environmental justice, economic autonomy and gender equality at the community level. Feminists also turned their attention to ethnic-minority women, such as South Asian migrants and foreign domestic helpers, widening their scope of concern. More importantly, to try to build a coalition among various feminist groups and consolidate solidarity, the Hong Kong Women's Coalition on Equal Opportunities (WCOEO) was founded in 1996 as a joint task force to connect women's groups and monitor the government's efforts in advancing gender equality.

In sum, three features can be observed from the development of the progressive feminist movement in Hong Kong. First, the movement is a decentralised effort with diverse agendas, organisations and tactics (Lim 2010). The coalition and connections between feminist organisations appear to be loose and issue-based, which allows flexibility for NGOs and pressure groups to focus on their own work. Yet, the lack of coordination also results in ideological or strategic discord and potential competition among groups with similar agendas. Second, the feminist movement maintains a position relatively independent from the state and political parties (Cho et al. 2020). As pointed out by feminist scholars, there has been an enduring tension between feminists and other social movement activists since the colonial era (Lee 2000; Lim 2015). Some prodemocracy supporters have even questioned the significance of the women's movement in the struggle for democratisation (Cho et al. 2020). Nevertheless, feminists are aware of the need to ally with other activists and politicians in achieving their goals—as reflected in the strategy of 'collaborating with a distance'—to lobby potential allies in civil society and the media to build ad hoc alliances and aggregating political influences that empower them to negotiate with the government (Wong 2000; Wong and Choi 2015). One example is the model of collaboration between the government, civil society and the media in the movement against sexual violence (Lai 2021). Last, as a colonial inheritance, the feminist movement in Hong Kong has sustained various forms of international affiliation, such as participating in transnational organisations. For example, one of the missions of the WCOEO is to prepare shadow reports and attend meetings organised by the United Nations to inquire into the application of the *Convention on the Elimination of All Forms of Discrimination against Women*, which was extended to Hong Kong in 1996 (see Kapai 2013). This three-pronged framework demonstrates the historical specificities of Hong Kong's feminist movement, but it also resonates with the women's movement in other Asian societies, particularly those with a colonial legacy (Roces and Edwards 2010).

Internal divisions and external challenges in the post-handover feminist movement

Since the 1990s, the gender equality agenda has been deemed socially acceptable and a 'politically correct' project that can not only improve women's wellbeing but also foster the modernisation of Hong Kong society. Even though some feminist perspectives, in particular those related to sexual rights and autonomy, may be controversial, these views can still be tolerated and even accepted by the public—a credit to the years of campaigning and awareness-building by the coalition of NGOs, scholars and the liberal media (Ho and Tsang 2012). Nevertheless, since the 2010s, the non–state-affiliated feminist movement has faced a new wave of challenges and risks. Whereas some of these originated from the internal shortcomings of the movement, others emerged within civil society and the political system along with the rapidly changing sociopolitical environment and were reinforced by the revival of a patriarchal ideology inherited from China's Confucian heritage and popularised by the global rise of the far right (Choi et al. 2020).

Awareness hierarchy within the feminist movement

Although decades of the women's movement have achieved substantive advancement of women's political, economic and social status, the benefits of gender equality are stratified. Those who have benefited the most are local, relatively young, educated, middle to upper-class women, while new immigrants, racial and ethnic minorities, older and less-educated working-class women may not receive the same privileges. As Lee (2000) pointed out, the women's movement in the pre-handover era was divided along class lines and class has continued to demarcate boundaries within the movement, which often are reflected in the activists' differing orientations and interests.

As described in the previous section, some feminist scholars observed a 'paradigm shift' in activism after the 1990s, in which considerable attention was gradually diverted from interest-based issues founded on macro-structural critiques of gender and class oppression to identity and sexual politics that promoted gender fluidity and sexual liberation (Choi 2012; Wong and Choi 2015). This emergent agenda expanded a new arena of feminist advocacy and generated transformative initiatives in the city. For example, the establishment of Zi Teng and AFRO not only advanced the rights of sex workers but also opened discursive space for the cultivation of more liberal sexual attitudes and the affirmation of sexual autonomy, particularly for women (Choi and Lai 2021). With the shift of attention, the 1990s also saw feminists' growing awareness of and sympathy for the LGBTQI+ community and, later, the two movements formed a strong coalition in their advocacy for issues such as antidiscrimination legislation and same-sex marriage, challenging heteronormativity and multifaceted heterosexism (King 2001; Kong et al. 2015).

Although the emphasis on sexual autonomy has recognised the subjectivities of women and sexual minorities and opened new forms of resistance, it has also drawn attention away from more 'conventional' concerns, many of which are associated with class and economic inequalities, such as the feminisation of poverty, the gender wage gap, women's underemployment and the gendered division of labour in the domestic arena. The sidelining of structural critiques of gender and class inequalities within the movement and in public discussion has led to an uneven hierarchy of focus. Advocacy for gender fluidity and sexual autonomy led by educated, middle-class feminists, who happen to possess greater discursive power and capital, was criticised by some feminists as being out of touch given the everyday oppression suffered by grassroots and working-class women (Cho et al. 2020; Choi 2012; Wong and Choi 2015). This shortcoming led to the limited support and resources invested in the consolidation and expansion of the efforts to organise grassroots women and reinforced the class division within the progressive feminist movement. Worse still, the lack of persistent criticism of the macro-structural oppression of women in the public discursive arena allows the circulation of a false assumption that gender equality has been satisfactorily achieved in Hong Kong. This misrepresentation thus incubates and legitimates the anti-feminist discourses that have undermined and denigrated feminism since the rise of right-leaning nativism in the territory in the 2010s (Choi et al. 2020).

Rise of anti-feminist sentiment

The 2010s saw the emergence of anti-feminist sentiment, particularly from right-leaning nativists as well as the wider public. To understand the rise of this trend of misogyny, one must examine it with respect to the developmental trajectory of the democratic movement in Hong Kong during the previous two decades. Since the July 1 Rally in 2003,[17] there have been successive mass demonstrations and issue-based participatory actions[18] that signified the growth of political participation across social positions and an increased awareness of social justice, democracy and local identity and heritage (Chen and Szeto 2015; Ku 2016; Ma and Cheng 2019; Veg 2017). It was believed that underscoring the emergence of this activism were the exacerbation of socioeconomic inequality, the government's inability to mitigate its repercussions (Cheng 2014) and the rapid integration with China that adversely affected Hongkongers' everyday lives and the city's political autonomy (Lee 2020; Ma and Cheng 2019). Despite successive attempts by civil society, progress in democratic and social reform stagnated. This gradually led to the division of the moderate and the radical factions within the movement. Whereas the moderate liberals and progressive left uphold democratic principles and electoral politics, the nativists—or localists—advocate prioritising the interests of Hong Kong citizens and promote an anti-China agenda through militant tactics (Lee 2020; Choi et al. 2020; Veg 2017). The moderates' conventional activism was heavily criticised and rejected by the nativists, who used the derogatory term 'leftard' to mock the progressive left and liberals for their stubborn embrace of inclusion and universal values regardless of the harsh political reality (Lee 2020).

---

17   The July 1 Rally was the first mass demonstration after 1997. It was triggered by citizens' discontent with the government's mishandling of the economic crisis and the outbreak of severe acute respiratory syndrome (SARS) and opposition to the passing of Article 23 of the Basic Law, which stipulates that the Hong Kong Government 'shall enact laws on its own to prohibit any act of treason, secession, sedition, subversion against the Central People's Government, or theft of state secrets, to prohibit foreign political organizations or bodies from conducting political activities in the Region, and to prohibit political organizations or bodies of the Region from establishing ties with foreign political organizations or bodies'. The proposed legislation sparked intense controversy as human rights groups and prodemocracy political parties considered the article a threat to the city's civil and human rights (Ma 2005).

18   Examples include protests against the demolition of the Star Ferry Pier and the Queen's Pier in 2006 and 2007 (Ku 2016); the campaign against high-speed rail transport in 2008–09; the 2012 Anti–National Education Movement; and the 2014 Umbrella Movement (Ma and Cheng 2019).

The nativists' resentment of the left also spilled over to feminists. The non–state-affiliated feminist movement has been close to the liberal and left-leaning activists since the early stages of the social movement development in the 1970s (Lee 2000; Chiu and Lui 2000). Despite conflict and scepticism, feminists have often joined forces with or lobbied support from the prodemocracy political parties and other pressure groups to advocate for their agendas and issues. Ideologically, both feminists and left-leaning liberals have adhered to the principles of equality and justice, which brought them closer in political orientation. This proximity to the moderates in terms of ideology and tactics led the nativists to view feminist activism as part of the progressive left, which should be condemned and dismissed. In addition, the unresolvable ideological divide between the nativists and the feminists, particularly on the issue of female immigrants from mainland China, fuelled the nativists' hostility towards feminists. The xenophobic discourse upheld by the nativists, which regarded female immigrants as spies or 'vaginas' sent by the Chinese party-state to recolonise Hong Kong (Choi and Lai 2022; Choi et al. 2020), contrasted with the feminist standpoint supporting the rights of vulnerable women.

The hostility of the nativists gave rise to two distinctive yet related forms of threat to feminism in Hong Kong. The first is the widespread tactic of claiming the irrelevance of gender (Choi et al. 2020), which is used to legitimise gender bias and misogynist nativist ideologies. In a study of male and female nativists' narratives and their perceptions of gender equality, my co-authors Choi and Pang and I found that gender irrelevance is accomplished through

> the misrepresentation of structural gender inequalities; the individualisation, naturalisation, and universalisation of gender inequalities and biases; the claim of sexual symmetry in gender biases; the development of the twin discourses of feminine privilege and male disadvantage; the compartmentalisation of gender biases; and the belief that gender equality is of secondary importance. (Choi et al. 2020: 492)

This proved to be an effective tactic to justify overt gender discrimination and sexist rhetoric because some of the female interviewees, despite having some degree of feminist awareness, still put up with the blatant misogyny within the nativist movement for the sake of their political pursuits.

The second threat is soft repression inflicted by nativist supporters on feminists, particularly on social media. Feminist sociologist Myra Ferree (2004) initially developed the concept of 'soft repression' to depict the 'mobilisation of nonviolent means to silence or eradicate oppositional ideas' by the regime in situations in which the state has not eradicated all the civil society institutions. This form of repression operates on three levels—ridicule, stigma and silencing—which interact with one another, often in highly informal ways, to dismiss and suppress ideas and identities that support 'cognitive liberation' or 'oppositional consciousness' in the public arena (Ferree 2004). Here, I apply this concept to delineate the nativist strategy of repressing feminist ideas and subjectivities in the public sphere. The fierce criticism and gender trolling by nativist supporters have been rampant on social media since the popularisation of the nativist movement. Feminists were called 'feminist dicks' (*neui kyun nan* in Cantonese) and were frequently stigmatised as hypocrites who manipulated the ideals of gender equality to advance their own interests and gain moral capital. These soft repressions, initially practised by nativists, spread into the public arena through social media and eventually appeared in day-to-day political and non-political conversations. In addition, anti-feminist commentators and key opinion leaders often prompted the silence of feminists by asking, 'Where are the feminist dicks?' Through questioning the views and actions of feminists on issues directly or vaguely related to their agenda, these anti-feminist commentators sought to expose the alleged self-centredness and moral flaws of feminists. In contrast to gender irrelevance tactics, these types of soft repression are actively, often aggressively, inflicted with the intent of demoralising, coercing, suppressing and marginalising feminist standpoints and identities. This can not only silence pro-feminist opinions in public discussion, but also dissuade people from aligning with feminism. The soft repression of feminists reached a peak during the #MeToo movement, when a huge backlash occurred against women and feminists who spoke up against sexual violence, becoming another ideological and emotional discord between the two blocks (Cho et al. 2020; Lai 2021).

The seemingly unbridgeable divide between the nativists and the feminists was temporarily narrowed during the 2019 Anti–Extradition Bill Movement. The #ProtestToo campaign, which was led by various feminist groups to demonstrate against political sexual violence inflicted by the Hong Kong Police, brought the age-long enemies together on the same line. It was seen as the 'grand reconciliation' between the right and feminists, and some even hoped for coalition-building between the two rivals, but others were sceptical of the genuineness of the nativists' support of the feminist agenda (Ho 2022; Lai 2021; Pang 2020). The hope for reconciliation has not yet been fulfilled and a revival of anti-feminist sentiment briefly appeared in the aftermath of the 2019 protests in the perpetuation of gender irrelevance tactics and soft repression in public and online discussions.

Diminishing of political space under democratic backsliding

It is believed that the political space in Hong Kong is quickly diminishing since the 2019 protests. Shortly after the movement, the National People's Congress Standing Committee unanimously approved the National Security Law (NSL), on 30 June 2020, which took effect on the same day. Although scholars are still investigating the impact of the strengthening of China's national security and the implementation of the NSL on Hong Kong's rule of law and its status as a liberal enclave (Chan and de Londras 2020; Fu and Hor 2022), in reality, civil society has been profoundly reshaped by the new law. For example, the prosecution of prominent opposition leaders and activists, the dismantling of NGOs and pressure groups, the arrest of journalists and the forced closure of prodemocracy and citizen media outlets—all reflected the sweeping impact of the NSL (Lee and Chan 2022; Lo 2021). In addition, the 2021 electoral reform eliminated the opposition's influence in formal political institutions and consolidated the control of the party-state, the city-state and the pro-establishment camp (Davis 2022). Moreover, demonstrations and protests were heavily curbed by Covid-19 prevention policies, and the repression of contentious politics continues even after the relaxation of the pandemic restrictions.

Facing such a sharp decline in democratic institutions, the conventional tactics used by feminists, such as coalition-building and demonstrations, may no longer be effective or feasible. First, a considerable number of civil society leaders, activists, organisers and scholars, including feminists, have been arrested or have emigrated overseas, diminishing the numbers of many NGOs and pressure groups. In addition, coalition-building has become difficult because of the elimination of the opposition inside and outside the political system. The closure of liberal and independent media outlets led to the shrinking of space for public deliberation. The disappearance of former allies in different domains heavily undermined the strength and impact of feminist advocacy, hampering attempts to promote a progressive agenda.

More importantly, the NSL created enormous uncertainty and political pressure on non–state-affiliated NGOs and pressure groups, including feminist groups, as they constantly struggle with risk calculation during their everyday operations and practise self-censorship to avoid violating the comprehensive yet vaguely defined law. For example, the NSL prohibits any acts of secession, subversion, terrorist activities or collusion with a foreign country or external elements to endanger national security. What is the exact definition of 'collusion with a foreign country'? Would using grants from international foundations—which is an established practice and an important source of funding for many NGOs in Hong Kong—be classified as 'collusion with a foreign country'? Activist groups know that red lines have been drawn, but many have no idea where exactly the lines are and what actions might be interpreted as crossing those lines, which are constantly being redrawn. This ambiguity and uncertainty generate fear that has crippled the advocacy work of not only feminist activists but also the remaining civic pressure groups.

Is self-limitation an answer? Feminist activism under political uncertainty

In the face of the repressive political reality, some activists and citizens have lamented the complete dismantling of civil society, while others imagine a future with a self-limiting movement by returning to the pressure group politics of the 1960s (see Chiu and Lui 2000). The notion of *self-limitation* originated from the Polish Solidarity Movement during the 1980s (Staniszkis 1984). It refers to a nonconfrontational method of approaching the authorities to achieve a 'revolution without blood, barricades, and violence through regaining the dignity of the people and the initiation of radical social change through a self-conscious coalition between the working class and intellectuals' (Grabowska 2012: 393). In practice, this approach was sustained by two political strategies. The first was the revitalisation of civil society through a strengthening of political consciousness across social classes, and the second involved the 'new evolutionism' (Arato 2000: 48) that prioritised reform and compromise with the ruling class (Grabowska 2012). Although it was deemed a pragmatic tactic to contain political risk under authoritarian rule and retain the strength of civic groups, Polish sociologist Staniszkis (1984) also described the self-limiting revolution as a period of 'painful, zigzag development' for the opposition, wherein the radical wave of protest and class war was crammed into a 'trade union formula' in which status-oriented policy always overwhelmed interest-oriented policy. Worse still, self-limitation perpetuates a culture of silence among activists, who may strategically or through fear avoid visibility because of political coercion (Staniszkis 1984).

What are the insights from the self-limiting movement for the feminist movement in Hong Kong under the recent democratic decline? Although self-limitation is certainly a way for feminist groups to play safe, how much should they limit themselves, and in what domains? Should self-limitation be deployed to moderate state–pressure group relations, to strategise movement tactics or to reposition and reframe their agendas? Would a self-limiting strategy undermine the core feminist principles and deviate the movement from its original promise and progressive essence?

As Grabowska (2012) noted, self-limitation is done not merely to compromise with state power but also to establish a self-conscious coalition across social classes. While Grabowska's proposition emphasises class identity and the transgression of class boundaries to cultivate collective resilience, scholars of intersectionality go beyond the class structure and problematise multi-structural inequalities (Collins 1990; Crenshaw 1989) and call for an intersectional collective resistance that synergises activism among diverse social groups. Capitalising on the theory of intersectionality, I propose a strategy of *intersectional specialisation* to complement the tactics of self-limitation. This strategy encourages feminist groups to adopt the intersectional framework to transform their existing agendas of concern and increase the degree of specialisation in their areas of interest.

Despite the shrinkage of a considerable part of civil society and the rejection of prodemocracy demands after successive political reforms since 2020, feminist agendas—including anti–sexual violence, equal rights and opportunities and sexual and reproductive health care—have been institutionalised and remain politically acceptable and legitimate in the city-state, which has retained valuable spaces for activists to manoeuvre in an increasingly repressive environment. The *intersectional specialisation* approach has two objectives. First, by intersectionalising existing agendas, it helps incubate new perspectives to reframe conventional agendas, diversify sources of support and secure potential allies in other sectors. By adhering to the past tactic of building situated coalitions, feminists could maintain a certain degree of independence in the political realm and at the same time share information, develop complementary strategies and muster resources inside and outside activists' circles. One example is to promote cultural sensitivity and address the experiences of ethnic and racial minorities in the movement against sexual violence. Second, increasing the specialisation of feminist campaigns—which could be achieved by professionalising research and service provision, consolidating organisational efforts in communities and member networks and maintaining persistent and opportune public engagements—could help develop the niche status and improve the bargaining power of feminist pressure groups in the public sphere, especially in policymaking and public education.

Nevertheless, these combined strategies may not resolve all concerns and could even lead to repercussions for the feminist movement. The first unresolvable challenge is the state–activist relationship. Feminist groups have been working with the government for years to advance policies and service provisions in many domains, such as anti–sexual violence legislation and legal reforms,[19] labour policies and the safety and protection of sex workers. Although there are practical needs for the continuation of these collaborations, how would these interactions between the government and pressure groups change after a political transition? Would non–state-affiliated feminist NGOs and pressure groups be completely replaced in policymaking with pro-China women's groups under a system that prioritises political loyalty over professionalism? Should feminist organisations resist or strategically accept cooptation when lobbying for policy reform?

This puzzle of state–feminist relations is inseparable from the second concern, which is the relationship between feminists and the fragmented civil society in the aftermath of the 2019 protests. Although many NGOs were dismantled and activists fled, there has been an emergence of local and overseas groups and individual initiatives to sustain the opposition forces. Some of these opinion leaders and groups, however, inherited the anti-leftist and anti-feminist sentiments from the former nativist movement. Against this backdrop, how should feminist groups navigate between different political factions within the opposition and among prodemocracy supporters? If self-limitation and compromise with the government are perceived as complicit acts by the prodemocracy block, it will certainly undermine support for the progressive feminist movement and appear to

---

19 One example is the review of substantive sexual offences conducted between 2012 and 2019. Feminist groups actively participated in the consultations initiated by the Law Reform Commission's Review of Sexual Offences Subcommittee.

legitimate the persistent misogyny and sexism ingrained in the opposition. Last, neither self-limitation nor intersectional specialisation will effectively moderate the risks of establishing or maintaining international connections under the NSL. However, severing international ties would accelerate the subsumption of Hong Kong under the geopolitics of China's relations with the world, isolating the city from the global feminist movement.

Solidarity beyond borders: Feminist collectives and informal resistance

These seemingly unresolvable challenges prompt us to seek insights from feminist movements in other places, one of which is the feminist struggle in mainland China. Between the 2000s and the early 2010s, there was a substantive growth in feminist activism on the mainland. However, the movement was disrupted by the crackdown on civil society in 2015 as prominent feminist activists were detained and many feminist and LGBTQI+ groups were disbanded (Wang 2022; Zheng 2015). Despite repression, scholars have identified various tactics deployed by activists and political agents to advance feminism in China's limited political space. One is *coalition-based gender lobbying*, in which political actors within and outside the formal political apparatus mobilise for women's interests that represent unified societal demands and build coalitions of state agency allies to substantiate these interests (Jiang and Zhou 2022). Another tactic is *differential coalescing* (Wang 2022), by which activists create new spaces and establish cross-sectoral coalitions among actors with different ideologies of social change to garner resources and advocate for their agenda. Although both approaches reflect 'institutionally anchored ways of thinking' (Ferree 2003) that may constrain the diversity of feminist pursuits (Jiang and Zhou 2022), they also illustrate that, by contextualising movement claims corresponding to the political and discursive opportunity structures, activists can advance feminist agendas and even substantiate women's interests within politically acceptable boundaries (Ferree 2003). These strategies offer insights for Hong Kong's feminists to rethink their relationship with the local and central governments in the face of increased direct control from the Chinese party-state.

Across the globe, feminist activism among marginalised groups who have little political power also offers valuable inspiration to feminist struggles under multifaceted constraints. In Chapter 13 of this volume, Diprose and her colleagues identify the significance of the 'webs of interdependence and solidarity' in the activism of marginalised women in rural Indonesia and depict how informal collective actions could foster women's empowerment and promote female leadership at the community level. As James Scott (1990) suggested, resistance can manifest in everyday practices and hidden narratives. In tandem with this, self-limitation does not necessarily mean the disappearance of resistance; it may imply the informalisation of resistance and the politicising of everyday life, which can occur in the domain of intimate relationships, economic life and the composition of self-identity. For example, economic cooperatives managed by migrant mothers living in subdivided units[20] in deprived neighbourhoods can generate subjective experiences of empowerment and counteract economic exploitation and, in turn, lead to changes in family power dynamics. Such informal resistance can also substantiate feminist ideas in the individual, relational, economic and sociocultural domains; rebut the tactics of gender irrelevance and soft repression; and consolidate a progressive ideological standpoint that stands in contrast to state conservatism. These everyday practices, though highly localised, also resonate with the lived experiences of women and other marginalised groups across societies and cultures. The practice of informal resistance with global awareness may incubate a global feminist collective by retaining existing formal international networks and weaving informal ties that help cultivate 'sequestered social sites' (Scott 1990: 20) that facilitate the exchange of progressive ideas across localities and nurture collective resilience.

To conclude, I have no intention of setting out a grand proposal for feminist activism in Hong Kong in the NSL era, nor will I attempt to motivate or incite concrete actions, both individual and collective, to challenge the existing political order. The aim of this chapter is modest. I have unravelled the legacies inherited from the earlier phases of feminism, to exemplify the present challenges faced by feminists and to suggest possible ways to revitalise the movement's legacies as valuable resources in re-strategising the approach to feminist advocacy in an uncertain future.

---

20 A housing unit subdivided from a larger domestic quarter, usually tiny and substandard, with a median floor area of about 11 square metres.

References

Arato, Andrew. 2000. *Civil Society, Constitution, and Legitimacy*. Lanham: Rowman & Littlefield.

Association Concerning Sexual Violence Against Women (ACSVAW). 2022. *Survey on Hong Kong Women's Experiences of Violence 2021. Executive Summary*. Hong Kong: Association Concerning Sexual Violence Against Women.

Bermeo, Nancy. 2016. 'On Democratic Backsliding.' *Journal of Democracy* 27, no. 1: 5–19. doi.org/10.1353/jod.2016.0012.

Caglar, Gülay. 2013. 'Gender Mainstreaming.' *Politics & Gender* 9, no. 3: 336–44. doi.org/10.1017/S1743923X13000214.

Carroll, John Mark. 2007. *A Concise History of Hong Kong*. Lanham: Rowman & Littlefield.

Census and Statistics Department. 2022. *Main Result*. Hong Kong: Census and Statistics Department.

Chan, Anita Kit-wa, and Wai-ling Wong. 2004. *Gendering Hong Kong*. Hong Kong: Oxford University Press.

Chan, Cora, and Fiona de Londras, eds. 2020. *China's National Security: Endangering Hong Kong's Rule of Law?* London: Hart Publishing. doi.org/10.5040/97815 09928187.

Chan, Shun-Hing. 2002. 'Interfacing Feminism and Cultural Studies in Hong Kong: A Case of Everyday Life Politics.' *Cultural Studies* 16, no. 5: 704–34. doi.org/ 10.1080/0950238022000025246.

Chen, Yun-chung, and Mirana M. Szeto. 2015. 'The Forgotten Road of Progressive Localism: New Preservation Movement in Hong Kong.' *Inter-Asia Cultural Studies* 16, no. 3: 436–53. doi.org/10.1080/14649373.2015.1071694.

Cheng, Joseph Yu-shek. 2014. 'The Emergence of Radical Politics in Hong Kong: Causes and Impact.' *China Review* 14, no. 1: 199–232.

Cheung, Fanny M. 1989. 'The Women's Center: A Community Approach to Feminism in Hong Kong.' *American Journal of Community Psychology* 17, no. 1: 99–107. doi.org/10.1007/BF00931206.

Cheung, Fanny M., and Eleanor Holroyd. 2009. *Mainstreaming Gender in Hong Kong Society*. Hong Kong: Chinese University Press.

Chiu, Stephen Wing Kai, and Tai Lok Lui. 2000. *Dynamics of Social Movements in Hong Kong*. Hong Kong Culture and Society. Hong Kong: Hong Kong University Press.

Cho, Joseph M.K., Trevor Y.T. Ma, and Lucetta Y.L. Kam. 2020. 'Feminist Activism in Hong Kong.' In *Routledge Handbook of East Asian Gender Studies*, edited by Jieyu Liu and Junko Yamashita, 95–105. London: Routledge. doi.org/10.4324/9781315660523-6.

Choi, Po-king. 2012. 'Xianggang Funu Yundong Huigu [Review of Women's Movement in Hong Kong].' In *Xingbie Juexing: Liang'an San De Shehui Xingbie Yanjiu* [*Gender Awakening: Gender Studies in China, Hong Kong and Taiwan*], edited by Maria Tam, Hon Ming Yip, Wai-ching Wong, and Sally K.W. Lo, 212–35. Hong Kong: Commercial Press.

Choi, Susanne Y.P., and Fanny M. Cheung. 2012. *Women and Girls in Hong Kong*. Hong Kong: Chinese University Press of Hong Kong.

Choi, Susanne Y.P., and Ruby Y.S. Lai. 2021. 'Sex Work and Stigma Management in China and Hong Kong: The Role of State Policy and NGO Advocacy.' *The China Quarterly* 247: 855–74. doi.org/10.1017/S0305741021000035.

Choi, Susanne Y.P., and Ruby Y.S. Lai. 2022. 'Birth Tourism and Migrant Children's Agency: The "Double Not" in Post-Handover Hong Kong.' *Journal of Ethnic and Migration Studies* 48, no. 5: 1193–209. doi.org/10.1080/1369183X.2020.1839397.

Choi, Susanne Y.P., Ruby Y.S. Lai, and Javier C.L. Pang. 2020. 'Gender Irrelevance: How Women and Men Rationalize their Support for the Right.' *Signs: Journal of Women in Culture and Society* 45, no. 2: 473–96. doi.org/10.1086/705006.

Collins, Patricia Hill. 1990. *Black Feminist Thought: Knowledge, Consciousness, and the Politics of Empowerment*. Boston: Unwin Hyman.

Crenshaw, Kimberlé. 1989. 'Demarginalizing the Intersection of Race and Sex: A Black Feminist Critique of Discrimination Doctrine, Feminist Theory, and Antiracist Practice.' *University of Chicago Legal Forum* 89: 139–67.

Davis, Michael C. 2022. 'Hong Kong: How Beijing Perfected Repression.' *Journal of Democracy* 33, no. 1: 100–15. doi.org/10.1353/jod.2022.0007.

Equal Opportunities Commission (EOC). 2009. *Study on Public Perception of Portrayal of Female Gender in the Hong Kong Media*. Hong Kong: Equal Opportunities Commission.

Equal Opportunities Commission (EOC). 2021. *Gender Equality in Hong Kong*. Hong Kong: Equal Opportunities Commission.

Ferree, Myra Marx. 2003. 'Resonance and Radicalism: Feminist Framing in the Abortion Debates of the United States and Germany.' *American Journal of Sociology* 109, no. 2: 304–44. doi.org/10.1086/378343.

Ferree, Myra Marx. 2004. 'Soft Repression: Ridicule, Stigma, and Silencing in Gender-Based Movements.' In *Authority in Contention*, edited by Daniel J. Myers and Daniel M. Cress, 85–101. Bingley: Emerald Publishing. doi.org/10.1016/S0163-786X(04)25004-2.

Fischler, Lisa. 2003. 'Women's Activism during Hong Kong's Political Transition.' In *Gender and Change in Hong Kong: Globalization, Postcolonialism, and Chinese Patriarchy*, edited by Eliza Wing-Yee Lee, 49–77. Vancouver: UBC Press. doi.org/10.59962/9780774851855-004.

Fu, Hualing, and Michael Hor, eds. 2022. *The National Security Law of Hong Kong: Restoration and Transformation*. Hong Kong: Hong Kong University Press. doi.org/10.1515/9789888754472.

Grabowska, Magdalena. 2012. 'Bringing the Second World In: Conservative Revolution(s), Socialist Legacies, and Transnational Silences in the Trajectories of Polish Feminism.' *Signs: Journal of Women in Culture and Society* 37, no. 2: 385–411. doi.org/10.1086/661728.

Ho, Petula Sik Ying. 2022. 'Connection at the Price of Collusion: An Analysis of "Hong Kong's New Identity Politics: Longing for the Local in the Shadow of China" (2020).' *Cultural Studies* 36, no. 2: 229–51. doi.org/10.1080/09502386.2021.1912802.

Ho, Petula Sik Ying, and Adolf Ka Tat Tsang. 2012. *Sex and Desire in Hong Kong*. Hong Kong: Hong Kong University Press. doi.org/10.5790/hongkong/9789888139156.001.0001.

Ho, Petula Sik Ying, and Minnie Ming Li. 2021. 'A Feminist Snap: Has Feminism in Hong Kong Been Defeated?' *Made in China Journal* 6, no. 3: 86–93. doi.org/10.22459/MIC.06.03.2021.10.

Hoe, Susanna. 1991. *The Private Life of Old Hong Kong: Western Women in the British Colony, 1841–1941*. Hong Kong: Oxford University Press.

Jiang, Xinhui, and Yunyun Zhou. 2022. 'Coalition-Based Gender Lobbying: Revisiting Women's Substantive Representation in China's Authoritarian Governance.' *Politics & Gender* 18, no. 4: 978–1010. doi.org/10.1017/S174392 3X21000210.

Kapai, Puja. 2013. 'The Human Rights of Women in the Hong Kong Special Administrative Region.' *William & Mary Journal of Women and the Law* 19, no. 2: 255–300.

King, Mary Ann. 2001. 'Nuxing/Tongzhi/Nuxing Zhuyi Yu Yundong [Female/ Tongzhi/Feminism and Movement].' In *Chayi Yu Pingdeng: Xianggang Funu Yundong De Xin Tiaozhan* [*Difference and Equality: New Challenges for the Women's Movement in Hong Kong*], edited by Chan Kam-wah, Wong Kit-Mui, Leung Lai-ching, Lee Wai-Yee, and Ho Chi-Kwan, 77–91. Hong Kong: Association for the Advancement of Feminism and Centre for Social Policy Studies, Department of Applied Social Sciences, Hong Kong Polytechnic University.

Kong, Travis S.K. 2018. 'Gay and Grey: Participatory Action Research in Hong Kong.' *Qualitative Research* 18, no. 3: 257–72. doi.org/10.1177/1468794117713057.

Kong, Travis S.K., Sky H.L. Lau, and Yin Li Cheuk. 2015. 'The Fourth Wave? A Critical Reflection on the Tongzhi Movement in Hong Kong.' In *Routledge Handbook of Sexuality Studies in East Asia*, edited by Mark McLelland and Vera Mackie, 188–201. London: Routledge. doi.org/10.4324/9781315774879-17.

Ku, Agnes Shuk-mei. 2016. 'Making Cultures and Places from Below: New Urban Activism in Hong Kong.' In *Making Cultural Cities in Asia*, edited by June Wang, Tim Oakes, and Yang Yang, 209–21. New York: Routledge.

Lai, Betty L.L., Kit-Chun Au, and Fanny M. Cheung. 1997. 'Women's Concern Groups in Hong Kong.' In *Engendering Hong Kong Society: A Gender Perspective of Women's Status*, edited by Fanny Cheung, 267–306. Hong Kong: Chinese University Press.

Lai, Ruby Y.S. 2021. 'From #MeToo to #ProtestToo: How a Feminist Movement Converged with a Pro-Democracy Protest in Hong Kong.' *Politics & Gender* 17, no. 3: 500–7. doi.org/10.1017/S1743923X21000246.

Lai, Ruby Y.S. 2023. *Premarital Abortion in China: Intimacy, Family and Reproduction*. New York: Routledge. doi.org/10.4324/9781003297833.

Lam, Wai-man. 2018. 'Hong Kong's Fragmented Soul: Exploring Brands of Localism.' In *Citizenship, Identity and Social Movements in the New Hong Kong: Localism After the Umbrella Movement*, edited by Lam Wai-man and Luke Cooper, 72–93. New York: Routledge. doi.org/10.4324/9781315207971-5.

Lam, Wai-man, and Luke Cooper, eds. 2018. *Citizenship, Identity and Social Movements in the New Hong Kong: Localism After the Umbrella Movement*. New York: Routledge. doi.org/10.4324/9781315207971.

Lee, Ching Kwan. 2000. 'Public Discourses and Collective Identities: Emergence of Women as a Collective Actor in the Women's Movement in Hong Kong.' In *Dynamics of Social Movements in Hong Kong*, edited by Stephen Wing Kai Chiu and Tai Lok Lui, 227–57. Hong Kong: Hong Kong University Press.

Lee, Francis. 2020. 'Solidarity in the Anti–Extradition Bill Movement in Hong Kong.' *Critical Asian Studies* 52, no. 1: 18–32. doi.org/10.1080/14672715.2020. 1700629.

Lee, Francis L.F., and Chi-kit Chan. 2022. 'Legalization of Press Control Under Democratic Backsliding: The Case of Post–National Security Law Hong Kong.' *Media, Culture & Society* 45, no. 5: 916–31. doi.org/10.1177/0163443722 1140525.

Lim, Adelyn. 2010. 'The Hong Kong Women's Movement: Towards a Politics of Difference and Diversity.' In *Women's Movements in Asia: Feminisms and Transnational Activism*, edited by Mina Roces and Louise Edwards, 144–65. London: Routledge.

Lim, Adelyn. 2015. *Transnational Feminism and Women's Movements in Post-1997 Hong Kong*. Hong Kong: Hong Kong University Press. doi.org/10.5790/hong kong/9789888139378.001.0001.

Lo, Sonny. 2021. 'Hong Kong in 2020: National Security Law and Truncated Autonomy.' *Asian Survey* 61, no. 1: 34–42. doi.org/10.1525/as.2021.61.1.34.

Luqiu, Luwei Rose. 2022. 'Female Journalists Covering the Hong Kong Protests Confront Ambivalent Sexism on the Street and in the Newsroom.' *Feminist Media Studies* 22, no. 3: 679–97. doi.org/10.1080/14680777.2020.1842481.

Ma, Ngok. 2005. 'Civil Society in Self-Defense: The Struggle Against National Security Legislation in Hong Kong.' *The Journal of Contemporary China* 14, no. 44: 465–82. doi.org/10.1080/10670560500115416.

Ma, Ngok. 2007. *Political Development in Hong Kong: State, Political Society, and Civil Society*. Hong Kong: Hong Kong University Press. doi.org/10.5790/ hongkong/9789622098107.001.0001.

Ma, Ngok, and Edmund W. Cheng. 2019. *The Umbrella Movement: Civil Resistance and Contentious Space in Hong Kong*. Amsterdam: Amsterdam University Press. doi.org/10.2307/j.ctvh4zj2n.

Pang, Lai-kwan. 2020. 'Identity Politics and Democracy in Hong Kong's Social Unrest.' *Feminist Studies* 46, no. 1: 206–15. doi.org/10.1353/fem.2020.0008.

Roces, Mina, and Louise Edwards. 2010. *Women's Movements in Asia: Feminisms and Transnational Activism*. New York: Routledge.

Scott, James C. 1990. *Domination and the Arts of Resistance*. New Haven: Yale University Press.

Sinn, Elizabeth. 1994. 'Chinese Patriarchy and the Protection of Women in 19th-Century Hong Kong.' In *Women and Chinese Patriarchy: Submission, Servitude and Escape*, edited by Maria Jaschok and Suzanne Miers, 141–70. Hong Kong: Hong Kong University Press.

Staniszkis, Jadwiga. 1984. *Poland's Self-Limiting Revolution*. Princeton: Princeton University Press.

United Nations Development Programme (UNDP). 2022. *Human Development Report 2021/2022*. New York: United Nations Development Programme.

Veg, Sebastian. 2017. 'The Rise of "Localism" and Civic Identity in Post-Handover Hong Kong: Questioning the Chinese Nation-State.' *The China Quarterly* 230: 323–47. doi.org/10.1017/S0305741017000571.

Walby, Sylvia. 2005. 'Introduction: Comparative Gender Mainstreaming in a Global Era.' *International Feminist Journal of Politics* 7, no. 4: 453–70. doi.org/10.1080/14616740500284383.

Wang, Di. 2022. 'Differential Coalescing: Re-Building the Coalition for "Single Women's" Reproductive Rights in China.' *The Journal of Contemporary China* 32, no. 143: 779–93. doi.org/10.1080/10670564.2022.2108680.

Wong, Pik-wan. 2000. 'Negotiating Gender: The Women's Movement for Legal Reform in Colonial Hong Kong.' PhD diss., University of California, Los Angeles.

Wong, Wai-ching, and Po-king Choi. 2015. *Xing/Bie Zhengzhi Yu Bentuqiyi* [*Gender/Sexuality Politics and Local Activism*]. Hong Kong: Commercial Press.

Zheng, Wang. 2015. 'Detention of the Feminist Five in China.' *Feminist Studies* 41, no. 2: 476–82. doi.org/10.1353/fem.2015.0001.

13

Webs of Interdependence and Solidarity: Growing marginalised women's influence and leadership in rural Indonesian villages

Rachael Diprose, Bronwyn Anne Beech Jones
and Ken M.P. Setiawan

Scholarship on Indonesian politics has primarily focused on efforts to increase Indonesian women's participation in electoral politics and formal leadership structures, and the networks and resources required to generate electoral success, highlighting how women candidates have negotiated multiple barriers (Aspinall et al. 2021; Bayo 2021; Prihatini 2019a, 2019b). However, a focus on women's representation in electoral politics is but one dimension of understanding women's political participation and influence in public life. Understanding how women challenge gendered institutional barriers and norms to widen their voice and leadership in rural Indonesia is especially important given that major studies on village governance under Indonesia's Village Law (2014) have described varied, but generally low levels of women's participation in community decision-making (for example, Syukri et al. 2017; Dharmawan et al. 2018), and that women feel afraid to contributing to planning forums (Akbar et al. 2020), indicating that barriers to women's participation remain difficult to circumvent.

In this chapter, we widen and enrich our understanding of women's local political participation by focusing on everyday village settings and how especially marginalised women navigate institutional and social barriers and opportunities for women's leadership, through women's groups. Village settings comprise complex and intimate social structures on which women depend and in which they are embedded but are often at odds to challenge, especially as countering structures of authority creates risks to women's reputations, safety and access to future support. We highlight how women's efforts to exercise influence in such settings take on more informal, amorphous forms that are less confrontational to village structures of power and authority, often taking place through women's groups and networks and in alternative 'spaces' for influencing powerholders. These groups foster solidarity among women from a range of backgrounds and can draw from supportive coalitions that include authoritative actors and men—a process we conceptualise as *women's networked collective action.*

We argue such strategies and spaces are essential to creating change and increasing women's political participation and influence at the local level. Although such strategies and actions may be accompanied by, or contribute to, other more institutionalised forms of collective action (such as electoral politics), we emphasise that the more informal strategies constitute the kernels from which women's solidarity and mutual support grow and are needed to overcome social and institutional barriers to gender equality.

Such strategies and spaces of influence, we also argue, are augmented by the support of supra-local women's civil society organisations (CSOs)—specifically those that focus on transformative change in gendered power structures. These CSOs can support poor women to grow their critical gender consciousness, skills and networks. They can also act as brokers, connecting marginalised women to power structures and helping facilitate the creation of new spaces of influence, both beyond and connected to those sanctioned by the state. In so doing, CSOs have an important role in supporting the formation of what we conceptualise as *webs of interdependence*: platforms and mechanisms for women, especially from marginalised groups, to exert influence in spaces of power and invite policymakers into newly created spaces.

To illustrate these arguments, we draw our empirical base from a large collaborative research project in Indonesia that explored women's collective action and empowerment and the role of women's CSOs in this process (Diprose et al. 2020). We examine women's influence in two villages in

East Java Province in Gresik District, only one of which one had the strong presence of a women's CSO, which helped establish and then supported a new women's group. A comparison of these sites helps us to draw out the role for women's groups and CSO influence in women's local political participation.[1] Our interdisciplinary team involved researchers from a variety of backgrounds, predominantly Indonesian, but also Dutch and Australian, and we used a feminist research approach involving qualitative mixed methods (long village stays, observation, semi-structured interviews and focus group discussions) that were designed to help vulnerable women feel safe and comfortable in sharing their stories and which sought to foreground the voices of women and represent and learn from women's lived experiences.[2] Women's CSOs were pivotal in the collaborative research design and analysis.

We first outline our conceptualisation of women's empowerment and collective action and provide a brief background on women's political participation in Indonesia. We then discuss various gendered social norms and attitudes towards women that constitute significant barriers for rural women to exercise their voice safely. These women are among the most marginalised and experience the most stigma in Indonesian villages. We illustrate these barriers through the experience of Lastri,[3] one of our research participants in Gresik District. Through the experiences of Lastri and other women in Gresik, the chapter then explores the practices and strategies through which women foster the solidarity, networks, resources, capacities, skills and knowledge necessary to counter challenges to shaping structures of power and decision-making in rural areas. In so doing, women exercise influence in different 'invited' and 'created' spaces and create positive change—transforming women's sense of self, renegotiating care work, claiming rights and influencing decision-making processes. Overall, we suggest that the informal spaces and strategies women use have transformational potential to challenge inequitable power relations.

---

1   On agreement with CSOs and research participants, we have chosen to refer only to the subdistrict rather than the village's name, and all interviewees have been given pseudonyms to protect their anonymity, especially taking into consideration the gendered social norms and stigmas women reported and the risks they take in expressing their voice and agency.

2   Funding for some of the initial data collection (2019–20) for this chapter was drawn from the Australia–Indonesia Partnership for Women's Empowerment and Gender Equality, although this did not contribute to the production of this chapter. The CSOs examined also funded parts of their initiatives from this partnership, although this did not influence published analysis or findings.

3   See Note 1.

Conceptualising empowerment and women's collective action

Examining the influence of poor women in villages demands attention to how multiple forms of marginalisation compound. The intersectional approach used in this research elucidates how multiple inequalities interact with one another and compound structural barriers for marginalised groups; identity categories of gender, class and location are not 'distinct but always permeated by other categories, fluid and changing' (Cho et al. 2013: 795). Intersectionality aligns with conceptualisations of women's empowerment as relational and multidimensional processes (Kabeer 2011) that aim to transform unjust gendered power relations, especially by building 'critical consciousness' of injustice and inequality among women (Cornwall 2016: 344; Batliwala 2007; Kabeer 1994). Different operations of power 'within', 'to', 'over' and 'with' are important in processes of growing women's individual agency and collective power and influence (Rowlands 1997; Kabeer 1994). Power 'within' is especially connected to developing a critical consciousness of unequal and unjust structures within women's everyday lives (Dulhunty 2021; Kabeer 1994; Cornwall 2016).

In supporting women to exercise agency,[4] intermediaries (for example, community associations, well-placed individuals, entrepreneurs) often link 'formal' (such as state actors and influential social leaders) and 'informal' actors and spaces by facilitating services for citizens and in filling gaps in state service provision (Davis 2017). In line with one of the co-authors of this chapter (Diprose 2023), we argue such intermediaries can be conceptualised as brokers—'network specialists' who understand and connect the perspectives of different actors (Bierschenk et al. 2002), navigate and connect knowledge systems and bridge gaps in social structures through networks across scales (Lindquist 2015; James 2011). CSOs can play multiple brokerage roles, opening spaces and strategies for women in villages, notably through supporting the creation of new women's groups.

---

4   Scholarship on the agency of women in their everyday lives in Asia has tended to focus on women's public activism, with everyday agency conceptualised as 'women's relational and emotional lives, their experience of domestic practices and daily social and sexual interactions, on the way they build relationships, and their involvement in forms of interdependence and mutual aid' (Parker and Dales 2014: 164).

Individual and collective transformation can occur through participation in women's groups built on a foundation of mutual trust, which in turn can become the basis for collective action (McGee 2016). Through groups, women can grow their confidence and self-belief (power 'within') and strengthen solidarity ('power with'), as well as engage in collective action (Dulhunty 2021: 734). As we will explore, these groups can function as alternative spaces where women—individually and together—increase their awareness and expand their senses of self, while also facilitating women to strategically move between spaces and apply strategies to effect change or disrupt local power structures. The brokerage role of CSOs, as Diprose (2023: 401) has conceptualised, is thus to 'traverse scales and perform brokerage functions in helping rural women from marginal groups to connect to and influence powerholders in Indonesia'. In this chapter, we examine one such initiative, the Women's Schools, where women have grown their power and influence both among themselves and with/over others.

Meanwhile, collective action scholarship has broadly distinguished between more formal forms driven through, or by, an organisation or government structure (Evans and Nambiar 2013), while informal collective action takes place within more 'amorphous social networks' and offers greater flexibility for members to participate and mould actions to their changing needs (Pandolfelli et al. 2008: 3), with women more likely to engage in informal collective action in low-income settings (for example, Agarwal 2000). Even so, the relationship between formality and informality is interconnected, uneven and messy (Davis 2017). Davis (2017: 316) argues that even when 'more universal norms, stable structures, and rationalised processes' become institutionalised, informal livelihoods, work, norms and practices (such as citizen activism, neighbourhood civil society and social norms) persist. As such, the binary between formal and informal groups and forms of collective action is in practice quite fluid.

Important in understanding the forms and processes of growing women's power is identifying the spaces available, or that can be constructed, for women to exercise influence over powerholders, and how women, particularly from marginalised groups, might connect to these spaces. Miraftab (2004: 3) conceptualises spaces and strategies of action together, arguing that grassroots groups and movements use a variety of spaces and forms depending on the context in which they act and what they deem as strategic to their aims.[5] Miraftab (2004: 1) also distinguishes between 'invited spaces'—where grassroots actors legitimised by donors (for example, funding agencies) or the state focus on coping mechanisms and propositions to support survival—and 'invented spaces' that are 'claimed by their collective action' and directly demand structural change. Groups occupy and use both sets of tools and spaces agilely and strategically, with invented spaces sometimes opening 'possibilities of citizen participation in invited spaces' (Miraftab 2020: 439).[6] Forming alternative invented spaces and practices in conjunction with invited spaces shows how women and CSOs shift between invited and invented spaces to 'assert their presence within spaces of invitation' (McEwan 2005: 977–78). This, we argue, occurs through the *webs of interdependence* forged via membership of groups and through networks with other women and coalitions of supporting men.

By forming new women's groups, supporting CSOs can strengthen women's organising structures and sources of knowledge/resources, and help broker networks with other women and authoritative actors to build supporting *webs of interdependence* and coalitions of influence. In our empirical analysis, we consider the more everyday micro-strategies that women use in contemporary Indonesia to garner support and build a critical mass to influence structures of power across a spectrum of spaces, and the roles CSOs play in growing these *webs of interdependence*. This is especially important for understanding how women seek to counter the historical influence of the state in structuring the nature and form of women's political participation.

Women's historical political participation in Indonesia

State gender ideologies have strongly influenced women's political participation in Indonesia at both national and grassroots levels, meaning that while the state has encouraged women's participation, the goals of state-sanctioned women's organisations often align with government priorities (Blackburn 2004; Davies 2005). The influence of state gender ideologies

---

5   These include 'formal channels', understood in this chapter as institutionalised, state-sanctioned spaces (for example, laws, local government, courts), oppositional practices (for example, protests) as well as what Miraftab refers to as more informal strategies of coping, resilience and opposing structures of power.
6   These spaces are also co-formed and relational in the sense that limited opportunities for participation and voice in invited spaces may push for the formation of alternative spaces (McEwan 2005).

on women's political participation was particularly pronounced during the authoritarian New Order regime led by president Suharto (1966–98), during which all leftist organisations were banned and their members imprisoned or killed,[7] which, alongside subsequent systematic 'demonisation' (Pohlman 2017), had a particularly detrimental effect on women's political activism. As a result, women's groups virtually disappeared from the grassroots level, except for religious groups and state-endorsed organisations such as the Pembinaan Kesejahteraan Keluarga (PKK, Family Welfare Guidance organisation).[8]

Instead, women's roles were constrained to that of wives, mothers and household managers, and women's political participation was limited to involvement in 'wives' organisations such as Dharma Wanita under the New Order's patriarchal gender policy conceptualised as 'state *ibuism* ['motherism']' (Suryakusuma 1987).[9] While these organisations offered some women certain forms of representation and voice, everyday women's influence over policies related to their lives and wellbeing was constrained (Diprose et al. 2020). State gender ideology, however, did not completely halt the development of women's organisations; religious organisations continued their social work by avoiding an overtly political stance (Blackburn 2004). New women's organisations and networks also emerged as the result of economic growth and increased education levels among women. Many of these new organisations were strongly influenced by feminist ideas and the global human rights movement and were critical of the state and women's subordination (Davies 2005).

The resignation of Suharto in 1998 heralded a shift to democratisation and a change in gender politics. Women's organisations rapidly grew— importantly, in areas where few had existed before (Blackburn 2004). State corporatist organisations, such as Dharma Wanita and the PKK, increased their focus on women's participation in politics and changed their structures, allowing for more democratic participation (Diprose et al. 2020). Greater state concern for gender issues was expressed through

7   This saw the end of the mass women's organisation Gerwani, which involved more than one million women, including many non-elite women in rural areas (Wieringa 2002: 179).

8   The PKK was endorsed by Suharto's authoritarian regime as a women's organisation with reach in villages. The PKK disseminated the state's official gender ideology, emphasising women's domestic roles, and organised female volunteers in state-led development programs. In 2000, the PKK changed its name to Family Welfare and Empowerment but remains largely connected to development priorities set by the central government.

9   Dharma Wanita is a state-corporatist organisation for wives of civil servants. Under the New Order, its activities echoed government priorities. Since the end of the New Order, membership is voluntary.

the establishment of new state bodies to promote women's rights, such as the National Commission on the Elimination of Violence against Women (Komnas Perempuan) in 1998, and legislative and policy change (Setiawan and Tomsa 2022). The introduction of a gender quota for legislative elections has increased the number of female candidates and seats won by women (Prihatini 2020).

Despite these changes, gender norms that emphasise traditional roles for women, especially as wives and mothers, remain deeply entrenched in politics and society. Indonesia's conservative religious turn has also constrained efforts to push for institutional and structural changes that benefit women (Setiawan and Tomsa 2022). This then raises the question of how women's organisations navigate entrenched norms, as well as more recent challenges, that impact women's political participation, especially beyond Indonesia's urban centres.

Contexts and methods

To explore these dynamics, we investigate women's voice and influence in two villages, one in each of two subdistricts in Gresik District: Wringinanom and Bungah. Both villages have high levels of poverty, have economies dominated by local markets, agriculture and fishing, and are geographically isolated, with limited access routes to the district capital and few public transport options. These conditions meant that before our study, village governments tended to prioritise funding for infrastructure development, especially paving roads.[10]

There were also three types of existing women's groups in both sites: integrated health posts (*posyandu*), the PKK and the religious women's organisation Fatayat (the women's affiliate of Indonesia's mass Islamic organisation, Nahdlatul Ulama). The PKK and Fatayat each had few members (often the same people) and none from marginalised groups.

---

10 In 2018, 40 per cent of the village budget in the Wringinanom research village was allocated to infrastructure projects.

Women occupied few leadership positions in either village over time and, when they did, they were positions of weak influence. In the Wringinanom village at the time of the research, only one woman held a role (of limited power) in the village administration (2019–25). In the Bungah site, two women held roles in the village government and one as a representative on the Village Consultative Council (Badan Permusyawaratan Desa, BPD), but her appointment resulted from a subdistrict directive in 2018 to include a female representative. All three were drawn from a small pool of elite PKK members.[11]

However, they differed significantly in one aspect: in the Wringinanom village, the CSO Women's Groups and Sources of Life (Kelompok Perempuan dan Sumber-Sumber Kehidupan, KPS2K), a local partner of the national organisation KAPAL Perempuan (Institute for Women's Alternative Education), established a women's group known as an informal Women's School (Prabaningrum and Abheseka 2020). By contrast, the Bungah village at the time of the research did not have a CSO-supported program or women's group and is thus used in our study as a counterfactual (or control) to the CSO intervention in Wringinanom (see Figure 13.1).

Figure 13.1 illustrates how we explore multiple forms of women's influence on development in these two villages. We chart the shape and extent of influence of women's individual leadership and existing women's groups, and then turn to more closely examine this CSO-facilitated new women's group. The figure illustrates key aspects of subsequent empirical analysis— the ways poor women grew their skills, knowledge and networks through new groups and by being connected to other women and powerholders outside their village. We argue that by growing these *webs of interdependence*, CSO-supported pathways of change, shown in Figure 13.1, helped spur transformative changes to the village and district context of women's political participation and influence on development.

---

11 For instance, the female BPD representative was chosen directly from the PKK by the village government and is the daughter of the PKK head. One PKK member described how she was perceived as a good fit because of her mother's position: '[P]eople like that have high loyalty. And that is passed on to her child.' The PKK has successfully nominated two women to become part of the village government, including an early childhood education teacher, who became section head of general administrative affairs in 2018.

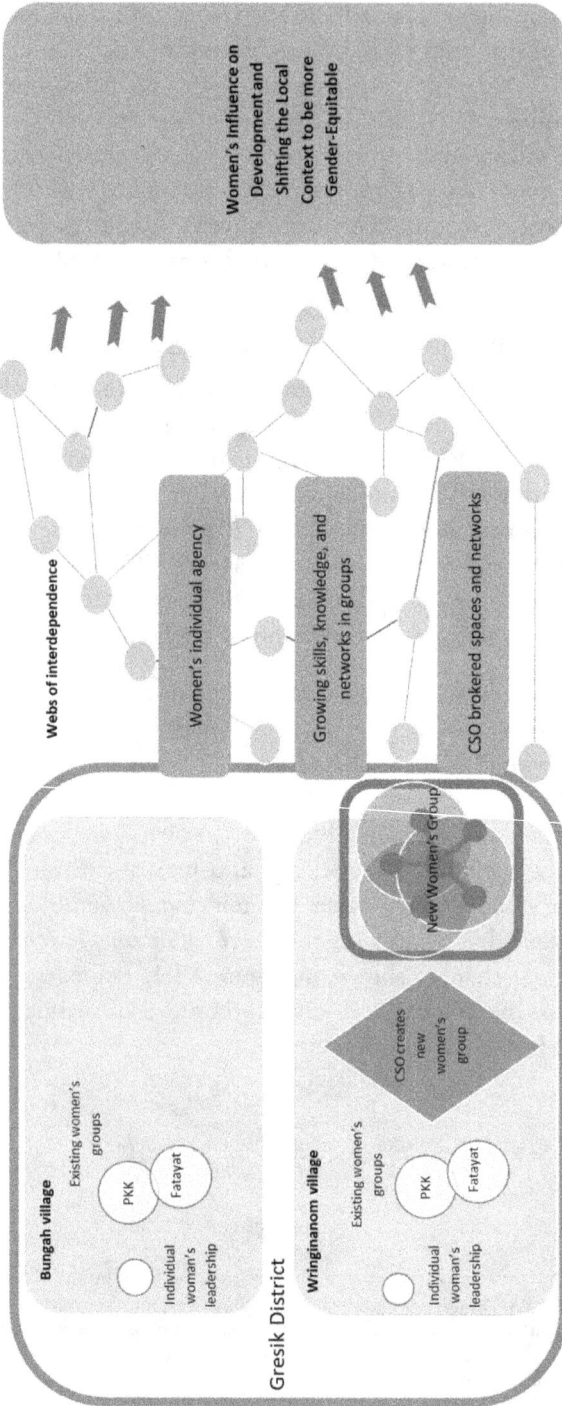

Figure 13.1: Conceptualising pathways of change and *webs of interdependence*

Gendered social norms, stigma and risks for women's participation

The two research villages are also characterised by strong patriarchal norms that create risks for women who challenge them. The embeddedness of such norms means that women's participation in group activities outside the household, beyond health clinics and prayer groups, often challenges deeply entrenched ideas about women's roles and obligations as daughters, wives and mothers. This illustrates the salience of state gender ideology discussed earlier in this chapter and shows how, in practice, women are primarily positioned within the domestic sphere, excluding them from more public-facing roles and decision-making.

One example of the entrenchment of patriarchal norms is the high prevalence of child marriage in both subdistricts.[12] Wringinanom subdistrict recorded 1,329 cases of child marriage in 2016 and 821 cases in 2017 (Radar Surabaya 2018). CSO staff noted that village government officials emphasise that marriage is preferable to pregnancy out of wedlock and prioritise respecting the wishes of parents.[13] One woman in Wringinanom, Nining, recalled:

> I was married at 13 and had children by 15. I had an arranged marriage. I stayed at the Islamic boarding school [*pesantren*] for four days, then I was taken and told that I was getting married. It was after I graduated from primary school, I was taken home right away and proposed to [for marriage]. I didn't know what my husband's face even looked like. After four days I was just taken … That's what the arranged marriage was like.

In both villages, even in private conversation, poor women very rarely were able to voice lived experiences of culturally taboo issues such as child marriage, frustrations with care work, illnesses (especially those related to reproductive health) and domestic violence, as this would contravene social norms that domestic and marital matters should not be openly talked about. As such, women had limited capacity to grow their political influence on issues important to their needs. As a result of entrenched patriarchal norms, in both villages, there was also a strong negative stigma associated

---

12   Until 2019, Indonesian state law defined the marriageable age for girls as 16 years old, in tension with international conventions.
13   Interview with KPS2K staff, Sidoarjo, East Java, 6 March 2019.

with women venturing outside the home for something other than socially sanctioned activities related to the running of the household, income generation (if approved by their husbands) or religious commitments.

We see the multiple barriers to women's participation in Lastri's story. While she later became the Gresik district coordinator of the Women's School introduced by KPS2K, Lastri encountered many challenges at the outset. First, Lastri's parents and husband did not give her permission to participate in the Women's School, arguing this would not generate income for the family. To prevent her participation, Lastri's husband gave her an increased load of household chores. This left Lastri feeling conflicted as she did not want to make a decision that was not supported by her family but did want to improve her knowledge and skills.

Second, Lastri lacked the confidence to participate in the Women's School. Coming from a poor family, she had received little formal education and had no experience in participating in village meetings. Third, resistance to women taking on leadership roles is reflected in the social stigma they encountered in even engaging with the Women's School group in Wringinanom. Lastri and others were accused of being 'improper' when they engaged with Women's School activities and were labelled as 'that "type" of woman' or what might be loosely translated as 'women of ill repute' (*perempuan nggak bener*) by members of the community, including other women.

These reactions also reflect deeply entrenched social attitudes towards women's political participation, as discussed earlier in this chapter. Often men spread rumours about group activities to tarnish the reputation of certain women's groups and the members involved, and to discourage other women from joining. Lasinem, a friend of Lastri and fellow member of the Women's School, recalled that her friend had been advised by her husband to not join the Women's School as he said it had taught Lasinem to 'challenge her husband'. After joining the Women's School group, Lastri continued to face negative reactions from villagers about her participation:

> Previously, I was tainted with that brush. If we went to the [activities held by the] Women's School outside the village, like in a hotel, we were deemed to be '*perempuan nggak bener*'. People labelled us like that so as to discourage [women from] attending the school.

Women such as Lastri particularly rely on their social networks and the support structures provided by communities to help them respond to the many challenges of poverty. Challenging norms risks being alienated from these support structures.

In both villages in Gresik, women also come up against gender norms that they are unsuitable for public-facing leadership roles. In Wringinanom, Aulia was the only woman among the 16 village government officials at the time of the research. She was initially elected hamlet head and later moved by the village head to a position he considered more suitable for a woman, the head of administrative and general affairs for the village government. Her male replacement explained that 'it was intended so [I could] be with the community, as "socialising is easier as a man than a woman"'.[14]

Equally, in the Bungah control village, whenever villagers were asked whether there were any female leaders or influential women in the village, as well as the head of the PKK, they also consistently referred only to Mafiroh, the first woman neighbourhood head, appointed in 1999, and one of only a handful in the area to have ever held such a leadership role; she operated with little support and constantly had to demonstrate her leadership worth. Now aged in her fifties, Mafiroh recounted how towards the end of the New Order era, she served in the village civil defence (*Hansip*) group. Only through demonstrating her skills in this group was she able to gain the neighbourhood head role.[15] Villagers reflected on how Mafiroh had challenged gendered preconceptions and proved her leadership skills, in doing so, somewhat reshaping how women's capacity for leadership was considered by others, with one man stating: 'We only knew women could become leaders because Ibu Mafiroh became the neighbourhood head. I now know that, and in fact, they are more agile and work faster than the male neighbourhood heads do.'

Mafiroh challenged widespread gender norms that suggest women do not have the capacity to be leaders. However, Mafiroh's story also shows the limited transformational capacity of individuals challenging gendered power structures alone: few women have held any leadership roles in Bungah since and have little support to do so. We later return to consider the participatory potential of 'invented' spaces and everyday strategies of solidarity building for poor women who are frequently excluded from state-sanctioned leadership roles.

14 Even the head of the village PKK—and wife of the village head—attended some village meetings but had little organisational role as her husband did not approve of her being active in this public role.
15 Positions of village defence were open to young people (between 20 and 40 years old) who had elementary education and no permanent employment or landownership.

Limited opportunities for organising

From the above discussion, it is clear that few organising opportunities and widespread gender norms limit women's participation in public life and capacity for political leadership compared with men. The few forms of women's organisations in these villages (the PKK, Fatayat and *posyandu*, each of which is state-sanctioned) are traditional, state-corporatist women's groups that constitute state-sanctioned 'invited spaces'.

Women from poorer families in both villages, such as Lastri, are less likely to be members of state-corporatist organisations, which are dominated by the wives of government officials—a legacy of compulsory membership under the New Order (Jakimow 2020). In Gresik, PKK leaders—at the village, subdistrict and district levels—are middle to upper class, with a district government official explaining that 'it is not possible that they [a PKK leader] would be from the middle to lower class'. Poor women in both villages expressed feeling excluded from the PKK, despite their interest in joining village-level organisations, or did not know about programs run by the PKK.

A focus group interview of five women farmers in Wringinanom captures how the selection of leaders, or cadres, limits who can join the PKK in their village:

> Interviewer: Why aren't you in PKK?
>
> Ratih: Because we aren't invited. You have to be selected.
> Per neighbourhood unit here, there can be one or two [selected].
>
> Interviewer: Who is selected usually?[16]
>
> Susi: The cadres, PKK cadres.

Similarly, in the Bungah control village, the PKK has comprised a small group of elite women, who tend to conform to the gender norms of women as wives and mothers. Leaders of the PKK were also prominent members of Fatayat's Qur'an recitation and prayer group. To even access the conditional cash transfer for children's education *Program Keluarga Harapan* ('Family Hope Program') women had to join the PKK. The village head framed this policy in punitive terms: '[I]t's like being warned, warned in the sense that if you do not go to PKK, it [cash transfers] will not be given.' While the

---

16 24 February 2019.

policy boosted the on-paper PKK membership to about 200–250 women, it meant group participation took a form sanctioned by the state and was only to access funds (few participated in activities); they did not gain a transformative sense of self or skills, knowledge or support from the group.

'How to become a leader inside myself': The Women's School in Wringinanom

Given these limited opportunities for women to organise and act collectively, the local CSO, KPS2K, in coordination with its national partner, KAPAL Perempuan, began work in Gresik District via an agreement with the district government in 2014. This enabled the CSOs to establish Women's School groups in villages, ensuring the involvement of the poorest village women to address their self-identified complex needs and grow their skills and opportunities. The Bungah village government rejected the creation of a Women's School there, as the village head was resistant to the work of CSOs, stating that 'empowerment programs create social conflict'.

To establish the Women's School in Wringinanom, access was granted but the village government was not strongly supportive. In initial discussions with KPS2K about potential members, the village government directed staff to the elite-dominated PKK for members. However, to instead connect with poor women, KPS2K went door-to-door, collecting data on poverty levels and inviting 80 women to attend a preliminary meeting at the village hall.[17]

Lastri recalled how the invitation to join the first Women's School gathering left her feeling confused: it was not a space with which she was familiar. Many women felt nervous about attending the meeting as it was held at the village hall; such spaces are normally for state-sanctioned activities from which women had usually been excluded. About 30 per cent of the women invited to participate in Women's School activities did not attend because their husbands did not give permission to do so. Despite these fears and barriers, other women forged new networks by participating in Women's School activities, growing their own power and that of the group, and later convincing friends to participate in activities.

---

17 At the district level, KPS2K also consulted with government planning and women's empowerment agencies to compare government poverty data with data collected through this social mapping. KPS2K selected Wringinanom subdistrict and this research village in particular because of its high poverty rates.

Growing skills, capacity, knowledge and confidence together

At Women's School meetings, KPS2K and KAPAL Perempuan provided training to members in public speaking, writing, advocacy, parenting, agricultural skills and the culturally sensitive issue of reproductive health. Through these training sessions, women built their confidence in speaking and deepened their understanding of gender and rights. Lastri recalled after the first training session being aware that 'women have the right to make decisions about what is right and wrong, like in the family environment. We have social protection, rights to be fought for.'

Deepening an understanding of gender roles as constructed, rather than natural, and how these norms shape women's everyday lives, had a profound impact on women's sense of self. One Women's School leader described how she returned home from training 'in a daze' as what she had learned contradicted what she had been taught since she was a child—'that you can't question your husband, you have to be obedient, your husband is like a god'. Women's School members have also built networks of trust and confidence by meeting regularly in more everyday, social forms at a group leader's house to share stories and seek advice, especially about how to handle problems they are facing at home and with their families.[18] Here, we see how the informal ways in which women gather and organise are important for growing their power 'within' and together as sources of mutual support: their *webs of interdependence*.

The self-confidence, gender awareness and capacities that women fostered together in their Women's School group led many to apply their new understandings and skills in their own lives and share their knowledge with neighbours. Interviewees described using new strategies of negotiation in their families, especially in expressing their opinions as well as negotiating household labour and mobility outside the home. Indah explained how after attending Women's School sessions, 'we realised what a woman's needs are and that there are ways to be able to discuss [these needs] with children and families. In the past I could not leave my child at home, but now I can negotiate with my husband to go out.'

---

18   The house where this takes place was chosen as a suitable meeting space because the leader lives alone with her children (her husband works outside the village), and because the house is far from the village office and close to the neighbouring village, which means that friends who live there can also attend.

By growing individual awareness of their rights through groups, women also supported one another to access services, particularly reproductive health care—again, growing women's power and the kernels of solidarity on which to build other forms of organising and influence.

Mutual support and accessing health services

The Women's School group's focus on reproductive health was shaped by Lastri's experience. Through participating in the Women's School, Lastri understood her rights to health care. After many years of not seeking medical treatment for symptoms, she was encouraged and supported by her friends in the Women's School to gain the relevant healthcare card and seek a free health check—despite her husband remaining unconvinced of their importance—at a hospital that partnered with the Women's School, at which she was diagnosed with cervical cancer.

Lastri's friend Endang captured the interconnectedness of these processes of building solidarity with other women (power with) and understanding and self-belief (power within) to engage in collective action for self-identified needs:

> I am 'aware' because *I* have learned at the Women's School that I also have rights. If I am not promptly referred to the hospital, *I* am the one who will be unwell. So, *I* have a right to make a decision that can make myself healthy. That's what I learned at the Women's School. Not how to become a public leader, but how to become a leader inside myself. To make decisions like those.

After Lastri's diagnosis, Women's School members discussed commonly disregarded symptoms of reproductive system diseases. Then, building on Lastri's experience, the Women's School group, together with hospital and district government networks described below, successfully implemented free annual early detection tests in 2015–17.

This example shows the messy, often-overlapping relationship of informal and formal spaces of organising. Lastri was able to form close friendships with other women who had a similarly marginalised position in the village by participating in the created space of the Women's School. These relationships were strengthened outside more formal training sessions through informal discussions about the challenges they faced. Through this *web of interdependence*, Lastri and her friends raised awareness about women's right to health care and challenged the boundaries of local political influence by drawing from her experience to spearhead the testing program partnership with the hospital and district government. The Women's Schools provided women with the skills and voice to demand and negotiate for more power in both the private and the public spheres. Lastri and her friends have also worked hard with KPS2K and the National Insurance Scheme staff to help community members process the cards needed to access *Indonesia Sehat* ('Healthy Indonesia') programs and other forms of government social protection.

'We worked together': Women's groups growing their power and influence in villages

Across the research sites in Gresik and beyond, there was significant diversity in the strategies used to participate in spaces of influence and to exercise voice and power on issues affecting women. Growing the confidence to approach authoritative actors was built on the skills, capacity, knowledge and mutual support developed through the new women's groups. This then saw more women than those involved in elite-dominated state-corporatist organisations being increasingly able to create or access spaces in which power is exercised in rural Indonesia, including more institutionalised, state-sanctioned spaces. Some of these different strategies and spaces of influence are discussed below.

Women's representation in structures of political power

In addition to women's limited representation in village government and other leadership positions described above, in both villages, historically few women attended village decision-making meetings (*musyawarah desa*, or *MusDes*) and village development planning meetings (*Musyawarah Perencanaan Pembangunan Desa*, or *Musrenbangdes*), at least before the establishment of the Women's School group in Wringinanom. In the Bungah control village, few villagers overall, and even fewer women, have been able to attend such 'community' meetings, as participation has been by invitation only and limited to the PKK chairperson and sometimes the secretary or treasurer. These women have rarely advocated for village development initiatives that are of priority to women, except for requesting a village fund allocation to fix the early childhood education building.[19]

In the Wringinanom site before the CSO interventions, there was low participation by women in village meetings as they were rarely invited and dared not just turn up. Attending and actively participating in *MusDes* was nerve-racking for many women interviewed, with Indah reflecting:

> [S]eeing them [government officials] in uniforms made us scared. Not only that, we felt reluctant to approach the village government. Back then it was really difficult for us. Even entering the village office is a rare thing for us to do.

Women's growing influence: Exerting pressure, using networks, negotiating spaces

Despite these barriers, through the Women's School, more women in Wringinanom have sought to grow their power and influence in these more institutionalised, state-led decision-making forums. This has included collecting and using poverty data to lobby the government, which gave women a useful and non-confrontational way to directly engage with the village government on pressing issues in their villages. This, together with other forms of action, grew the legitimacy of the women's groups in villages, which was crucial for them to develop their activities and to later have increased presence and voice in village forums. These processes were absent in the Bungah village.

The public speaking skills, gender awareness and confidence fostered via the Women's School helped members and other women participate in public forums and in their advocacy (together with KPS2K staff) to be invited to *MusDes* and *Musrenbangdes*, in which women's social and gender development priorities were generally overlooked. Building on their growing engagement with village leaders, they repeatedly contacted the village head via WhatsApp, called him for updates and found ways to meet

---

19 Very few other villagers go to these meetings and, even then, they only tend to participate when financial incentives are offered; programs that offer no incentives lack participants in meetings or other activities. Moreover, when the income generated from the villagers' livelihood surpasses the incentives offered for participation in government programs, villagers are less inclined to give up their time to participate. One villager explained: 'In this village, with a little bit of work, they can get money … It is difficult to encourage [the villagers] to participate [in activities] when there's no money offered.'

him in everyday settings, also reaching out to other leaders to advocate on their behalf. Using such a relational approach through informal, everyday spaces and relationships, and leveraging new and expanding networks, is one strategy women used to access and influence more formal decision-making strategies and forums.

Such pressure eventually resulted in Women's School representatives being invited to attend the *Musrenbangdes*. During the forum, Women's School members for the first time were brave enough to read out the 10 key women's needs they had identified before the *Musrenbangdes*. Partway through, they were instructed to stop by organisers, who considered their contribution to be too long and wasting time:

> At the beginning I went with friends. We were not invited, but we always asked the village head, 'When is the village *Musrenbang*? When is it? When is it?' So, because we asked so often, after a while he was overwhelmed … The Women's School also wanted to attend the *Musrenbangdes* … In the end, we were invited … There were 10 proposals, but the four suggested [by a Women's School cadre] were rejected.

Women's priorities were not initially accommodated by the village government and, as is common, infrastructure was prioritised. The Women's School cadres thus shifted their lobbying attention to the district government for support, highlighting how Women's School participation and influence in village development were aligned with the district's gender-inclusion priorities. The women leveraged their growing networks with district leaders developed through participation in district events, workshops and planning efforts—often initially facilitated by KPS2K.

For example, KPS2K had informally engaged and gained the commitment of influential actors in the district government to be gender-responsive in their programs and allocate funds. In 2016, under a new district government, KPS2K personally engaged key young actors in the District Development Planning Agency (Bappeda) and the Family Planning, Women's Empowerment and Child Protection Office. These actors were considered to be both open-minded and in strategic positions of influence, particularly given their authority in developing the District Medium-Term Development Plan and their capacity to navigate the bureaucracy and frame women's empowerment in the appropriate language for the bureaucracy.

Slowly, Women's School members from villages were drawn into planning and advocacy processes. This resulted in not only new networks for village women and access to powerholders, but also new government efforts to accommodate the interests of women and children by initiating a district *Musrenbang* especially for women. One of the Bappeda staff explained:

> Recommendations related to women's needs are heard [in the forum]. [For] the women's *Musrenbangdes*, besides inviting women's organisations, we also invite women at the grassroots level, because we want to have a clear picture of what their basic needs are. Their needs are not usually echoed in the media, nor heard in [conventional] forums, so women are more reluctant to have a voice. When they are among fellow women, we can know, 'Oh, what women need is this, or that', so we can focus more on what they actually need.

Later, when their participation and funding were blocked by the village, Women's School lobbying (with KSP2K) to the district government through their networks saw the village government acquiesce to district pressure. Indah explains:

> The district head supported us … We had proven the function of the Women's School to the district and the district government officials. It wasn't just us in the Women's Schools who did the work, there were also district committees like the monitoring committee. So … we worked together. That is why in 2017 we began attending the village *Musrenbang*. At the *Musrenbangdes* we really pursued village funding. It was in 2017 that such goals began to be realised [with a fund allocation].

Here, we see how women worked together and used multiple strategies to exercise leadership and influence, also tapping multiple networks for support—or what we call women's 'networked collective action'. The outcome of such leadership and multiple sources of pressure on the village government was the official recognition of the Women's School members as participants in village meetings and funding for initiatives. Further, despite the entrenchment of patriarchal norms, after five years of collective efforts, women in Wringinanom also influenced village development by working with KPS2K and village leaders to develop new regulations to support gender inclusiveness and support for the Women's School, including a funding allocation for the schools to build women's knowledge and skills. Again, such processes of change were not observed in the Bungah control village.

Networked collective action

In the discussion above, we can see the ways women in the Wringinanom research village made significant efforts to establish relationships and networks of trust with authoritative actors with influence over governance processes and social norms, which contributed to what we conceptualise as women's *networked collective action*.[20] That is, the efforts taken by women and other actors to collectively influence governance, development, policy programs and structures of power to be more gender inclusive. *Networked collective action* involved women building or strengthening *webs of interdependence* with other women (through groups and informal spaces), and webs of trust with other community members, especially authoritative actors, often through engagement in everyday settings. It then involved women leveraging their newly established or existing networks to garner support for their cause.

This support then created multiple sources of pressure on authoritative actors such as the village government and, ultimately, decision-making forums and other power structures, to influence outcomes. Such processes were helpful for overcoming challenges, particularly resistance to gender inclusiveness among authoritative and influential figures. Women's informal spaces and more formal groups bolstered this process by extending networks, providing a new arena in which to build individual and collective agency through shared knowledge, skills and resources, providing mutual support and a source of protection, and fostering a sense of solidarity and collective agency.

Women's networked collective action across scales also influenced district actors to make greater investments in women's health issues as well as education extension programs for women. Such action has also influenced the regulatory environment in relation to child marriage, as one school member explains:

> We made recommendations in the subdistrict and district *Musrenbang*. KPS2K has always advocated for eliminating child marriage. We approached district government offices and we alerted them to the consequences of child marriages for women's economic wellbeing, domestic violence, maternal mortality and children's health.

---

20 Our findings on processes of 'women's networked collective action' were like those for other research sites in the larger study (Diprose et al. 2020).

As a result, in 2018, the district government published a circular letter on the elimination of child marriage, which gives instruction to government officials to wind back endorsement of such marriages.

Brokering spaces and networks

We can also see from the case above how KPS2K and KAPAL Perempuan performed a brokerage role for the poorer, more marginalised women in Wringinanom in connecting them to the structures of power across scales (Diprose 2023), such as to the district government and the National Insurance Scheme. These CSOs supported poor women to grow their power and influence in ways that were not observed in Bungah, where individual women and existing elite-dominated women's groups were limited in their ability to counter power structures without diversified mobilising structures.

The CSO's role in connecting women to structures of power was also interrelated with networked collective action among grassroots members. We also saw this in the ways the Women's School connected to the district officials to in turn pressure resistant village elites, but also for wider-scale development planning in the district to give increasing attention to women's needs (cf. Diprose 2023). CSOs brokered spaces for women's influence on powerholders by negotiating with powerful state and non-state actors, so women were increasingly recognised and invited into spaces where power was exercised (cf. Diprose 2023). Working with strategic actors in the bureaucracy also resulted in changes to the nomenclature and priorities outlined in the District Family Planning, Women's Empowerment and Child Protection Agency budget in 2018 to provide support for KAPAL Perempuan/KPS2K's Women's Schools and a district policy to replicate the Women's Schools in 10 other villages. This was given further endorsement through its inclusion in the 2016–21 Gresik District Medium-Term Development Plan. Women's Schools have been replicated in other places with funding from districts, with the women in Wringinanom sharing their knowledge and experience with other women in this process.

Conclusion

For women in rural Indonesia who are deeply embedded in intimate social networks on which they rely, collective action does not necessarily involve overt public demonstrations of protest against powerholders from whom they are personally distant. Rather, it involves creating connections both among women and with others to mutually pursue change in status quo power relations in ways that minimise overt confrontation—for example, by seeking new everyday interactions with other authoritative social and political actors to build trust for later support and *networked collective action*.

Growing the confidence of women to approach authoritative actors in our intervention site was built on the skills, capacity, knowledge and mutual support developed through the new CSO-supported women's groups. Our study therefore shows interrelations between the space of the Women's School, created through the CSO intervention, and more amorphous everyday spaces and strategies. The formation of coalitions of influence also relied on growing support from influential powerholders through everyday interactions. Building trust and multiple sources of pressure together then saw women increasingly able to create or access spaces in which power is exercised in rural Indonesia, including more institutionalised, state-sanctioned spaces.

Women in the villages discussed above, and in many other villages in our wider study (Diprose et al. 2020), have traditionally been less represented in 'invited', state-sanctioned spaces where power is exercised, such as in electoral politics, holding office or participating in village decision-making. It was only in the empowerment-focused CSO intervention village in Wringinanom where significant change in women's influence in village development was observed.

The Women's School and its networks have contributed to significant impacts on women's wellbeing, including changes in gendered household relations, gaining access to services, new village and district funding and regulations, group recognition, the assertion of women's rights and slowly changing gender norms. These dynamics were not present in our Bungah research village, where only poorly attended state-sanctioned women's groups were permitted and legitimated. Limiting support to certain women's groups such as the PKK constrains who can voice their concerns and effect change, as well as perpetuating norms about the 'types' of participants in governance and politics.

Creating new groups aimed at growing women's sources of mutual support and power, and augmenting more amorphous spaces for women to connect, allows for reflexive possibilities in which participants, especially those from marginalised groups, can identify shared problems as well as imagine alternative realities. In Wringinanom, these interactions have sown seeds of solidarity on which women have drawn to exercise their collective influence to create positive change for themselves, their peers and their community.

In finding opportunities and through more amorphous social arenas of engagement with powerholders, women disrupt overwhelmingly male-dominated sites of decision-making, which often cause women to feel afraid and unwelcome, such as spaces associated with the village government. Feminist scholars have long problematised binaries between private/public spheres and formal/informal politics, arguing that often politics involving the private sphere (for example, gendered divisions of labour, reproduction and parenting) is delegitimised by imparting certain values and capacities on this sphere (Volpp 2017). A formal/informal binary also risks deeming some forms of community participation in decision-making and policymaking legitimate and other types of organising as illegitimate (Miraftab 2004; McEwan 2005). We must therefore be attuned to how distinguishing between formal and informal politics can, if treated uncritically, associate formal, organised politics with 'male forms of political organising' and confine women's organising to 'informal organising', denying 'the struggle which took place to redefine the personal into the political' (Brownill and Halford 1990: 397).

The *webs of interdependence* we have examined grew out of everyday interactions and friendships between group members, training programs and the multiple spaces where women exercised their influence, including households and hospitals as well as village and district forums. By centring the formation of *webs of interdependence*, we have complicated a binary between formal and informal spaces, instead emphasising how poor, marginalised women claimed space for themselves, together forming solidarity and exercising strategies across multiple issues and spheres, from reproductive health to participation in village development.

We have also shown how women's CSOs can take on an important role in augmenting, structuring, resourcing and organising processes of recruitment, knowledge, trust-building and network creation among women, in contexts where groups are otherwise absent, fragile or less inclusive for the most marginalised women. In so doing, CSOs broker marginal groups' power bases through strengthening organising structures and sources of knowledge/resources and their horizontal networks, connecting women across space, class and social issues (Diprose 2023). They also broker spaces for women's influence on powerholders through direct negotiations and brokering networks with authoritative actors to build supporting coalitions of influence.

References

Agarwal, Bina. 2000. 'Conceptualising Environmental Collective Action: Why Gender Matters.' *Cambridge Journal of Economics* 24, no. 3: 283–310. doi.org/10.1093/cje/24.3.283.

Akbar, Aulia, Johannes Flacke, Javier Martinez, and Martin F.A.M. van Maarseveen. 2020. 'Participatory Planning Practice in Rural Indonesia: A Sustainable Development Goals-Based Evaluation.' *Community Development* 51, no. 3: 243–60. doi.org/10.1080/15575330.2020.1765822.

Aspinall, Edward, Sally White, and Amalinda Savirani. 2021. 'Women's Political Representation in Indonesia: Who Wins and How?' *Journal of Current Southeast Asian Affairs* 40, no. 1: 3–27. doi.org/10.1177/1868103421989720.

Batliwala, Srilatha. 2007. 'Taking the Power Out of Empowerment: An Experiential Account.' *Development in Practice* 17, nos 4–5: 557–65. doi.org/10.1080/09614520701469559.

Bayo, Longgina Novadona. 2021. 'Women Who Persist: Pathways to Power in Eastern Indonesia.' *Journal of Current Southeast Asian Affairs* 40, no. 1: 93–115. doi.org/10.1177/1868103421989712.

Bierschenk, Thomas, Jean-Pierre Chauveau, and Jean-Pierre Olivier de Sardan. 2002. *Local Development Brokers in Africa: The Rise of a New Social Category.* Working Paper 13. Mainz: Department of Anthropology and African Studies, Johannes Gutenberg University.

Blackburn, Susan. 2004. *Women and the State in Modern Indonesia.* Cambridge: Cambridge University Press. doi.org/10.1017/CBO9780511492198.

Brownill, Sue, and Susan Halford. 1990. 'Understanding Women's Involvement in Local Politics: How Useful is a Formal/Informal Dichotomy?' *Political Geography Quarterly* 9, no. 4: 396–414. doi.org/10.1016/0260-9827(90)90036-A.

Cho, Sumi, Kimberlé W. Crenshaw, and Leslie McCall. 2013. 'Toward a Field of Intersectionality Studies: Theory, Applications, and Praxis.' *Signs: Journal of Women in Culture and Society* 38, no. 4: 785–810. doi.org/10.1086/669608.

Cornwall, Andrea. 2016. 'Women's Empowerment: What Works?' *Journal of International Development* 28, no. 3: 342–59. doi.org/10.1002/jid.3210.

Davies, Sharyn Graham. 2005. 'Women in Politics in Indonesia in the Decade Post-Beijing.' *International Social Science Journal* 57, no. 184: 231–42. doi.org/10.1111/j.1468-2451.2005.00547.x.

Davis, Diane E. 2017. 'Informality and State Theory: Some Concluding Remarks.' *Current Sociology* 65, no. 2: 315–24. doi.org/10.1177/0011392116657301.

Dharmawan, Leni, Gregorius D.V. Pattinasarany, and Lily Hoo. 2018. *Participation, Transparency and Accountability in Village Law Implementation: Baseline Findings from the Sentinel Villages Study*. Jakarta: Local Solutions to Poverty and The World Bank.

Diprose, Rachael. 2023. 'Brokerage, Power and Gender Equity: How Empowerment-Focused Civil Society Organisations Bolster Women's Influence in Rural Indonesia.' *Journal of International Development* 35, no. 3: 401–25. doi.org/10.1002/jid.3770.

Diprose, Rachael, Amalinda Savirani, Ken M.P. Setiawan, and Naomi Francis. 2020. *Women's Collective Action and the Village Law: How Women are Driving Change and Shaping Pathways for Gender-Inclusive Development in Rural Indonesia*. Working Paper. Melbourne: The Australia–Indonesia Partnership for Gender Equality and Women's Empowerment, University of Melbourne, and Universitas Gadjah Mada. doi.org/10.46580/124326.

Dulhunty, Annabel. 2021. 'Gendered Isolation, Idealised Communities and the Role of Collective Power in West Bengal Self-Help Groups.' *Gender, Place & Culture* 28, no. 5: 725–46. doi.org/10.1080/0966369X.2020.1754167.

Evans, Alison, and Divya Nambiar. 2013. *Collective Action and Women's Agency: A Background Paper*. Washington, DC: World Bank Group. hdl.handle.net/10986/21032.

Jakimow, Tanya. 2020. *Susceptibility in Development: Micropolitics of Local Development in India and Indonesia*. Oxford: Oxford University Press. doi.org/10.1093/oso/9780198854739.001.0001.

James, Deborah. 2011. 'The Return of the Broker: Consensus, Hierarchy, and Choice in South African Land Reform.' *Journal of the Royal Anthropological Institute* 17, no. 2: 318–38. doi.org/10.1111/j.1467-9655.2011.01682.x.

Kabeer, Naila. 1994. *Reversed Realities: Gender Hierarchies in Development Thought*. London: Verso.

Kabeer, Naila. 2011. 'Between Affiliation and Autonomy: Navigating Pathways of Women's Empowerment and Gender Justice in Rural Bangladesh.' *Development and Change* 42, no. 2: 499–528. doi.org/10.1111/j.1467-7660.2011.01703.x.

Lindquist, Johan. 2015. 'Brokers and Brokerage, Anthropology of.' In *International Encyclopedia of the Social and Behavioral Sciences*, edited by James D. Wright, 870–74. 2nd ed. Amsterdam: Elsevier. doi.org/10.1016/B978-0-08-097086-8. 12178-6.

McEwan, Cheryl. 2005. 'New Spaces of Citizenship? Rethinking Gendered Participation and Empowerment in South Africa.' *Political Geography* 24, no. 8: 969–91. doi.org/10.1016/j.polgeo.2005.05.001.

McGee, Rosie. 2016. 'Power and Empowerment Meet Resistance: A Critical, Action-Oriented Review of the Literature.' *IDS Bulletin* 47, no. 5: 103–18. doi.org/10.19088/1968-2016.170.

Miraftab, Faranak. 2004. 'Invited and Invented Spaces of Participation: Neoliberal Citizenship and Feminists' Expanded Notion of Politics.' *Wagadu* 1: 1–7.

Miraftab, Faranak. 2020. 'Insurgency and Juxtacity in the Age of Urban Divides.' *Urban Forum* 31: 433–41. doi.org/10.1007/s12132-020-09401-9.

Pandolfelli, Lauren, Ruth Meinzen-Dick, and Stephan Dohrn. 2008. 'Gender and Collective Action: Motivations, Effectiveness and Impact.' *Journal of International Development* 20, no. 1: 1–11. doi.org/10.1002/jid.1424.

Parker, Lyn, and Laura Dales. 2014. 'Introduction: The Everyday Agency of Women in Asia.' *Asian Studies Review* 38, no. 2: 164–67. doi.org/10.1080/10357823. 2014.899313.

Pohlman, Annie. 2017. 'The Spectre of Communist Women, Sexual Violence and Citizenship in Indonesia.' *Sexualities* 20, nos 1–2: 196–211. doi.org/10.1177/ 1363460716645789.

Prabaningrum, Galih, and Norin Mustika Rahadiri Abheseka. 2020. 'Increasing Women's Political Capacities and Advocacy for Accessing Village Fund Allocations through the Women's School.' In *Membuka Jalan untuk Pembangunan Inklusif Gender di Daerah Perdesaan Indonesia: Bunga Rampai Kajian Aksi Kolektif Perempuan dan Pengaruhnya pada Pelaksanaan Undang-Undang Desa* [*Forging Pathways for Gender-Inclusive Development in Rural Indonesia: Case Studies of Women's Collective Action and Influence on Village Law Implementation*], edited by Amalinda Savirani, Rachael Diprose, Annisa Sabrina Hartoto, and Ken M.P. Setiawan, 111–36. Working Paper. Melbourne: The Australia–Indonesia Partnership for Gender Equality and Women's Empowerment, University of Melbourne, and Universitas Gadjah Mada. doi.org/10.46580/124328.

Prihatini, Ella S. 2019a. 'Women Who Win in Indonesia: The Impact of Age, Experience, and List Position.' *Women's Studies International Forum* 72: 40–46. doi.org/10.1016/j.wsif.2018.10.003.

Prihatini, Ella S. 2019b. 'Women's Views and Experiences of Accessing National Parliament: Evidence from Indonesia.' *Women's Studies International Forum* 74: 84–90. doi.org/10.1016/j.wsif.2019.03.001.

Prihatini, Ella S. 2020. 'Islam, Parties, and Women's Political Nomination in Indonesia.' *Politics & Gender* 16, no. 3: 637–59. doi.org/10.1017/S1743923X 19000321.

Radar Surabaya. 2018. 'Nikah Dini, Janda Gresik Makin Banyak [Early Marriage, Gresik Widows Increasing].' *Radar Surabaya*, 2 February. radarsurabaya.jawapos. com/jatim/02/02/2018/nikah-dini-janda-gresik-makin-banyak/.

Rowlands, J. 1997. *Questioning Empowerment: Working with Women in Honduras.* Oxford: Oxfam. doi.org/10.3362/9780855988364.

Setiawan, Ken M.P., and Dirk Tomsa. 2022. *Politics in Contemporary Indonesia: Institutional Change, Policy Challenges and Democratic Decline.* London: Routledge. doi.org/10.4324/9780429459511.

Suryakusuma, Julia. 1987. 'State Ibuism: The Social Construction of Womanhood in New Order Indonesia.' MA thesis, Institute of Social Studies, The Hague.

Syukri, Muhammad, Palmira Bachtiar, Asep Kurniawan, Gema Satria Mayang Sedyadi, Kartawijaya, Rendy Adriyan Diningrat, and Ulfah Alifia. 2017. *Study on the Implementation of the Law No. 6/2014 on Villages: A Baseline Report.* April. Jakarta: SMERU Research Institute. smeru.or.id/en/publication/study-implementation-law-no-62014-villages-baseline-report.

Volpp, Leti. 2017. 'Feminist, Sexual, and Queer Citizenship.' In *The Oxford Handbook of Citizenship*, edited by Ayelet Shachar, Rainer Bauböck, Irene Bloemraad, and Maarten Vink, 153–77. Oxford: Oxford University Press. doi.org/10.1093/oxfordhb/9780198805854.013.7.

Wieringa, Saskia. 2002. *Sexual Politics in Indonesia.* New York: Palgrave Macmillan. doi.org/10.1057/9781403919922.

14

Resistance Through Care: Japan's Technical Intern Training Program

Serena Eleonora Ford

Facing a demographic crisis because of its ageing population and declining birthrate, Japan has been pressured to introduce a number of reforms to increase the labour force, while keeping its typically restrictive immigration policies in place (Oishi 2021; Endoh 2021). Migration scholars working on Japan have typically noted the use of 'side-door' or 'backdoor' channels for workers to enter the country via 'unofficial immigration' avenues (Tian 2019: 1496; Chung 2021; Endoh 2021), wherein visa categories or migration programs are not formally recognised as labour migration programs or avenues for guestwork, but are concealed with the use of ambiguous or unclear language to appease potentially xenophobic voters (Endoh 2019, 2021; Surak 2018; Roberts 2018). One program under which migration to counter the labour shortages is possible is the Technical Intern Training Program (TITP). The TITP is a government initiative that ostensibly upskills young people from neighbouring Asian countries in Japan, but also serves as a stopgap measure to counter critical labour shortages in small and medium-sized enterprises across the country (Hironaka and Yamada 2022; Tian 2019; Mazumi 2019; Demelius 2020; Oishi 1995).

For nearly 30 years, the TITP has attracted criticism from activists in Japan and abroad. Advocates for TITP trainees in Japan have vocally argued for the abolition of the program and pushed for reform, directly challenging the state and working as activists to promote TITP trainees' labour rights, including demonstrating on the street or outside government offices after cases of alleged labour rights or human rights abuses (Surak 2018; Kremers 2014). However, another, quieter coalition of advocates across Japanese and Vietnamese communities supporting TITP trainees works in solidarity to reverse the harms generated by the TITP, through the provision of care—including affective support, housing, reproductive support and so on—to trainees, without necessarily targeting the TITP itself.

This division between those who challenge the program and those who supplement the gaps is also captured in the literature, with some scholars condemning the program outright and arguing for its immediate dismantlement and others suggesting more reform and care practices be implemented to mitigate the harsh consequences of the scheme. For instance, Tian (2019: 1508) refers to the TITP as 'an extremely restrictive, exclusionist, and profoundly illiberal guest worker programme that does not even fully recognise its participants as labourers'. Liu-Farrer (2020: 5) argues that the '[d]emographic crisis is a long-term structural problem that can't be addressed by temporary labor imports'—a point stressed also by Ogawa (2020: 121), who suggests that 'the whole society will collapse without an adequately regulated labor migration channel, sustainable through ensuring decent working conditions and strengthening human rights protection'. These scholars clearly condemn the TITP as an unsustainable and damaging system and their arguments sit squarely within the consensus in TITP scholarship that the program is controversial and problematic (Yoshida 2021; Shipper 2002; Roberts 2018; Kim 2021; Sasaki 2020; Bélanger and Giang 2013; Oishi 1995, 2021).

Other scholars, while not overtly promoting the TITP, argue for a different approach in caring for and supporting trainees, without necessarily dismantling the TITP itself. Kuwano and McMaster (2020) argue for new approaches in both medical services and welfare, to ensure the provisioning of culturally sensitive care to TITP trainees in need, while Shinohara et al. (2021) suggest that Japan's immigration system is immature relative to Western countries, leading to an insufficient level of support in healthcare provisioning for trainees in the system. They suggest an improvement in the accessibility of resources for TITP trainees, rather than an overhaul of the whole system (Shinohara et al. 2021). Arita et al. (2022) also write on TITP trainee wellbeing and acknowledge that trainees face increased risks of mental health issues due to participation in the program, compared with other migrant groups in Japan. They argue that improved social supports are fundamental for improving trainees' mental wellbeing in Japan (Arita et al. 2022). While these scholars identify and acknowledge problems within the TITP, they still argue for changes to the system's design as it stands and promote increased inflows and supports for trainees to mitigate some of the program's harmful effects.

Drawing on these bodies of literature, this chapter attempts to bring both perspectives together to argue that trainees in Japan's TITP experience harm from a lack of care from the Japanese state, but that by providing care and inflows to support trainees, Japanese and Vietnamese advocates resist the depletive status quo of the TITP without taking on an overtly revolutionary tone. First, this chapter examines the origins of the TITP, then introduces a feminist international political economy theory as a framework to understand the lack of care and support for TITP trainees, known as 'depletion through social reproduction', and combines it with studies of everyday resistance to understand quieter forms of subversion in the TITP. Next, this chapter looks specifically at a civil society organisation known as Tomoiki (Japan–Vietnam Tomoiki Support Association), which provides support for Vietnamese trainees in Japan and suggests that by so doing, depletion in the TITP is mitigated, trainees are replenished and proposals for societal transformation to reverse the harmful effects of the TITP are made.

I first came across the TITP as a 20-year-old student a few years into my Bachelor of Asian Studies degree. For several weeks, I interned at a feminist organisation in Tokyo, the Asia–Japan Women's Resource Centre, which works closely with transnational feminist groups in the Asia-Pacific to support Vietnamese trainees entering Japan through the program. It was this initial exposure to transnational feminist activism in Japan that sparked my interest in the interrelationship between advocacy, social reproduction, depletion and labour migration.

Being neither Japanese nor Vietnamese and engaging with Asia-Pacific advocacy groups as an undergraduate from a Global North university, my analysis of the TITP involves risks. These include blind spots that might essentialise the experiences of Vietnamese workers in the program or the advocates who work alongside them (Rajan and Thornhill 2019; Lee and Chang 2023). I also risk positioning Vietnamese trainees as lacking agency in terms of their views of the program and its outcomes (Rajan and Thornhill 2019).

For these reasons, my aim is to maintain dialogue with the advocates and trainees about whom I write (Lira et al. 2019; Au 2019). My honours thesis, on which this chapter is based, was sent to Tomoiki and the Asia–Japan Women's Resource Centre. Their insights and perspectives on the TITP are ones that I bring with me into this chapter.

The Technical Intern Training Program in Japan: An overview

According to Japan's Ministry of Justice, there were 181,957 Vietnamese trainees residing in Japan at the end of June 2022, accounting for 55 per cent of total TITP trainee numbers in Japan (MOJ 2022). Vietnamese remain the largest proportion of foreign workers in Japan (Vietnam News Agency 2023). The latest figures show women constitute 42.5 per cent of the TITP trainee workforce (OTIT 2022) and it is generally believed that Vietnamese women (and other women migrant workers in Japan) tend to work in feminised industries including manufacturing, agriculture, food processing and service-oriented work in restaurants (CGD 2021)— consistent with other regions in the Asia-Pacific (Vijeyarasa and Liu 2022; Bourke-Martignoni et al. 2018). In 2022, 23.2 per cent of Vietnamese trainees worked in food processing, 21.6 per cent in construction, 15.8 per cent in assembly and welding and 6.8 per cent in agriculture, among other sectors (MOJ 2022). These Vietnamese workers enter Japan as 'trainees' under the auspices of the TITP.

The TITP originated from a labour transfer scheme in the 1950s under which workers in Japanese companies situated abroad could come to Japan temporarily and learn skills to improve work performance at home. This intraregional training scheme was possible due to Japan's involvement with the Colombo Plan for Cooperative Economic and Social Development in Asia and the Pacific beginning in 1954, which allowed thousands of trainees from South Korea, Taiwan, Indonesia, Thailand and Malaysia to enter Japan and upskill in certain technologies for the benefit of their home countries' developmental advancement (The Colombo Plan Secretariat 2024; Surak 2018).

The program was operated largely under the management of the Japan International Cooperation Agency and attracted some 48,000 trainees between 1954 and 1977 (Surak 2018). Surak (2018) notes that, by 1982, there were 10,000 intracompany trainees, which increased to 23,000 by 1988. By the late 1980s, Japan started to experience severe labour shortages in small manufacturing firms, which lacked access to capital for investing in labour-saving equipment or the option to invest in the labour market abroad (de Carvalho 2003). Concurrently, the number of overstaying migrants increased to more than 10 million people, at which stage the trainee system was reformed to allow Japanese companies with no international operations to also recruit trainees through mediating institutions, including chambers of commerce and industry and small enterprise associations (Shipper 2002; Yoshida 2021). Over the following decade, the TITP system was reformed and expanded several times to increase the intake of trainees into small and medium-sized enterprises across Japan, often coinciding exactly with periods of economic downturn and labour shortages, which explains Japan's dependency on the TITP (Shipper 2002; Oishi 1995; Surak 2018). Nevertheless, the system has never ceased to be described as an initiative for upskilling trainees to improve the economic development of their home countries (OTIT n.d.; JITCO n.d.).

These days, the TITP is widely acknowledged by activists and scholars in both Japan and Vietnam as a thinly veiled guestworker program, which serves to counter the demographic woes facing contemporary Japan and does not deliver on its stated aims of upskilling foreign workers but rather appoints them to sectors and industries where there are critical labour shortages (Mazumi 2019; Tian 2019; Bélanger et al. 2011; Bélanger and Giang 2013; Tran 2020). Vietnamese workers started working in the TITP in greater numbers in the early 2010s and, in 2016, overtook Chinese workers as the largest cohort of foreign labourers living in Japan through the TITP (Tran 2020). The TITP, while sustaining its public mission statement as being designed for international cooperation and development (JITCO n.d.; OTIT n.d.), has attracted international condemnation from civil society groups, foreign governments and human rights advocates for facilitating widespread abuse and exploitation of trainees (Department of State 2020, 2021, 2022; Sasaki 2020; Tian 2019). Some scholars have referred to the TITP as a form of 'modern-day slavery' (Sasaki 2020: 247).

One sobering fact to illustrate this is the rate of deaths on the program. Between 2012 and 2017, the Ministry of Justice of Japan reported that 171 trainees had died while undergoing training through the TITP (MHLW 2017; Osumi 2019). This reporting prompted immediate condemnation from the US Department of State, which declared Japan a Tier 2 country for human trafficking in 2017—namely, identifying Japan as a country that does not meet the minimum standards for the elimination of trafficking (Department of State 2017). In response, Japan introduced several new laws and labour protections for TITP trainees and established the Organization for Technical Intern Trainees (OTIT) to monitor and audit companies recruiting TITP trainees (JITCO n.d.; Yoshida 2021; Department of State 2018). This resulted in an improved standing in the US State Department's rankings from 2018 to 2019, when Japan ranked in Tier 1—meeting the minimum standards. Nevertheless, reports of abuse continued. By the end of 2018, 9,052 trainees had 'fled' their workplaces, with half of these being Vietnamese workers (Tran 2020), followed by another 8,796 in 2019 (MOJ 2021). From 2020 to 2022, Japan has continuously been ranked as a Tier 2 country for failing to counter human trafficking through the TITP, among other measures. The US State Department's ranking system also merits caution as a tool for measuring human trafficking. The *Trafficking in Persons* report does not provide explanation of how national data have been compiled or whether it has comparative analysis in other languages, and it is questionable whether the US Government is adequately neutral to make accurate assessments of other states (Vijeyarasa 2015; Gallagher 2011). Even at Tier 1 status, it is possible that trainees' situation in Japan was dire.

An underlying factor of the level of abuse reported on the TITP is the Japanese Government's failure to account for trainees' wellbeing. The OTIT sits underneath the Ministry of Justice and the Ministry of Health, Labour and Welfare, but observers have continued to argue that the agency is far too understaffed to make a difference. For example, in 2020 there were just 350 staff in the OTIT, covering more than 7,300 companies (Department of State 2019). In this environment of poor regulation, employers are not penalised sufficiently to incentivise proper conduct within the workplace in terms of providing adequate living space or inflows to sustain trainees' wellbeing. The reported insufficient and unsanitary housing provided for trainees by their employers (CCC 2020), as well as constant oversight of trainees' personal lives and overwork in the workplace, can lead to depletion— what feminists define as the harmful outcome of a devaluation and lack of inflow to support the social reproduction of individuals, households and communities (Rai et al. 2014). The next section will elaborate on depletion in the TITP and the ways it is resisted in the context of Japan.

Depletion and everyday resistance

Depletion through social reproduction theory is a feminist framework developed by Shirin Rai, Catherine Hoskyns and Dania Thomas (2014), which emerges out of ongoing debates about the unacknowledged contributions of individuals and communities performing social reproductive work. It focuses on the negative consequences for people who perform this labour, when excessively relied upon, in global economies (Rai et al. 2014). Social reproduction here is defined as biological reproduction, unpaid production of goods and services within the home and the reproduction of cultural beliefs and ideologies (Rai et al. 2014). Depletion of an individual occurs when they are performing excessive amounts of both productive (wage labour) work and social reproductive work in a given context, without the inflows (such as adequate rest, leisure time or maintenance of social networks) needed to recharge and replenish after labouring hours (Rai et al. 2014). Depletion has been mapped in cases of dispossession (Fernandez 2018), natural disasters (Tanyag 2018), in export-oriented zones (Gunawardana 2016) and in settler-colonial settings (Chilmeran and Pratt 2019). Depletion can also occur in cases where individuals and communities cannot or are prohibited from biologically reproducing, performing unpaid work in the home or practising cultural beliefs freely, given the crucial roles these activities play in supporting healthy social relations and individual health (Chilmeran and Pratt 2019; Rai et al. 2014).

In the past, scholars working on the TITP have frequently attributed the bodily harm and suffering of trainees to insufficient labour laws (Shipper 2002; Bélanger et al. 2011; Sasaki 2020; Hayakawa and Barnes 2017), but beginning in 2017, the Japanese Government introduced a new law to protect trainees' labour rights, the *Technical Intern Training Act*, which grants trainees the same rights as Japanese workers, including maximum working hours, a minimum wage and parental leave (Department of State 2017; JITCO n.d.). Nevertheless, reports of abuse and harm have not reduced (see the next section). This is suggestive of a deeper structural issue that transcends work rights issues. To this end, depletion is a useful framework for analysing how trainees' lives and treatment in the workplace, where productive work takes place, intersect with their social reproduction outside training spaces. Depletion acknowledges violence and bodily harm even in contexts where trainees may consent to the work or are not engaged in obvious forced labour as such. This is because the framework is used to measure 'invisible' harms that stem from the unacknowledged overwork that occurs outside formal workplaces, as well as inside them, and is less reliant on more 'visible' indicators of forced labour (Rai et al. 2014; Johnston and Lingham 2021).

Beyond the 'obviously depleting effects' of labour under poor conditions, depletion sees productive and social reproductive labour as intimately connected to each other, and labour time and wages, rather than the effects of certain kinds of labour, as the main indicators of and risk factors for bodily harm (Johnston and Lingham 2021: 12). Under Japan's TITP, where reports of overwork are rife and trainees do not have sufficient hours for rest (Verité 2018; Yoshida 2021; Kamibayashi 2013), there is also a lack of sufficient support from the Japanese Government to provide inflows to help Vietnamese trainees recover or replenish from their labouring hours, which has been noted by civil society organisations across Japan (Solidarity Network with Migrants Japan 2019). This has a cumulative effect on trainees' bodies, with individuals unable to keep up with the labouring demands of the system and simultaneously practise social reproduction or simply replenish from their hours of output. The consequence of this unsustainable lifestyle is a deterioration in the health and wellbeing of individuals (Rai et al. 2014), which is evident in the statistics of trainee distress, discussed in the next section.

As with other contexts in the Asia-Pacific (Vijeyarasa and Liu 2022), in Japan, regulation and oversight of the labouring conditions of TITP trainees are very poor and often the government defers the responsibility to care for and attend to the needs of Vietnamese trainees to civil society groups. These groups fill the gap by providing inflows to support trainees where they are missing (Tian 2019) as well as vocally resisting the status quo of the program. Civil society groups have made overt demands to the government to reform or scrap the program and this work has largely been undertaken by lawyer-advocates (Kremer 2014), labour unions and migrant advocacy groups, such as the well-known Zentoitsu Workers' Union and Solidarity Network with Migrants Japan, both headed by Trafficking in Persons Hero Ippei Torii, who uses methods such as public protest and coalition-building with other civil society groups across Japan to condemn the TITP (TIP Report Heroes 2022). However, this resistance also takes place in much quieter forms at an everyday level, which helps reverse the depletion of trainees.

Resistance to depletion is complex and multifaceted. Due to the complication of measuring and identifying depletion in the first place (Rai et al. 2014), resistance against its negative effects should not be understood as manifesting in overt expressions of political protest but takes the form of everyday negotiation and struggle. To this end, discussions of everyday resistance prove a fruitful starting point to begin unpacking resistance against depletion in the TITP.

Everyday resistance is a theory posited by James C. Scott in 1985, exploring resistance that is quiet and less visible to the state or mainstream society and that is often not overtly politically articulated (Johansson and Vinthagen 2019). While everyday resistance has been explored and defined in a multitude of different ways, this chapter agrees with the theory posited by Johansson and Vinthagen (2016; Vinthagen and Johansson 2013) that this form of resistance, while still an oppositional activity against forms of domination, does not require a shared political consciousness or a coherent form of action or coalition-building. Everyday resistance is not an act that intends to fundamentally disrupt hierarchies of power that subordinate particular groups, but it can nevertheless carve out a space for these groups to create systems that serve their own interests within the constraints imposed by their subordination (Elias 2005; Johansson and Vinthagen 2015).

In the case of Japan's TITP, everyday resistance against depletion takes form through attempts to reverse it by Vietnamese and Japanese activists, who work together to care for Vietnamese trainees afflicted by abuse and harm in the system. If we draw on the theory of everyday resistance to understand the context of the TITP, we must first identify the power relationship that underpins the program and where the power lies. In the TITP, there is a power hierarchy between the state and trainees. Because the state neglects to provide adequate services and protections for trainees, it ultimately facilitates depletion within the system, which trainees therefore endure. Trainees are subordinated by this depletion, which is generated by the state, and it should therefore be seen as an effect of an unequal and dominating relationship. Framing depletion in the TITP as a form of domination, or at least a product of unequal power relationships that subordinate trainees, allows us to see the reversal of depletion by activists as a form of everyday resistance.

By assisting trainees to mitigate the stresses of their workload, providing support and inflows for trainees to recover from their labours and highlighting the lack of care afforded to these trainees by simply providing it themselves, activists challenge depletion in the everyday without overtly voicing their political resistance to the TITP. They carve out spaces for TITP trainees and other groups to recover from the dominating effects of depletion in the program. One association in Tokyo, the Japan–Vietnam Tomoiki Support Association (hereinafter Tomoiki), provides support to trainees and is a good site to examine everyday resistance and solidarity against the TITP through the provisioning of care. The next section builds on Tomoiki's work to illustrate the reversal of depletion and the resulting acts of everyday resistance contained therein.

Tomoiki: Mitigating, replenishing, transforming

Nisshinkutsu Temple (colloquially known as the Vietnamese Temple in Tokyo) first became a safe haven for Vietnamese migrants who had become homeless in Japan after the Tohoku earthquake in 2011, which formed part of Japan's triple disaster earthquake, tsunami and nuclear meltdown (Murakami 2020). Members of the temple formed the civil society organisation Tomoiki to promote positive Japan–Vietnam relations across the citizenry of Japan. However, they increasingly focused their energy on the TITP, starting in 2013, when the number of Vietnamese people entering Japan began accelerating and the abuse that other foreign trainees had faced before them began to surface more prominently in the Vietnamese community (Tomoiki n.d.[a]; Tran 2020). These days the temple serves as the headquarters of Tomoiki and as a place for trainees to seek refuge, with most of the organisation's members also running the temple, including head nun of Nisshinkutsu and leader of Tomoiki, Jiho Yoshimizu. Tomoiki states that, since 2014, its mission has been to support and protect the lives and human rights of Vietnamese trainees, prompted by a feeling of indignation at the number of young Vietnamese people losing their lives in Japan (Tomoiki n.d.[a]).[1] As Yoshimizu shared in 2020: 'We do everything. We take care of people from when they're inside the womb to when they're inside an urn' (Murakami 2020). Care is a key framework informing the activities of Tomoiki and works to reverse and resist the depletion of trainees in several ways.

---

1   Original quote in Japanese:「ベトナム人技能実習生、留学生などが若くして命を落とすことに憤りを感じ2014年より『命と人権を守る』支援活動を行う。」(Tomoiki n.d.[a]).

Tomoiki's activities align with Rai et al.'s (2014) original theory for reversing depletion—namely: mitigation, replenishment and transformation. Mitigation includes communities and collectives sharing stressful work; replenishment includes groups and institutions voluntarily assisting people to cope with depletion through social reproduction by providing inflows when they are missing; and transformation is the society-wide change needed to dismantle structures that generate depletion.

Mitigation

Mitigation is the first layer of care that Tomoiki provides to trainees. Rai et al. (2019) describe mitigation as a short to medium-term response to depletion, in that it reallocates care without necessarily challenging the underlying factors that generate depletion in the first place. Tomoiki mitigates the pressure for trainees to find sufficient housing or food to replenish from their often-traumatic experiences working in intensive labour settings with poor accommodation, particularly in cases of emergency departure from their workplaces. Housing on the TITP visa is connected to one's employers (MOJ 1990), so if a trainee is unfairly fired from a workplace or must escape a violent situation, they lose both their income and their housing in the same instant (Kamibayashi 2013). Tomoiki provides accommodation to trainees to stay safely in the temple and supports them in finding alternative arrangements. They also provide emergency food packages and meals to trainees, sending food assistance to 6,038 people in 2021 alone (Tomoiki n.d.[a]).

By providing housing and unpaid labour within the home (namely, the provisioning of nutritious food for overworked bodies), the organisation tends to the immediate consequences of depletion and harm but, in so doing, forms part of the wider infrastructure of the TITP's functioning, as the government increasingly relies on these resource-poor civil society groups to tend to trainees' needs, rather than taking action itself to address the pitfalls of the system for trainee wellbeing (Tian 2019; Kremers 2014). This confirms Rai et al.'s (2014) observation that inequalities are inbuilt within mitigation despite mitigation remaining the most available method of reversing depletion. It also echoes the feminist global care chain literature that notes how the redistribution of care labour intensifies the risk of 'depletion of the weakest down the care chain' (Rai and Goldblatt 2020: 177; Yeates 2009). In other words, the care burden falls onto individual advocates in Tomoiki, who themselves may begin to experience depletion from their advocacy output in support of trainees. Despite Tomoiki's best efforts at mitigating depletion to lessen the negative consequences of the TITP on trainees, there is limited potential for everyday resistance given this method of reversing depletion still forms part of the larger harmful ecosystem that is the TITP.

Replenishment

Rai et al. (2014) posit a second strategy for reversing depletion, which is replenishment. Replenishment is understood here to mean the role of public and private entities 'filling' the gaps that are systematic consequences of depletion (Rai et al. 2014: 99) and lessening its effects. In this case, Tomoiki replenishes trainees as a kind of 'social resource' (Fernandez 2018: 160) in that it provides options for trainees over a longer term and in a systematic way, compared with their work in mitigating depletion in emergencies. This provisioning of information about trainees' rights to parental leave or legal rights to biologically reproduce is an inflow that supports trainees in their practice of social reproduction. This conforms with Rai et al.'s (2014: 99) vision of replenishment as a fill-in for systemic causes of depletion, but, as they note, 'these interventions are extremely variable and always in danger of cutbacks in times of economic crises'.

Tomoiki attends to the needs of pregnant Vietnamese trainees working through the TITP in Japan who lack sufficient access to sexual and reproductive health services and information, particularly about their access to childcare services or parental leave. To this end, Tomoiki volunteers source childcare centres for trainees and disseminate materials, as well as holding sessions to explain the legal rights to parental leave to which trainees are entitled under the TITP. The inflows to sustain the form of social reproduction that is biological reproduction are lacklustre within the structure of the TITP. Apart from a few passages in TITP handbooks given to trainees on arrival in Japan and some campaigns to try to make trainees aware of their right to parental leave, as with many other trainee rights, the government leaves it up to employers to make their workers aware and does not sufficiently audit organisations to ensure those rights are being protected (Department of State 2020, 2021). For example, reports of trainees being laid off on discovery of their pregnancy are widespread across activist groups (Sasaki 2020; Oie 2016). One government survey found that between 2017 and 2020 as many as one-quarter of pregnant trainees were told by their companies to repatriate on discovery of their pregnancy and 25 per cent of the surveyed participants said they had not received explanation of their maternal and sexual health rights (Kyodo News 2022).

In this context, Tomoiki replenishes trainees' social reproduction by providing longer-term care options for pregnant trainees, including providing institutional arrangements for women to using childcare once they return to their traineeship in the TITP (Tomoiki n.d.[c]), sorting visas for trainees and their newborns and finding alternative means of employment so that mothers can stay in Japan for longer (Tomoiki n.d.[c]).

This strategy of reversing depletion cannot rest on its own and must be accompanied by broader structural change. This is where transformation of depletive systems, potentially generated by forms of visible everyday resistance against the TITP and the visible provisioning of care where it is lacking, might generate deeper change compared with mitigation or replenishment.

Transformation

Rai et al.'s (2014) third and final vision for reversing depletion is transformation, which is the promotion of structural change within depletive systems. Transformation can be viewed as a reconfiguration of power relationships within a society (with an emphasis on gendered social relations in depletion theory), but it can also be viewed as the result of incremental and minor changes that lead to changes in societal perspectives in the longer term (Rai et al. 2014). To this end, the visible inflows that Tomoiki provides to trainees should be seen as a potential avenue for deeper change in public perceptions of the program and its effects on trainees.

Tomoiki (n.d.[a]) engages near-weekly in media discussions highlighting the lack of care within the TITP. It disseminates articles that highlight the lack of support infrastructure for trainees who have been laid off and personal stories of interactions between the Japanese and Vietnamese people within Tomoiki to highlight the systemic issues of the TITP and its depletion. This dissemination of materials is performed without the revolutionary tone that some other organisations take (see Tomoiki n.d.[a]). For example, one high-profile nun who has worked closely with Tomoiki at the Nisshinkutsu Temple, Thich Tam Tri, has stated openly:

> As a nun, my efforts aren't based on a political motive or wanting to criticise a system, but simply from a humanitarian perspective. If there is someone in front of me who needs help, it is natural that I want to help them, and I am happy to. (Lee and Inuma 2022)

This approach to seeking change vis-a-vis TITP's challenges has interesting implications for resistance in that the advocacy promoted within the organisation is not overtly confrontational to the TITP but rather negotiates with its depletive consequences in a more discreet way.

By highlighting a lack of care within the system of the TITP, the members of Tomoiki advance a subversive truth (Lilja and Johansson 2018): that the TITP is not a development initiative but is systemically depletive, as proven by the uncared-for figures of Vietnamese trainees with whom they work. Through the repeated imagery and media engagements in which Tomoiki participates to emphasise this lack of care, it circulates a narrative that challenges the veneer of what the TITP professes to be to the Japanese public. Lilja and Johansson (2018) argue that dominant narratives are challenged when resistant voices repeatedly articulate an alternative understanding of power relationships. Resistance may take the form of a challenge to the vocabulary used by the dominating voice, by subverting the status quo (Lilja and Johansson 2018). By visibly and publicly providing inflows to trainees' social reproduction, Tomoiki highlights its systematic lack within the TITP and resists the dominant narrative that this program benefits Vietnamese trainees. In this sense, the dissemination of materials is one of the more subversive undertakings of Tomoiki and is evidence of its resistance to the TITP in a more direct manner compared with mitigation or resistance.

Limitations of the theory? Resistance, change and the future of care in Japanese guestworker programs

In 2018, the Japanese Government introduced a new status of residency for accepting migrants into Japan, including those without tertiary education, known as the Specified Skilled Worker (SSW) visa (Oishi 2021). The SSW visa allows workers to enter the country in 12 different fields, including nursing, construction, accommodation and agriculture (MOFA n.d.[b]). After years of using the TITP and other avenues, it seemed Japan was finally opening its 'front door' to labour migration (Oishi 2021). Partnered with the new visa categories was the introduction of 126 programs designed to support workers adapting to Japanese society, including provisions for their everyday life, the recruitment process to companies and support with foreign residence controls (Endoh 2021). Not only this, but SSW workers will be able to change company and workplace without the administrative hurdles that the TITP has traditionally had in place; they are guaranteed wages and conditions that match those of Japanese citizens, and they can be hired directly by a company rather than using intermediaries, which has been generative of exploitation in the past (Endoh 2021).

Further, on 29 July 2022, then justice minister Yoshihisa Furukawa pledged to overhaul the TITP and create a new system (potentially sitting within the SSW visa) that would have no difference between its stated aim and its reality in practice (Tauchi 2022). These positive changes must be viewed as partly, if not completely, the outcome of vocal activism and advocacy on the part of Japan's loudest groups supporting trainees, who have resisted the system and attracted the attention of international organisations that put pressure on Japan to make policy changes improving conditions for migrant workers (Kremers 2014).

Nevertheless, these positive inroads are not perfect and there is still work to be done at a micro-scale and in support of trainees' social reproduction. For example, there are two different visa categories under the SSW scheme. The first, SSW-1, allows migrants to enter Japan and work for a maximum of five years with no possibility of family reunification or contract renewal—effectively mirroring the rotating labour migration layout of the TITP (Oishi 2021). If migrants demonstrate 'improved' skill levels by passing Japanese-language and skills tests in their sector, they are eligible to apply for the SSW-2 visa, which enables them to work permanently in the country and also allows for family reunification (Oishi 2021). On the announcement of the visa categories, then justice minister Yamashita Takashi's staff testified in the Upper House that the jump from SSW-1 to SSW-2 would be made into a 'fairly high' hurdle (Endoh 2021: 293), suggesting that the Japanese Government does not intend for migrants and their families to live in Japan without first going through challenging administrative steps.

TITP trainees will be able to seamlessly apply for the SSW-1 visa without the initial Japanese-language test and occupational examinations required of other migrant groups in the country (MOFA n.d.[b]). One NGO reported that more than 90 per cent of migrant workers in Japan under the SSW were former TITP interns in vulnerable sectors prone to human trafficking

(Department of State 2022). This suggests the SSW might be, as Endoh (2021: 292) describes, 'the same wine (a de-facto guest worker program) in a different bottle'. Without the easy option of family reunification, trainees are likely to experience the same isolation and inability to practise, for instance, their social and cultural reproduction—one of the categories of social reproduction that Rai et al. (2014) identify as key to sustaining wellbeing.

To this end, depletion through social reproduction theory is useful in understanding Tomoiki's contributions in supporting trainees. Even if its efforts to sustain the day-to-day life and social wellbeing of trainees and provide emergency care do not appear as a direct challenge to Japan's guestworker programs on the surface, Tomoiki's contributions should nevertheless be acknowledged through the prism of social reproduction. Looking at the TITP through depletion allows us to analytically step back from a focus on production, labour issues and resistance to labour exploitation, to look at the workers' lives in the micro, everyday level beyond the workplace. Tomoiki is valuable for its resistance to the depletion that hides within the TITP and which may hide within the SSW in future, because it illustrates the lack of care for trainees' social reproduction by the state by providing that care itself. This type of resistance may not appear as revolutionary as the more vocal advocates in Japan whose work seems to be linked to wide-sweeping policy change and reform, but their work is likely to become increasingly important in the next stage of Japan's labour migration visas. This will be particularly the case if depletion continues to hide in incremental policy reforms that still do not account for or cater to the social reproductive needs of workers in Japan.

References

Arita, Kuniko, Akira Shibanuma, Rogie Royce Carandang, and Masamine Jimba. 2022. 'Competence in Daily Activities and Mental Well-Being among Technical Intern Trainees in Japan: A Cross-Sectional Study.' *International Journal of Environmental Research and Public Health* 19, no. 6: 3189. doi.org/10.3390/ijerph19063189.

Au, Anson. 2019. 'Thinking about Cross-Cultural Differences in Qualitative Interviewing: Practices for More Responsive and Trusting Encounters.' *The Qualitative Report* 24, no. 1: 58–77. doi.org/10.46743/2160-3715/2019.3403.

Bélanger, Danièle, and Linh Tran Giang. 2013. 'Precarity, Gender and Work: Vietnamese Migrant Workers in Asia.' *Diversities* 15, no. 1: 16.

Bélanger, Danièle, Kayoko Ueno, Khuat Thu Hong, and Emiko Ochiai. 2011. 'From Foreign Trainees to Unauthorized Workers: Vietnamese Migrant Workers in Japan.' *Asian and Pacific Migration Journal* 20, no. 1: 31–53. doi.org/10.1177/011719681102000102.

Bourke-Martignoni, Joanna, and Elizabeth Umlas. 2018. *Gender-Responsive Due Diligence for Business Actors: Human Rights-Based Approaches.* Academy Briefing No. 12, December. Geneva: Geneva Academy. www.geneva-academy.ch/joomla tools-files/docman-files/Academy%20Briefing%2012-interactif-V3.pdf.

Center for Global Development (CGD). 2021. *Migration Pathways: Technical Intern Training Program (TITP).* Policy Brief. Washington, DC: Center for Global Development. gsp.cgdev.org/wp-content/uploads/2021/07/CGD-Legal-Pathways-Database_Technical-Intern-Training-Program-TITP.pdf.

Chilmeran, Yasmin, and Nicola Pratt. 2019. 'The Geopolitics of Social Reproduction and Depletion: The Case of Iraq and Palestine.' *Social Politics: International Studies in Gender, State & Society* 26, no. 4: 586–607. doi.org/10.1093/sp/jxz035.

Chung, Erin Aeran. 2021. 'The Side Doors of Immigration: Multi-Tier Migration Regimes in Japan and South Korea.' *Third World Quarterly* 43, no. 7: 1570–86. doi.org/10.1080/01436597.2021.1956893.

Clean Clothes Campaign (CCC). 2020. *'Made in Japan' and the Cost to Migrant Workers.* Amsterdam: Clean Clothes Campaign. www.cleanclothes.org/file-repository/ccc-made-in-japan-report.pdf/view.

de Carvalho, Daniela. 2003. *Migrants and Identity in Japan and Brazil: The Nikkeijin.* London: Routledge. doi.org/10.4324/9780203220719.

Demelius, Yoko. 2020. 'Multiculturalism in a "Homogeneous" Society from the Perspectives of an Intercultural Event in Japan.' *Asian Anthropology* 19, no. 3: 161–80. doi.org/10.1080/1683478X.2019.1710332.

Department of State. 2017. *Trafficking in Persons Report: June 2017.* Washington, DC: US Department of State. www.state.gov/wp-content/uploads/2019/02/271339.pdf.

Department of State. 2018. *Trafficking in Persons Report: June 2018.* Washington, DC: US Department of State. www.state.gov/wp-content/uploads/2019/01/282798.pdf.

Department of State. 2019. *Trafficking in Persons Report: June 2019.* Washington, DC: US Department of State. www.state.gov/wp-content/uploads/2019/06/2019-Trafficking-in-Persons-Report.pdf.

Department of State. 2020. *Trafficking in Persons Report: 20th Edition*. Washington DC: US Department of State. www.state.gov/wp-content/uploads/2020/06/2020-TIP-Report-Complete-062420-FINAL.pdf.

Department of State. 2021. *Trafficking in Persons Report: June 2021*. Washington DC: US Department of State. www.state.gov/wp-content/uploads/2021/09/TIPR-GPA-upload-07222021.pdf.

Department of State. 2022. *Trafficking in Persons Report: July 2022*. Washington, DC: US Department of State. www.state.gov/wp-content/uploads/2022/08/22-00757-TIP-REPORT_072822-inaccessible.pdf.

Elias, Juanita. 2005. 'The Gendered Political Economy of Control and Resistance on the Shop Floor of the Multinational Firm: A Case-Study from Malaysia.' *New Political Economy* 10, no. 2: 203–22. doi.org/10.1080/13563460500144751.

Endoh, Toake. 2019. 'The Politics of Japan's Immigration and Alien Residence Control.' *Asian and Pacific Migration Journal* 28, no. 3: 324–52. doi.org/10.1177/0117196819873733.

Endoh, Toake. 2021. 'Immigration Easing or Restriction? A Consideration of Japan's Foreign-Worker Acceptance Policy.' *The Bulletin of the Graduate School of Josai International University* 24: 289–98. www.jiu.ac.jp/files/user/education/books/pdf/2020-24-018.pdf.

Fernandez, Bina. 2018. 'Dispossession and the Depletion of Social Reproduction.' *Antipode* 50, no. 1: 142–63. doi.org/10.1111/anti.12350.

Gallagher, Anne T. 2011. 'Improving the Effectiveness of the International Law of Human Trafficking: A Vision for the Future of the US Trafficking in Persons Reports.' *Human Rights Review* 12, no. 3: 381–400. doi.org/10.1007/s12142-010-0183-6.

Gunawardana, Samanthi J. 2016. '"To Finish, We Must Finish": Everyday Practices of Depletion in Sri Lankan Export-Processing Zones.' *Globalizations* 13, no. 6: 861–75. doi.org/10.1080/14747731.2016.1155341.

Hayakawa, Takeshi, and Jon Barnes. 2017. *Learning Experience? Japan's Technical TITP and the Challenge of Protecting the Rights of Migrant Workers*. Research Report, 16 October. London: Institute for Human Rights and Business. www.ihrb.org/focus-areas/mega-sportingevents/japan-titp-migrant-workers-rights.

Hironaka, Chikako, and Kazuyo Yamada. 2022. 'Foreign Workers and Overseas Production for Japanese Manufacturing SMEs.' *Journal of the International Council for Small Business* 3, no. 1: 56–61. doi.org/10.1080/26437015.2021.1951144.

Japan International Trainee & Skilled Worker Cooperation Organization (JITCO). n.d. 'What is the Technical Intern Training Program?' [Online]. Tokyo: JITCO. www.jitco.or.jp/en/regulation/index.html.

Johansson, Anna, and Stellan Vinthagen. 2015. 'Dimensions of Everyday Resistance: The Palestinian *Sumūd*.' *Journal of Political Power* 8, no. 1: 109–39. doi.org/10.1080/2158379X.2015.1010803.

Johansson, Anna, and Stellan Vinthagen. 2016. 'Dimensions of Everyday Resistance: An Analytical Framework.' *Critical Sociology* 42, no. 3: 417–35. doi.org/10.1177/0896920514524604.

Johansson, Anna, and Stellan Vinthagen. 2019. 'Everyday Resistance as a Concept.' In *Conceptualizing 'Everyday Resistance'*, edited by Anna Johansson and Stellan Vinthagen, 17–32. London: Routledge. doi.org/10.4324/9781315150154-2.

Johnston, Melissa, and Jayanthi Lingham. 2021. *Inclusive Economies, Enduring Peace: The Transformative Role of Social Reproduction: An Annotated Bibliography*. Educational resource. Melbourne: Monash University. doi.org/10.26180/137 28475.

Kamibayashi, Chieko. 2013. *Rethinking Temporary Foreign Workers' Rights: Living Conditions of Technical Interns in the Japanese Technical Internship Program (TIP)*. Working Paper Series 169 (March). Tokyo: Institute for Comparative Economics, Hosei University.

Kim, Kyunghwan. 2021. 'Framing Immigrant Rights in Politics: Comparative Evidence from Japan and South Korea.' *Pacific Focus* 36, no. 2: 287–315. doi.org/ 10.1111/pafo.12187.

Kremers, Daniel. 2014. 'Transnational Migrant Advocacy from Japan: Tipping the Scales in the Policy-Making Process.' *Pacific Affairs* 87, no. 4: 715–41. doi.org/ 10.5509/2014874715.

Kuwano, Noriko, and Rosanna McMaster. 2020. 'Knowing Ourselves: Self-Awareness and Culturally Competent Care.' *Nursing & Health Sciences* 22, no. 4: 843–45. doi.org/10.1111/nhs.12735.

Kyodo News. 2022. 'Quarter of Trainees in Japan Told to Return Home if Pregnant: Survey.' *Kyodo News*, 23 December. english.kyodonews.net/news/2022/12/f51 c0921e45c-quarter-of-trainees-in-japan-told-to-return-home-if-pregnant-survey. html?phrase=trainee&words=trainee,trainees.

Lee, Jaeyeon, and Ruwen Chang. 2023. 'Torn Apart! Transnational Feminist Researchers' Geopolitical Positionality in (Pre-)COVID-19 Times.' *Gender, Place & Culture* 30, no. 8: 1147–69. doi.org/10.1080/0966369X.2022.2158178.

Lee, Michelle Ye Hee, and Julia Mio Inuma. 2022. 'The Vietnamese Workers Japan Depends on Are Falling through the Cracks. One Buddhist Nun Is Trying to Catch Them.' *Washington Post*, 3 February. www.washingtonpost.com/world/2022/02/03/japan-pandemic-vietnamese-migrants-nun/.

Lilja, Mona, and Evelina Johansson. 2018. 'Feminism as Power and Resistance: An Inquiry into Different Forms of Swedish Feminist Resistance and Anti-Genderist Reactions.' *Social Inclusion* 6, no. 4: 82–94. doi.org/10.17645/si.v6i4.1545.

Lira, Andrea, Ana Luisa Muñoz-García, and Elisa Loncon. 2019. 'Doing the Work, Considering the Entanglements of the Research Team While Undoing Settler Colonialism.' *Gender and Education* 31, no. 4: 475–89. doi.org/10.1080/09540253.2019.1583319.

Liu-Farrer, Gracia. 2020. *Immigrant Japan: Mobility and Belonging in an Ethno-Nationalist Society*. Ithaca: Cornell University Press. doi.org/10.7591/cornell/9781501748622.001.0001.

Mazumi, Yusuke. 2019. 'What Shapes Local Demand for "Guest Worker" Migrants in Japan? The Case of the Seafood Processing Industry.' *Contemporary Japan* 31, no. 1: 2–20. doi.org/10.1080/18692729.2018.1563346.

Ministry of Foreign Affairs of Japan (MOFA). n.d.[a] 'Procedures Required Before Working as a SSW.' [Online]. Tokyo: Ministry of Foreign Affairs of Japan. www.mofa.go.jp/mofaj/ca/fna/ssw/us/introduction/.

Ministry of Foreign Affairs of Japan (MOFA). n.d.[b] 'What Is the SSW?' [Online]. Tokyo: Ministry of Foreign Affairs of Japan. www.mofa.go.jp/mofaj/ca/fna/ssw/us/overview/.

Ministry of Health, Labour and Welfare (MHLW). 2017. 外国人技能実習生の実習実施者に対する　監督指導、送検等の状況(平成29年) [*Status of Supervision, Guidance and Referral to Prosecutors for Foreign Technical Intern Trainees (2017)*]. Tokyo: Ministry of Health, Labour and Welfare. www.mhlw.go.jp/file/04-Houdouhappyou-11202000-Roudoukijunkyoku-Kantokuka/besshi.pdf.

Ministry of Justice (MOJ). 1990. *Ministerial Ordinance to Provide for Criteria Pursuant to Article 7, Paragraph (1), Item (ii) of the Immigration Control and Refugee Recognition Act*. Ordinance of the Ministry of Justice No. 16, 24 May. Tokyo: Ministry of Justice. www.japaneselawtranslation.go.jp/en/laws/view/2006/en.

Ministry of Justice (MOJ). 2021. 'For Technical Interns and Prospective Technical Interns.' *MOJchannel*, [*YouTube*], 25 March. www.youtube.com/watch?v=0p3E0cJnFx4.

Ministry of Justice (MOJ). 2022. '令和4年6月末現在における在留外国人数について [Number of Foreign Residents as of the End of June 2022].' Press release, 14 October. Tokyo: Immigration Services Agency. www.moj.go.jp/isa/publications/press/13_00028.html?hl=en.

Murakami, Sakura. 2020. 'In Tokyo, a Temple Offers Pandemic-Hit Vietnamese Workers a Safe Haven.' *Reuters*, 7 July. www.reuters.com/article/health-coronavirus-japan-temple-idUSL1N2ED035.

Ogawa, Reiko. 2020. 'Use and Abuse of Trafficking Discourse in Japan.' *Journal of Population and Social Studies* 28: S106–25.

Oie, Kosuke. 2016. '監理団体の実態と法的責任 [The True State of and Legal Responsibilities of Supervising Organisations].' *M-Net* 187, no. 8.

Oishi, Nana. 1995. 'Training or Employment? Japanese Immigration Policy in Dilemma.' *Asian and Pacific Migration Journal* 4, nos 2–3: 367–85. doi.org/10.1177/011719689500400210.

Oishi, Nana. 2021. 'Skilled or Unskilled? The Reconfiguration of Migration Policies in Japan.' *Journal of Ethnic and Migration Studies* 47, no. 10: 2252–69. doi.org/10.1080/1369183X.2020.1731984.

Organization for Technical Intern Training (OTIT). n.d. 'About OTIT.' [Online]. Tokyo: OTIT. www.otit.go.jp/about_en/.

Organization for Technical Intern Training (OTIT). 2022. 令和3年度外国人技能実習機構業務統計 概要 [*FY2021 Foreign Technical Intern Training Organization Business Statistics Overview*]. Tokyo: OTIT. www.otit.go.jp/files/user/docs/%EF%BC%88%E4%BF%AE%E6%AD%A3%EF%BC%89%E4%BB%A4%E5%92%8C%EF%BC%93%E5%B9%B4%E5%BA%A6%E6%A6%82%E8%A6%81%EF%BC%88%E6%A5%AD%E5%8B%99%E7%B5%B1%E8%A8%88%EF%BC%89.pdf.

Osumi, Magdalena. 2019. 'Probe Reveals 759 Cases of Suspected Abuse and 171 Deaths of Foreign Trainees in Japan.' *Japan Times*, 29 March. www.japantimes.co.jp/news/2019/03/29/national/probe-reveals-759-cases-suspected-abuse-foreign-trainees-japan-171-deaths/.

Rai, Shirin M., and Beth Goldblatt. 2020. 'Introduction to the Themed Section: Law, Harm and Depletion through Social Reproduction.' *European Journal of Politics and Gender* 3, no. 2: 171–84. doi.org/10.1332/251510820X15855860254106.

Rai, Shirin M., Catherine Hoskyns, and Dania Thomas. 2014. 'Depletion: The Cost of Social Reproduction.' *International Feminist Journal of Politics* 16, no. 1: 86–105. doi.org/10.1080/14616742.2013.789641.

Rai, Shirin M, Jacqui True, and Maria Tanyag. 2019. 'From Depletion to Regeneration: Addressing Structural and Physical Violence in Post-Conflict Economies.' *Social Politics: International Studies in Gender, State & Society* 26, no. 4: 561–85. doi.org/10.1093/sp/jxz034.

Rajan, Hamsa, and Kerrie Thornhill. 2019. 'Dilemmas of Feminist Practice in Transnational Spaces: Solidarity, Personal Growth, and Potential Solutions.' *Gender, Place & Culture* 26, no. 10: 1345–52. doi.org/10.1080/0966369X.2019. 1618246.

Roberts, Glenda S. 2018. 'An Immigration Policy by *Any* Other Name: Semantics of Immigration to Japan.' *Social Science Japan Journal* 21, no. 1: 89–102. doi.org/ 10.1093/ssjj/jyx033.

Sasaki, Ayako. 2020. 'Are "Trained" Migrants and "Educated" International Students at Risk? Understanding Human Trafficking in Japan.' *Journal of Human Trafficking* 6, no. 2: 244–54. doi.org/10.1080/23322705.2020.1691875.

Shinohara, Aya, Ryoko Kawasaki, Noriko Kuwano, and Mayumi Ohnishi. 2021. 'Interview Survey of Physical and Mental Changes and Coping Strategies among 13 Vietnamese Female Technical Interns Living in Japan.' *Health Care for Women International* 45, no. 2: 265–81. doi.org/10.1080/07399332.2021.1963966.

Shipper, Apichai W. 2002. 'The Political Construction of Foreign Workers in Japan.' *Critical Asian Studies* 34, no. 1: 41–68. doi.org/10.1080/146727102760166590.

Solidarity Network with Migrants Japan. 2019. 'Who We Are: The Solidarity Network with Migrants Japan (SMJ)].' [Online]. Tokyo: 移住連 [Solidarity Network with Migrants Japan]. migrants.jp/english.html.

Surak, Kristin. 2018. 'Migration Industries and the State: Guestwork Programs in East Asia.' *International Migration Review* 52, no. 2: 487–523. doi.org/10.1111/ imre.12308.

Tanyag, Maria. 2018. 'Resilience, Female Altruism, and Bodily Autonomy: Disaster-Induced Displacement in Post-Haiyan Philippines.' *Signs: Journal of Women in Culture and Society* 43, no. 3: 563–85. doi.org/10.1086/695318.

Tauchi, Kosuke. 2022. 'Technical Intern Program Will Be Overhauled, Says Justice Minister.' *The Asahi Shimbun*, [Osaka], 29 July. www.asahi.com/ajw/articles/ 14682662.

The Colombo Plan Secretariat. 2024. 'The Colombo Plan: A Brief History.' [Online]. Colombo: The Colombo Plan Secretariat. colombo-plan.org/who-we-are/.

Tian, Yunchen. 2019. 'Workers by Any Other Name: Comparing Co-Ethnics and "Interns" as Labour Migrants to Japan.' *Journal of Ethnic and Migration Studies* 45, no. 9: 1496–514. doi.org/10.1080/1369183X.2018.1466696.

TIP Report Heroes. 2022. 'Ippei Torii: Japan, Class of 2013.' [Online]. US Department of State Trafficking in Persons Report Heroes. www.tipheroes.org/ippei-torii/.

Tomoiki. n.d.[a] '日越ともいき支援会について [What is the Japan–Vietnam Friendship Support Association]? [Online]. Tokyo: NV Japan–Vietnam Tomoiki Support Association. www.nv-tomoiki.or.jp/about.

Tomoiki. n.d.[b] '新着情報 [What's New].' [Online]. Tokyo: NV Japan–Vietnam Tomoiki Support Association. www.nv-tomoiki.or.jp/news.

Tomoiki. n.d.[c] '生活支援事業 [What You Can Do].' [Online]. Tokyo: NV Japan–Vietnam Tomoiki Support Association. www.nv-tomoiki.or.jp/support.

Tran, Bao Quyen. 2020. 'Vietnamese Technical Trainees in Japan Voice Concerns Amidst COVID-19.' *Asia-Pacific Journal: Japan Focus* 18, no. 11. apjjf.org/2020/18/tran.

Verité. 2018. *Forced Labor Risk in Japan's Technical Intern Training Program: Exploration of Indicators among Chinese Trainees Seeking Remedy.* Amherst: Verité. www.verite.org/wp-content/uploads/2018/09/Forced-Labor-Risk-in-Japans-TITP.pdf.

Vietnam News Agency. 2023. 'Vietnamese Nationals Account Largest Proportion of Japan's Foreign Worker Population.' *VietnamPlus*, 27 January. en.vietnamplus.vn/vietnamese-nationals-account-largest-proportion-of-japans-foreign-worker-population-post247509.vnp.

Vijeyarasa, Ramona. 2015. *Sex, Slavery and the Trafficked Woman: Myths and Misconceptions about Trafficking and Its Victims.* London: Routledge. doi.org/10.4324/9781315608501.

Vijeyarasa, Ramona, and Mark Liu. 2022. 'Fast Fashion for 2030: Using the Pattern of the Sustainable Development Goals (SDGs) to Cut a More Gender-Just Fashion Sector.' *Business and Human Rights Journal* 7, no. 1: 45–66. doi.org/10.1017/bhj.2021.29.

Vinthagen, Stellan, and Anna Johansson. 2013. '"Everyday Resistance": Exploration of a Concept and its Theories.' *Resistance Studies Magazine* 2013, no. 1: 1–46. www.resistance-journal.org/wp-content/uploads/2016/04/Vinthagen-Johansson-2013-Everyday-resistance-Concept-Theory.pdf.

Yeates, Nicola. 2009. *Globalizing Care Economies and Migrant Workers: Explorations in Global Care Chains.* London: Palgrave Macmillan.

Yoshida, Mai. 2021. 'The Indebted and Silent Worker: Paternalistic Labor Management in Foreign Labor Policy in Japan.' *Critical Sociology* 47, no. 1: 73–89. doi.org/10.1177/0896920520924102.

Collective Afterword: Listening, re-storying, reanimating research and action

Ramona Vijeyarasa, Sonia Palmieri,
Margaret Jolly and Tanya Jakimow

This afterword traverses our collective thoughts as we have reflected on what we have learned from this process of bringing together scholars and scholarship from across Asia and Oceania. Our lessons are substantive and methodological and, in most cases, both, as we have come to appreciate how methodological predispositions shape which and whose stories are told and, in turn, whose are not. We attempt here to identify synergies across the chapters in ways that can help move us forward.

The language of difference: Epistemic violence and injustice

The chapters in this volume attest to the emergence of profound questions of epistemic justice. The dominance of researchers from certain countries and English as the privileged language of publication is palpable. Moreover, in acknowledging our positionality in a very unequal world, further questions stem from the language we use to describe our differences and how those differences have sedimented in the *longue durée* of Euro-American colonialism and its aftermath. Several chapters critique dominant modes of classification and categorisation, posing ethical questions about the epistemic violence in such choice of language.

In 1952 amid the Cold War, the French geographer Alfred Saury coined 'the Third World' to describe those countries, many of which were erstwhile colonies, that were not in the camps of the rival powers of the Soviet Union and the Eastern Bloc or the United States of America and its Western allies. Although embraced by many individuals in 'non-aligned countries', its bipolar, geopolitical foundations and then the collapse of the Soviet Union meant this term was contested and ultimately obsolete. Alongside this ternary partition, in the period after World War II, we saw a proliferation in binary labels, 'developing' and 'developed', as poles of a projected continuum. In English the usage of the word 'development' exponentially rose after World War II alongside the establishment of institutions following the Bretton Woods Conference, including the World Bank and the International Monetary Fund, to regulate international commercial and financial relations. This notion of development was widely criticised for envisaging linear progress on a Western model, for privileging economic indicators and for failing to see how the relations between the developing and developed worlds were predicated on the inequalities created by a colonising and globalising capitalism (for example, Escobar 1995).

Despite such trenchant critiques, the language of development survives in many national policies and programs and notably in the language of the United Nations, as in the Sustainable Development Goals. Still, the language of Global North/Global South surged from the 1970s and 1980s. Coined by American writer and activist Carl Oglesby in connection to the Vietnam War, 'Global South' was used to depict those countries with dense populations, low cash income, poor infrastructure and little industrialisation. In critical development studies, Global North/ South refer to nations *and communities* of relative wealth and deprivation, accounting for pockets of extreme wealth in 'developing countries' and of poverty in 'developed countries', with explicit attention to the relations between them (Dirlik 1997). These categories have nonetheless, in wider usage, become synonymous with developing/developed, used as a descriptor for countries rather than as a basis for transnational solidarity (Mohanty 2002). The use of geographic hemispheres to depict these relations was not only confusing (since many countries of the Global South were in the Northern Hemisphere and vice versa), but also threatened to naturalise geopolitical relations that were far more fluid and contested (see Jolly 2008). The dichotomy tended to homogenise diverse countries and, despite the attempt to neutralise disparaging language, it sustained pejorative values in ways akin to developing/developed.

More recent language avowed by many of the authors in this volume is that of the majority/minority worlds. Coined by Bangladeshi photographer and journalist Shahidul Alam in the 1990s (see Alam 2008),[1] the terminology of majority/minority worlds aspires to reframe from the perspective of the majority—that is, the overwhelming demographic majority of people on Earth. Alam asserted that previous framings including Third World and developing/developed stigmatised the majority through a capitalist, material lens as 'icons of poverty'. This resonates with compelling critiques of how this negative lens was further darkened for women of the 'Third World'. They were too often seen as victims of poverty, of male domination and gender violence in a way that denied their individual and collective agency, their political engagement and efficacy (see Mohanty 1988, 2002; Pailey 2020; Spivak 1988). While terminology may vary, our collective ambition has been to challenge a singular and hegemonic approach to acknowledge these abovementioned tensions.

Positionality and privilege: Seeking justice

As foregrounded in Chapter 1 of our volume, mainstream theorising about gender and politics has come predominantly from 'white', minority-world women. We do not suggest this scholarly project was inessential or uncomplicated; indeed, the sustained struggle to present a cogent critique of male dominance in political institutions has ultimately made a significant contribution to women's gradually increasing political participation, especially in the minority world. In some ways, it appears we four co-editors embody that tradition: we *are* all women from the minority world, employed by Australian universities.

Yet, we are also not the same: our individual and collective scholarship is informed by vastly different experiences—theoretical and practical— as well as diverse cultural backgrounds. Ramona and Sonia grew up in 'ethnic communities' in Australia, respectively, from Sri Lankan-Malaysian and Italian ancestry, grappling with what it meant to be different and the same in an evolving, albeit not always progressive, acceptance of Australian multiculturalism. Although her Ukrainian father was subject to exclusion as

---

1   Alam's photo agency is called Majority World. 'The term majority world, now increasingly being used, challenges the West's rhetoric of democracy. It also defines the community in terms of what it has, rather than what it lacks. In time, the majority world will reaffirm its place in a world where the earth will again belong to the people who walk on it' (Alam 2008: 89).

a young migrant in Australia, Tanya was afforded social invisibility through her 'whiteness'. Margaret has Scottish and north English ancestry; she grew up in a working-class family and benefited from the brief era of free tertiary education in Australia in the 1970s. While Margaret and Tanya have deep disciplinary roots in anthropology, Ramona and Sonia are grounded in the terrain of law and political science. All of us have been involved in feminist activism as well as scholarship, variously in street protests, in collective movements in Australia and overseas, in international organisations, in government work and in challenging perduring patriarchal practices in curricula, scholarly assessments and organisational culture in the universities in which we work.

It is not surprising, then, that we deliberately sought new entry points from which to elucidate our understanding of gender and politics in Oceania and Asia. Indeed, the heart of this edited volume lies in its diversity. Together, our contributors bring new voices, new questions and, we suggest, a new justice to this field of study.

Our volume includes the voices of emerging authors, queer authors, authors from both Oceania and Asia, authors with a disability, legal scholars, anthropologists, political economists, journalists, public servants, development specialists and practitioners, political scientists and early, mid and late(r) career scholars. From these varied positionalities, our authors asked new and fascinating questions. How can the disciplines of anthropology, history, development studies, political economy and media studies inform our understanding of gender, culture and politics? How can the study of gender and politics itself be broadened to include those who participate in alternative ways? How can the experience of people in Oceania and Asia, including their colonial and decolonial experiences, speak back to minority-world theories and concepts? How can local and domestic spaces be leveraged as political spaces in majority-world settings? How can non–state-affiliated feminist movements be sustained, even in states that are increasingly or totally authoritarian? How can we capture, in culturally respectful ways, the lived experience of those women who engage in formal politics in the majority world? How can the theoretical contributions of scholars from Oceania and Asia on gender and politics be better cited and celebrated? These questions point to an obvious injustice in the narrower focus of political scientists in particular, but also of minority-world scholarship in general.

Linguistic injustice: Challenging Anglophonic bias

That language is loaded is self-evident in the discussions captured in the pages of this book. In many respects, the entire collection is a response to Tanya Jakimow's call (in Chapter 1) to 'inquire into how this [linguistic] imbalance impacts the field of gender and politics'. We have sought to bring visibility to the language bias that in some disciplines is acknowledged as 'underexplored' topics (Ammann 2022: 811) and which, while well recognised by feminist scholars, continues to persist across disciplines.

International legal scholar Odile Ammann defines language bias as not just being about the inclination or prejudice towards one language but also an association with that language as good, strong and trustworthy and therefore others as weak and of less value (Ammann 2022: 823). An English 'imperialism' in teaching and research, Ammann argues (2022: 823), has contributed to a type of linguistic injustice. We see such injustices play out in the scholarship about gender in politics across both Oceania and Asia. The struggles of marginalised groups to be represented and accepted in political spaces—many of them hard won—are paralleled by the struggle to be accounted for in scholarly writing.

We are reminded of the consequences of such linguistic bias, as Jaemin Shim (Chapter 2) demonstrates the extent to which the increasing spaces carved out for 'gendered' scholarship have not been matched by a representation of scholarship from all regions and languages of the world. A bias towards the minority world permeates. Authors from particular countries—the United States, the United Kingdom, Canada and Australia—dominate scholarly debates, amplifying a narrowness concerning who is cited and about which countries. This is a critique we rightly direct at ourselves as authors from Anglophone Australia, as dedicated as we have been individually to studying countries in Asia and Oceania in as grounded ways as possible, using local languages where we can. Batalibasi et al. (Chapter 7) show how using local languages creates a sense of comfort for interlocutors but also attunes researchers to the need to listen carefully and to hear nuances and cultural silences. Given the hegemonic nature of these Anglophonic experiences and standpoints, what are authors whose first language is not English left to do? Either bear the financial cost of communicating in one's first language and translating into English or embrace the challenge of writing in English, even though certain pivotal concepts or cultural nuances may not adequately translate.

If we fail to challenge the boundaries and demarcations that language can create, we lose the potential to share knowledge as a result. We can acknowledge that '[p]eople, materials, and ideas move more easily within linguistic communities than between such communities' (Roberts 2017: 3). Yet, when debates that may be vibrant and robust in one set of nations speaking the same language are not making their way across borders to others, there is a notable loss for knowledge generation (Vijeyarasa 2024). Anna Kwai (Chapter 3) has reminded us of what is lost in translation— or, in this case, overwhelmed by the dominance of cultural precepts, frameworks and gatekeeping of the minority world, deliberate or otherwise. A monolithic approach to language—in which English dominates—can lead to a monolithic approach to culture, Kwai warns for Solomon Islands. Cultural experiences are incorrectly narrated by minority-world 'experts' and development agencies and certain women's stories may be erased altogether from oral, written and photographic histories. Selected languages and, in turn, perspectives bury others in telling an allegedly 'bigger' and more comprehensive story about women and development in Solomon Islands.

Challenging English as the lingua franca of gender and politics research raises a further problem. English-language concepts, developed elsewhere, may not have localised meaning. Mema Motusaga and Elise Howard (Chapter 9), in their project of re-storying through a Pacific narrative women's experiences of politics in Samoa, require us to revisit and arguably challenge a framing of women's rights and gender equality as Western outsider ontologies that have little to offer. Margaret Jolly's work on Vanuatu (Jolly 2000: 134) and the 'powerful allure' of the 'language of human rights' for educated, elite ni-Vanuatu women is suggestive. She proposed that this might eschew the individualist character of some dominant Western models of the person. A broader traction for such language might entail articulating with Indigenous ideas of the human person in *kastom* (tradition, ways of the place) and the collective Christian projects of women's groups, which aim at improving women's lives. Perhaps, then, a middle path can be plotted to embrace both 'tradition' and human rights (see Biersack et al. 2016; Leach 2021; and below on vernacularisation).

How do we alter such practices to move forward? Language bias is not easy to overcome; moreover, it is something that all English-language scholars perpetuate and amplify (Ammann 2022: 823), to a degree. We may want to forgive a reluctance among minority-world scholars to give due attention to Asia and Oceania, since combining feminist scholarship and political action might seem easier if one is a citizen. Moreover, to truly compare across borders requires scholars and activists to contextualise, to seek local meanings and to interpret sociocultural practices, policies and laws—both formal and informal—that may be specific to a culture (Rosenblum 2006: 778). Such depth of critical engagement often requires a fluency in language alongside a deeper cultural knowledge than may be available to an outsider (Vijeyarasa 2024). Yet, we cannot ignore the degree to which language bias is felt both across countries and regions and within nations. The Philippines, for instance, is a nation with 175 individual languages. While Tagalog-based Filipino is the national language according to the 1987 Constitution, it has made few inroads into the Filipino legal system (Pefianco Martin 2012: 1). In the Western Pacific, linguistic diversity is extreme: Papua New Guinea has 834 Indigenous languages, Vanuatu has 134 and there are 73 in Solomon Islands. In all these countries pidgins are widely used as a lingua franca and, in some, are recognised as national languages. Nonetheless, the educated elites and the political classes are fluent in English and in Vanuatu English and/or French.

Is the trap, then, to tread around rather than plunge head-on into the complex terrain of language, culture and rights? Serena Ford (Chapter 14) speaks to a Japanese Government intervention that is depicted as a 'training program' and yet is highly depleting of women's energy, time, resources and skills. Ford describes what in the eyes of many is the exploitation of the rights of migrant workers from Vietnam. Yet, what we consider a euphemism may better reflect the discomfort or lack of universalism or resonance of the language of human rights. Ruby Lai (Chapter 12) reminds us that a further challenge lies with the coopting of human rights language. In Hong Kong, the language of 'gender equality' has been deemed socially acceptable and feminist activists are even forced to 'professionalise' their feminist claims through the nature of their research or public engagements to strengthen feminist bargaining power.

At the same time, these chapters illustrate that language can be transformed and new meanings given. Both Asia and Oceania call on us to give new meaning to terms whose definitions seem entrenched. 'Housewives' can become presidents in Indonesia and the Philippines (Vijeyarasa, Chapter 8).

Meanwhile, the matrilineal cultures of the South Tetun–speaking communities of West Timor transcend the very concept of 'housewife' as female 'housemasters' hold authority and influence (Bayo, Chapter 10; and below).

We ultimately seek scholarship—on singular countries and comparative ones—that is rigorous, nuanced and both global and localised. This is an overwhelming ask for many scholars. That subaltern scholarship from Asia (by Mohanty 1988, 2002; Spivak 1988; and others) appears throughout the chapters in this book reflects the extent to which we have sought to revisit, revalue and re-centre non-Western forms of knowing that are upheld by such linguistic bias.

Masculinist states, gendered binaries and vernacularisation

An aim of this volume has been to identify theoretical lenses that can illuminate the common processes in which masculinist states become dominant. As outlined in Chapter 1, a key concept in the anthropology of democracy—the vernacularisation of democracy (Tanabe 2007; Michelutti 2007)—can be repurposed for both analytical and transformative ambitions. Common models and institutions of liberal representative democracy have spread globally, yet the forms they take are anything but uniform. Rather, 'the moment democracy enters a particular historical and sociocultural setting, it becomes vernacularized; producing new social relations and values, which in turn become the raw material for new relations, political rhetoric and political cultures' (Michelutti 2010: 67). Local idioms, folk values and practices come to influence how people perceive the political world; in turn, the political world transforms social and cultural practice. It is through the comparative method of revealing convergences and divergences in processes of vernacularisation that we can help to explain, in the hopes of redressing, male political dominance.[2]

The chapters in this volume tell stories of historical forces and cultural continuations that have profoundly shaped contemporary democracies. The impact of *colonialism* on the marginalisation of women in politics today is increasingly recognised (for example, Celis et al. 2013; Hawkesworth 2012)

---

2   Vernacularisation also works as a lens to understand how other 'universal' frameworks have taken different forms (see Merry 2006a, 2006b, 2009).

and is a central theme in chapters by Anna Kwai (Chapter 3), Salmah Eva-Lina Lawrence (Chapter 5), Margaret Jolly (Chapter 6), Mema Motusaga and Elise Howard (Chapter 9) and Longgina Novadona Bayo (Chapter 10). These authors also point to how colonialism extended far beyond the institutions of formal politics. *Missionisation and Christian conversion* pervasively transformed gender relations with political consequences across Oceania and in several parts of South and South-East Asia. During processes of *decolonisation*, new states drew on colonial models of governance that favoured men's political leadership and devalued 'women's relevance in political affairs' (Jolly, Chapter 6). *Postcolonial state and nation-building* have also introduced novel gender ideologies that are often framed as being 'traditional', as seen during Suharto's New Order regime in Indonesia (Bayo, Chapter 10). Hong Kong's complex colonial and postcolonial histories (Lai, Chapter 12) have led to a point where women's movements struggle with subtle ideological dissonances, particularly between elite and grassroots activists.[3]

Centring Asia and Oceania has revealed the significance of these forces, not as experiences unique to these regions, but as often converging with other national and regional histories (Vijeyarasa, Chapter 8). Moreover, despite the myriad possibilities that could arise from the assemblage of cultural norms, ideologies and practices, vernacular democracies seemingly everywhere have produced, or produced anew, male political dominance. At critical junctures, vernacular democracies have been scripted by, and to the advantage of, men.[4]

These vernacular democracies share a common feature, albeit with local particularised characteristics. Binaries of male/female and public/domestic that relegate women to their 'natural' position within the domestic sphere have enabled men's near monopolisation of formal politics (Segato 2018; Vogel 2013). Feminists have problematised the separation of and opposition between public and private as, for example, not capturing the politics that occurs within the home or other forms of informal, localised and collective politics-making (Diprose et al., Chapter 13). The binary nonetheless remains an analytically productive and consequential distinction 'linking

---

3   In navigating these challenges, Hong Kong has also witnessed a persistent but not fully achieved desire among feminist and queer groups struggling against the patriarchy to represent a diversity of interests while overcoming discord.

4   By scripted, we do not mean purposeful writing. Rather, we allude to how male hegemony, including greater ideational power, allowed an organic emergence of vernacular democracy that advanced male interests and power.

the cultural valuations given to the category "woman" to the organization of women's activities in society' (Moore 1988: 23). For example, across Oceania, precolonial gender roles, in which reproductive and productive roles were valued equally and not separated, were disrupted by 'novel gendered binaries between domestic and public life' (Jolly, Chapter 6). The 'cult of domesticity' established the domestic sphere as the basis for women's contributions in Solomon Islands, resulting in a devaluing of women (Kwai, Chapter 3). The public/domestic distinction introduced during colonial times in Papua New Guinea by white male officials, excluding women from colonial enclaves, plantations and mines, continued through decolonisation. As Anne Dickson-Waiko avers, men were allowed to enter states as citizens and individual agents, while women were instead cast as 'relational beings', their relational labour devalued and afforded a lower status (Lawrence, Chapter 5; Jolly, Chapter 6). While these experiences are from Oceania, they are shared with other regions. Rita Segato (2018), an Argentinian feminist, scholar and activist, argues this binarism is a feature of colonial modernity more generally. As the 'public' became a totalising space in which all else was separated into the 'private', the masculine was made primary and the feminine secondary. The long-term consequences for women's position in politics in postcolonial democracies have been profound.[5]

Comparison can reveal the mechanisms introducing, solidifying and producing anew these novel binaries into durable political arrangements. Reading across chapters, four mechanisms are evident. First, is the lack of recognition of women's sources of power, and a separation of the domains in which women's power lies from the secular-formal-political. Missionaries lacked understanding of women's power in Samoan *feagaiga* (complementary brother–sister) relationships. In emphasising 'dutiful wifehood and domestic life', they 'effectively wiped out pathways for women to gain status through the *feagaiga* relationship' (Motusaga and Howard, Chapter 9). Women's power was further diminished through the separation of secular and spiritual power, weakening the importance of the latter, in which women held greater authority, and enabling men to monopolise the former. Women's spiritual power was also unrecognised in West Timor (Bayo, Chapter 10). Here, the failure to comprehend or appreciate Timorese gender diarchy based on difference and interdependence led to its

---

5   As these binaries reflected European models of social organisation, it is also the case that the impacts of this binary are found in the politics of former colonising countries, with women's subjugation in imperial countries mutually reinforced by the ideological forces of colonialism (see Levine 2004).

displacement by a gender hierarchy based on dominance and subjugation. Women's spiritual authority was undermined and they were relegated to a secondary role in political affairs.

Second, these distorted configurations of gendered power came to be institutionalised and solidified through language and representation. In Solomon Islands, Kwara'ae men were edited out of photos that showed them in childcaring roles (Kwai, Chapter 3). In Samoa, early versions of the Bible used the term *fafine* ('female' or 'wife') for women, with its negative connotations, rather than *tamaitai* ('lady'), which held equal status to *matai* (male chiefly titleholders). This lower status was then codified and formalised in the Constitution (Motusaga and Howard, Chapter 9), with governance modelled on the *matai* system in which men dominate with only *matai* titleholders eligible for political candidacy.

Third, gendered exclusions from power are further solidified through space (Crewe 2021). Gender diarchy in West Timor (Bayo, Chapter 10) was disrupted by the imposition of uniform housing styles during Indonesia's New Order. The building practices of an outer platform and inner house of the *uma kukun* ('dark house') were symbolic of the gender diarchy of Timorese political organisation. These were displaced by the *rumah Malay* (or 'Malay house'), transforming these political arrangements and undermining the authority of women. In Samoa, the national parliament *Fono* is modelled on local-level *fono* spaces dominated by men, and coded masculine through oratorical registers and 'men jesting' (*tala tau sua*) (Motusaga and Howard, Chapter 9). The striking National Parliament building in Port Moresby, Papua New Guinea, is similarly modelled on a men's house from the Sepik, from which women were excluded. Few women have held a seat in the 'men's house' in the decades since independence in 1975. Parliaments and other spaces of politics can thus exclude through their very architecture— 'built for specific forms of masculinity' (Crewe 2021: 115).[6] These are often based on, and solidify, a distinction between the public and the private (see Batalibasi et al., Chapter 7).

Fourth, practices based on men's experiences and sensibilities reproduce that space as masculine. For example, the oratorical strategies and language of the national *Fono* are learnt in the male-dominated *fono*, while practices of 'men jesting' are seen as inappropriate in front of women (ironically

---

6   Motusaga and Howard's presentation at the 2022 workshop gave details of the architectural features of Samoa's National Parliament building.

drawing on their status as sisters in the *feagaiga* relationships) (Motusaga and Howard, Chapter 9). Politics in this way is (re)inscribed as dirty, and thereby an inappropriate domain for women—an inscription that serves to exclude women from politics throughout much of the world (Jakimow 2023). Discomfort in inhabiting political spaces or navigating the formalities of bureaucracies is also evident in Indonesia and India. Deepak Mishra and Aparimita Mishra (Chapter 11) observe how the rituals, practices, performative obligations and temporality of political life in a border state in India are modelled on men's life experiences, with women facing challenges adapting to the required modalities and sensibilities. 'Public space' is marked 'as a different territory from life at home or in the village' (Mishra and Mishra, Chapter 11), a distinction that they argue is an additional frontier that women must cross to participate in politics. More optimistically, Diprose et al. (Chapter 13) show similar challenges in Indonesia, but also how initiatives to move political processes to everyday spaces enabled women to conduct their business with greater ease and comfort.

These four mechanisms—lack of recognition of women's power; solidifying distorted gender power dynamics in representation and language; the masculinisation of political spaces; and masculinist repertoires and sensibilities to navigate these spaces—have established and solidified the separation of public/domestic while sustaining male political dominance.

Tools of justice: Re-storying and rescripting inclusion

Women consummately navigate these dynamics to carve out space in politics. For example, assuming a political style as a 'good housewife' draws on local idioms to create a place for women in politics, which is 'not *too* great an affront to social expectations' (Vijeyarasa, Chapter 8), although it comes with attendant limitations (see also Ghosh and Lama-Rewal 2005; Kidu and Setae 2002). Other women exercise political influence in the home through elected husbands and/or play a role in constituency work or conflict resolution (Bowie 2008; Manderson 1991). Bayo (Chapter 10) instead shows how women challenge the separation itself. Cooking for and with other women builds connections through shared affective experiences while creating communal spaces for discussion and deliberation. Bayo terms these practices '"public domesticity", whereby domestic practices extend beyond private spheres and intersect with public life', thereby challenging 'any conception of the domestic realm as being apolitical', while also remaining true to their roles within the community. Although not explicitly stated by Bayo, the establishing of affective ties with 'voters' and building women-based support teams can substantially reduce the financial costs of campaigns by avoiding the vote-buying that is considered inescapable in Indonesian elections (Aspinall et al. 2021; Harahap et al. 2022). In this way, 'public domesticity' not only removes a significant barrier to electoral participation for women; it also has the potential to transform the political culture that privileges elite men and women.

Feminist social action would centre women in rescripting vernacular democracies, including challenging the public/private binary. Rita Segato (2018) argues not for a disavowal of the domestic, but for its elevation. Rather than seek entry to and equal status within masculine spaces of politics, 'we should instead recognize and reclaim the plurality of spaces and the politics of different styles offered by communal life' (Segato 2018: 206). She advocates an approach of '*domesticating politics*, de-bureaucratizing it, humanizing it by transposing it into a domestic key, but where the "domestic" is re-politicized' (Segato 2018: 205), as urged here, too, by Bayo (Chapter 10) and Diprose et al. (Chapter 13) among others. In this way, we must seek those areas of feminine politics that have always existed but have been rendered outside formal politics. The goal is not inclusion of women into politics as usual, but a disruption of the way politics can be: both the dramatic and the 'quieter, more localised and negotiated forms of opposition' (Vijeyarasa, Part IV Introduction). Scholar-activists have a role in seeking these alternatives, not simply to write about them, but also to expand knowledge of 'the conditions and possibilities of being human' (Ingold 2014: 391). The chapters in this volume have advanced that knowledge.

Women's rescripting of politics as usual gives hope for more transformative change. Processes of vernacularisation are in a constant state of becoming and, as such, can become otherwise. Across Asia and Oceania, women are questioning the taken-for-granted nature of masculine-dominated politics and the narrow conception of what democracy could be. For example, writing about their losses in the 1997 PNG election, Carol Kidu and Susan Setae (2002) argue that electoral politics has taken a form derived from Western institutions and a narrow reading of Melanesian cultures. They call for a reimagining of democracy to be based on the diversity of cultures in the region. Motusaga and Howard (Chapter 9) provide a valuable tool to do just this. Re-storying is 'to reframe narratives, to draw out new meanings from old stories and to identify the way forward'. They show how Samoan concepts can be retold in ways that create possibilities for politics to be otherwise, through understanding and practising political power 'as relational (based on obligation) rather than competitive (based on conquest)', and 'engaging with the concept of *teu le vā* to re-story politics as a safe and respectful, rather than dirty, space'. These practices allow for the creation of new political idioms or the reclamation of cultural concepts and their repurposing for greater gender equity within reimagined vernacular democracies.

Several contributors to this volume also underline the importance of who writes these new scripts for democracies. Starting from the diagnoses of what needs fixing, Anna Kwai (Chapter 3) shows that the 'spotlight' of an outsider casts a narrow beam that leads to narrow (mis)understandings. To continue the analogy, in contrast, the work of local scholar-activists is more akin to 'stadium lights' that illuminate the different elements of culture and history and the connections between them, as Margaret Jolly (Chapter 6) perfectly demonstrates, in her conjoint celebration of the work of Anne Dickson-Waiko, J. Kēhaulani Kauanui and Teresia Teaiwa.

In a similar vein, the collaboration between Batalibasi and colleagues (Chapter 7) centres local scholar-activists, producing rich analysis of the challenges facing women. Researching across Cambodia, Bougainville, Fiji and Solomon Islands, they unpacked the experiences of the relatively small number of women in parliament and executive government through interviews and autoethnographic methods. They frankly observe the difficulties in accessing such women and, even more so, those who have failed to be elected, due to both institutional and personal reasons. Attuned to cultural sensitivities, they found many of their interlocutors were restrained in official surroundings and more relaxed in informal or domestic settings. This methodological observation led to an important insight: the very space around parliaments seems to contribute to a sense of exposure and vulnerability for women politicians, while spaces outside felt more 'physically and emotionally safe' (Batalibasi et al., Chapter 7).

Not only women, but also youth, LGBTIQ+, Indigenous and ethnic minorities are challenging their exclusion from formal politics by disrupting the gendered binaries of public and domestic, and the masculinism of states (Stephenson, Chapter 4). As Elise Stephenson shows, across South-East Asia and Australia, 'trans and nonbinary individuals [are] almost entirely unrepresented and invisible'. As a critical feminist friend and drawing on large-scale participant observation of thousands of people at ASEAN–

Australia workshops across the region and in-depth qualitative interviews, Stephenson gives value to these political agents, who, while excluded from formal politics, are not disengaged passive victims. Young, gender-diverse people have been politically active through alternative pathways, including creative industries, non-profit activism and entrepreneurial activity. '[T]raditional politics still matters, but it is not all that matters' (Stephenson, Chapter 4). Diverse actions challenged 'the deeply ageist, ableist, gendered, heteronormative and ethnically homogeneous political context' in which these change agents operated. These alternative pathways afford political proxies for marginalised identities and have created safe spaces for political participation in diverse vernacular voices. The conventional 'political pipeline' must be wrenched open but, more crucially, alternative ways of conceiving of and doing politics should be revalued.

Within this volume perhaps the most powerful tool of justice is *Indigenisation*. Salmah Eva-Lina Lawrence (Chapter 5) develops this concept to mean 'a nonlinear social process undertaken by people Indigenous to that context, which involves identifying, adapting and adopting what is useful from the new and introduced, and building on what already exists'. This process of Indigenisation can be both systemic and organic, thereby pointing to the possibilities of purposeful action, as well as interventions into immanent processes of change. It is by understanding the processes of vernacularisation, the mechanisms resulting in male political domination despite a melange of possibilities and the search for new alternatives scripted by and for the benefit of women and gender-diverse people that such knowledge can become the social action for which Collins called (2019).

Addressing gaps

We are proud of the diversity evident in this volume. Yet, we could only go so far. Drawing from international scholar and queer theorist Dianne Otto (2017), we concede how limited we have been in our ability to use queer theory to challenge the heteronormative nature of gender and politics discourses. We are grateful for and acknowledge the contributions of queer scholars and particularly welcome Elise Stephenson's queer, feminist 'insider' perspectives on how diverse and otherwise marginalised young people are making themselves heard from increasingly powerful alternative spaces (Chapter 4). We know, however, that this one chapter is far from what a broader queer contribution to this body of knowledge could make.

Regrettably, many contributors to this collection have been largely confined to dualistic understandings of male and female belonging and exclusion in various political domains. We acknowledge the profound inequalities and dangers facing queer communities in both Asia and Oceania. Without excusing, but perhaps explaining, the source of our conundrum, consensual same-sex relationships are criminalised in a vast number of nations in both regions, shaping a lack of open gender diversity in formal political systems, including in Afghanistan, Brunei, Malaysia and Singapore (Vijeyarasa 2022: 9), as well as in Solomon Islands and Samoa (ILGA 2017–25). The criminalisation of both gender and sexual fluidity often dates to colonial legislation, especially in the erstwhile colonies of the British Empire (see Stewart 2014). Yet, there are many who identify as transgender, nonbinary, intersex or otherwise non-cisgender across Asia and Oceania, where associations of transgender and queer activists have been active in challenging discrimination and promoting human rights for their constituents (see Hamer et al. 2018; Besnier and Alexeyeff 2014; Boellstorff 2005; Kihara 2022).[7]

We are inspired by J. Ann Tickner's identification of the four principles of feminist research: which *questions are asked and why*; whether that research is *useful to women* (and men); a commitment to *reflexivity* and the *subjectivity of the researcher*; and knowledge as *emancipation* (Batalibasi et al., Chapter 7). But we might ask after Stephenson how those feminist principles can be expanded to embrace gender and sexual diversity beyond the binary that has been entrenched in so many masculinist, heteronormative states. As Stephenson argues, researching and writing only about cis-women, in majority or minority worlds, continue to 'silence and render invisible gender diversity in politics' (Chapter 4), and present an incomplete analysis of the gendered dynamics of politics. A future ground for research therefore remains in how LGBTIQ+ sexual politics interacts with both formal and informal politics.

---

7   The film *Leitis in Waiting* (Hamer et al. 2018) is the story of Joey Mataele and Tongan *leitis*, an intrepid group of transgender women fighting a rising tide of religious fundamentalism and intolerance in their South Pacific kingdom. The film follows Joey, a devout Catholic of noble descent, as she organises an exuberant beauty pageant presided over by a princess, provides shelter and training for a young contestant rejected by her family and spars with American-financed evangelicals threatening to resurrect colonial-era laws that criminalise the *leitis*' lives. Yuki Kihara is a Samoan fa'afafine and a prominent artist. Her exhibition 'Paradise Camp', mounted first at the Venice Biennale in 2022, subsequently travelled to Sydney in 2023 and to Upolu Island, Samoa, in 2024 (Kihara 2022).

Naturally, in one volume we could only traverse a segment of the more than 60 countries (depending on where one chooses to draw their boundaries) that make up Asia and Oceania. Yet, we believe that this collection reflects the experiences of both formal and informal politics in ways that are common to many of the nations not included in the collection. We are proud, too, of our successful efforts to bring greater visibility to Oceania than may be typical of volumes on Asia and Oceania and even our comparative contribution across the two regions that draws together the experiences of Cambodia, Bougainville, Fiji and Solomon Islands (Batalibasi et al., Chapter 7). This chapter showcases a diversity not just of countries but also of researchers collaborating across the borders of scholarly and political practice. It confronts the vulnerability of both research subjects and researchers and the challenges of navigating the research process in an ethical, feminist way.

Capturing the diversity of women and including those excluded from mainstream political thought and action are further challenges that this volume has not resolved. Women at the intersection of multiple forms of discrimination and marginalisation have often been among the most creative and forceful in challenging male political dominance in their quest for rights, recognition and redistributive justice. Dalit feminism, for example, offered a sharp critique of feminism in India, highlighting the connections of patriarchy to other institutions—including but also beyond caste—and insisting that intellectual projects not be divorced from political projects (Ganesh 2016). Similarly, an Islamic feminist movement has been critical to legal reform in India and, more recently, in resisting political Hindutva and state-sanctioned violence against Muslims (Kadiwal 2023; Narain 2008). Ruby Lai's contribution (Chapter 12) reminds us that there is a need to negotiate space and to be heard among different feminist groups rather than a goal of supplanting one with the other. These examples remind us that we must not only decentre Euro-America and respond to the critiques of 'white' feminism, but also be attentive to other forms of erasure within national feminist movements and scholarship. We have barely touched on the richness that comes from the diversity of lived experiences across Asia and Oceania, and from which we can learn.

So, finally, our collection has sought to explore not only the outcomes of research—the 'findings'—but also the process of researching. We have sought dialogue across disciplines, rather than valuing singular and non-representative lenses. We acknowledge the inequities that exist within academia and hence have sought a diversity of contributors—from honours students to emerita professors—and have attempted to privilege researchers in-country and their participation, as a means of both acknowledging and challenging such hierarchies. We have sought to blur the neat lines too often drawn between practitioners and academics, at times even pursuing a 'pracademic' methodology (Stephenson, Chapter 4). We are cognisant of the purposeful strategies involved in bringing together such a diverse collection of authors.

A way forward

To conclude we ask: how, then, might a diversity of voices be guaranteed in research related to gender and politics, and how do we expand the gender and politics community in our regions of Oceania and Asia? We have a few suggestions. First, we must continue to create collaborative conversation spaces that invite in—as Tanya Jakimow did in 2022—'people working in nongovernmental organisations, feminist organisations, government departments and elected representatives' (see Chapter 1, this volume). But further, in these conferences, workshops and seminars, we must amplify the voices of those traditionally marginalised, make way for a diversity of language, and support, when we are asked, their compounding, complicated struggles against oppression. In these spaces, we must be honest about our complex positionalities, understanding that many of us see the question of power and privilege through contradictory lenses, and that it is only through dialogue with one another that we come to recognise what Motusaga and Howard (Chapter 9) call our 'insider and outsider perspectives'. In 2020, amid the Covid-19 pandemic, Tongan activist and scholar 'Ofa Guttenbeil-Likiliki published, through the International Women's Development Agency, a manifesto for what she called 'equitable South–North partnerships' (Guttenbeil-Likiliki 2020). To this end, she suggests a reconceptualisation and recalibration of power in these relationships towards women in the Global South (or majority world), recognising and privileging their knowledge, agency and autonomy.

Second, we must advocate for research funding that builds in equitable collaboration. Feminist research is, by definition, that which seeks to understand the role of power in any given situation. In Oceania and Asia, ethical feminist research—specifically, that which does not exploit, marginalise or jeopardise our partners or participants—is often expensive. Research grants—primarily available through highly competitive bidding—

are increasingly dependent on the leadership and guidance of 'expert scholars' from the minority world who design, in advance, questions and methods that will be used to explore issues. And, in some contexts, depending on the source of funding, the significance of issues must be framed in the 'interest' of the donor or funding body, albeit a government, an international agency or an NGO. This does not allow for co-designed, participatory or even exploratory research driven by the needs of equitable research partners. Unless grant proposals and aid programs build in opportunities for adaptive research projects—meaning research that responds at opportune moments to the identified needs of local groups—the community of practice will continue to privilege the few so-called experts of the minority world.

Third, we must include those who have traditionally been seen as 'non-traditional' researchers in our field. Research teams, like all working groups, benefit from the inclusion of very different skill sets such as communications specialists and facilitators, graphic designers, youth group officers and local civil society activists and administrators, to name a few. Including unusual suspects in gender and politics research teams broadens the way we do research, the topics we research, the participants we engage and our analysis, because the discussions of the groups will necessarily be informed by different experiences and localised knowledge. Moreover, those discussions enrich the participants of the group, extending everyone's research capabilities.

We humbly offer these suggestions and look forward to being a part of the collective reimagining and re-storying of gender and politics.

References

Alam, Shahidul. 2008. 'Majority World: Challenging the West's Rhetoric of Democracy.' *Amerasia Journal* 34, no. 1: 88–98. doi.org/10.17953/amer.34.1. 13176027k4q614v5.

Ammann, Odile. 2022. 'Language Bias in International Legal Scholarship: Symptoms, Explanations, Implications and Remedies.' *European Journal of International Law* 33, no. 3: 821–50. doi.org/10.1093/ejil/chac044.

Aspinall, Edward, Sally White, and Amalinda Savirani. 2021. 'Women's Political Representation in Indonesia: Who Wins and How?' *Journal of Current Southeast Asian Affairs* 40, no. 1: 3–27. doi.org/10.1177/1868103421989720.

Besnier, Niko, and Kalissa Alexeyeff. 2014. *Gender on the Edge: Transgender, Gay and Other Pacific Islanders*. Honolulu: University of Hawai'i Press. doi.org/10.21313/hawaii/9780824838829.001.0001.

Biersack, Aletta, Margaret Jolly, and Martha Macintyre, eds. 2016. *Gender Violence & Human Rights: Seeking Justice in Fiji, Papua New Guinea and Vanuatu*. Canberra: ANU Press. doi.org/10.22459/GVHR.12.2016.

Boellstorff, Tom. 2005. *The Gay Archipelago: Sexuality and Nation in Indonesia*. Princeton: Princeton University Press. doi.org/10.1515/9781400844050.

Bowie, Katherine. 2008. 'Standing in the Shadows: Of Matrilocality and the Role of Women in a Village Election in Northern Thailand.' *American Ethnologist* 35, no. 1: 136–53. doi.org/10.1111/j.1548-1425.2008.00010.x.

Celis, Karen, Johanna Kantola, Georgina Waylen, and S. Laurel Weldon. 2013. 'Introduction: Gender and Politics: A Gendered World, a Gendered Discipline.' In *The Oxford Handbook of Gender and Politics*, edited by Georgina Waylen, Karen Celis, Johanna Kantola, and S. Laurel Weldon, 1–19. Oxford: Oxford University Press. doi.org/10.1093/oxfordhb/9780199751457.013.0034.

Crewe, Emma. 2021. *The Anthropology of Parliaments: Entanglements in Democratic Politics*. London: Routledge. doi.org/10.4324/9781003084488.

Dirlik, Arif. 1997. *The Postcolonial Aura: Third World Criticism in the Age of Global Capitalism*. Boulder: Westview Press.

Escobar, Arturo. 1995. *Encountering Development: The Making and Unmaking of the Third World*. STU edn. Princeton: Princeton University Press. www.jstor.org/stable/j.ctt7rtgw.

Ganesh, Kamala. 2016. 'No Full Circle: Revisiting My Journey in Feminist Anthropology.' *Contributions to Indian Sociology* 50, no. 3: 293–319. doi.org/10.1177/0069966716657456.

Ghosh, Archana, and Stéphanie Tawa Lama-Rewal. 2005. *Democratization in Progress: Women and Local Politics in Urban India*. New Delhi: Tulika Books.

Guttenbeil-Likiliki, 'Ofa-Ki-Levuka. 2020. *Creating Equitable South–North Partnerships: Nurturing the Vā and Voyaging the Audacious Ocean Together*. Research Report. Melbourne: International Women's Development Agency. iwda.org.au/resource/creating-equitable-south-north-partnerships/.

Hamer, Dean, Joe Wilson, and Hinaleimoana Wong-Kalu, dirs. 2018. *Leities in Waiting*. [Film].

Harahap, Aida Fitra, Tanya Jakimow, Asima Yanty Siahaan, and Yumasdaleni. 2022. 'Is Money an Insurmountable Barrier to Women's Political Representation in Transactional Democracies? Evidence from North Sumatera, Indonesia.' *Politics, Groups and Identities* 11, no. 4: 733–49. doi.org/10.1080/21565503. 2022.2041442.

Hawkesworth, Mary. 2012. *Political Worlds of Women: Activism, Advocacy and Governance in the Twenty-First Century*. London: Routledge.

Ingold, Tim. 2014. 'That's Enough about Ethnography.' *HAU* 4, no. 1: 383–95. doi.org/10.14318/hau4.1.021.

International Lesbian, Gay, Bisexual, Trans and Intersex Association (ILGA). 2017–25. *ILGA World Database*. [Online]. Geneva: ILGA. database.ilga.org/en.

Jakimow, Tanya. 2023. 'Dirty Politics and Political Care in Local Politics: Gendered Barriers to Moral Boundary Crossing in Dehradun, India.' *Contemporary South Asia* 31, no. 2: 165–78. doi.org/10.1080/09584935.2023.2206995.

Jolly, Margaret. 2000. 'Woman Ikat Raet Long Human Raet o No? Women's Rights, Human Rights and Domestic Violence in Vanuatu.' In *Human Rights and Gender Politics: Asia-Pacific Perspectives*, edited by Anne-Marie Hilsdon, Vera Mackie, Martha Macintyre, and Maila Stivens, 124–46. London: Routledge.

Jolly, Margaret. 2008. 'The South in *Southern Theory*: Antipodean Reflections on the Pacific.' *Australian Humanities Review* 44: 75–100. doi.org/10.22459/ AHR.44.2008.

Kadiwal, Laila. 2023. 'Critical Feminist Resistance to the Politics of Hate in India.' *Globalisation, Societies and Education* 21, no. 5: 734–53. doi.org/10.1080/147 67724.2023.2222074.

Kidu, Carol, and Susan Setae. 2002. 'Winning and Losing in Politics: Key Issues in Papua New Guinea.' *Development Bulletin* 59: 51–53.

Kihara, Yuki. 2022. *Paradise Camp by Yuki Kihara*. Edited by Nathalie King. Wellington: Creative New Zealand, Toi Aotearoa, with Thames & Hudson.

Leach, Timothy. 2021. 'Human Rights of People Living with HIV, Men with Diverse Sexualities and Transgender Women in PNG.' PhD diss., The Australian National University.

Levine, Philippa, ed. 2004. *Gender and Empire*. Oxford: Oxford University Press.

Manderson, Lenore. 1991. 'Gender and Politics in Malaysia: Reflections on Order, Knowledge and Enquiry.' In *Why Gender Matters in Southeast Asian Politics*, edited by Maila Stivens, 43–60. Melbourne: Monash University.

Merry, Sally Engle. 2006a. *Human Rights and Gender Violence: Translating International Law into Local Justice.* Chicago: University of Chicago Press. doi.org/10.7208/chicago/9780226520759.001.0001.

Merry, Sally Engle. 2006b. 'Transnational Human Rights and Local Activism: Mapping the Middle.' *American Anthropologist* 108, no. 1: 38–51. doi.org/10.1525/aa.2006.108.1.38.

Merry, Sally Engle. 2009. *Gender Violence: A Cultural Perspective.* Chichester: Wiley Blackwell.

Michelutti, Lucia. 2007. 'The Vernacularization of Democracy: Political Participation and Popular Politics in North India.' *Journal of the Royal Anthropological Institute* 13, no. 3: 639–56. doi.org/10.1111/j.1467-9655.2007.00448.x.

Michelutti, Lucia. 2010. 'Wrestling with (Body) Politics: Understanding "*Goonda*" Political Styles in North India.' In *Power and Influence in India: Bosses, Lords and Captains*, edited by P. Price and A.E. Ruud, 44–69. London: Routledge.

Mohanty, Chandra Talpade. 1988. 'Under Western Eyes: Feminist Scholarship and Colonial Discourses.' *Feminist Review* 30, no. 1: 61–88. doi.org/10.1057/fr.1988.42.

Mohanty, Chandra Talpade. 2002. '"Under Western Eyes" Revisited: Feminist Solidarity through Anticapitalist Struggles.' *Signs: Journal of Women in Culture and Society* 28, no. 2: 500–35. doi.org/10.1086/342914.

Moore, Henrietta. 1988. *Feminism and Anthropology.* Cambridge: Polity Press.

Narain, Vrinda. 2008. *Reclaiming the Nation: Muslim Women and the Law in India.* Toronto: Toronto University Press. doi.org/10.3138/9781442688964.

Otto, Dianne. 2017. 'Introduction: Embracing Queer Curiosity.' In *Queering International Law: Possibilities, Alliances, Complicities, Risks*, edited by Dianne Otto, 1–11. London: Taylor & Francis. doi.org/10.4324/9781315266787-1.

Pailey, Robtel Neajai. 2020. 'De-Centring the "White Gaze" of Development.' *Development and Change* 51, no. 3: 729–45. doi.org/10.1111/dech.12550.

Pefianco Martin, Isabel. 2012. 'Expanding the Role of Philippine Languages in the Legal System.' *Asian Perspectives in the Arts and Humanities* 2, no. 1: 1–14. archium.ateneo.edu/english-faculty-pubs/20/.

Roberts, Anthea. 2017. *Is International Law International?* Oxford: Oxford University Press. doi.org/10.1093/oso/9780190696412.001.0001.

Rosenblum, Darren. 2006. 'Internalizing Gender: Why International Law Theory Should Adopt Comparative Methods.' *Columbia Journal of Transnational Law* 45, no. 3: 759–828.

Segato, Rita. 2018. 'A Manifesto in Four Themes.' *Critical Times* 1, no. 1: 198–211. doi.org/10.1215/26410478-1.1.198.

Spivak, Gayatri. 1988. 'Can the Subaltern Speak?' In *Marxism and the Interpretation of Culture*, edited by C. Nelson and L. Grossberg, 271–313. Urbana: University of Illinois Press.

Stewart, Christine. 2014. *Name, Shame and Blame: Criminalising Sex in Papua New Guinea*. Canberra: ANU Press. doi.org/10.22459/NSB.12.2014.

Tanabe, Akio. 2007. 'Toward Vernacular Democracy: Moral Society and Post-Colonial Transformation in Rural Orissa, India.' *American Ethnologist* 34, no. 3: 558–74. doi.org/10.1525/ae.2007.34.3.558.

Vijeyarasa, Ramona. 2022. 'Flamer-Caldera v Sri Lanka: Asia-Wide Implications of an Essential Evolution in CEDAW's Jurisprudence.' *Asian Journal of International Law* 13, no. 2: 209–19. doi.org/10.1017/S2044251322000583.

Vijeyarasa, Ramona. 2024. 'Comparing Whose Laws? Interrogating Biases in Comparative Law and Scholarship through the Lens of Domestic Violence Workplace Leave.' *International Journal of Comparative Labour Law and Industrial Relations* 40, no. 2: 249–74. doi.org/10.54648/IJCL2024010.

Vogel, Lise. 2013 [1983]. *Marxism and the Oppression of Women: Toward a Unitary Theory*. Chicago: Haymarket Books. doi.org/10.1163/9789004248953.